Betrayed

Linda Diebel

BETRAYED

The Assassination of Digna Ochoa

CARROLL & GRAF PUBLISHERS
NEW YORK

BETRAYED
The Assassination of Digna Ochoa

Carroll & Graf Publishers
An Imprint of Avalon Publishing Group Inc.
245 West 17th Street
11th Floor
New York, NY 10011

AVALON
publishing group incorporated

Library of Congress Cataloging-in-Publication Data is available.

ISBN-10: 0-7867-1753-X
ISBN-13: 978-0-78671-753-8

9 8 7 6 5 4 3 2 1

Printed in the United States of America
Distributed by Publishers Group West

To my mother, Ethel Lyman Diebel,
the other writer in the family

Contents

List of Principal Characters

Both surnames are cited for most people listed below. Within this book, however, I have used only one surname for those more commonly known by only that name, such as President Vicente Fox.

THE PROTAGONIST
Digna Ochoa y Plácido

HER FAMILY
PARENTS
Eusebio Ochoa López
Irene Alicia Plácido Ochoa

SIBLINGS

Carmen	Ismael
Jesús	Esthela
Luz María	Roberto
Eusebio	Juan Carlos
Guadalupe	Ignacio
Elía	Agustín

COUSIN
Juan Carlos Cruz Plácido

List of Principal Characters

HER BOYFRIEND
Juan José Vera Mendoza

POLITICIANS
MEXICO
President Vicente Fox Quesada
Attorney General Rafael Macedo de la Concha
Defense Secretary Gerardo Clemente Vega García
Interior Secretary Santiago Creel Miranda
Marieclarie Acosta Urquidi, undersecretary, human rights and
democracy

MEXICO CITY/FEDERAL DISTRICT
Mayor Andrés Manuel López Obrador
Attorney General Bernado Bátiz Vázquez

JOURNALISTS
Maribel Gutiérrez Moreno, *El Sur*
José (Pepe) Reveles, *El Financiero*
Blanche Petrich, *La Jornada*
J. Alberto Nájar Nájar, *La Jornada*
Regina Martínez, *El País/La Jornada*

HUMAN RIGHTS ORGANIZATIONS
MEXICO CITY
Miguel Agustín Pro Juárez Human Rights Center (PRO):
Founded by Jesuits to investigate human rights abuses
Edgar Cortez Moralez, S.J.
Mario E. Patrón Sánchez
Jesús González Alcántara
Carmen Herrera García
Jorge Fernández Mendiburo

Former PRO Directors:
José de Jesús (Chuche) Maldonado García, S.J.
David Jesús Fernández Dávalos, S.J.

Federal District Human Rights Commission (CDHDF)*:
Arm's length Mexico City governmental organization
Emilio Álvarez Icaza, director
María del Pilar Noriega García

National Human Rights Commission (CNDH)*:
*Arm's length commission operating within the framework of the Mexican
national government*
José Luis Soberanes Fernández, director

WASHINGTON
Center for Justice and International Law (CEJIL):
Investigates human rights abuses in the Americas
Viviana Krsticevic, director

HUMAN RIGHTS LAWYERS
MEXICO
Víctor Brenes Berho
José C. Lavanderos Yáñez
Bárbara Zamora López
Gerardo González Pedraza
José Lamberto González Ruíz
Leonel Guadalupe Rivero Rodríguez
Enrique Flota

WASHINGTON
Ariel E. Dulitzky
Denise Gilman

Spanish acronyms

List of Principal Characters

Robert Warburton, Ontario Centre of Forensic Sciences
Dr. Peter I. Collins, Ontario Provincial Police, Centre for Addiction and Mental Health

STATE OF GUERRERO, MEXICO
Organization of Peasant Ecologists of the Sierra of Petatlán and Coyuca of Catatlán:
Teodoro Cabrera García
Rodolfo Montiel Flores
Eva Alarcón Ortiz
Felipe Arreaga Sánchez
Juan Bautista Valle
Perfecto Bautista Martínez

HEMISPHERIC RIGHTS ORGANIZATIONAL STRUCTURE
The key rights body in the Americas is the Inter-American Court of Human Rights, which is the judicial arm of the Organization of American States (OAS) and based in San José, Costa Rica. It receives cases through the Inter-American Human Rights Commission, a body of the OAS.

PROLOGUE

"Every Bone in Her Body, Every Ounce of Her Being"

Motors throbbed in the distance and the villagers of the Sierra Madre strained to listen. They had been waiting since dawn on this most auspicious day and there was a buzz of excitement. *Is that her? Is she finally here?*

A few moments later, two squat red all-terrain vehicles bounced up the path and into view. Children shrieked with pleasure at the rare sight of strangers in this remote place and the even rarer prospect of chicken to eat. The four-wheelers roared into the village and rattled to a noisy stop. Everyone got their first glimpse of the important guests.

A woman struggled to hoist herself from the back of the first vehicle. She was not from these mountains and looked worn out from the rigors of an arduous trip. She was covered with mud, her sweatshirt hanging like a sack and drenched with sweat, her hair plastered to her skull. Her face, with its high cheekbones and large eyes, was red and glistened with beads of perspiration. She was a small woman, wearing army pants and big black boots. She walked stiffly to the clearing where villagers wait, followed by a tall and skinny *gringo*, who picked his way through the muck like a stork. The men barely came up to his chest and they stared at him with incredulity.

Thus, amid great expectations from the people, the lawyer Digna Ochoa y Plácido arrived in the village of El Zapotillal in the mountains of the state of Guerrero, Mexico, on this first day

1

of October 2001. This region is called Costa Grande and it's rough, inaccessible, and usually ignored. Here, there are no roads, no potable water, a health clinic with no medicine, and a school-house with no supplies. In this village, a blind boy has waited his lifetime of six years to see a doctor who never came.

The *gringo* was Harald Ihmig, a German theologian and aid worker, whom Digna brought with her to hear about the lives of the people of the Costa Grande. They would visit four communities over two days, including La Pasión, which takes its name from the suffering of its inhabitants as much as that of Jesus Christ. There is no sound for the letter *h* in Spanish, so nobody could pronounce Harald's name. He was stooped, with a bushy gray beard and a cross that dangled around his neck on a leather string. He winked at the children, who giggled at his strangeness, stealing glances and then hiding their eyes.

A robust woman, who was on the second four-wheeler, came bustling up the trail behind them. She was heavyset, with a mournful look that belied her infectious energy. She was Eva Alarcón and, having organized this expedition for Digna into the mountains, she took immediate charge of the situation.

"Come, come, come," she said, clapping her hands. "We must get started. Time is short, and soon we have to go."

Eva beckoned everyone to gather round. It was only mid-morning but already as hot as an oven. The dogs were passed out in the dirt as if dead. Wooden benches had been set out in rows and people began to take their seats, men in tattered shirts and straw hats, women with babies dangling off their hips, and, everywhere, the children. This was an event. About two hundred people had come to see Digna and Harald, many walking stony trails from the surrounding villages with no shoes on.

They began to recount their stories. Their problems were twofold: They lived in all-encompassing poverty and in fear for their lives, terrified of the soldiers and the death squads. They said these mountains run red with their blood and the government does

2

nothing to protect them. Everyone knew the army has impunity in Mexico.

A little boy had been chosen to welcome the distinguished visitors on behalf of the community. He was about eleven, maybe twelve, barefoot and dressed in white. He said his name softly, almost in a whisper. "I am . . . Everardo." He wrapped his arms around his body and stared at the ground. But he lost his nervousness when he spoke.

"*Bueno.* Welcome *Señoras* and welcome *Señores*," he began. "I would like you to know that in our village, we don't have the resources to do anything. We can't put out the awful fires in the forest or even find work because, well, you know"—he shrugged—"in order to get a job, you have to have clean hands." And he held out his own dirty little palms to show Digna. An old man's hands, scarred and worn. Everardo was only a child but he already knew these dirty hands condemned him to a life without opportunity.

"We can't get anywhere," he said. "Here, we can't even study, you know–just to *be* somebody in life."

To *be* somebody. It's all he wanted.

He said there was no secondary school in the village and no money to go to school anywhere else. He finished with another shrug: "Well, for my part, that's all."

There was scattered applause and Digna beamed at the boy. She smiled at everyone. Over two days, she was thrown off a bike into the river, devoured by bugs, burned by the sun, scraped, bruised, cut, and battered but she always seemed to have a joke.

Eva invited Digna here on behalf of the Organization of Peasant Ecologists of the Sierra of Petatlán. It is an organization of poor villagers—Eva was recording secretary—begun a few years ago because they wanted to save the forests. Logging companies were making deals with Mexican politicians and the trees were coming down like there was no tomorrow. A U.S. company's trucks were hauling the timber out of the Costa Grande day and night. The land was drying up and their babies were thirsty. They feared for the futures of their children and grandchildren.

They fought back and they stepped on big toes. They took on the governor and the local political bosses. Huge interests are at stake in the volatile state of Guerrero: money, narco-trafficking, gun-running, timber, land. Throughout this state, crude wooden crosses mark the graves of the victims of massacres. Poor villagers organized protests, appealed to the national government, and sent petitions, signed with rough initials or thumbprints. Ultimately, they blocked the logging roads into the mountains. The governor sent in the army and members of their organization were arrested and thrown in jail on charges that everyone said were trumped up by the authorities.

Others who were charged went into hiding. They lived in caves, fleeing from the soldiers who pursued them in the canyons. Some who were there that day were wanted men, with arrest warrants hanging over their heads. Like ghosts, they materialized at stops along Digna's route to give her their statements. They were frightened but they had come because they believed this lawyer from Mexico City could help them. Their cases were politically charged, involving as they did powerful interests, and it could be extremely risky for an outsider like Digna Ochoa to become involved.

These villagers knew a little about her. They knew she defended two men from these same mountains, Rodolfo Montiel and Teodoro Cabrera, who were imprisoned in the battle over the forests. Digna fought to have the soldiers who captured them brought to justice to face allegations of torture and the cases against the two men dismissed. She worked hard for their release (a goal that would be achieved within a few weeks, although in a manner that nobody here today could possibly predict).

Digna listened, waiting her turn to speak. She looked fragile,

Harald towering over her like a giant. There was nothing remarkable about her demeanor or dress. The villagers knew that she was respected and that her visit was important, but they had no idea that Digna was famous, or that she ranked among the world's most distinguished human rights lawyers—that special breed of individuals who dedicate their lives to the right of people to be free of oppression, illegal imprisonment, torture, and murder.

They didn't know she had spent her life working to tear down the wall of impunity around the Mexican Army and security forces. It was Mexico's Berlin Wall, built to keep its victims unseen and their voices unheard.

She has won many accolades and awards; she had been feted and admired. Kerry Kennedy, the U.S. human rights defender and author, described Digna as a person who gave everything she had, her heart and soul and sinew. She struggled with "every bone in her body, every ounce of her being."[1]

Eva introduced Digna and she stepped forward, smiling. There was a hush.

"Well, as Eva said, I am a lawyer and I worked on the case of Rodolfo and Teodoro," she began, as she would in three other communities over the next two days. She told them that nobody stops the soldiers and death squads from coming after them because they were people without faces.

She was inspired by their courage, she told them. Perhaps she could help.

"There is a very strong environmental movement in the United States, and there is a very strong environmental movement here. But there is a fundamental difference between the two, and that is resources," she explained. Her aim was to seek the resources they needed.

"I am going to knock on doors. I can't promise you that they will open, or that everyone is going to help us, but it is worth trying, no? I can promise nothing. But I can try to help you and we can try together, no?"

Digna talked with her hands. They were graceful, with slim, tapering fingers, and seemed almost to flutter. Several times she said she would knock on doors, each time lifting her right hand and knocking on the air.

Her words were a revelation to her listeners. She explained that, as impoverished and isolated as they were, they were powerful and the authorities had reason to fear them. Nobody had ever told them they were powerful.

"For many years, the Mexican government has been extremely worried about keeping its good image abroad, and I can tell you this from experience," she said. It was her only reference to the considerable irritant she had been to the Mexican government and the price she had paid.

"The government spends a great deal of money to maintain this good image with political parties in other countries, especially since 1994 (and the free trade deal with the United States and Canada)," she continued. "But other countries will take notice that there is another Mexico behind the Mexico of the tourists. This other Mexico bears the face of suffering. These are your faces.

"Great pressure is put on the government—it is already happening—when these situations of social injustice, of people being taken prisoner, of being hunted, become known outside of our country. It is very strong pressure and it is beginning to bring special attention to Mexico. It would be a big step to get your situation known and it is a step that we can take immediately. We can tell your stories to people in other countries. They carry political weight and, let's hope, they can help you. More than anything else, this is what I can offer to you."

By promising to tell their stories, she gave them hope. They were no longer alone. They had a champion in Digna. She was their ally, both as a lawyer and a communicator, an ambassador, as it were, for this other face of Mexico.

It was the face of poverty, torture, and persecution. It was the blood-soaked countenance of a country whose violence seemed almost unimaginable to people living safe lives in Canada or the United States. This face was hidden away from tourists who relaxed under swaying palm trees on white sand beaches.

She would knock on doors on their behalf. She was accustomed to opening doors and she would use her clout—her contacts with powerful people and organizations in Washington, New York, Los Angeles, and elsewhere—to bring their faces to life outside of Mexico.

On Tuesday, October 2, Digna went back down the mountain the same bumpy way she came up, on the rump of a vehicle she had grown to dislike intensely. She said good-bye to Harald and stayed overnight at Eva's house, in Petatlán, on the Pacific Ocean. It was small and humble and sat near the highway, about a ten-minute drive from the gleaming hotels of the resort town of Ixtapa-Zijuatenejo, on the Mexican Riviera. Acapulco was about three hours south. Tourists were ferried along this road in air-conditioned buses and limousines, staring out at blue Pacific waters, with margaritas on their minds.

Digna and Eva talked of somber things. Digna carried with her a letter from the wife of a prisoner in Acapulco, in which she wrote that her husband, an *ecologista*,[2] was tortured by the soldiers who arrested him. She wanted to take the case before the Inter-American Human Rights Commission in Washington.[3]

They also talked of life, family, food, and men. Digna was thirty-seven. She loved children but she said she would never have a child because her life was too dangerous. She didn't want to leave an orphan.

She opened up to Eva, talking about her boyfriend, Juan José Vera, and how much she was in love with him. She longed for him. He was a teacher and mathematician in Mexico City. She laughed as she described J.J. and how much he loved to eat. And then, turning serious, she said he was intelligent and tender and unlike

7

anyone she had ever known. He changed her way of thinking, opening her up to the idea they could share a future together.[4]

The next morning, she boarded a bus for the sixteen-hour ride home to the capital. She was excited, full of plans and eager to throw herself into helping the villagers of the Sierra Madre. She set to work and, on October 10, sent an e-mail to her friend Ariel Dulitzky in Washington, a lawyer with the Inter-American Human Rights Commission.

"I have just returned from Guerrero," she wrote, "and things are much clearer to me."

Digna has given her word to people who endured the same poverty she knew as a child. For many reasons central to her own existence, they were her people and she intended to keep her promise to them.

One of the first things she planned to do, with Harald's help, was get medical attention for the little blind boy. Digna had no time to lose.

CHAPTER ONE

"They Just Killed Digna"

On a Friday afternoon, a seemingly ordinary afternoon in Mexico City, lawyer Gerardo González Pedraza hurried into the courtyard of 31-A Zacatecas Street. It was late and he was impatient, merely stopping by to pick up some legal papers before catching the bus home to Cuernavaca for the weekend. He began to climb the outdoor staircase to a suite of offices on the first floor of the apartment building.

Nothing appeared amiss. The October weather was seasonally mild, the skies were partly cloudy, it was smoggy, and traffic was dreadful, as it always was in the capital, except for the few days over Christmas and Holy Week when the city blissfully emptied. It was getting dark and he glanced at his watch, surprised to see it was not yet six.

The office was located in a run-down part of Colonia Roma, a once-magnificent district that had seen better days. Roma was hit particularly hard by the 1985 earthquake in Mexico City and some sections were never rebuilt. More than ten thousand people died, tens of thousands more were injured, whole blocks of the capital were destroyed, and political bungling and the mishandling of relief money left a sour aftertaste in the mouths of most Mexicans.

Gerardo and his colleagues, Pilar Noriega and Lamberto González Ruíz, opened an office here, in a nondescript building with muddy brown paint, bars on the windows, and a general air of seediness. They handled cases most other lawyers wouldn't touch, mainly human rights issues that were challenging and morally rewarding, but hardly profitable. There wasn't enough money for a receptionist, and the cleaning woman, who lived with her family on the floor above, didn't come often enough. The offices were grimy and cluttered, overflowing with books and files. There was a parking lot across the street, a few spindly trees and rows of narrow apartment buildings. It was an ordinary street, memorable, perhaps, only for a peculiar absence of birdsong.

Gerardo reached the first floor and stood on the veranda, fishing for his keys. For a moment, he was frozen on the other side of the door, unaware that his life was about to change. Once he opened this door, he will never be able to close it. In the days and months to come, perhaps for the rest of his life, he would remember the next few hours with chilling clarity.

Many people would remember what happened at 31-A Zacatecas Street on October 19, 2001. But it was Gerardo, a soft-spoken and unassuming middle-aged man, who would be the first witness to a crime that stunned the nation with its sheer brazenness.

He unlocked the black metal door and pushed it inward, disregarding a couple of flyers stuck in the door frame. They fluttered to the ground, and he swept them aside with his foot. Only later would these seemingly insignificant pieces of paper become important. He closed the door, squinting into the dimness. There is a desk in front of him and, to his right, a passageway that ran the length of the space and was divided into cubicles, a small bathroom and kitchen, storage closet and a reception area for meeting clients. It had floor-to-ceiling bookcases, a couple of threadbare couches facing each other, a small wooden cabinet, and two white, plastic chairs, the kind you'd see on a beach.

Gerardo had a sense of foreboding. Peering into the gloom, he could just make out a dark figure lying against the far sofa or, as it would come to be known in countless forensic reports, the south sofa. He assumed it must have been a child, the figure was so small. It looked like a little boy. He believed his eyes were playing tricks on him.

He flipped on the light. He looked down and saw a woman's headband, a single arc of what looked like plastic, lying on the floor, just inside the door. Odd, he thought. There was a white, powdery substance around the headband, and an intermittent trail leading to the couch where, by now, he could make out the slumped body of a woman. He studied her from a distance, before walking toward her, his heart pounding.

She was small, with chin-length black hair. She was lying on her left side, with her torso against the couch and her legs splayed on the carpet. Her head rested on the cushion, with the right side of her face turned upward. He couldn't see who it was because her hair had fallen over her face. She was wearing a white blouse with black piping around the collar, dark pants, and black, zip-up ankle boots. Gerardo didn't notice this, but her black ankle socks were frilly, like a child's, with a white floral design on the flap. They peeked sadly over her boots.

He saw white powder on her pants, on the couch, on the floor around her legs. There was even powder on the soles of her shoes. He looked around, and noticed it was sprinkled on the couch opposite and on a large, black bag sitting on one of the plastic chairs. The bag had three zippered pouches and the one nearest to him gaped open. What was this stuff? he wondered. Flour? Cocaine? His mind raced and he could hardly breathe.

"Ay Dios," he thought, and in this instant, he was sure he was looking at the body of Digna Ochoa y Plácido. She was a colleague, another lawyer who specialized in human rights cases. He didn't know Digna well, but human rights lawyers made up a small world in Mexico and, besides, Digna was famous. He remembered Pilar telling him that Digna would be taking over her caseload at the Zacatecas Street office. Pilar had just accepted a senior position with the Mexico City Human Rights Commission, a government job that would take all her time.[1] She was working full-time on Zacatecas Street, while Gerardo and Lamberto (as well as other colleagues who occasionally shared the space) had

positions elsewhere, Gerardo with a small human rights organization and Lamberto with the Mexico City department of labor. They were used to greeting each other on the run, as they juggled cases here with other responsibilities.

Yes, Pilar told him the week before that she'd given Digna a key.

Gerardo leaned in toward the woman's face. He saw blood on the couch, a large stain that had spread out around her head onto the tatty brown and gray striped surface. He saw thick gobs of blood matted in her hair. There was something dark—maybe a coat—partially hidden underneath her body. Maybe she was holding it, he couldn't tell; he couldn't see her hands. He knew better than to touch anything (he would later insist to police) and he backed away slowly. He is not a robust man and he was trembling, almost fainting.

He walked to the reception desk, picked up the phone to call Pilar and, rattled, misdialed several times before he remembered her number at the human rights commission. She was not there, and he left an urgent message. He tried Lamberto at the labor ministry. They'd appeared together at an arbitration hearing earlier in the day, before having a late lunch at a restaurant on Isabel la Católica Street. Lamberto's office was not far from the restaurant; he should have been back by now.

"Please, Beto, be there, be there," Gerardo prayed as he dialed his friend's number. His hands shook.

Lamberto, a thin-faced man with a pencil moustache, was in his office, chatting with colleague Gonzalo Mejilla. He picked up the telephone immediately, listened to his friend's frantic voice, and tried to calm him. "I'll be right there," he said. He slammed down the phone and the two men sprinted to the street, hailed a taxi, and within twenty minutes were pounding up the spiral staircase at 31-A Zacatecas Street and into the office, where Gerardo was waiting for them. He pointed to the inert body on the couch.

At first, like Gerardo, Lamberto thought it was a child. Looking closer, he realized that this was a woman and, most certainly, Digna. "She looks peaceful," he thought. "Maybe she's just unconscious." To the others, he whispered, "Maybe she's not dead."

He tried to rouse her, calling her name. "Digna! Digna! Wake up!"

Lamberto saw the white powder everywhere, even a trail leading in the direction of the bathroom door around the corner.

Somebody—and later, no one would remember exactly who—noticed there was a cell phone sticking out of the bag that rested on the plastic chair. They assumed it belonged to the woman. It was a chunky black Nokia and it was turned on. Its face glowed green.

* * *

Perhaps, at this point in the story, with this fragile body lying motionless and the minutes ticking by, there was an obvious question. What about the police? They had not been called by the first witnesses, and they wouldn't be for some moments yet, when others in a rapidly expanding cast of characters placed calls from various locations.

It is not an oversight. It was enough to say now that Digna Ochoa's colleagues were human rights lawyers and activists whose experiences with authority in Mexico had been bleak. These people had no reason to believe they could either trust, or count on, the police. Over the next week, everyone from President Vicente Fox to the most senior members of his cabinet, with the power to turn the country upside down if they so chose, would promise them that, this time, the outcome of this crime against one of their own would be different than the litany of unsolved assassinations in Mexico. The same promise would be made by Mexico City Mayor Andrés Manuel López Obrador.

Both the conservative president and the leftist mayor gave their solemn word.

* * *

At 6:40 P.M., Pilar Noriega, a confident, energetic woman, strode into her office after giving a class on general trial law at the Pontifical University of Mexico in the southern suburb of Tlalpan. Friday traffic was a nightmare, and looping north on the *Periférico* was a dusty, grinding, sweaty mess of honking horns and blaring music. It was the last day of a tough first week in her new job as "first visitor"[2] at the human rights commission, and she was looking forward to the weekend. An assistant gave her Gerardo's urgent message, and she dialed the Zacatecas office.

Lamberto picked up.

"There is a woman here in the office and we think she is dead," he told her. "There are bloodstains and she doesn't appear to be breathing. We can't see her face, Pilar, but we think it's Digna."

Pilar felt her legs crumble. She and Digna had been friends for years. They'd worked on cases together, partied together, spent weekends hanging around the pool at her home in Cuernavaca, an hour's drive south of the capital. A few weeks earlier, another friend, lawyer José Lavanderos, had thrown a birthday party for Pilar at his apartment. Everyone was in a great mood that night. There were lots of photographs taken and Digna, wearing a soft orange sweater and pearls, was laughing in each of them. She was radiant. Everybody said it was because she was in love. Over the summer, she had lost weight, making jokes about her willpower to turn down her favorite *chiles rellenos* and savory sausage from her home state of Veracruz.

In one photo, she stood with her right arm around her new boyfriend, Juan José Vera, while Pilar grinned on her left. Pilar was shorter than Digna, with curly brown hair, a wide brow, and an intelligent face. She was wearing jeans, and a silk scarf fastened with a clip at a jaunty angle. Click-click. Moments were forever captured. Nobody seemed to have a care in the world.

But, of course, that's not true. Far from it. Their real lives were different, full of fear and pain. Their work had been exceedingly difficult, particularly cases they handled for an organization called the Miguel Agustín Pro Juárez Human Rights Center, known by its Spanish acronym, PRODH, or simply PRO.[3] They had comforted one another in the worst days and faced death threats with courage, even bravado. They took on the untouchables—the police, intelligence agencies, and the army.

Death threats against them (and other members of PRO) began in the mid-1990s.

"Condolences for the much-felt deaths of Digna and Pilar . . . To all sons-of-bitch attorneys. We are already sick of you. When will you stop? . . . We are having a party and you are our special guests."[4]

Shortly before they were scheduled to fly to Washington, D.C., to meet on one case with officials at the Inter-American Human Rights Commission, they received a threat, the letters clipped from newspapers and crudely glued to spell out: *"Those two shrews will find themselves someplace other than Washington—in a thousand pieces. Remember, airplanes have accidents."*[5]

Digna put on a brave face. She even made jokes. Once, in the car on the way to Pilar's house in Cuernavaca, she picked up the newspaper and saw that Pilar's photo was mistakenly used in a story about her. She started to giggle. "Oh, good, it's not going to be me they get," she said, almost rolling off the seat with laughter.[6]

Now, on the phone, Pilar was still trying to grasp what Lamberto was telling her from the Zacatecas office. She heard him talking about a cell phone in the woman's bag. He told her it might be Digna's.

"Do you have her number?" he asked.

Pilar cupped her hand over the receiver and instructed her secretary to pick up another line. "I want you to call this number," she told her. Slowly, she dictated.

"Zero-four-four . . . one-nine-oh . . . zero-two-three-four-nine."

She knew the number by heart. She had called it a thousand times.

On the other end of the phone line, Lamberto and the others waited silently. Seconds passed. They stared at the cell phone, the same mantra running through their minds: *Don't ring! Don't ring! Don't—*

But the phone did ring. Loudly, insistently.

"Pilar, Pilar, can you hear me?" asked Lamberto.

But Pilar didn't answer. She had heard the ringing of the cell phone in the Zacatecas office.

All in an instant, her secretary hung up, Digna's cellular went silent, and Lamberto was speaking to a dial tone.

* * *

Pilar's offices were on Chapultepec Avenue, the fabled street that cuts across the city and ends in the lush greenery of Chapultepec Park. Pilar slumped into her chair and, from her desk, called another lawyer, Víctor Brenes, who was special assistant to Emilio Álvarez Icaza, director of the Mexico City Human Rights Commission, where Pilar now worked. Víctor's office was directly above hers and they were old friends.

"Víctor, they just killed Digna," she told him. "They just killed Digna in her office. Gerardo found her dead."

"Don't move, Pili," he said, before hurtling out the door and down the stairs, taking them two at a time, to her office on the floor below.

He burst in to see Pilar at her desk, holding her head in her hands. She looked up, her face drained of blood, and burst into tears. She rushed into his arms, almost knocking him over. Víctor was a compact man with a baby face that made him appear much younger than his forty years. In shock himself, he supported Pilar in his arms.

"Tell me what happened," he said, and she recounted Gerardo

finding a body, the cell phone ringing, and the likelihood that Digna was dead.

They hurried downstairs, where Pilar's driver was waiting. He swung the car over to Cuauhtemoc Avenue, which links the city's historic center to the southern suburbs. Tonight's events all took place within a few hundred square blocks in the heart of the capital city. Zacatecas Street wasn't far away, but Cuauhtemoc was clogged with bumper-to-bumper traffic. Víctor had never seen it so bad. Besides the normal Friday rush hour, motorists were using Cuauhtemoc as an access route for the Eric Clapton concert at the Foro del Sol.

On weekends in the capital, there's always excitement in the air. The last weeks of October are a wonderful time, with the rainy season almost over, the skies clearing, and the upcoming Day of the Dead heralding a festive season that lingers through Christmas and New Year's Day to the Feast of the Three Kings in January. No city relishes its festivals like Mexico City.

In the backseat of Pilar's car, however, the mood was leaden.

En route, Víctor called his boss, Álvarez Icaza, who at that moment was doing an interview in the nearby offices of the city's largest newspaper, *Reforma*. He told Víctor he would telephone Mexico City attorney general Bernardo Bátiz himself. He would make sure, he promised Víctor, that Bátiz understood the significance of the crime.

Pilar was white. She looked fifty. She'd aged ten years, her face already taking on the ghastly, ashen cast it would wear throughout the next terrible days. In all the newspapers, in the TV coverage, she would look the same—shell-shocked, her features set in grief.

Shortly after arriving at Zacatecas Street, Lamberto made another call, this time to the offices of PRO, the Jesuit-founded rights organization where this tight network of lawyers had met and become friends. PRO's offices were a few blocks away on

Serapío Rendón Street, on the north side of Mexico City's most famous avenue, Paseo de la Reforma, where the golden Angel of Independence soared above the traffic.

Digna had worked for many years at PRO, so long and with such intensity that her name had become synonymous with the organization, especially in the eyes of international rights organizations and the media. There would be confusion in coming weeks about her status, with the press apparently unaware she had left PRO a full year before her death. It was an impression that, oddly, nobody attempted to correct.

Lamberto reached senior litigator Carmen Herrera, who held Digna's former job at PRO. Carmen instructed a colleague to telephone the police, and dialed the pager number of Dr. Jorge Arturo de León, one of Digna's closest friends.

Dr. de León was in his car, driving south to his home. He was almost there in Mixcoac when his phone rang. He was a family doctor who taught medicine at the National Autonomous University of Mexico and worked with human rights organizations. He had documented cases of physical torture and worked on environmental issues, including a groundbreaking study of a Veracruz pesticide factory explosion ten years earlier and its impact on the health of the local population. He was a big man with a kind face and gentle manner, and it's not surprising Digna went to him when the death threats began again in August.

She was scared. These threats were especially unnerving because they arrived where she thought she was safe—her new apartment, far from the city center where she lived before going into exile in 2000. She'd just come home to Mexico in March, after spending seven months in the United States. Digna fled Mexico after she was kidnapped twice and the death threats became more persistent. The last time she was abducted, in October 1999, unknown assailants overpowered her in her apartment, questioned her all night, and left her tied up beside the open valve of a portable gas tank. She managed to untie herself and escape.

"If they had wanted to kill me, I'd be dead," Digna said about that night.[7] She believed state agents were behind it.[8] She thought they were trying to frighten her into dropping a particular case in Guerrero, where she was attempting to prosecute two soldiers on charges of torture and sticking her nose in some important people's business. The case made her prominent and an even bigger target. Death threats arrived at her PRO offices, but she didn't back down. She kept slugging away, trying to ignore her fears, until her friend Edgar Cortez, a Jesuit priest and director of the PRO rights center, insisted she leave Mexico for her own safety and that of her colleagues. Digna didn't want to go, but she trusted Edgar and, in the summer of 2000, flew into exile in Washington, D.C.

She had no reason not to trust Edgar.

When she returned in the spring of 2001, she moved into a one-bedroom apartment in the southern suburb of Lomas de Plateros and, for five months, everything was fine. Or maybe, with a new life and a new love, that is what she wanted to believe.

Then, on August 7, she found a letter in her mailbox. It was dropped off; there was no stamp or postmark. There would be two more letters: one on August 10, and a third only a few days before her death.

"You son of a bitch, we know very well where you are . . . Did you think you were free of us? . . . Very soon, you're going to get screwed. Do you want to know how?"

Dr. de León turned his car around and headed north, squeezing tears from his eyes as he drove. He was thinking about those letters, and about how Digna was so frightened she couldn't sleep at night. He had prescribed a mild sedative.[9]

He arrived at the Zacatecas office some time before seven.

Inside, he gently lifted the woman's hair to confirm his worst fear. Yes, it was Digna. He searched for a pulse and found none. He saw that there was congealed blood in her nostril. He thought she had been shot, but could not see her wounds.

He made mental notes. There was blood spatter on the bookcase and blood on the sofa across from Digna. It would become known in the forensic lexicon as the north sofa. He did not move the body. About this he was careful now, and would be clear later when police asked him, as they would many times, "Did you move the body?"

No, he insisted, over and over.

Just as insistently, they replied: "Well, then, who did?"

That he didn't know.

But he did notice something strange at the scene of the crime. Digna's hands were underneath the couch, almost stuffed there. He couldn't quite see them. It looked to him as if her body had been "arranged." That is the word he would use later with detectives from the Public Prosecutor's Office. "If I fall unconscious," he explained, "my body will unconsciously choose a more comfortable position. Her position was not an anatomically natural position." He had a creepy feeling, looking down at his dear friend, that her killers enjoyed arranging her corpse. "This was a professional job," he thought. "This was a *hit*."[10]

He turned to the others.

"She's dead," he said simply.

* * *

News traveled fast across the city that night. Rights commissioner Emilio Álvarez Icaza had telephoned and left a message for Mexico City Attorney General Bátiz, who was tied up in an evening meeting with his deputy, Renato Sales. "It appeared to me that what happened was extremely serious, especially in light of the climate of death threats against human rights activists," Álvarez Icaza later told the weekly newsmagazine *Proceso,* confirming that he spoke directly with Bátiz, the capital's top law enforcement officer.

Police received a Code 33 homicide call at 7:39 P.M. (although the time would be disputed) and opened file FDCUAHT/03/USD04/ 2576/ 01-10 into the death of a woman under suspicious circumstances at 31-A Zacatecas Street.[11] A squad car was dispatched. It's not clear when the first officers arrived at the crime scene but, by eight, the place was crawling with cops. They cordoned off the reception area with yellow police tape and began numbering evidence tabs with green felt markers.

Martín Valderrama Almeida, from the Public Prosecutor's Office (which fell under Bátiz and the attorney general's department),[12] was lead investigator that night. From the beginning, this looked to him like murder. Forensic photographers Renato Hernández Jiménez and Carlos Barajas Colín photographed Digna's body from various angles. They photographed the white powder on her trousers, on the couch around her head, on the rug, and on the floor around the woman's headband found by the door. They photographed the blood spatter, the black nylon bag with its zippered pouches (also sprinkled with white powder), and, in an interior office, a desktop computer with two red lollipops placed beside it, still in their wrappers. They dusted for fingerprints and measured and bagged evidence, including the flyers that Lamberto kicked aside on his way in.

They took everything, even a used sanitary napkin from the bathroom wastebasket. DNA testing later matched it to Digna's blood. No semen was found on the pad.

The killer(s) had left their calling card. Police found a death threat on the desk just inside the door. It was a computer printout in capital letters, apparently for the lawyers at PRO, the human rights organization where Digna had worked for so many years.

"PROs, you sons of bitches, if you keep it up we're going to screw another one of you too. We're warning you, this is no trick."

An off-kilter red cross was slashed across the bottom of the page.

* * *

There was something else, something macabre.

Digna was wearing a pair of thick, red rubber gloves. They were much too big for her small hands with their slender fingers, and they appeared to investigators that night as if they had been shoved on, haphazardly, after death. They were rolled over at the cuffs and covered in an unidentified white powder. There was powder on her wrists and it looked like it coated her hands inside the gloves, apparently the same white powder found everywhere else. The gloves were an American size 8 and the fingers, well past Digna's, bobbled grotesquely when police lift her body onto a stretcher.

The gloves were a creepy touch and they soon became a hallmark of the case. What sick, twisted bastards did this? What did the gloves mean? Mexico City newspapers reported that a death squad operating in Guerrero, in the mountain villages Digna visited before her death, left red gloves on the hands of victims. *La Jornada* reporter Alberto Nájar wrote that Digna's kidnappers put similar gloves on her hands in October 1999, before tying her up and opening the gas valve.

There were reports, too, that the index and middle fingers on her left hand had been arranged in a "V."

A police source told *Reforma* that death squads used the "V" sign during the Dirty War years of the seventies and eighties. That's how they used to find corpses in the state of Guerrero. "It was a signal they were leaving the person in peace, as it were. In this case, it could mean the killers were signaling the job was done and they didn't want to be disturbed—or it could mean somebody *inside* the system did it."[13]

* * *

José Lavanderos, a tall man with a neatly trimmed salt-and-pepper beard and a patrician manner, was at the downtown Río

Guadalquivir cinema when his cell phone rang. He answered and PRO director Edgar Cortez told him, "José, I don't want to give you bad news, but they have killed Digna."

José and Digna were close, and he raced over to Zacatecas Street, arriving some time between seven and eight, to see police already on the scene. He was an experienced lawyer, a veteran of human rights work for PRO, and currently handling complicated cases for the Mexico City government under Mayor López Obrador and the left-wing Democratic Revolutionary Party (PRD). As a senior lawyer for the city government, José spent much of his time in court, knew high-level police officers, and was used to police procedure. He recognized a "contaminated" crime scene when he saw one, and this was what he witnessed that night, as he stood inside the office, behind the police tape. Police were falling all over themselves, he said later.[14]

"I entered, but I couldn't see Digna's body because it was obscured by the number of people who were there. There were ten or twelve of them, all from the prosecutor's offices. They were taking photographs, taking fingerprints. I could see many people crouching down looking for things, looking for fingerprints on the floor. There were many people there, and they had not secured the area very well."

Víctor Brenes was thinking the same thing. He saw that the police appeared disorganized and the crime scene was not being properly protected. Víctor realized that officers on the scene had no idea who Digna was, or that her life had been threatened over her high-profile human rights work. He heard them talking about a threatening letter against the PRD government of Mexico City and knew they had gotten it wrong. Later, he noticed their consternation when the heavyweights arrived.

Around ten, well after Digna's corpse had been removed, the beefy body of Attorney General Bátiz would be seen puffing up the stairs, his small, bald-headed deputy, Sales, toddling up behind him. The beat cops didn't know what to make of it. This must be an important case to pull the bigwigs out on a Friday night.

* * *

Police followed procedure in removing the body.[15] Detectives traced Digna's remains with chalk, then turned her over and lifted her lifeless form onto a stretcher. They recorded what they saw. She had been shot in the head, and there was blood on her left pant leg, front and back, at thigh level. She appeared to be holding a bloody navy overcoat, with a red cotton scarf rolled at the collar.

They found a gun under her legs. It was a strange-looking little weapon, a semiautomatic handgun with illegible markings on the grip. One officer described it as a "museum piece."[16] The gun's frame was black plastic or fiberglass, and the barrel looked like a sawed-off rifle barrel. There were five bullets in the magazine.

Police found three shells, two on the floor between the couches, and a third wedged into a corner between the south sofa and the wall. One shell had been flattened, as if stepped on. They found two bullets, one in each sofa. They believed the third bullet would be found in the victim's head.

They located a single white button. Possibly from a woman's blouse, it lay close to where Digna's head rested on the sofa.

On the floor was a small piece of chewed gum.

* * *

A somber knot of friends, colleagues and journalists gathered in the courtyard below. It was an overcast night, starless, and already turning chilly. People were in shock, speaking in hushed tones. There were muffled sounds of weeping, the noise of traffic on nearby Cuauhtemoc Avenue, the ringing of cell phones, dogs barking and distant music from the downtown clubs.

They had rushed to this place from all over the city, Lamberto, Pilar, Víctor, José, Dr. de León, and another friend of Digna's from the rights movement, Rafael Álvarez, rumpled and blinking in disbelief. From PRO, there were young lawyers Jorge Fernández, Mario Patrón, and Carmen Herrera, as well as director Edgar Cortez, who had played such an important role in Digna's life.

Pilar was weeping. "What a blow this is," she said, choking out the words.

"A bigger blow for Digna," said Lamberto. "As big as her life."

Bárbara Zamora, another lawyer, was here, her beautiful face red and swollen from crying. She'd been trying to reach Digna all day to finalize plans for their meeting with prisoners tomorrow at Almoloya de Juárez Prison, in a northern suburb of the capital region.[17] Bárbara and Digna had been long-time friends who often worked together. This time, they were defending three brothers accused of planting a bomb at a Mexico City bank, and Bárbara had left several messages. Police stenographers would transcribe her words from the microcassette in Digna's answering machine at Lomas de Plateros, building H-2, apartment No. 21.

"Digna, it's Bárbara! It's three in the afternoon. I just want to know what time is convenient for you to leave tomorrow for Almoloya. I'll be on my cell or home. Thanks, ciao."

At 6:07 P.M.: "Digna, it's Bárbara again, please give me a call so we can agree on going to Almoloya tomorrow. Thanks."

And, finally, at 6:43 P.M., a last message: "Digna, it's Bárbara again. I urge you to call me . . ."

Across the city and around the world, people were getting the news. "Human rights activist Digna Ochoa has been found dead," evening anchors from Televisa and TV Azteca told their audiences.

In a little house with a flower garden in the south of the city, Sister Brigitte, a French nun with the Dominicans of the

Incarnate Word, answered the telephone to hear the voice of Sister Luz calling from Cuernavaca. "Quickly, turn to Channel 40," said Sister Luz, before uttering the same awful sentence as so many others this night: "They just killed Digna."

Sister Brigitte sat down heavily and began to cry. Digna had lived in this very house for eight years before leaving the order almost three years earlier. But she had stayed in touch with the nuns and Sister Brigitte thought of the last time she saw her, at Digna's birthday party in May. She loved Digna.

President Vicente Fox was in Shanghai, where he and First Lady Martha Sahagún were finishing up a world tour. His attorney general, General Rafael Macedo de la Concha, whose life had intersected with Digna's more than once, was in his office in Colonia Lomas de Sotelo. Other political players were in the capital too, Defense Secretary Gerardo Clemente Vega García, Interior Secretary Santiago Creel Miranda, and Marieclaire Acosta, the former rights activist who, the previous December, had taken her seat at the Fox cabinet table with fanfare as the nation's first undersecretary for human rights and democracy.

The news was really shocking. Digna was Mexico's most high-profile human rights lawyer, recognized nationally and internationally, awarded and admired, known to Washington politicians and Hollywood actors. She had been involved in Mexico's most politically charged and controversial cases, cases that focused on allegations of torture, rape, and murder by members of the army and other security forces.

On this very night, on the other side of the Atlantic, Pulitzer Prize–winning playwright Ariel Dorfman's production of *Speak Truth to Power* was staged in Cheltenham, in western England. It was based on the book of the same name by U.S. activist Kerry Kennedy about human rights leaders, including Digna herself.

"I am filled with sorrow to think that showing her on the stage could not help her to live, and not die," Dorfman told the Associated Press.

Kerry Kennedy got the news in New York. She was stunned, unwilling to believe someone so full of life and vitality, seemingly bigger than life, was gone. She knew she shouldn't have been shocked though, given what Digna had been through. "She lived in the line of fire," she would say later about the woman who had become her friend.[18]

Eva Alarcón was watching TV in her home in Petatlán, Guerrero, on Mexico's Pacific coast. A little over two weeks earlier, she had accompanied Digna on her last journey into the mountains, where she promised villagers she would "knock on doors" on their behalf. On the last day at the bus station, Eva had wrapped her big arms around Digna and given her a hug. "Be careful," she told her.

Now she was frozen at the news. Her lips moved but no sound came out. She stumbled into the bedroom and woke her husband. "Oh God, they've killed Digna," she cried out, before sinking to the floor in tears.

In Misántla, a town in eastern Veracruz state, in the house where Digna was born, a ringing phone interrupted the American League playoff game Eusebio Ochoa was watching on TV. He loved baseball and got up reluctantly to answer the phone. The news was the worst a father could get. He was a tough, old man, a former political prisoner who had lived through torture, but nothing was as bad as this. He gulped for air, then put on his old straw hat and walked stiffly out the front door and down the street to the town square. He sat on a bench, his head bowed, for a long time, struggling to compose himself before returning home to tell his ailing wife that their fifth child was dead.

* * *

The heavy metal door at the top of the spiral staircase at 31-A Zacatecas Street swung open and four men began to maneuver a stretcher through the narrow frame. On the stretcher was a small body, covered by a sheet and tied in place. It looked like the body of a child. They banged the stretcher against the door frame as they angled it out onto the narrow landing.

From the courtyard, heads strained upward. Nobody spoke. Time stood still, images forever indelible. Tears flowed, and nobody bothered to wipe them away.

Carefully, the men navigated the winding stairs. In Spanish, a spiral staircase is called *escalera de caracol,* literally "snail stairway," for the shape of the shell. And, aptly, it was at a snail's pace that the men came gently down, working against the perilous steepness in an effort to keep the body level.

On the ground, they loaded the stretcher into a waiting ambulance. Slowly, it pulled away, carrying Digna Ochoa into the night.

CHAPTER TWO

La Llorona

Under a waxing moon, as Digna's body was borne away, there were bad omens in the Valley of Mexico. The city shed its modern skin and sliped back into the mists of Tenochtitlán, the great capital city of the Aztecs, so named in the Nahuatl tongue before the Spanish Conquest. Ancient voices moaned from the depths of the earth. On the wind, and in fire, they lamented the betrayal of their most beloved daughter.

"Ay de mis hijos," wailed *La Llorona*. "My poor children," the Weeping Woman cried, on the night of the murder of Digna Ochoa.

For this night, when the sun set and the birds stopped singing in the floating gardens of Xochimilco in the south of the city, the legend of *La Llorona* was performed, as it is every year at this time, in the rituals leading up to the Day of the Dead. There are fireworks first, then torches and flickering candles to light the darkness, as spectators draw near in gondolas to watch a troupe of actors re-create the legend of *La Llorona*. They perform the play on a small island, amid canals dug more than half a millennium ago by the Aztecs and still beautiful.[1]

She is a phantom who rises out of the depths and walks among the people, wailing for her lost children. She has many forms and incarnations, in pre-Hispanic and modern times, this Earth Mother, this demon, this angel of death who beats her breast over the murder of her children. She is both nurturer and destroyer. Under the spotlight in the floating gardens of Xochimilco, *La*

Llorona holds the bloody knife in her upraised hand, slaying her own children rather than permit them to be taken by the Spanish conquerors. It is a story that continues to resonate in the hearts of Mexicans.

According to Aztec legend, she is Cihuacoatl, daughter of Coatlicue, all-powerful goddess of life and death. It is told by the elders how, long ago, she appeared in the night, dressed in flowing white robes, her skin coated with chalk, weeping over her loss. She was the all-powerful Mother who created the first man and woman to walk upon the earth, and her children and her children's children were the inhabitants of the shining city of Tenochtitlán. And so it was that the ancient priests understood the apparition of the Weeping Woman and, through her coming, foretold the fall of their empire and the aborning days of conquest and death by foreign invaders.[2]

The legends of *La Llorona* are abundant. But none bodes well. It is as if, on this night, Mother Earth herself had been violated.

"My poor children," wept *La Llorona*, as Digna's body was placed on a table in the amphitheater of Public Ministry No. 4,[3] 100 Chimalpopoca Street, Colonia Doctóres, in the heart of the modern city. By Mexican law, forensic investigators from a special unit of the prosecutor's office performed the first medical examination of a body, limiting their work to external observation. The autopsy and coroner's report would come later, well after midnight, at Mexico City's Medical Forensic Service, after her poor body had been transported once again through the dark streets of the city.

* * *

On Chimalpopoca Street, Digna's clothes had been removed and fabric samples sent for testing. They were stained with white powder and what appeared to be blood. Items were cataloged: a white, long-sleeve blouse with black piping at the neck and wrists; a pair of black ladies' slacks, with a front zipper and a hole surrounded by (what proved to be) powder burns in the upper part of the left leg; black boots with low heels; black socks with a white floral design; a beige brassiere and white panties.[4]

When they pulled off the big red rubber gloves, they saw that both hands were coated in powder. It was so thick it looked like she was wearing another pair of gloves.

The body was covered with a sheet, ready for identification. Juan Carlos Plácido, Digna's cousin, entered and stood over the table as the sheet was drawn slowly back from the corpse. He inhaled deeply and nods. "Yes," he said. "It's her, it's Digna, my cousin." *She looks so serene,* he thought to himself. *She looks like she's sleeping.*[5]

Ministry officials examined Digna's jewelry. She was a small woman, with small bones, and her jewelry was delicate. There were tiny, gold-colored earrings, flower clusters with a red stone at the center; a slim silver ring; a watch, brand-name Swerve, with a stainless steel head, white face, and black hands.

A police photo was taken of the watch. The hands read ten to nine.[6]

The black nylon bag with three zippered compartments was emptied of contents that were the accouterments of a life. The first side pocket contained six small bandages, eight lozenges, a roll of toilet paper, two wrapped sanitary napkins, a miniature bottle of hand lotion, two packets of toothpicks from the Mexican store chain Sanborns, a sewing kit, a toothbrush and toothpaste, and a black pen. In the other side pocket, there was a small black umbrella, a folded white plastic bag, a key chain with seven keys, a plastic hairclip, a nail file, two boxes of caramels, two faxes addressed to Digna Ochoa, three sheets of paper with legal notations, and a red pen.

Police didn't specify, but one of the faxes was likely a map to a little girl's birthday party on the morning of Saturday, October 20. Brigadier General José Francisco Gallardo, an internationally recognized prisoner of conscience, had been in jail as long as his daughter, Jessica, had been alive. This year he missed her eighth birthday. She was born a few months after he went to jail, following a military tribunal on trumped-up charges and a sentence of twenty-six years. His crime was daring to speak out about human rights abuses by the military.

His wife, Leticia—he calls her Lettie—telephoned Digna on Wednesday to invite her to the party and she said she would be delighted to attend. Lettie was pleased. Digna had visited her husband in jail and was trying to help him. Lettie admired her, believing her immensely brave for standing up to the Mexican Army. She faxed a map to Digna's office, showing the location of their apartment, in an army housing complex in the south, near the exit to Cuernavaca, and looked forward to Digna's arrival on Saturday morning.

In the third pocket of Digna's bag, there is a small denim-covered agenda with the brand name Mead. An appointment for *"Papás"* was entered for the evening of Thursday, October 18, and for 9:30 the next morning, there was a single entry: *"w/Sra. Marisol Rodríguez."* There is no explanation of either entry, the last arranged for the day of Digna's murder.

There was a zippered compartment, with a black leather wallet inside. It contained a driver's license, a phone card, a Mexican voting card for Digna Ochoa y Plácido, a man's photograph, two Metro tickets, 14 pesos, red and blue pens, sweets, and the black Nokia cell phone.

Digna loved this bag. She lugged it everywhere. There was a photograph of her with it on the beach in Acapulco, taken by her boyfriend on a sunny March day soon after they began seeing each other earlier that year. She was barefoot and laughing in the surf, wearing her pants rolled to her knees, a wide-brimmed straw hat on her head and that bag slung over her right shoulder.

Its contents offered clues to her personality and taste. Digna had a sweet tooth; she always did, perhaps even when she sold candy on the street as a seven-year-old, a little Totonaca Indian girl in

Misántla, in the state of Veracruz. She was meticulous and organized, ready with her sewing kit to mend a tear or replace a button, and savvy enough to know it's wise to carry one's own roll of toilet paper in Mexico. She cared enough for her boyfriend, Juan José Vera, nicknamed J.J., to carry his photo in the innermost secret compartment of her bag.

Police sent the white powder to the lab for testing. Samples were taken from Digna's hands, as they had been from the bookshelf, carpet, couches, black bag, and navy overcoat. The powder would turn out to be common starch, used for washing by women all over Mexico.

Fingerprint testing would show that a fragment found on the anonymous death threat left at the scene was insufficient for identification, as were other fragments collected at the crime scene. Police would say there were no leads.

* * *

By 11 P.M., in the Public Ministry amphitheater, Digna lay naked and faceup on a stainless steel table; the medical team was ready to proceed. Cold facts were recorded. The body, it was written, was that of a female, thirty-eight (Digna was in fact thirty-seven), with some muscular rigidity in her back and the body at room temperature—a notation made this night whose significance I wouldn't understood until much later in Digna's story.

They didn't record height or weight. I don't know how much she weighed at the time of her death but, in 1986, on forms for the Veracruz attorney general's office, where she was working, she listed her height as 1.60 meters (five feet three inches) and 54 kilos (118 pounds) as her weight.

No cause of death was listed. That was left to the coroner's report.

It was noted, however, that the victim had two gunshot wounds, one described as being in the left temporal region and the second in the left upper thigh. The head wound was shaped like a star with irregular borders, 1.5 by 2 inches. There was a .03 by .028

inch puncture of the skull bone, and powder burns within the star's perimeter and around the pericranium, which indicate the weapon was fired into Digna's head at point-blank range. There was no exit wound.

The victim also had a gunshot wound with an irregular border in the front of her upper left thigh, measuring 3.14 by 4.00 inches, and a smaller oval-shaped hole on the underside of the same thigh, measuring .028 by .026 inches. There was no attempt, in this examination, to identify entry and exit wounds. That, too, was left to the coroner's team.

Some time after midnight, Digna's naked body was rolled onto a stretcher, loaded into a hearse from the Gayoso Sullivan Funeral Home, retained by Digna's friend José Lavanderos, and driven once again through the dark city to the coroner's office on nearby Niños Héroes Avenue.

* * *

It was after two on Saturday morning when she was placed on another table for the autopsy, which, when it was written up later that morning, would list the cause of death as a gunshot wound to the head.

Her head had been shaved. A forensic photographer had taken pictures of the star-shaped entry wound on the left side, with its jagged borders and ugly plug of yellow bone showing at its center. There were close-ups of the sooty powder ground into the edges of the star and speckled around her scalp. Thick, clotted blood had dried in the wound, which looked raw and savage, a shockingly large hole from such a small bit of metal. That's the first thing that occured to me when I saw the photos a few months later. The small caliber bullet removed from Digna's skull wasn't much more than half an inch long.

The bullet, according to the coroner's report, passed through the skull from left to right, as makes sense from an entry wound on the left side of her head, and moved on a slight angle from up to down and from back to front. It remained embedded in her right temporal bone. Forensic personnel, wearing red latex gloves not dissimilar to the color of the gloves found on Digna's own hands, made an incision, pulled her scalp and hair forward over her face, and dissected her head with a saw in order to extract the bullet, by now battered and squashed into the shape of a fan. The bullet clattered onto a tray and was sent off to ballistics for testing.

The bullets and shells found at the scene would be analyzed in the lab, along with the gun found under Digna's body. Closer examination of the weapon showed that the grip was stamped "DUO," which means that the gun, or at least part of it, was made in Czechoslovakia. The registration number was M13711, and Mexican police sent out an alert through Interpol to trace its origins. The bullets were .22-caliber and the shells were stamped with an "A" on the bottom.

The second bullet entered Digna's thigh from the front and exited from the back. The autopsy report detailed the appearance of the wound, noting that it was not life-threatening and would have healed in two weeks.

Many months later, in March 2002, sitting in his office at the Medical Forensic Service on Niños Héroes, beneath a portrait of Mexico's most famous president, Benito Juárez, director Dr. José Ramón Fernández Cáceres[7] described for me what the .22-caliber bullet did to Digna's brain. On the desk in front of him was the coroner's report, dated October 20, 2001, and he scanned it before folding his arms and beginning to speak. He said the force of the bullet was so great that it split the cranial base of Digna's skull.

"It pierced everything and there was hemorrhaging and destruction of brain tissue and of the nervous system," he said. "The bullet passed through the brain, causing internal bleeding in the ventricle, and there was a fracture in the middle of the cranial base."

The bullet pulverized everything in its path. It smashed into the temporal bone, ripped through the meninges—the layers of membrane that cover the brain—and into the left temporal lobe, creating a pressure wave of devastation in its wake. Before it, brain tissue exploded outward into a quivering mass larger than the size of the projectile, and then collapsing inward, leaving a jagged tract.

The energy created by a bullet to a brain is so great that it is "as if internal tissue is running away as fast as it can from the bullet,"[8] a race it is doomed to lose. It couldn't run fast enough to save Digna.

It plowed through the gelatinous tissue of the brain—eight hundred times the density of air—and, in the minutest fraction of a second, damaged capacity for speech, memory, and motor skills, as if any of that mattered to Digna by the time its lethal journey was over. All in a split second, rampaging onward, it entered the ventricular chamber, where spinal fluid is produced, and caused massive, rushing bleeding inside Digna's brain.

It ripped through the corpus callosum, the carpet of nerve fibers that connects the left and right lobes, allowing them, in essence, to speak to each other. Finally, it entered the right temporal lobe, mashing brain tissue that controls spatial functions, and continued until, at last, the bullet thudded into the thick right temporal bone, where it stopped.

Digna would likely have succumbed in an instant, bleeding to death in her brain from the massive trauma of the mortal shot. It's also likely, although neurologists cannot know for sure, she would have felt nothing.[9]

The bullet to her thigh, however, would have caused pain, unless she was pumped so full of adrenaline that she was past feeling. The reports did not estimate how long she lived after she was shot the first time, and Dr. Fernández said he didn't know.

He did confirm, however, during our interview in 2002, that forensic examiners at the Public Ministry on Chimalpopoca Street estimated the time of death to be between noon and 2 P.M. He again perused the file and said the autopsy began about twelve hours after death. He explained that they would have based their estimate of the time of death on the temperature and characteristics of Digna's body, such as the degree of muscular rigidity that had settled into her back. (Mexico City is seventy-five hundred feet above sea level and, at this altitude, rigor mortis takes about fifteen hours to set in completely before a body begins to go flaccid again. This reverse process starts at the head and, after about twenty-four hours, rigor has disappeared and the corpse is flaccid again.)

There were differences but, to my later chagrin, I thought little of them during my only chance to interview Dr. Fernández. Right after Digna's murder, for example, he told reporters that she died between 1 and 3 P.M.—but I let it pass. Neither did I press him when he said that nobody recorded Digna's actual body temperature.

The contents of Digna's stomach showed she ate about six hours before death. The food was too well digested to be identifiable.[10] "Here in Mexico," Dr. Fernández told me, "the custom is to eat at three in the afternoon and ten at night, and to have something in the morning."

Digna's last meal was breakfast.

* * *

It was a grim conversation about the clinical evidence with the esteemed Dr. Fernández on a warm March afternoon, five months after the crime. But there was comic relief. Dr. Fernández, who headed the Medical Forensic Service for a capital city of twenty-two million people, taught at the National Autonomous University of Mexico, and has performed thousands of autopsies, smoked like a fiend. A veritable smokestack. A heavy man, with a sad dog demeanor and large glasses, he chain-smoked throughout a long interview about Digna's murder, lighting each new prospect with the smoldering stub of the last.

I was unable to resist the urge to ask him about his habit.

"Doctor, how many pairs of lungs have you examined? It must be thousands and thousands, and yet you *still smoke?*"

He grunted. "Ahhh, but I will tell you what I told my students during an autopsy once when they asked me what caused all those little black dots on the lungs. I told them there are two explanations: those who don't smoke say they're from cigarettes and those who do, say it's from smog. Well, this autopsy was on a baby of six months. And so, you see, there can be no doubt—it's the smog."

* * *

On the morning of October 20, 2001, Digna's autopsy took an hour and a quarter, a feat that would, much later, be snidely described by an international investigative team as "record time." Dr. Fernández said it began at 2:15 A.M. and, at half past three, Digna's family was allowed to claim her remains. Juan Carlos Plácido filled out the paperwork.[11]

The autopsy time did seem unreasonably short, I suggested to Dr. Fernández, especially given who Digna was and the circumstances of her death. "Not at all, not at all," he said, taking off his glasses and wiping them with a tissue.

"Here in Mexico, we have a different custom, a different way of doing things than in Canada or the United States," he began.

"Up there," and he gestured vaguely skyward, "you can keep the body for a whole week to carry out the studies. Here, if we keep the body for more than two hours, the family starts making noises. Here in Mexico, the custom is to have the wake immediately. . . . People spend the whole night with the body. In some parts of the country they have parties, dinner, music, because the custom is to recognize the person is going away to a better life. . . . Nobody leaves until the body is buried.

"So, on one hand, one needs to respect the customs and, on the other hand, the public prosecutor is in a hurry for us to hand in our reports, which is what happened in this particular case. . . . Of course, the doctors who perform the autopsy take samples from the organs, the blood, and we send them to the laboratory and the results of these tests we call the amplification of the autopsy report."

Such tests on Digna revealed that she was not pregnant and there was no semen in her body. Nor were there traces of drugs or alcohol in her bloodstream. Her blood type was O Rh-positive.

* * *

Shortly after eleven on Friday night, Juan José Vera was leaving the Eric Clapton concert at Mexico City's best rock venue, Foro del Sol. He had seen Digna only once since she returned to the capital from Guerrero more than two weeks earlier. Both had been busy with work and they had to cancel a date the previous weekend when he came down with the flu. But they had spoken every day on the telephone, and had plans for Saturday after she returned to the city from Almoloya prison.

The night before she died, Digna called him around nine, as she was finishing up her work in the Zacatecas Street office. "I'm done. I'm going to go home," she said. Then she laughed. "I'm calling you now because if I call you later, you will be asleep. And when you are asleep, you say 'yes' to everything."

Juan José was a round-faced man, made rounder by round spectacles. He was as blind as a bat without them. He had regular features, a goatee and moustache, and a little bit of a pot, which he was trying to lose. It was hard, though, when both his mother and his girlfriend fussed over him with his favorite dishes. Mexican mothers treasure their boys. They call them their *varones* and as such they are treated, like little barons. Juan José, in his early forties, separated and in the middle of a divorce, moved back home with his widowed mother, Raquel Mendoza, who had a spacious home in a northern suburb. He lived at the absolute opposite end of the capital city from Digna's apartment building in the south.

He was in high spirits that night, buoyed by the concert, and belting out an off-key version of "Over the Rainbow," when his cell phone rang. He had just turned it back on after the concert and picked it up to hear the voice of Digna's young niece, Miranda.

"They've killed her," she told him. "They've killed Digna."

People had been trying to reach him all night. "*Hola,* Juan José, if you're there, or pass by there, give me a call. It's Carmen Herrera, Digna's friend, and I need to talk to you. Please get in touch with me as soon as possible, please, it's a serious issue," said a message left on Digna's answering machine at 8:23 P.M.

J.J. barely had time to grasp Miranda's words when his cell phone rang again. This time, it was his mother. "Tell me it's not true, Mother. Please, it can't be true," he gasped, before Raquel had a chance to speak. She told him she'd just seen Digna's murder reported on Televisa. She was crying. She had a good relationship with her son's girlfriend. Digna often referred to her as *mi suegra,* letting the word roll deliciously off her tongue, even though Raquel wasn't her real "mother-in-law."

"*Uf!, Mi suegra,* what problems she gives me," she would say to Eva Alarcón in the Guerrero mountains, and chuckle, as if savoring the many aspects of having a relationship with a man after so many years alone. For eight years, she was with the Dominican nuns in Mexico City, leaving in 1999 without taking her final vows. Now she had fun complaining about a woman she adored. "My poor mother-in-law, I know she doesn't agree with me but she won't say that to me," she told Eva. "She respects me and my way of thinking—although she wishes I were different."

"Digna, it's Raquel, I am trying to communicate with you. I wish you would please give me a call. Thanks," said her message on Digna's machine at 10:32 P.M. *It can't be her,* Señora Mendoza was thinking as she spoke slowly into the receiver, her mind flashing on the TV report.

Digna was helping Raquel draw up her will. She worked on it the evening before. At 5:23 P.M., Thursday, October 18, in what would turn out to be her last hours, she sent an email to J.J. "*Hola, mi amor,* please give this to your mother. Thanks. I love you."

Digna sent a blank will for Raquel, with detailed instructions on filling it out. "If you want we can follow through with this. I propose that, once it's completed, I can review it and you can go ahead and have it witnessed. If you like, I can accompany you. . . . I suggest you don't date the will until the day that you file it. . . . If you have any doubts, ask me, and we will figure it out together. *Saludos,* Digna."

Digna made a joke in the way she wrote "ask me," drawing out the verb in Spanish *(pregúntame)* to become "*Preguuuuuuuúntame,*" talking like her favorite character, Donkey, in the movie *Shrek*.

J.J.'s phone wouldn't stop ringing now. Maybe it's what saved him that night. Moments later, Juan Carlos Plácido called. They exchanged words of disbelief, and Juan Carlos asked him to drive to Digna's apartment in Lomas de Plateros and pick out something for her to wear, which he did. He was on automatic pilot, unlocking Digna's door, reaching into her closet, and pulling out a dress that would be suitable for a funeral. Later, he remembered nothing about it, except that it was dark and he was sobbing as he stuffed it into a bag. He drove to the coroner's offices on Niños Héroes, where he waited with Juan Carlos for the invasion of the autopsy to end and the procession to the funeral home to begin.

He waited at a location where, just as *La Llorona* signaled this night's beginning, the gods of the Aztecs gazed upon its sad end. Outside the capital's forensic building, there was a large and famous statue of Coatlicue, mother of Cihuacoatl, her clawed feet on a pedestal of black marble. Her name means "Serpent Skin" and she is horrible to behold, a two-headed snake with the body of a woman. Human hearts and hands are strung around her neck and a skull dangles from her belt.[12] She is Life and Death, the duality of existence, and she keeps vigil over the images of the swimming child in the womb and the skeleton drawn up in death, which are carved into the façade of the building where the dead give up their secrets to the living.

* * *

By Saturday afternoon, detective Martín Valderrama Almeida and forensic photographers Renato Hernández Jiménez and Carlos Barajas Colín, from the prosecutor's office, wrapped up their findings. These investigators, fresh from the scene, signed a preliminary report on the death of Digna Ochoa y Plácido, in which they detailed conclusions and presented the most probable scenario of the day before at 31-A Zacatecas Street, Colonia Roma, in the Federal District.[13] They had compiled twenty-two points, followed by a twenty-third, which recounted the most likely chain of events.[14]

Their report began: "On the basis of thanatological [in death] observations of the deceased, it is estimated that death occurred no more than eight and no less than six hours before our investigation." They began their work at 8 P.M., and therefore calculated that Digna died between noon and 2 P.M. They determined that her assailant(s) entered by the main entrance, and that the lock was not forced, indicating free entry. There would be speculation that she knew the killers, or one of them. The premises were not greatly disturbed and nothing was missing, indicating that robbery was not the motive. The white button, found on the couch and confirmed to be from Digna's blouse, along with the headband found on the floor near the door, indicated that there was "a struggle between the killer and the victim."

Three bullets were fired, one into the south couch, another into the victim's thigh, and a third into her skull. Positive nitrate testing (the Walker test) and the presence of powder burns on the skin indicated the mortal bullet to her skull was fired at point-blank range.

The weapon was a semiautomatic handgun, with "DUO" stamped on the grip. At this point in the investigation, police were calling it a .22-caliber lr (for long rifle). It's a hybrid, a sawed-off rifle barrel stuck on the body of a handgun. The magazine is located in front of the trigger and the team traced the trajectories of the three shells they found, based on the fact that this particular gun ejects cartridges upward and to the right. One of the shells was flattened and the detectives duly reported that someone probably stepped on it.

There was a particularly gruesome dimension to Digna's murder. The gloves, they wrote, "were pulled onto the hands of the deceased after she was murdered."

Somebody moved Digna's body. Or, as the detectives noted, "based on lividity [the pooling of blood through gravity after death], bloodstains, the arrangement and state of the clothes, as well as related signs, we can establish that the position of the body observed when the criminal investigation was undertaken was not the same position in which the victim died."

Point #23 concluded their report. It detailed "with a high degree of probability" what happened to Digna:

The victim enters the building and walks toward the office, carrying her bag and over-coat (found in her right arm), enters the office, closes the door, and proceeds down the passage to the chairs located against the west wall of the reception area. She leaves her bag on one of the chairs.

Some time later, there is a knock at the door. She opens it and, in that instant, is surprised by the killer, who threatens her with a gun. He pulls her into the reception area where, to intimidate her, he fires a shot, having first placed the barrel's mouth against a cushion of the couch, which is against the south wall, in order to muffle the sound.

Then, still threatening the victim, the killer sits her on the couch against the north wall (and) placing himself on her left, pushes the barrel of the gun into her left thigh, a distance of no more than one centimeter, and fires. This accounts for the bloodstains, the hole in the cushion, and the recovered bullet in the couch.

Then, the killer places the victim in the center of the room, he's on her left, and presses the barrel of the gun to her left temporal region and fires point-blank into her skull, killing her. It is most likely that the deceased was positioned with her trunk leaning slightly forward, and the killer simply released her and let her fall forward onto the carpet, with her head on the couch.

The killer places the gun in the position where it was later found and carries out a series of maneuvers to mess up the scene, such as strewing about the powder, which, possibly, he brought with him.

He puts powder in the gloves and pulls them up to cover the hands of the victim and repositions her head, which is on the corner of the couch, onto its side. He completes the final act of leaving the white paper with text in capital letters on the reception desk, and leaves the office by the main door.

The detectives knew that the killer repositioned Digna's head because the bloodstains under her head were dry, indicating that the cushion where she lay had been exposed to air.

This report by Team No. 1, as it would become known, was not made public. (I wouldn't see it until July 2003, when the Mexico City Attorney General's Office published it online.) It was confusing in parts and left many unanswered questions, as might be expected in a report compiled within twenty-four hours of a homicide. In the coming weeks and months, details would be leaked to the media, including crime scene photos of Digna's corpse, creating controversy around an increasingly problematic investigation.

It was clear, however, that Digna was murdered. Mexico City attorney general Bernardo Bátiz emphasized that fact at a press conference the following Saturday morning, promising that his authorities would not rest until Digna's killers were brought to justice. He said the crime is "undoubtedly political in nature— a violent attack against a person who dedicated her life to the defense of human rights and people who she felt were persecuted for political reasons. Her murder is a loss to the entire human rights community, as well as to those who were touched by her work."

A few days later, senior Mexico City investigator Patricia Bulgarín revealed another intriguing piece of information. At a press conference, she said Digna's body showed significant bruising, which she characterized as "signs of a violent struggle" before she was shot.[15]

It was more proof of Digna's agonizing final moments, proof that not everyone would remember in the months to come.

* * *

Mexico is rich in the surreal, and so the Bátiz press conference, held shortly before the funeral mass that Saturday afternoon, provided a layer of bizarre and inadvertent comedy. Digna surely would have appreciated it.

The attorney general was a most serious man, a lawyer who wore thick glasses, a thick beard, and the distracted air of the scholar deep in thought. He was a man given to stern pronouncements and a lack of levity, as befitted a former professor at Ibero-American University in Mexico City, a college founded and run by Jesuits.

"*San Bernardo* (Saint Bernardo)," reporters called him. His sidekick, the Jesuit-educated Renato Sales, was *Beato Renato* (Blessed Renato).

On that Saturday morning, speaking about Digna's murder, he opined that the crime was "undoubtedly political" because the killers left an anonymous threat addressed to his own political party, the Democratic Revolutionary Party. The leftist PRD had come to power in the Federal District four years earlier when Cuauhtémoc Cárdenas became the first mayor to be democratically elected, in 1997. Political scientist Andrés Manuel López Obrador won again for the PRD in 2000. Bátiz was the most senior officer of the law in the Federal District and a significant player in the López Obrador cabinet. An important man.

He informed reporters gathered at City Hall that Digna's killers left an anonymous threat at the crime scene—*"This is no trick"*—aimed at members of the PRD. He said that it was left by "somebody who felt persecuted by members of the PRD, who weren't named, but who were warned the same thing would happen to them if they continued."[16]

The assembled journalists took their notes and reported the story.

But it was PRO that was mentioned in the note, not PRD—*PRO!*

The threat was directed at other lawyers with Miguel Agustín Pro Juárez Human Rights Center, not at the political party in power in the Federal District.

It would take several days for the error to be sorted out and for officials to explain that it was a natural mistake. The "O" looked like a "D." Perhaps, given that so many PRD activists have been murdered in this country over the past decade, the mistake was understandable for the Mexico City attorney general and his department to make.

However, a queasy feeling was already settling into this investigation, the same malaise Víctor Brenes and José Lavanderos felt the night of the murder, watching police fall over themselves at the crime scene. There was a cockeyed, Keystone Kops quality to the investigation, and it was going to be difficult to shake in the days ahead.

Perhaps it was nothing, this apparent ineptitude, but it was, alas, another bad omen in a city of bad omens that had just begun to weep for Digna Ochoa.

CHAPTER THREE

Smile, Life Is Marvelous

Late Saturday afternoon, a lonely caravan journeyed east from Mexico City to Jalapa and then wound northward through the mountains to the village of Misántla in Veracruz. Digna's family and friends were bringing her home.

J.J., at the wheel of his white Tzuru, never imagined he would be burying this woman who burst into his life the previous February. They talked about the dangers of her work but she always seemed so full of life that he came to believe she was invincible.

Digna's mother, Irene, wasn't happy with their relationship— after all, J.J. was still legally married and a former Protestant lay pastor—but others close to Digna were delighted. Her younger sister Esthela embraced J.J. wholeheartedly. These two sisters had a special bond. They used to chat on the telephone almost every day, sharing their secrets. They looked alike, with the same high cheekbones, dark eyes, and delicate features. Esthela could see that Digna was happy and was glad for her. She worked at the Bital Bank in Martín de la Torre near Misántla and, when she could, she visited her sister in Mexico City. She had spent the long weekend with Digna and J.J. over Holy Week in April, getting to know them and joining them for day trips outside the city.

It was a short romance, barely nine months, but during their time together, Digna brought J.J. into her circle of friends. "She was very happy," said José Lavanderos. "I think her relationship really did help her. We used to make jokes and I would say to her, 'What is J.J. giving you, you look so happy?' And she would blush and say, 'I am very well, I am very happy.' It was true, I had never seen her so happy. She was so in love. It is obvious in the photographs. She was truly radiant."

Indeed she was. Digna shone in that photo taken on the beach in Acapulco, with her straw hat akimbo, pants rolled up, and feet in the sea. J.J. took the picture. It was their first romantic weekend, a couple of weeks after Digna returned to Mexico City from Washington in March 2001, and she looked relaxed and happy. There was J.J., sitting under a *palapa* (straw umbrella), wearing rose-colored glasses and making a funny face, goofy and vulnerable.

Theirs was an unusual love story, if one dares comment on the secrets of the human heart. They met online in a chat room for Spanish speakers thirty-five and older. It was February 2001, and Digna was living in exile in Washington and working for the Center for Justice and International Law (CEJIL), a job that was arranged for her before she went into exile. At work, she was very busy, researching cases in preparation for the upcoming spring sessions of the Inter-American Human Rights Commission, which was based in Washington, D.C. Digna worked on files involving people who had been tortured, kidnapped, and threatened with death because of their political activities, and the hours were long and intense. Still, she was lonely and desperate for Mexico, where she felt she truly belonged. By this time other events, shadowy and inexplicable, had occurred in her life and she was feeling particularly isolated.

From her studio apartment in Adams Morgan, she entered a virtual world, calling herself Diana, and soon began corresponding with a man back in Mexico City. He introduced himself as Antonio, before telling her that his real name was Juan José and that he was a mathematics teacher in the Mexican capital. When she told him she was living north of Mexico City, he guessed Monterrey. "Further north," she said, letting him guess other places before she finally told him it was Washington. It didn't take long for Digna's colleagues to realize something was up. CEJIL director Viviana Krsticevic remembered: "There was a light in her eyes."

J.J. saved most of Digna's e-mails, but only a few of his own. He didn't want to use up the memory on his e-mail account. Besides, at the time, he didn't think they were relevant. It is chilling to read her words now—to share her hopes and passion for life—when we know how little time remained to her.

Her letters were playful, eloquent, and full of exuberance. She loved puns, slang, risqué humor, and anglicisms (her favorite word was "super") and she was a great fan of capital letters and screaming punctuation!!!!!!!! She adored the French language. She lived for six months in France, at the motherhouse of her order, the Dominicans of the Incarnate Word, and occasionally slipped in a word in French. She was sentimental; that much was clear. And, at times, an almost girlish yearning crept in and one remembers that Digna was only a year out of the convent, where she spent eight years before deciding against taking her final vows as a Dominican nun.

One can imagine her on a wintry (compared to Mexico City) Washington afternoon in early 2001, sitting down at her computer and beginning to write.[1] These two were not long into their relationship, the forty-something, bespectacled math teacher who had moved back in with his mother in Mexico City and Digna, coming up on her thirty-seventh birthday in May, and longing to connect with someone who understood her as a woman.

Sunday, February 11, 2001, 2:03 P.M.[2]

Hola Juan José,

You give me a good vibe when you talk to me and make me realize that, indeed, yes, you do exist and that, even more, I believe I will get to know you in person. This experience gives me pleasure. Now, I must get back to work but I am thinking of you. The truth is that you unsettle me a little today, but it's a good feeling. My window looks out over a little park and there is lovely sunshine, even though it is slightly cold. Of course, not inside, but I can feel the cold air because the window is open. I have to prepare several things for the upcoming week but I look forward to receiving your e-mails. I feel a little childish, but quite content really. I think it is worthwhile to give ourselves an opportunity to enjoy and make the most of life. Behave as you like and as best you can. I will get to work and merely imagine you. I am going to banish you from my mind for a while so that you will let me work.

Ciao, Diana

Monday, February 12, 3:49 P.M.

Hola, Juan José,

I was pleased that you telephoned to talk to me on Saturday and I hope we can maintain this contact. I check my e-mail every day. In this way, we'll begin to get to know each other a little better, don't you think? I would like that very much. I don't know what will come of this, but I do want to do it. A kiss—and you can put it wherever you want.

Diana

There was a gap in the correspondence. This mysterious "Diana" appeared to have disappeared and J.J. was annoyed. He fired off an e-mail:[3]

Diana,

Another day without any news from you. What's going on? Are you okay? Don't you want to chat with me anymore?[4] I'd be grateful if you'd just let me know.

J.J.

Their correspondence resumed with e-mails from Digna after President Day's, Monday, February 19. She alluded to her work with the center but she was careful not to say too much about who she was or what she did—at least, for now. Given the importance of Digna's work in her life (and what we would later learn about her suffering while in exile in Washington), such caution rather limited the scope of her letters and kept them, for the most part, breezy and superficial. Perhaps she was more forthcoming on the telephone, but it didn't seem so. She appeared to be careful about not revealing too much to this man she had never met.

She finally wrote back.

Tuesday, February 20, 1:07 A.M.
Hola, I'm here and I do apologize but I just arrived and got your message, and I'm answering you right away. But I must get to bed so I will write you tomorrow.

Good night, Diana

In the morning, she kept her promise. Curiously, she reverted to calling him Antonio. Was she chiding him a little for his impatience? As we would soon see, it did not escape his notice.

Tuesday, February 20, 9:22 A.M.
Hola Antonio,
Today I am more awake than I was last night when I wrote you my *petit message*.[5] I was away from the city and I just came back last night, which is why I didn't write to you before. How are you? How have you spent these last few days? I have been super, I had a lot of fun and a lot of Mexican food because I got together with Mexican friends so it was just super. For me, it's wonderful finding people from home, people whom I love a lot.

Yesterday was a holiday here so I took advantage of the opportunity and I got back at midnight. Another thing I'd like you to know is that I haven't returned to the chat room. I hope to get to know you better and if our relationship turns out, I'd prefer not to look for anybody else.

51

I am pleased to perceive that you go after what you want most. I think it is so important in life to be who we want to be and to do what makes us most happy—even if it exhausts us, which is completely normal.

I will be back home in Mexico soon but there's going to be a great deal of work for me over the coming days. I think I am going to be busy all the time. Consequently, I'll be able to write you this week, but next week I can't guarantee anything. I hope that you understand. Work is work and usually I arrive home so exhausted that the only thing I want is sleep. I know the kind of meetings that await me. At a later date, I will speak to you in more detail about exactly what it is I do.

Well, I am going back to work. It's what I must do.

Talk to you soon,

Diana

SMILE, LIFE IS MARVELOUS!!!!!!!!!!

Thursday, February 22, 9:05 A.M.

Hola Juan José,

I have more time to write you now and, rereading your e-mail, I can see you are a bit upset with me because I called you Antonio. But you sent me an e-mail in which you said you were Antonio and it made me think that, when you did tell me your name, it wasn't your real name either.

Look, for me sincerity and trust are important. But I figured that you hadn't given me your real name and so, if I offended you, I'm sorry. That was never my intention.

Diana

Friday, February 23, 11:26 A.M.

Hola Juan José,

The truth is that I would like us to be able to continue our virtual friendship and I hope it is real and sincere. Even if this is all it turns out to be, I believe that we will have gained something, me an *amigo* and you an *amiga*[6]—someone with whom we can share and confide, especially since I know that one has to build trust and feed it continuously with sincerity.

You tell me you'll be away for the weekend. I hope you'll be okay. You didn't tell me that you give classes in mathematics or that you were a teacher.[7]

Tell me, where do you give classes?

You know, I'm currently in New York and it's a very cold day with a lot of snow, but in only 20 days I will be back home. I want to keep in touch with you, so that we can get to know each other little by little and then, we shall see.

Well, hope everything goes well, Diana

Monday, February 26, 2002, 11:24 P.M.

Hola, I was delighted to receive your message and, despite the fact I'm in a hurry, I don't want to leave without telling you that I am thinking of you. Yes, I am returning around the middle of March and I'll let you know exactly when so that we can meet. How does that sound to you? And in the meantime, I would like to keep exchanging e-mails in order to get to know each other better.

You must understand that, as I told you, I have so much work to do all this week. That's just how it is. But I will write you with more attention later. I am thinking about you and I hope that you are doing the same with me.

Diana

J.J. left Mexico City for a few days. Upon his return, he wrote to Digna.

Hola guapísima (most attractive)!!!!!!!!!!!
I am back again in our Mexico City where the news, by popular decision, is that we don't have to change the clocks.[8]

The conference was 50-50: some meetings were very good and a couple were very bad, but such is life in tropical countries.

Yes, of course, among my activities I also teach. I have been doing that for years and it's like a hobby for me despite the fact that I take it very seriously. Right now I am teaching mathematics and computer science at the secondary level.

I suppose that you will be back in Mexico around the 15th of the month? I hope everything is all right and that you will be able to leave that freezing weather behind you very soon. Here it is spring and it is becoming more apparent every day.

I would like you to tell me what you expect of our imminent meeting, and please tell me a little more about what you are doing in New York, if you can. My message won't be as long as I'd like today because I want to get to bed early. I am sending you a hug and a kiss in anticipation of our next encounter.

Sweet dreams,

Juan José

Thursday, March 1, 1:55 A.M.

Hola Juan José,

How are you, how's it going, how's your work? Look, every day I am happier to be going back to Mexico and the truth is that I would like you to tell me a little more about yourself in these coming days so that I will be able to know you better and, in that manner, if we do meet each other, it will be more enjoyable. You know, I do feel that we know each other already, even if it's only slightly.

Look, these days I'm back in Washington, D.C., at the sessions of the Inter-American Human Rights Commission.[9] This week has been rather heavy, but with a lot of personal satisfaction because I have learned many new things. Moreover, I saw all my friends, some from Mexico, who flew in for the sessions. Well, then, I will be able to talk to you in more detail about all of these complicated things in the future.[10]

Last night I watched the soccer game between Mexico and the USA with friends. We had a Mexican dinner even though we are all from different countries—Colombia, Venezuela, Brazil, Argentina, USA, Spain,

Italy, and Mexico—and very cosmopolitan, as you can guess. After dinner, we talked, laughed, and sang and it was just super. I love these kinds of get-togethers because they bring together so many different people who are, above all else, my *amigos* and *amigas*. We share our experiences, our political vision, our interests, but nobody ever discusses their romantic life.

I am thinking about you. I try to imagine you but I can't quite conjure up your features in my mind.

Are you still going into the chat room where I talked to you the first time? Not me. On one hand, because I want to meet you personally and, on the other, because of all the absorbing work that I have had. But I can't complain because I do what I want.

You told me that you were married and that you have two children. What's your relationship like with them now? Is there any possibility of reconciliation with your ex-wife? Do you still see her? Do you want to go back with her?

What do you like to do on the weekends, for example?

Okay, I hope you will have a little free time so that you can write and tell me more about yourself. That is, of course, if us getting to know each other better is what you want too. Beyond that, one day we'll talk about a torrent of different things.

Will write again soon, Diana

Digna was preparing to leave Washington. Without telling J.J., she had booked a flight home for Sunday, March 4. She wanted to surprise him. But her last days turned into an emotional rollercoaster, beginning on Friday when she logged into the chat room where she met J.J. and got a shock. One can imagine her seething all day at work before, in the early hours of the next morning, she blasted off this note.

Saturday, March 3, 1:42 A.M.

Juan José,

More than anything, please forgive me for being a foolish dreamer.

55

Really, I don't think you can possibly know or guess what has happened, nor would I expect you to. Well, I am going to tell you now.

Since the very first time I chatted with you, I never went back into that chat room, first because of all my work, and second, because I had begun to exchange e-mails with you and I believed that we could try to build something between us. Yesterday, I arrived at the office after a morning loaded with work, very tense and tired (of course, you can't have foreseen this) and, while eating a sandwich (nutritious meal??), it occurred to me to check my e-mail and reread your last message to me. And, I don't know why, but at that moment I figured it would be fun to talk with you and, since I was alone, I went into the chat room again and realized that you were there. To tell you the truth, I was very happy to see that you were there but what really bothered me was that you thought I was somebody else. Certainly, my mistake was to ask you to guess who I was.

You guessed that I was "The Woman from Monterrey," and then you called me by a different name.

I don't know if I am being objective or not, but I felt offended. It's made me realize I can't continue with something that perhaps won't work out. Moreover, I told you that it was my first and only experience in the chat room and that I didn't want to meet anybody else. I don't think this sort of relationship makes sense to me anymore.

I know that if I want to begin an intimate relationship with somebody, it has to be by making contact with the person in a normal fashion. I believe that I will have that eventually.

In simple terms, please forgive me for giving up at the first obstacle but I prefer to leave it there for my own good. Thank you for making me think I could dream with you. I think you are a good person and you surely will find somebody who will love you and who will accept everything. I thought I could do it, but I see now that I can't.

Thanks for everything.

Sincerely, Diana

J.J. fired back a response:

No, no and no. I don't accept your decision. Don't I have an opinion here? Don't I have any voice or vote in this? I have no doubt that you are going to do what you decide to do, but don't be unfair. You're not the only one with a dream. I have one too. At least give me a chance to defend myself. Please, I've never asked anything of you. Today, I ask you to come back into the chat room and give me a chance. Don't you want one too?

Please.

J.J.

J.J. was trying, but he knew he was in trouble. He had, in fact, guessed the names of several different women he'd met in the chat room, not just the woman from Monterrey. He waited for Digna's answer, which didn't take long.

Saturday, March 3, 10:16 A.M.

Hola Juan José,

I am reading my mail and, of course, your message. Again, I say, forgive me, I feel silly, and I think I must be silly for having sought to find someone in this way.

It's true that we never made any major commitments; we simply agreed to write to each other in order to get to know each other better and then attempt to meet.

I took it so seriously that I was thinking about you, trying to imagine you from your description of yourself. There's no doubt in my mind that I am still dreaming but I can tell you, at the least, that it is a lovely dream. And yes, you have the right to think and say whatever you want to me even though, in the end, I think it's better that we leave it here. I don't want to keep thinking about what will happen between us.

Well, I guess in the end it was nothing. It's all virtual and it's as if it doesn't exist, don't you think?

I think that you're a good guy and that you'll find the person you're looking for and I'll try to do the same. But not through this medium because it can never be anything but virtual.

Today is a new day and each day is a gift, a new opportunity for us to do what we want, what we can and what we should do. Everybody has to try and take advantage of each day. I'm convinced that this life is marvelous and beautiful. As long as we're alive, we take the good with the bad, sadness as well as happiness—that's life and we just have to know how to enjoy it.

And of course you have the right to answer as you wish, but I don't think it is going to change anything. Moreover, I don't believe I have any right to ask anything of you so don't stop going into the chat room just because I am being foolish.

Again, forgive me.

Good luck. Diana

J.J. wrote back rapidly, apparently telling her that he was the one feeling upset and playing on her sympathy, and she responded again.

Saturday, March 3, 1:50 P.M.

Look, Juan José,

It is not that I consider you bad news; it's just that I think that I am. And to tell you the truth, I felt really bad when I received your last e-mail. Maybe you're right. But this little incident made me feel bad about myself—you know, not only for you, but for me.

It's true that I felt I was starting to know you and that I was pleased. You seemed sincere and I prayed to God that it was true, and began to dream and think about you. You make me happy and I smile when I think about you, and my friends noticed and began to ask me what was happening but, clearly, I didn't tell anything to anyone. They imagined that it was because there was somebody in my life but still, I didn't share this relationship that I was starting with you with anyone.

Tell me, do you really think that we can continue and honestly try again?

Well, here is the way I feel now: I am happy to be thinking about you. I realize that I am afraid of falling in love and maybe it is because of fear that I don't want to allow myself this chance. I know that I don't want to suffer, at least not for this. Normally, I feel very confident—I decide, I speak, and I do—but in this realm, I have been quite reserved lately because I haven't wanted to risk being disappointed.

I don't know if it is right telling you all these things but I do want to speak to you with my heart in my hand, because this is how I feel at this point.

I am in my apartment alone and thinking about all this, about myself, about what to do and the truth is, I don't know.

Today, there's sunshine, with a few clouds and they are saying that it's going to snow tomorrow. I'd like to see it snow, as long as I am in the apartment and I don't have to go out. Last week, it snowed a lot and I had to go out and it was freezing. Imagine, it was snowing so much that I carried my umbrella. The problem is that the snow didn't stay on my umbrella, but rather on my coat, which turned completely white. It was really windy and the snow was hitting me in the face, which wasn't very pleasant at all. If I hadn't had a meeting, I wouldn't have gone out for anything.

When it's snowing and I'm here, I love to sit in front of the window. I have a view of the park and an intersection and it's quite lovely. The park turns white with the snow, as do the trees, and I am enchanted by this spectacle. But I wouldn't trade Mexico for anything.

Tell me all the news from Mexico for it could be that it's the only reason that I am writing to you.

Thank you for understanding me and, above all, for being patient.

Diana

Whatever J.J. wrote in response this time, it would be enough for Digna. Plus, he told her about Mexico City. She was mollified (as if she really meant her good-byes) and eager to share her life again. It was her last weekend in Washington, but she didn't tell J.J. exactly when she was coming home. She wanted her arrival to be a surprise.

Saturday, March 3, 8:30 P.M.

Juan José,

I just got back from shopping and I am going out again. My friends are preparing a good-bye party for me. I tell them they're happy to be rid of me and then they get upset. But the person who is really happy is me.

Really, I think you're right and I do want to give it a try. When we finally meet, we'll realize that everything was a figment of our imagination. Life goes on, but at least we are going to give ourselves a chance.

I will telephone you when I arrive, and I'll write before, too. Thanks for sharing with me a piece of the landscape of my beautiful and beloved Mexico. When I read it, I could really imagine it and I was transported to the city. Even with all its corruption, insecurity, noise, pollution, I realize that I love D.F. and, soon, I will be able to enjoy for myself the landscape you described today.

Thanks, too, for beginning to share your life with me. These everyday things are what's really important—I believe it's the little details of life that are the most important. The big ones are always quite obvious, but sometimes we don't give enough value to the little ones.

Thanks again for your honesty. I think it is an essential element when you are sharing, whatever the relationship may be.

Until next time, Diana

The next day, Sunday, March 4, Digna took the late afternoon United Airlines flight from Washington-Dulles Airport to Mexico City. Her cousin, Juan Carlos Plácido, met her at the airport. She was excited to be home and fairly bursting to share her secret with J.J.

Monday, March 5, 2:41 P.M.
New day, new week, full of hope and happiness

Hola Juan José,

I am reading you now. It is 2:30 in the afternoon and I have a problem with my computer so I am at an Internet café really close to where I am living. Do you like surprises? Well, I have one for you. Can you give me your telephone number again? Maybe I'll call you one of these days. I won't be able to check my e-mail again until tomorrow at midday.

You didn't go to the office today? Don't you take the bus if your car breaks down?

I don't know but I have been thinking about you. Did I tell you that they're asking me why I am so happy, more than just returning? Of course, I haven't told any of my friends about you.

So, do you think we can go to Sanborns?[11] What do you think? I love milk shakes and it's been such a long time since I've tasted one. Well, if I start to eat all the things I haven't eaten for so long, I don't know if I can stop. But I know that I have to prioritize and take small doses of everything I want to taste and eat.

My friends tell me they don't know how I can eat the way I do and not get fat. Hey, I'm not trying to scare you. Sometimes I behave decently and eat less.

Well, see you soooooooooonnnnnnn!
Very soon!

Diana

Later that same day . . .

Monday, March 5, 11:23 P.M.
Surprise!!!!!!!!!!!!!!!!
Hola Juan José,

My computer was repaired today and it's okay again. And, at this very moment, I am reading your e-mails and answering you. Hey, see how urgent it is? You have to see how interested I am in answering you!

61

I'm glad to hear that your car is okay because I know how indispensable it is to you, especially when you have to do so much traveling.

I will call you tomorrow during the day. What do you think about getting together for coffee on Thursday? Can you? I don't think I'll have a problem with any time you suggest. Well, we can decide later.

I am nervous about our meeting. It's such a crazy and daring thing that I'm doing right now. The truth is that I don't know what will happen. But what is supposed to happen will happen, and if it's not supposed to happen, it won't, don't you think? That seems logical to me. Do you have any plans for Sunday? I am inviting you to the Zócalo[12] for the indigenous gathering. Does that interest you, or not?

Well, see you soon, Diana

Tuesday, March 6, 1:37 P.M.

Juan José, another surprise—I am in Mexico today!
I tried to call you a couple of times but I couldn't get you. To tell you the truth, I am in a bit of a jam with where I am going to live. I found an apartment and they told me it was okay, but it isn't. So I am in the middle of painting, brushes, soap, and all the cleaning stuff, above all because I made the big mistake of buying my furniture yesterday. The first thing I did when I arrived was to go to a furniture store and buy what I needed, at least the most important things. So they are going to deliver them tomorrow and I have to have the apartment clean and in good condition. So today I am like Cinderella. I don't recommend seeing me as I am today. It was nice of you to send me your photo. I like your smile.

I will call you in a little while. Look, I am at my cousin's house now. If I can, I will talk to you tonight. What is happening is that he is here and it's difficult to talk. You understand? I haven't told him anything about you because we haven't even met each other yet. But I hope to have my apartment ready this week.

I bought a whole set of rustic furniture, which I absolutely love. I bought a stove and a fridge. The rest will come little by little. I have to get curtains, though, because they are urgent. I hope I can do it on

Thursday. Right now, I am killing myself cleaning the floors. Maybe I will have to install linoleum or something, but they will do for now. I was a fool for trusting my cousin to rent the apartment for me. What happened is that before I rented a furnished apartment but this time I wanted something in the south, and cheaper.

When we talk again, can we agree on where we shall meet, yes?

Well, talk to you later.

A kiss, Diana

Digna's new apartment was in Lomas de Plateros, a district in the south end. Juan Carlos found her a modest one-bedroom flat in his complex. It was a whitewashed low-rise, hidden from the street by pine and yucca trees. Digna soon made it feel like home. She tacked a little sign to her living room wall: "Here, where God has put me, I will flourish."

Tuesday, March 6, 10:53 P.M.

What do you think about my surprise?

Just imagine, I arrived Sunday night. I didn't want to tell you because I wanted to phone you myself but then I wasn't able to get in touch with you. I will try to call you tomorrow when I get into my new apartment. Today I cleaned and one of my cousins came over to help me. And then, my cousin Juan helped in the afternoon and we just finished a little while ago. To tell you the truth, it is has turned out quite different than what I saw yesterday.

Tomorrow I will be there all day waiting for the furniture. You know, I am very happy. It isn't the place I would have preferred but, well, at least it will be my place. I am very demanding about my space. I always need to have it. My cousin is super but I prefer to be alone. I will invite you over as soon as I finish getting settled in.

So when shall we see each other? Here's my telephone number at the apartment: 56-51-89-75. Tomorrow, I will be alone. On Saturday, my aunt and uncle and their daughters probably will help me move my things. I ask you not to call me that day until I talk to you personally, but tomorrow you can call me, or I will try to call you. What time do you get home from work? Today I called twice and then I felt uneasy about insisting. As well, once I started working, I didn't occupy myself with anything else. If the furniture arrives early tomorrow, I will try to get the curtains and accessories I need, and look for any other items I require urgently. On Thursday, I will be at my apartment again because the plumber is supposed to come to install the stove and the sink, and do some repairs on the windows.

I hope to see you soon.

I just looked at your photo again, and it's a pity I don't have any of myself in the computer. If I had one, I would send it to you. But you will soon see the flesh-and-bones. That's better, no?

See you soon,

Diana

She rang him at his mother's Wednesday night and they arranged to meet the next day, Thursday, March 8, at a VIPS restaurant near her apartment, off the *Periférico*, in Colonia San Jerónimo. VIPS, a chain of moderately priced restaurants, is a touchstone in the lives of Mexicans. The most important rites of passage are celebrated at the local VIPS, and so it was with Digna and J.J.

"How will I recognize you?" he asked her on the telephone.

"I am thin, dark and a *Veracruzana*. I have the style of a *Veracruzana*," she told him, most certainly aware the women of Veracruz are said to be the most beautiful in all Mexico. She said she would be wearing a flowered dress.

They were to meet at 5 P.M. and he was late. (It would be a pattern. Meticulous, Digna was never late.) He was driving down from Tlanepantla, in the city's north end, and the traffic, as usual, was terrible. He called her on his cell phone to ask her to wait for him. He recognized her the moment he walked in and hurried to the table where she sat alone.

It was a difficult moment. They were, at first, shy and awkward.

But they ended up talking for hours, mostly about their families. He told Digna about his late father, a teacher from Durango, and about his mother, whose home he shared. He had moved back in after separating from his wife and was in the process of getting a divorce.

Over the next few days, there were no e-mails, only phone calls, as Digna got herself settled, caught up with her family in Mexico City, talked long-distance with Esthela in Misántla, and made plans to see J.J. at the indigenous gathering she had mentioned to him a few days before.

This was no small event. The whole city is abuzz with anticipation, waiting for the Zapatista rebel caravan, led by Subcomandante Marcos, to arrive in the capital on Sunday. Marcos and the Zapatistas were Mexico's most famous rebels, largely viewed by a sympathetic public as a modern-day Robin Hood with his Merry Men.

The air was electric. It was the first time the Zapatistas had left their jungle hideout in the southern state of Chiapas since their rebellion began seven years earlier. For days, their progress had been charted by the media, with maps and graphics showing their starting point in the Lacandon jungle and a zigzag march toward Mexico City. They are being followed by supporters on foot, on horseback and in every manner of vehicle. Some observers say it's a trick and that the national government has offered safe passage to Marcos and the Zapatistas in order to deceive and capture them. However, President Fox had given his word and he would be true to it.

On Sunday, March 12, thousands line Miguel Angel de Quevedo Avenue in the capital to cheer the arrival of the popular rebels and follow them, in a pushing, honking, seething mass, to the historic city square, the *Zócalo*, for an afternoon of speeches and celebrations.

J.J. agreed to accompany Digna, with no idea of who she was, or how much her life story was part of the great saga of modern

Mexico. She had not told him, not yet, that she had been a defense lawyer in the 1995 case of the "presumed Zapatistas," in which teachers, union leaders, and social activists were accused of being revolutionaries, thrown in jail, and tortured. She and her colleagues won their release in what became a landmark human rights case in Mexico.

On Sunday, moving through the city was almost impossible and, when they did meet, the *Zócalo* was so packed they couldn't get near it. They didn't mind, deciding to go to a movie instead. J.J. wouldn't remember the movie but he would remember the heady rush, the urgency, of their fingers touching in the dark. When they emerged, they were holding hands.

The next day, Digna wrote him using her own name for the first time. She was Digna. Diana of the virtual love affair had vanished.

Monday, March 12, 1:17 P.M.

Hola Amor (Love),
Hola Mi Amor
It still feels so strange to write those words, "*mi amor*," but I am answering my mail and I feel like sending you one even though we will talk later. I just want to tell you that I am thinking about you and how much I love being with you. I feel super today.

Yesterday was very special for me. The truth is that I didn't think it would be like that but I am so happy that we met.

I hope everything will be okay with your meetings. I am working and waiting for the guy to come repair the stove. See you soon.

A kiss,

Digna

Wednesday, March 14, 6:26 P.M.

Hola Amor,
Hola Juan José,
I, too, have been thinking a lot about you. I talk about you now with my

cousin, Juan Carlos. You can imagine that we were talking this morning because he needed me to help him with a loan. It was urgent and I had to bring the money to the municipal hall. I came home around noon and then we went to buy a telephone to replace the one that was here. We came back home to install it and that's why my phone was disconnected. Then, we went out to eat to my Aunt Tana's and afterward, I came back home, and here I am.

Amor, I think about you so much. It is something I didn't really want, however here I am, thinking about you and I have no remorse. I love you and I miss you. I began to miss you so quickly.

A kiss, love, a great big hug,

Digna

Thursday, March 15, 3:43 P.M.

Hola Juan José,

I am working, going through my mail and I wanted to tell you that I LOVE YOU, *Amor*. I don't know exactly what's happened, but I love you. I think about you only. I miss you, I desire you.

I am waiting for my cousin. He is coming to eat. Really, I am dying of hunger. I hope he's not too late.

A kiss, no, better, a lot of kisses,

Digna

Tuesday, March 20, 12:09 A.M.

Hola,

Does it make any sense to say 129 times, I LOVE YOU? WELL, I AM ONLY ASKING.

Juan José, it is midnight and I remember that you told me that you sent an e-mail and I wanted to see it. I found it and it said: I LOVE YOU.

I love you too, *amor*. I love you a bunch and two bunches. Can you imagine how much that is? It is A LOT, HUGE, MORE THAN HUGE. Um . . . well, it is to say, enough.

WHY? I DON'T KNOW.
TRULY,

MEEEEEE

Tuesday, March 20, 3:48 P.M.

You act like a mathematician. Well, you did that thing of adding up all the hours, but you missed a few minutes.

My love, I am at home. I LOOOVE YOU.

Me

* * *

Their romance grew. Over the spring and summer, they took road trips, first to Acapulco for a weekend in March and then, in July, to the United States for a week. They drove north through Mexico's desert and misty mountains, crossed the border at Laredo, and toured Texas, stopping in Houston, San Antonio, and Galveston. Texas in July. It was 113 degrees and they were stuck in a car with no air-conditioning, but it didn't bother them. It was all a big lark. They were like a couple of teenagers in love.

At J.J.'s urging, Digna bought running shoes for the trip. She'd never owned a pair before. "You are changing me," she told him.

"That upsets you?" he asked.

"No," she replied, "I like that you are changing me."[13]

It was the summer of Digna's transformation, the summer of rushing to meet J.J. in the afternoon rain, of showing him off to friends, of walking with a spring in her step and a smile on her lips. She changed her style, adding splashes of color, shedding a few pounds, and acquiring the glow that everyone soon noticed. She let her hair grow to please him, though she teased him often about chopping it all off. (Months later, when J.J. and I met, it would be difficult to hear him talk about Digna's beautiful hair, knowing that gloved and clinical hands shaved it all off before the autopsy.)

One day at Digna's apartment, J.J. found a photograph of her with President Bill Clinton.

"What is this?" he asked, incredulous, holding up the photo.

"It's nothing. Really, it's nothing," she replied.

"How can you say it's nothing?" he said. "Digna, *who are you?*"

But she just laughed and leaned in for a kiss.

"I'm the woman you love," she whispered.[14]

CHAPTER FOUR

Don't Fail Us

A murder like this wasn't supposed to happen in the Mexico of Vicente Fox.

A year earlier, in 2000, the immensely popular Fox, from the opposition National Action Party, won the presidency, ending more than seven decades of one-party rule. The mighty Institutional Revolutionary Party (a deliciously Mexican oxymoron) was defeated by a politician who promised real democracy and an end to crushing years of corruption, violence, and impunity under the PRI.

Mexicans were jubilant. They delighted in this six-foot-four rancher politician, with his jeans, embroidered shirts, silver belt buckles stamped "FOX," and his penchant for campaigning out of the backs of pickup trucks. He was populist and comfortable with everyone, a man who lived large, with a booming voice, a big moustache, broad shoulders, and mud on his boots. He was a man *con huevos* (with balls), which is pretty much the highest accolade in macho Mexico. He loved to be photographed riding one of his muscular little horses that were so full of grace and fire. His favorites were El Rey, Bayo, and the mare, Maximiliana.

Fox was well educated but spoke in a rich, vernacular Spanish, without airs. In the election campaign of 2000, he was the opposite of his PRI opponent, Francisco Labastida, with his perfect hair and fussy tailoring. Fox laughed at him and the people laughed with him, the kiss of death for a politician.

Sounding like a pusillanimous schoolboy, Labastida accused

Fox of making "obscene gestures" at him during a nationally televised campaign debate.

"You called me shorty. . . . You said I was a girlie man," he whimpered,[1] about being called, among other more graphic terms, "*la vestida*," slang for a female in a dress.

"My esteemed Mr. Labastida," intoned Fox, "I can always stop being rude, but you people can never stop being the tricky, corrupt incompetents that you are."[2]

Mexicans lapped it up. "In that moment, Labastida was like a kid who couldn't handle a few nasty words and was crying in the schoolyard," observed Sergio Aguayo, a leading political analyst and author. "It was very, very bad. He reminded everyone of what Fox thinks of him."[3] Fox didn't put a foot wrong. Throughout the campaign, he seemed charmed, with Mexicans even going to the polls on his birthday. He turned fifty-eight on July 2, 2000, and what a fiesta it was. A *Foxifiesta.*

After midnight, as his supporters laughed, wept, and shouted his name, the president-elect went to the symbolic heart of the nation, the gilded statue of the Angel of Independence on Paseo de la Reforma, and raised his hands high in the V-sign for victory, for Vicente.

"*Ya, ya, ya, ya, ya, ya, ya, ya!*" shouted the crowd, echoing his campaign slogan. *Ya!* Enough already, enough of the PRI.

The night was magical, full of sizzling summer heat and energy. It felt like a dream. People were delirious over the fall of the PRI, hugging one another, kissing, and dancing conga lines along Paseo de la Reforma.

"I have never been so in love with my country, and with each and every one of you," Fox yelled, his voice hoarse, almost inaudible over the chants of his supporters. Tears coursed down people's cheeks; they loved him too.

There was a warning, though, on that hot July night.

"Don't fail us," the people called over and over, their raised faces lit by TV lights. "Don't fail us. Don't fail us."

Mexicans put their faith in Fox. He took 42.7 percent of the popular vote over Labastida's 35.8 percent and analysis of the results revealed the depth of the passion for change among the young and educated. He won the support of 50 percent of voters between the ages of eighteen and thirty-four, and 60 percent of college-educated voters, compared to 32 percent and 22 percent in the same categories for his rival, Labastida.[4]

The polls had indicated Fox would win, possibly in a squeaker. But polls are notoriously wrong in Latin America and, besides, Mexicans didn't really believe the PRI could be dislodged so easily. The upcoming election was all people talked about in Mexico over the first half of 2000. At market stalls and cantinas, they would shake their heads and predict the PRI would pull something from their bag of tricks at the last minute. Hadn't they always?

It had happened on July 6, 1988, when, in the early hours of the vote count on election night, the computers went down, or so they said. Some time later that night, without releasing any results, PRI party president Jorge de la Vega appeared on television to simply declare that ruling party candidate Carlos Salinas was the president-elect of Mexico and would become the eleventh consecutive *priísta* president.

Of course, everybody knew there had been massive electoral fraud, and that the PRI had stolen victory from leftist candidate Cuauhtémoc Cárdenas, leader of the Democratic Revolutionary Party (another delicious oxymoron). The PRD coalition was new, cobbled together to take on the ruling PRI, and wouldn't unite as a permanent party until after the vote. Election headquarters leaked like a sieve and people knew very well Cárdenas was trouncing Salinas when the PRI shut down the vote. No wonder Mexicans call their election officials "*mapaches*" (raccoons), after an animal that wears a mask and steals things in the night.

Nobody believed the official results when they were announced a week later, apparently fabricated out of thin air to give Salinas a rather robust win. The numbers had Salinas at 50.4 percent of the vote, while Cárdenas was at 31.1 percent and *panista* Marcel Clouthier (Fox's political mentor, who was killed in a car crash) at 17.1 percent.[5]

Many blamed the debacle on outgoing president Miguel de la Madrid, who had picked Salinas to succeed him. He carried on the ruling party tradition of figuratively pointing his finger—*el dedazo*—at the anointed one, who always managed to carry the vote, and another six years of power for the PRI, on election day.

Mexicans would have to wait until de la Madrid published his memoirs in 2004 for the official version of what happened that night. He wrote that the PRI brass, fearful that the huge lead for Cárdenas and the PRD would hold throughout the night, simply shut down the computers rather than risk defeat. The ballots were destroyed, without ever having been counted. De la Madrid recalled being told: "You have to proclaim the triumph of the PRI. It is a tradition that we cannot break without causing great alarm among the citizens."[6]

It took twelve years after the fraud of 1988, but the tradition of *el dedazo* was finally broken. On election night in 2000, at the Angel of Independence celebrations, a victorious Fox basked in the affection of a nation. *Viva Fox! Viva Mexico! Viva!* Yes, he told the crowd, he would do his duty for the people and the Republic of Mexico.

"I would have been happy to go stay on my ranch," he said, "but the country called me—and here I am."

* * *

Fox made it sound as if his decision to run was recent, but the truth was he had been the preferred candidate among the cognoscenti in Mexico and the United States for some years. He strode onto the political stage in 1988 when he won a seat in the federal Congress for the National Action Party, a firebrand who shook up Mexican politics. He scoffed at protocol and made headlines when he walked onto the floor of the Chamber of Deputies, tossing half-burned ballots onto the floor to protest the discredited elections.

In August 1991, he ran for governor of his home state of Guanajuato but, in a repeat of the 1988 national scandal, local PRI bosses stole the vote. There was an uproar and, from the presidential palace of Los Pinos in Mexico City, Salinas was forced to install an interim governor. Fox lost the next state election but he kept plugging away until, finally, in 1995, he won the governor's mansion by a 2-to-1 margin.

Fox had star power. I heard the buzz about him soon after I arrived in Mexico in February 1995 to become Latin American correspondent for the *Toronto Star*. I'd been based in Washington for five years and, naturally, one of my first stops was the U.S. embassy near Paseo de la Reforma to sniff the political winds. Fox's name was on the lips of U.S. officials, and in Latin America as elsewhere in the world (and especially in the countries in Washington's own backyard), one learns to pay attention to the opinions of U.S. diplomats.

The political power-brokers and intellectuals of Mexico City talked about his potential. Despite his cultivated "man of the people" image, he was a member of the high-profile San Angel Group, an eclectic coalition of political and economic thinkers who met regularly in an upscale neighborhood of the capital. And, in perhaps the most telling clue that a Fox victory had been ordained, President Ernesto Zedillo, elected in 1994, changed the Constitution to allow a Mexican with foreign-born parents to become president. How propitious for Fox, whose mother was Spanish. The scene was set for 2000 by a PRI president who understood perfectly the dynamic of power in Mexico.

I set off in February 1996, a year after my arrival, to interview him at the governor's mansion in Guanajuato, 220 miles northwest of Mexico City. It is a lush agricultural state and, for the sixty miles or so, the car was filled with the unmistakable aroma of manure over greening pastures. In my report, I described Fox as the "man to watch" in Mexico, picking him as the politician with the potential to break the PRI grip on the country.[7] It was not a difficult call; I simply did my homework.

Fox couldn't have been more charming, welcoming me with a bear hug and inviting me to lunch at the governor's residence, where he reminisced about holidays in Canada and the United States. He switched easily from Spanish to English, telling jokes in both languages. He showed me around the capital city, Guanajuato, where folks slapped him on the back and shouted greetings to the neighbor they still called "*Don* Vicente." He's hard to miss, standing close to six-foot-six with his boots on.

I found him immensely likeable and, after our afternoon together, kept in contact with his advisers, interviewing him several times and meeting with him again before the elections in 2000. By then, the dust of Mexico had settled on my heart, as the saying goes, and I was hopelessly in love with the country. I understood the joy of the crowd on that July night at the Angel of Independence as they cheered for Fox.

"My father only ever gave me one piece of advice: Study anything but agriculture because a farmer's life is too hard. And, please don't ever get into politics. It's rotten, it's corrupt." He told me this over lunch. Then he laughed his big, booming laugh, slapped his thigh, and said, "So, I'm a politician and a farmer. I'm a very obedient son."[8]

He described his "very simple" approach to life. "In politics, you've got to be a democrat. In business, you've got to be a capitalist. That's my philosophy."

His favorite subjects were his kids and his ranch. He was separated from his wife and the children lived with him at the governor's residence. "It's not my life's work to be a politician," he said. "My life's work is farming, bringing up my kids, horseback riding, and enjoying my life. But I have one burning commitment—and that is to kick them out of Los Pinos. . . . That is why I am here."

There had to be an end to *el sistema,* he said. That's what everybody called the PRI stranglehold on power: the system. Peruvian writer Mario Vargas Llosa nailed it when he famously called Mexico the "perfect dictatorship."

"The PRI is like the Mafia," Fox said after lunch, stretching out long legs on a leather recliner in his study. "If you get out of the party, they kill you. If you stay in, you're well paid and protected for life. They're like gangsters."

He had paid a price for challenging the party. During the 1988 congressional campaign, local party heavies closed down his family's vegetable freezing plant, citing health regulations, and fomented labor problems at the Fox Western Boot factory. He talked about the risks in taking on the PRI power structure.

"They could frame me—or worse," he said. "All I can say is that I am a Roman Catholic, I am devout, I go to Mass every Sunday, and I am confessed at all times. I don't take chances."

His faith shaped his politics. As a teenager, he studied for a year at a Jesuit college in Minnesota and went to the Guanajuato campus of the Ibero-American University. Breaking from Mexico's secular political tradition, Fox was open about the importance of religion in his life. He was a natural fit with the National Action Party (known by its Spanish acronym, PAN), which was conservative and close to the Catholic Church and only beginning to be influenced by business leaders like Fox who would take it to Los Pinos four years later. Fox chose PAN under the influence of its former leader Marcel Clouthier, who had been the party's presidential candidate in 1988.

He showed me a photo of an unidentified Cristero rebel facing a firing squad in Guanajuato. It was taken during the Cristero Rebellion of the 1920s, one of the bloodiest chapters in the struggle between church and state in Mexico. The war began in 1926 when the government banned the practice of Roman Catholicism and, by the time it ended in an uneasy standoff, more than seventy thousand Mexicans were dead.[9] It would simmer, without resolution, until full rights were granted to the Catholic Church in 1992, during the *sexenio* (six-year term) of Carlos Salinas.

The photo is riveting. The condemned man appears unafraid of his impending death. He stands upright, his eyes fixed on the soldiers with their raised rifles, his sombrero in his hand. "He looks brave, doesn't he?" commented Fox. He told me he kept the photo on his desk to remind him what courage looks like.

* * *

We had a long interview and I asked him about his special ties to Washington. Why was his name being bandied about the American embassy in Mexico City as the next president a full four years before the vote?

Fox had been director of operations for Coca-Cola in Mexico for fifteen years, before leaving the company and returning to his ranch and a run at politics. He left Coca-Cola when an offer to head the Latin American division meant he would have to move his family to Atlanta, Georgia, which he said he didn't want to do. Over those fifteen years with Coca-Cola, he got to know a lot of people and, by the time I met him, the U.S. State Department was helping him build on those connections by sponsoring "get acquainted" trips to Chicago, New York, and Washington, as well as arranging private meetings with American opinion-makers like Ted Turner from CNN.[10] It appeared to me that he was being groomed.

(In more ways than one, it would turn out. After his election victory, the *Dallas Morning News* reported that Fox had hired a team of top Texans to prepare his presidential campaign. Veteran Republican political consultant Rob Allyn, from Dallas, revealed he'd worked secretly for Fox for three years, "shaping and honing his message of change." He and others had slipped in and out of Mexico, undetected by the media, using false identifies and other tricks. He described his work for Fox as his "second life."[11])

"Look," Fox replied to me that afternoon in 1996, "nobody gets to be president of Mexico without the goodwill and support of the U.S. president, as well as public opinion in the United States and Europe. That's just the way it is. The problem is that Mexicans resent that closeness with the United States, and the politician who does it too much gets rejected. It's a double-edged sword."

Of course, he hadn't answered my question. But Fox didn't have to explain why he was the perfect Washington candidate. That much appeared obvious to me.

By this time, pressure was building on all sides for the PRI hegemony to end in Mexico. A revolt was simmering in the south and opposition to the government was growing stronger and more insistent. It was time for a president from the opposition, and smart U.S. diplomats understood that very well. They liked Fox, he was a known commodity—fifteen years is a long time to spend at blue-chip Coca-Cola—and they clearly felt comfortable with his politics and confident of the predictability of a Fox presidency.

Mexican leaders also grasped the need for political change at the beginning of the new century. It was no surprise on election night in 2000 when President Ernesto Zedillo ended any chance of a repeat of the 1988 fiasco by going on national television to announce a Fox victory over the PRI. He went live at 10:30 P.M., setting the victory in stone and even enabling many foreign print journalists to make first-edition deadlines. It was a bold move and it was clear he knew exactly what he was doing.

Zedillo, who would go on to postings at the United Nations and the Center for Globalization at Yale University, was widely criticized from within his own party for jumping the gun on a count that wasn't finished and wouldn't be for another week. PRI party "dinosaurs," the old hard-liners who were used to having their way, accused him of being a traitor. They were most resistant to opening up the country politically and economically and feared this new wave of Ivy League presidents—Salinas from Harvard, Zedillo from Yale—with their savvy advisers and new economic blueprint for the country.

But Zedillo was too wily for the PRI's old guard. By announcing a Fox victory he preempted the dinosaurs and locked in a peaceful transition. There was no going back.

* * *

On election night in July 2000, Mexicans—and specifically *capitalinos*—had another reason for optimism. It came with the election of Andrés Manuel López Obrador in Mexico City, only the second democratically elected mayor in the history of the capital. He was a political scientist by profession, former head of an indigenous organization and *priísta* from the southeastern state of Tabasco, who left the party in the late 1980s after losing a race to become the PRI's gubernatorial candidate. He joined the nascent Democratic Revolutionary Party under Cuauhtémoc Cárdenas, won the leadership of the party in Tabasco, and became a full-time political activist. Already considered the left's strongest hope for the presidency in 2006, he lost no time in launching a series of populist campaigns in the capital, going so far as to bring a court challenge to Daylight Saving Time, which was imposed by President Zedillo in 1996.[12] People cheered when he sent in bulldozers to begin construction of a highway overpass in Mexico City against moneyed interests. "We lick no one's boots," he declared. "Deliver to the people, that's all we have to do."[13]

A compact man, of long nose and dour expression, López Obrador, forty-seven when he was elected mayor, was known as a hard worker who held daily press conferences at City Hall at 6:30 A.M. and eschewed the lavish trappings Mexicans had come to expect from their politicians. People called him "AMLO" for his initials and *"el peje,"* which is short for *pejelagarto*, a fish native to Tabasco. He was adept at publicity and, later, would pull off such events as bringing in former New York mayor Rudolph Giuliani to walk the streets as part of his campaign to clean up crime.

I first interviewed him at his home in Villermosa, Tabasco, on the Gulf of Mexico, in February 1996. I was in Tabasco to write about escalating violence over a campesino blockade of oil roads. The Gulf Coast was a major oil-producing region for the national oil company, Petroleos Mexicanos (PEMEX), with two thousand miles of gas and oil pipelines snaking through the state and a history of oil spills into the tropical lowlands of the Gulf of Mexico. International agencies, including the World Health Organization, blamed PEMEX for environmental degradation of mangrove swamps, farmlands, lakes, and marine life, and the company eventually was ordered to pay millions of dollars in compensation to displaced farmers.[14] I saw entire rivers on fire and interviewed health officials who spoke of leukemia rates among children rising by over 1,000 percent during two decades of oil production. Tabasco PRD leader López Obrador backed the campesinos who, by that time, were blocking routes into sixty-four PEMEX wells, arguing that the oil company hadn't begun payment of the compensation money. The federal government sent in the army from neighboring Chiapas, where the Zapatistas simmered, and 106 protestors were arrested and jailed, many later claiming they were tortured.

I got López Obrador's address from a local PRD organizer and, to my surprise in a country of bodyguards and assassinations, simply drove up to his very modest house, knocked on the door, introduced myself, and spent an hour or so interviewing him about the protest and state and national issues. He criticized PRI governor Roberto Madrazo (who may well be his opponent for president in 2006) for ignoring social needs, and we talked about a series of lawsuits in which it was alleged that PRI bigwigs skimmed off millions in PEMEX compensation money for illegal state campaign contributions.[15] That was apparently the reason there was no money to pay the campesinos. He was articulate and passionate and juggled phone calls and staff interruptions with ease. The interview over, he hurried down his front walk, squeezed himself into the backseat of a car with half a dozen party workers, and was driven away.

The next time I covered him, it was 2000, and he was running for mayor in Mexico City.

* * *

Mexico was changing before President Zedillo's election in 1994, but at an agonizingly slow pace. In 1989, his predecessor, Carlos Salinas, allowed a controversial victory by the National Action Party to stand in the state of Baja California Norte. It was the first time an opposition party held power in any of Mexico's thirty-one states and the Federal District. In his book *Mexico: Biography of Power*, historian Enrique Krauze called that decision the "first test—which the Salinas government passed with flying colors."

But it was Zedillo, the accidental president, who laid the groundwork for the first post-PRI administration. He was thrust into the spotlight after presidential front-runner Luis Donaldo Colosio was assassinated on March 23, 1994, during a campaign stop in Tijuana, just across the border from California. It was a shocking crime, five months before the elections, and Mexicans were reeling. They liked Colosio, with his populist appeal and promise of reform. In style, he was the Mexican politician most like the ebullient Fox, a natural orator who whipped up the crowds with his pledge of putting the PRI dinosaurs out to pasture. He had been "fingered" to succeed Salinas and, when he was murdered, the PRI had to come up with an alternative candidate for the August vote.

The murder of Donaldo Colosio is considered to be Mexico's John F. Kennedy assassination. One man, Tijuana factory worker Mario Alberto Martínez, was convicted and sentenced to forty-five years in jail. Few believe, however, that only one shooter killed

Colosio, who was hit in the abdomen and head, and the case remains shrouded in mystery and violence. There were at least eight murders of principle investigators in the immediate aftermath of Colosio's death, including José Arturo Ochoa, in charge of the Tijuana attorney's office.

When Salinas replaced Colosio with Zedillo, Mexicans didn't know who he was. He had been Colosio's campaign manager, an unassuming former finance bureaucrat and education secretary, more comfortable in the party's back rooms than on the campaign trail. When he left office in 2000, his *sexenio* completed, most people didn't know much more about him.

And yet, he signed an election reform pact with the opposition parties that changed the rules of politics and laid the groundwork for the Fox victory. "Today, united, we take an essential step toward the democracy that all Mexicans need and that all Mexicans want," Zedillo said at the signing ceremony at Los Pinos, in the summer of 1996. Looking back, it is stunning to realize how easily the PRI had been able to use its rules to dominate the country for so long. Under the reform pact, the greatly feared Interior Ministry, with its massive intelligence network and links to the military, no longer ran the country's electoral system. Instead, the nonpartisan Federal Election Institute was established to oversee the national vote and ensure that elections would never again be stolen. As well, the president could no longer simply appoint the mayor of Mexico City, which paved the way for the 1997 election of Cuauhtémoc Cárdenas and the opposition PRD in the first free vote in the Federal District.

Zedillo was highly praised for these reforms; however, many insisted they were forced on the nation's elites by grassroots movements within Mexico,[16] an analysis that appears to be borne out by years of struggle. "The impulse to change is due far more to the force of our society than to President Zedillo," argued Luis Gómez, head of the postgraduate political science department at the National Autonomous University of Mexico, on the day the pact was signed. As Gómez saw it, Zedillo's destiny was to be the "gravedigger" for *el sistema*.[17]

* * *

There was another set of gravediggers, less obvious perhaps to those working inside the republic, but lined up with some pretty hefty shovels just the same. The push to change Mexico was coming from outside the country as well, from powerful people who could not be ignored. It came from the U.S. and Canadian capitals, from Wall Street, and from the head offices of corporate America, and it, too, would help change the face of Mexican politics.

It all began with a free trade deal.

The North American Free Trade Agreement (NAFTA) became law in Mexico, the United States, and Canada on January 1, 1994. The goal of free trade, originating with American financiers and business leaders and articulated by former president Ronald Reagan as early as 1984, was to create a hemispheric trading bloc to stretch from Alaska to Tierra del Fuego and include all the nations of the Americas (except for Cuba as long as Fidel Castro was around).

The agenda, however, included far more than trade, or the movement of goods and regulation of services in the Americas. Instead, its purpose was to give the force of treaty law to an economic system, known as neo-liberalism, which was developed by influential American economist Milton Friedman and his Chicago School during the 1960s and 1970s. NAFTA's creators wanted a greater stake in the economies of Latin America. They wanted its leaders to open up their nations to unfettered foreign investment, sell off state companies, cut social spendings and adhere to strict debt repayment plans, which would keep high interest fees flowing from the developing to the developed world and, in particular, to the financial houses of Wall Street.

This was the economic blueprint favored by a new generation of politicians in Mexico, beginning with Carlos Salinas.

The genesis of free trade lay in the Latin American debt crisis of the early eighties. There was panic in the Americas; Mexico defaulted on its international debt in 1982; and as bailout packages were being cobbled together (largely through Washington's Brady Plan), American financial leaders were looking for a more stable framework for their investments in the hemisphere. They realized the crisis could be used as a lever to pry open future gains from indebted governments. Debt didn't have to be seen as negative. The leading proponent of turning an economic blueprint into international treaty was the American industrialist David Rockefeller, former chair of the Chase Manhattan Bank, whose family has a long history in the Americas.[18] They lost millions when Mexican President Lázaro Cárdenas (father of Cuauhtémoc) nationalized the oil industry in 1938 and scooped up the holdings of their Standard Oil Company, along with other American, Dutch, and British interests.

By the mid-1980s, corporate titans from such blue-chip firms as American Express, Eastman Kodak, and Caterpillar Inc.[19] joined what turned into a free-trade crusade. They lobbied legislators in Washington and worked with like-minded individuals at universities and think tanks, whose research was often funded by their own corporations. It was all very cozy. Rockefeller turned his foundation, the Americas Society, into an advocate for free trade, sponsored conferences on the subject, and ferried politicians, including Mexico's Salinas, to his family estate in Tarrytown, New York.

Former Secretary of State Henry Kissinger, a Rockefeller family protégé who helped shape U.S. policy on Latin American through several U.S. administrations, was a powerful advocate of free trade. His consulting group, Kissinger Associates, whose clients included American Express and the Chase Manhattan Bank, had interlocking interests in Latin America[20] and Kissinger supported free trade.

Washington implemented these trade deals incrementally—first with Canada in 1987 and then, in 1994, folding the agreement into a larger deal to include Mexico. By the year 2000, the debate was over another proposed treaty, which would roll the NAFTA into the so-called Free Trade Area of the Americas and realize Reagan's original plan. After his reelection in 2004, President George W. Bush turned his attention to the issue of a final free trade deal locking in the entire hemisphere. NAFTA-plus, they called it.

Back in 1989, at a conference at Toronto's stately King Edward Hotel, Kissinger explained the importance of free trade to the Americans. It was a matter of survival. "We've all been brought up on free trade principles, but the fact is that the world is organizing into regional trading blocs," he said.[21] "We have to create a potential trading bloc in North America to protect our economic interests."

Throughout a decade of negotiations, there was one guiding principle: free trade could not be perceived as an American plan. And it certainly couldn't be seen as a corporate blueprint. Canadians and Mexicans had to think it was their idea, or it wouldn't fly. As it turned out, that wasn't all that difficult to achieve.

Journalists Carol Goar in the *Toronto Star* and Peter C. Newman in *Maclean's* magazine, revealed how, beginning in 1983, the U.S. ambassador to Canada, Paul Robinson, sold the concept to Canadians.[22] "I realized, of course, that the public initiative had to come from Canada because, if it came from us, it would look as if we were trying to gobble up our neighbor," Robinson told Newman.

The same rule applied to Mexico. There is nothing more odious to Mexicans than the idea of being dominated by *gringos*.

At a 1992 conference of the Forum for the Americas, an elite gathering of corporate and political heavyweights, Kissinger told a story: "A few years ago, at the beginning of the Salinas term in Mexico, I spoke to one very highly placed individual, and he was outlining some of the ideas which would dominate the new administration. And I said, 'What about a free trade area?'"

According to Kissinger, the individual replied: "Don't ever mention that in Mexico. That will be perceived as exploitation by America. We can go step-by-step. We can make sectoral agreements. But don't ever mention a free trade area if you don't want to damage all of us who believe in free trade."[23]

It was good advice and Washington listened. At the 1992 conference, held in the U.S. capital, Kissinger was able to boast: "A few years ago, if anyone had talked about a North American Free Trade Area, it would have been treated as a clever device of economic exploitation by the United States of its weaker neighbor to the south. We have come so far that now the political debate in the United States is that those devious Mexicans are taking us for a ride (*laughter*) and that they're exploiting us in the free trade discussion (*more laughter*)."[24]

Talks sailed to a successful conclusion. With barely a ripple of protest, the free trade deal was signed in December 1992, in San Antonio, Texas, not far from the Alamo, by the so-called Three Amigos—Salinas, Canadian Prime Minister Brian Mulroney, and U.S. President George Bush, who had just lost his bid for a second term in office.

* * *

The beginnings of free trade south of the border, however, were anything but smooth.

On New Year's Day, 1994, the day the agreement became law, some two thousand Zapatista rebels, led by the charismatic and media-savvy Subcomandante Marcos, burst onto the international stage from Chiapas in southern Mexico. Tourists in the colonial capital of San Cristóbal de las Casas were the first to hear about this new Indian rebellion, fitting perhaps, given the importance of tourists to the Mexican economy. The Subcomandante held court in front of the cathedral in San Cristóbal, a modern-day revolutionary telling tourists that rebels from the Zapatista Army of National Liberation (EZLN) had taken four towns in the region, including San Cristóbal itself.

Marcos spoke colloquial English and he wowed them. He was young and masked, wearing a black balaclava and fatigues, and he smoked a pipe of maple tobacco. He had two bandoliers of red shotgun shells that looked like they could take down a moose, although they didn't match the pistol-grip shotgun or vintage revolver stuck in his belt. He seemed bemused by the success of his ragtag army. It had taken him some time on New Year's Eve to convince local police, in an overly celebratory mood, that the Zapatistas weren't holiday revelers dressed up as guerrillas.

Nobody had paid much attention to the decision under Salinas to bring Mexico into NAFTA. And now, here was this dashing rebel leader, soft-spoken and sexy, with a great sense of humor, conducting political science classes in the town square. He explained that the rebels were named for the revolutionary war hero Emiliano Zapata. He said Indians were the forgotten people of Mexico and talked about how their corn and coffee, already selling at rock-bottom prices on world markets, would not be able to compete with big farming conglomerates springing up under new NAFTA rules. They would be wiped out, he said, calling the trade deal a "death certificate" for the Indians of Chiapas.

Already, their land was being bought up from under them by rich landowners, a practice that the Salinas government made legal in the run-up to free trade by rewriting Article 27 of the Constitution. The change allowed traditional, constitutionally guaranteed communal lands, or *ejidos*, to be sold to private buyers. It didn't take long for capitalism to arrive full-blown in the remote highlands of the ancient Maya, often pitting villager against villager. Wealthy landowners gobbled up more land, quickly pushing fifteen thousand *expulsados* (expelled people) off property that had been communally farmed for generations. These refugees drifted to the outskirts of cities, adding to the *cinturónes de miseria,* literally "belts of misery," growing ever larger and poorer.

And it was done with the stroke of a pen in Mexico City.

For the campesinos, the landless farmers who worked the land across Mexico, life turned out to be much more difficult after free trade. They couldn't compete against the conglomerates, and the government turned a cold face to their pleas for help. Over the next six years, tariffs on imported agricultural products would be drastically slashed, or eliminated, driving down the price of coffee, corn, and vegetables for Mexican farmers. Imported U.S. corn syrup nearly wiped out the Mexican sugar crop within three years.[25] By the end of the century, Javier Usabiaga, agriculture secretary in the Fox government, would blithely tell farmers they had five years to become efficient. "We give you a choice. Either you become efficient and competitive on an international scale, or you choose another activity."[26] He didn't say what that might be.

Marcos simplified things. He made Mexico's most important struggle—the war over land—understandable to tourists. It was ironic that faceless rebels were putting a face, and a sympathetic one, to the Tzotziles, Tojolobales, Tzeltzales, and other descendants of the Mayan people of Chiapas, and the romance of this was not lost on the media. This was a made-in-Hollywood scenario. Castro was getting old; in the age of globalization, Marcos was the new guerrilla prince.

Soon, luminaries were trekking to the jungle highlands. If they were lucky, they got to see Marcos (known in another life as Rafael Sebastién Guillen Vicente, university professor). Filmmaker Oliver Stone posed with him on horseback, French presidential widow Danielle Mitterrand sat at his campfire, rice and beans on her lap, and assorted groupies of the international left came away with autographs.

It was a public relations disaster for the Salinas government.

In the first days of the war, national and foreign reporters rushed to Chiapas. Images of government warplanes and attack helicopters bombing Indian villages made news broadcasts around the world. Thousands of Mexican troops poured into the region, moving in convoys of tanks and armored trucks along mountain roads as far as the eye could see. Refugees, with nothing but the clothes on their backs, holding crying children and waving white flags, fled the Lacandon jungle highlands as the army moved in. The international press documented the exodus and the portrayal was brutal.

In one heart-stopping shot, Peter Power from the *Toronto Star* photographed a woman lying on the ground beside her newborn twins, one stillborn and the other dying. She had walked for miles down a mountain trail after soldiers took her village and, terrified and exhausted, went into premature labor. There was nothing for Peter to do except record the image of a scene that would be forever burned in his memory.

We were working together on that Chiapas trip and, years later, he told me: "I don't even know if I have a print in my files but I don't need one. It's difficult for me to even speak of that day or my emotions. I don't need the photograph to remember every detail—every face, every smell, every emotion."

He remembers us being hustled by a pleading woman into the rear of what was an old farm building now being used as a makeshift shelter for refugees.

"A woman has had her baby. They are dying. You must come. You must see. You must take pictures," she cried, and he felt refusal was not an option. But his own wife was pregnant with their first child at the time, and he dreaded what we would see.

"What struck me at first was the group of midwives standing politely to one side of the room, their somber faces lit only slightly by the light coming through the door. They had moved aside to allow the journalists into the room. There, on the mud floor, was a young woman, a new mother, named Aborlia Domínguez. She was motionless, possibly in shock, lying facing the wall. A few feet away from her, on a blanket, lay two tiny, wet, baby girls—one appeared to be dead, the other struggled to breathe. We were told they were born prematurely and saving either one of them was impossible."

He took his photographs and emerged into the sunlight. Tears were streaming down his face.

Later, he had trouble getting the photo out. The Associated Press photo editor at a nearby site, who'd sent Peter's earlier photos, refused to send the image through to AP in New York. He said it was too graphic and he didn't want it on the wire. But Peter was able to file it directly to the *Toronto Star*, where editors placed it on the front page of the next day's edition.

Such images of the human cost of the war—and I've seen none more powerful—brought international condemnation of the Salinas government and pressure to negotiate with the rebels. On Wednesday, January 12, a truce ended the hot war and the Zapatista uprising settled into a simmering dispute over land and indigenous rights. A solution would evade Salinas and his successors.

* * *

The Zapatista rebellion revealed the myth of free trade.

It was supposed to herald a new era of economic gains and political freedom for Mexicans—indeed, the Three Amigos had promised a "win-win-win" scenario for working people in the United States, Canada, and Mexico[27]—but people began to see that just the opposite was happening.

Mexico was supposed to be the poster child for free trade, the foundation upon which to expand the treaty to the rest of the Americas. But who could point to success in Mexico? In NAFTA's kickoff year, Indians revolted in Chiapas in January, a presidential candidate was assassinated in March, the ruling party steamrolled to another victory in August, even as one of its highest officials was murdered, the peso crashed in December, and horrific human rights abuses occurred all year long. Not a good record.

There was no economic miracle. Rather, the country was in turmoil after the peso crash[28] and soon was spiraling out of control. As events soured, external pressure for change in Mexico began to build, adding strength to domestic activists who had been protesting for years.

The push for change intensified because, after free trade, there was an added dimension: people were now paying attention to Mexico—particularly people in the capitals of her new trading partners, Canada and the United States. Their leaders spent a great deal of political capital selling free trade with Mexico and they needed this crisis to go away. While the United States was putting together a $50 million bailout package for Mexico, New York Democratic senator Alfonse D'Amato warned that it was pointless. "Mexico has collapsed already," he told the *New York Times*. "The rescue plan has failed and we are just perpetuating a myth if we think we are helping anyone but rich investors."

It can be argued, as the country crawled out of 1994 with the economy in shambles (at one point, there was only $3.8 billion in the national treasury[29]), tens of thousands thrown out of work, the middle class devastated, Mexican-owned businesses going belly-up at a staggering rate, and interest rates topping 145 percent, that this newfound international attention was the only real benefit of free trade to the average Mexican.

It did make a difference, however. Marcos understood that very well. Free trade helped Mexicans in a way nobody had imagined. It made them visible; it gave them faces.

This was the point Digna Ochoa would be making seven years later, in 2001, to villagers in the Guerrero highlands, a couple of weeks before she was assassinated. She could help them, she said, by broadcasting the Third World devastation of their lives and the persecution they faced while the national government stood idly by and state officials were shown by human rights investigators to have been complicit in abuses by the army and death squads. The Mexican government cared about its image abroad, she assured them, particularly since the 1994 trade deal. The stakes were too high for Mexico to be seen as a country where human rights were trampled and there was impunity for the torturers.

Before free trade, the PRI had always been able to stuff the genie of human rights abuses—no matter how gruesome—back into the bottle, even when the authorities themselves were responsible. That is the essential nature of crimes that are labeled as human rights abuses: they are committed against citizens by the very authorities bound by the laws of the country, international laws, and human morality to protect them. These crimes were being committed by the army and police, or by the unholy alliance of state agents working with the death squads.

In one of the most infamous chapters of modern Mexican history, on the eve of the Mexico City Olympics in 1968, thousands of students were surrounded by tanks and machine-gunned by the army in what became known as the Massacre of Tlatelolco. Hundreds, if not thousands, died and the death toll remains unknown. The army high command pretended to know nothing about the massacre, sending out a communiqué to all barracks, blaming the killings on communists[30] and advising vigilance against the shadowy forces of darkness.

Mexican writer Elena Poniatowska's twenty-one-year-old brother Jan was killed that night of October 2, and she dedicated her tour de force about the massacre, *La noche de Tlatelolco* (*The night of Tlatelolco*), to him. She included a description from *El Universal*, October 4, 1968:

"At the Medical Forensic Service, autopsies showed that the great majority of victims died . . . as a consequence of having been bayoneted. . . . Others from gunshots fired at close range. . . . Three cases caught the attention of the doctors, a child of about 13, who died from a bayonet wound to the head . . . an old woman who succumbed after having been bayoneted in the back . . . a young woman who was brought in with a bayonet wound in her left side. The wound started in her armpit and ended in her hip."

Yet the Olympics proceeded with little awareness, if any, by Mexico's distinguished visitors, of bodies piled up in the morgue or the somber mood of the city. It was the army's elite Olympic Battalion, trained in the United States, that opened fire, sending fifteen thousand rounds into crowds of students trapped in the square.

Those responsible for the Tlatelolco massacre have never been punished.

The tourist campaigns continued to burble on about Mexico's white beaches, blue seas, and *fiesta* time while, year after year, human rights groups churned out prodigious research documenting a reality of systemic torture.

Certainly, Mexican society was not oblivious. By the late 1980s, activists were coming together, among them the founders of the Miguel Agustín Pro Juárez Human Rights Center, to begin the extremely perilous and difficult struggle of using the law to fight for fundamental human rights of citizens, including the right not to be hauled off by the authorities, executed, and buried in shallow graves, as if their country were some hick dictatorship, existing only for the benefit of a bunch of wealthy thugs who made deals with foreign powers who looked the other way.

In 1991, Amnesty International called its report on Mexico "Torture with Impunity" and documented cases of abuse and extrajudicial killings. Soldiers, police, and paramilitary death squads, the report said, tortured civilians: they routinely used electric shock, cut off testicles and tongues, shot soda or chili water up noses, covered people with honey and buried them in anthills, and held victims with their heads in toilet bowls, repeatedly hauling them up, in the last seconds before drowning, to continue the interrogations. A variation was pulling half-dead victims out of an ice box so that a doctor could revive the "patient" for another round. Or, there was a technique called "the telephone." Torturers slapped both ears at once, hard, trying to burst the eardrums.

At the time of free trade's introduction in 1994, and after, human rights abuses continued unabated.

In its 1998 annual report, Amnesty International reported that "scores of people, including children, were extrajudicially executed by security forces and paramilitary groups" in Mexico the year before. Another twenty people, again including children, were tortured to death by security forces. The rights agency sent a high-level delegation to Mexico City to plead with the Zedillo government to recognize the need to "halt gross human rights abuses, bring an end to impunity and implement reforms to the administration of justice."

Amnesty investigators were able to document thirty reported disappearances in 1997, considered to be only a fraction of what was occurring. *Los desaparecidos* (the disappeared ones)[31] entered the lexicon of Latin America in the latter half of the twentieth century, when thousands of citizens were taken by the security forces of their own governments to be imprisoned, tortured, and killed, their bodies found grotesquely disfigured or, as was often the case, never found at all. Undiscovered bone yards of the disappeared are scattered throughout Latin America.

Mexican newspapers carried stories of political assassinations that, after the touchstone "stolen" election of 1988, mostly involved opposition activists from the leftist PRD. Politicians and organizers were falling like flies, with 447 documented murders between 1988 and 1996, and certainly a much higher number unofficially. They were being wiped out for their political beliefs, on the doorstep of the United States, often a stone's throw away from the sun 'n' sand tourist packages of Acapulco, Mazatlán, and Ixtapa-Zihuatenejo, on the Mexican Riviera.

Mexico was awash in blood. I kept a file on political murders at the *Toronto Star* bureau in Mexico City, beginning on May 9,

1995, and by December 1996 it was crammed to overflowing with stories of activists found murdered (or shot to death in front of their families) and massacres of civilians by state police, soldiers, and the death squads. And that didn't count separate files I kept on open investigations into famous unsolved crimes, including the 1993 murder of Cardinal Juan Jesús Posadas Ocampo at the Guadalajara Airport, a cardinal in his robes allegedly mistaken for a Tijuana drug cartel kingpin and gunned down in broad daylight, and the 1994 killing of presidential candidate Colosio. Files were exploding out of my filing cabinet. Many of the stories were from *La Jornada,* the leftist Mexico-based daily whose justice reporters tracked human rights issues. However, I also clipped from the financial daily *El Financiero,* the popular centrist broadsheet *Reforma,* English daily *The News* and more right-leaning publications, including *El Universal* and the daily *Milenio.*

* * *

In addition, kept an ever-thickening dossier—which branched off into separate files on drug cartels and internecine PRI battles—on the August 1994 murder of PRI general secretary José Francisco Ruíz Massieu in Mexico City. He was a former governor of Guerrero and divorced from Adriana Salinas, sister to then-president Carlos Salinas. Thousands of tons of cocaine are shipped through Guerrero (also a huge marijuana- and opium poppy-growing area) to the United States and Canada every year, the bulk making its way along the drug highways of the hemisphere, en route from Colombia, Peru, and other South American countries.

The extraordinary Ruíz Massieu saga offers a taste of that other constant story line in Mexico, and one that is directly linked to the issue of human rights abuse—drugs, crime, corruption, staggering amounts of money, involvement of leading political players, including military officers, and efforts to protect privileged fiefdoms. To briefly summarize the highlights of a case that reads like a dark soap opera:[32]

In August 1994, President Salinas appointed the dead man's brother, Deputy Attorney-General Mario Ruíz Massieu, as special prosecutor in charge of the case. Ruíz Massieu later resigned, accusing the PRI hierarchy of orchestrating a cover-up. His claims buttressed widespread rumors in Mexico that the PRI brass was also behind the murder of Colosio, who apparently intended to investigate high-level involvement in drug trafficking. (None of this has been proven.) Ruíz Massieu fled to the United States, where he was eventually arrested and charged with money-laundering, convicted by a Houston jury of having taken bribes from narco-traffickers, and, facing more charges, supposedly committed suicide in jail in 1999.

In February 1995, newly installed president Ernesto Zedillo ordered the arrest of Raúl Salinas, brother of Carlos and Adriana, for the murder of José Francisco Ruíz Massieu. Carlos Salinas, three months out of Los Pinos, promptly disappeared, turning up in Monterrey, where he staged a hunger strike at the home of a party volunteer.

(This event marked my arrival in Mexico: the man who had been president of the country three months prior now on a hunger strike in some bungalow in Monterrey and his brother in jail facing a murder rap. I would learn a great deal about Mexico in the years to come, but no image would better illustrate for me the sheer savage nuttiness of the place.)

From Monterrey, Salinas gave a radio interview, sounding confused and saying he had nothing to do with the murder of Luis Donaldo Colosio. President Zedillo met with him in Monterrey and, after thirty-six hours, Salinas ended his hunger strike. It is not known what was promised, if anything. By this time, Salinas was the most hated man in Mexico for his role in the peso crash. He went into exile, living mostly on his farm in Ireland over the next few years; sightings of him in Mexico, or in Cuba where he vacationed with his friend Fidel Castro, always caused a stir.

His brother remained in jail as his in camera trial proceeded, amid press reports of his alleged involvement—along with his brother, the former president—in narco-trafficking and money-laundering. "Carlos was head of the Mafia—the *capo di tutti capi* as they say in Chicago," Porfirio Muñoz Ledo, president of the Revolutionary Democratic Party, told reporters.[33]

In November 1995, Raúl's wife, Paulina Castañón de Salinas, a Catherine Deneuve look-alike, was arrested in Geneva when she tried to withdraw $84 million in cash from a Swiss bank. She was acting on the instructions of her husband, in jail in Almoloya. At the same time, police were trying to trace the spectacular wealth Raúl had amassed during his brother's presidency. One of Paulina's former bodyguards characterized the lifestyle of Mexico's elite families for the *Toronto Star*: "These people hold their distance. They are in the clouds. They don't say hello. They have armored cars and motorcycle escorts and lovers. We open and close their doors for them, and they don't talk to us."

In October 1996, Raúl's former mistress, Spaniard María Bernal, accompanied by her spiritual advisers, two Spanish witches, led special prosecutor Pablo Chapa Benzanilla to a skeleton in a shallow grave on Raúl's ranch. She claimed it was the body of a missing PRI deputy who was supposed to have been involved with Raul Salinas in the murder of Ruíz Massieu. Instead, the corpse turned out to be a relative of one of the witches. Chapa Benzanilla, who also investigated the murders of Cardinal Posadas Ocampo and Colosio, was fired and, eventually, disappeared.

In February 1997, the *New York Times* won a Pulitzer Prize for a series of stories that detailed involvement in the drug trade by the governors of Morelos and Sonora. The stories also reported that Raúl Salinas was the go-between for drug interests and Mexican government officials, apparently lugging suitcases full of cash. Also in 1997, a brigadier general in the Mexican Army was arrested on bribery charges related to narco-trafficking.

On January 21, 1999, Raúl Salinas was convicted of having masterminded the murder of José Francisco Ruíz Massieu and sentenced to fifty years in prison, a term that was later reduced to twenty-seven and a half years. In June 2005, the conviction was overturned and Salinas walked out of jail after his family posted $3 million in bail. He still faces illegal enrichment charges involving $100 million.

* * *

By 1999, five years into free trade in Mexico, there could be no doubt that human rights abuses continued. The crisis was deepening, in fact. That year, Amnesty International, which had been doing reports for years on Mexico and had a strong basis of comparison, determined that the human rights situation in Mexico was "seriously deteriorating."[34]

Amnesty analyzed the reasons, concluding that the most intrinsic cause was the expanding militarization of Mexico and the increasing role of the army in law enforcement. Soldiers were the new sheriffs in town, and theirs was a rough justice.

However, under the microscope of the all-important trade agreement, with its importance to business in North America and the role it was expected to play in winning a larger deal for the hemisphere, these crimes were no longer going unnoticed by politicians outside of Mexico. Amnesty itself pointed out that international organizations, including United Nations agencies, were showing greater interest in Mexico's human rights situation.

There was also a new and different tone to the reports. Investigators put blame squarely on the shoulders of the country's leaders, without that deferential "but they're trying" chorus of past years. In 1999, the Washington-based Human Rights Watch criticized the indifference of Mexico's leaders to a savage legacy perpetrated by their own state agents. The report, titled "Systemic Injustice," began: "Torture, disappearances and extrajudicial executions remain widespread in Mexico. . . . Political leaders have been unwilling to ensure that existing human rights–related laws are applied vigorously. Authorities are more likely to close ranks and deny that even well-documented abuses ever took place, than they are to insist that those responsible be brought to justice."

Before a state visit to Mexico by Canadian Prime Minister Jean Chrétien in 1999, a coalition of Canadian rights groups wrote to him, saying: "Canada must speak with a strong voice to raise human rights violations which are of international concern. The economic, social and political links which Canada has promoted with Mexico over recent years (particularly in the context of the NAFTA) afford you, Prime Minister, with both the opportunity and the responsibility to put human rights on the agenda. It is essential that Canada's voice not be silent."[35]

It was cold comfort to the people being tortured and murdered in Mexico that the foreign public was paying more attention, cold comfort indeed. And the debate continues over whether this attention has done any good, or merely raised the bar for the quality of the reporting of the crimes, both by the rights community and the media.

Still, things had changed after 1994. The murder of Luis Donaldo Colosio, photographed with his brains oozing onto a Tijuana street, was the first post-NAFTA political assassination. Instead of being able to deal with it relatively quietly, President Salinas (before his hunger strike began) was forced to maneuver with more foreign reporters covering the story and representatives of his NAFTA trading partners peering in from the sidelines.

Prime Minister Chrétien and his entourage arrived on schedule in Mexico City, a few days after the murder. The trip was intended as a little publicity boost to free trade in Mexico, a bonbon as it were from its Canadian political supporters. But the prime minister had to give his press conference at the Canadian embassy in Polanco, even as Salinas and PRI strategists were meeting at Los Pinos to settle on the reportedly unwilling Zedillo as Colosio's replacement. Chrétien found himself on the hot seat over the grave situation in Mexico.

"Well," he observed, "in Mexico, they have a democracy which is not our democracy in many ways."

A few days later, over Holy Week, I traveled to the Lacandon jungle to interview Subcomandante Marcos in a guerrilla encampment not far from Mexico's border with Guatemala. I waited three days for him to appear and on the third day, just as the sun was setting, there he was on his bay horse, silhouetted against the sky, like the hero in an old western movie. (I imagined him waiting in the brush for the perfect dramatic moment to appear.) He galloped into camp and settled down for the interview. He lit his pipe and fragrant smoke curled upward. More than three hours passed before he would announce, *"Ya basta* (Enough),"* jump back on his horse, and gallop off into the night.

When I asked him about Chrétien's comment, he laughed.

"How many kinds of democracy are there? That is my question to the prime minister," said Marcos. "Democracy that looks like democracy but is *not* democracy? That is democracy in Mexico—it looks like democracy but nobody believes in it."

He continued: "Democracy means government of the people for the people by the people. Ask him, 'What does it mean in Canada?'"

As the 1990s drew to a close, Mexicans were being quoted in the foreign press talking about democracy. Human rights crimes and political murders were no longer slipping under the radar and, frankly, it was embarrassing for Canadian and American politicians, who had sold free trade with such gusto, to have to keep fielding messy questions about the affairs of their newest friend and trading partner.

* * *

Vicente Fox's victory should be viewed in this broader context. The pressure cooker of Mexican politics had to blow off steam, and it finally did, with the election of somebody other than a ruling party *priísta*. That somebody was selected long before 2000.

On December 1, when the green, red, and white presidential sash was slipped over the shoulders of the new president at the palace of Los Pinos, it carried with it the hopes and dreams of ordinary Mexicans that life really would be different.

This being Mexico, Inauguration Day was full of omens. A mild earthquake, originating in the Pacific coastal state of Oaxaca, rumbled through the capital in the morning, causing buildings to sway, but little damage.

Fox went in the early hours to the Basilica of Guadalupe to pray to Mexico's patron saint. It was the first time a president-elect publicly sought the blessing of a priest, and he did so at the most sainted location in Mexico, the site where, in 1531, the dark Virgin, Our Lady of Guadalupe, is said to have appeared to the Indian peasant Juan Diego. Her image is everywhere in Mexico, in homes and shop windows, and bobbing on the dashboards of hundreds of thousands of little green-and-white Volkswagen beetle cabs.

At noon, in a portent duly noted by the pious and interpreted as auspicious, the volcano Popocatepetl, the sleeping woman of Aztec legend, released a plume of white smoke into the atmosphere from her mountain, just south of the capital city.

In the afternoon, Fox gave his inaugural speech to a visitors gallery crammed with dignitaries, including Cuban President Fidel Castro, U.S. Secretary of State Madeleine Albright, Canadian Foreign Affairs Minister John Manley, Spanish Crown Prince Felipé de Borbón, Chilean President Ricardo Lagos, former Soviet leader Mikhail Gorbachev, and writers Carlos Fuentes of Mexico, Mario Vargas Llosa of Peru, and Nobel Prize winners Nadine Gordimer from South Africa and Gabriel García Márquez of Colombia, who has a home in Mexico City. (Márquez was then undergoing successful treatment for lung cancer. It was rumored in the bohemian writers' cafés of Coyoacán that the master gave up, with great reluctance, his five packs of cigarettes a day.)

There was much goodwill toward Fox.

Early in the new year, Fox visited Ottawa and Washington, where he met with human rights organizations and promised to deal personally with the most high-profile human rights cases before his government. He was at ease with newly elected U.S. president George W. Bush. Both were ranchers, one from Guanajuato, the other from Crawford, Texas. Both are gangly men, with a fondness for silver belt buckles. Bush chose Fox's ranch for his first foreign outing to what would be dubbed the "Cowboy Summit," although his Mexican hosts were perturbed when the bilateral agenda was blown out of the water by the Bush administration's decision that weekend to bomb Iraq, accusing President Saddam Hussein of having illegal radar command-and-control sites near Baghdad. On the summit's first day, Bush's time was consumed by U.S. and British fighter jets pounding Iraqi targets, in what turned out to be a small-scale dress rehearsal for war with Iraq two years later. "We are going to watch very carefully as to whether or not [Saddam] develops weapons of mass destruction," declared Bush, the Mexican president at his side.

(I had my doubts about the budding friendship between Fox and Bush. Living in Mexico, one gets swept up in the appreciation of omens. As I was writing my summit wrap story back in Mexico City, a bird hit the window of my office and fell down dead onto the terrace. I knew something was up.)

Fox continued to shine. Later that spring of 2001, at the Summit of the Americas in Quebec City, he carried the banner for free trade throughout the hemisphere. It was now possible for Mexico to be proclaimed the harbinger of true democracy via free trade. The Mexican miracle could indeed come to pass elsewhere in Latin America.

In his inaugural address, he made solemn promises to the people of Mexico.

"In Mexico and Chiapas, there is a new dawn," he said, pledging to respect the rights of Mexico's Indian peoples. "Nevermore" would there be a Mexico without them.

"The fight against corruption begins today," said Fox, promising to overhaul Mexico's shadowy intelligence services, including the Center of Investigation and National Security (CISEN), which keeps files on politicians, journalists, union leaders, and activists of all stripes at its offices within the Interior Secretariat. "An administration that spies on its people to learn what they are thinking has not learned to listen," the new president said, and the people cheered.

He made a simple vow to safeguard the nation's human rights activists.

"We are going to protect them like never before and respect them like never before."

With all their hearts, Mexicans wanted to believe him.

* * *

And now, only ten months into his term, Digna Ochoa y Plácido was murdered in her offices in the heart of the capital, in the shadow of Los Pinos. José Luis Soberanes, president of the National Human Rights Commission, an agency of the national government, called it the "the first political crime of the Fox *sexenio*."[36]

Everyone seemed to grasp its significance. Not only had a human rights activist been murdered, but the victim was someone who took on the army and spoke often and openly about how political assassinations go unpunished in Mexico. It would be the ultimate irony if her killers were able to get away with it. This time, under this president, there must be no impunity. Her assassination is a supreme test for the Fox administration, and it was quickly characterized as such by the *New York Times, Washington Post, Los Angeles Times,* and other leading opinion-makers in the United States.

This was not a crime to be swept easily under the carpet. Digna's profile was far too high, especially in Washington where opinions mattered to the leaders of Latin America, even to those who liked to pretend they didn't.

Digna was associated with the magic of the Kennedy name.

Kerry Kennedy, niece to America's martyred President John F. Kennedy and daughter to his slain brother, Bobby, was pivotal to Digna's success in the United States, at least in the beginning. A human rights activist herself, Kerry interviewed Digna for her book, *Speak Truth to Power: Human Rights Defenders Who Are Changing Our World.* Digna's name was soon on short lists for prestigious honors, her extraordinary work recognized and applauded.

"This is a terrible, terrible day," Kerry Kennedy told *La Jornada* the day after Digna's murder. "Once, I asked her where she found the courage to defend cases when she herself had been tortured and she knew the consequences of her actions. She told me, 'You know, it's because I am angry. When I think about what they do to my people, my country, it makes me so indignant that I feel a sense of peace and calm, and I have the ability to confront whatever comes.'"

She included Digna in her book because she felt that, as a woman, an Indian, and a former nun, hers was a unique perspective. "She was working in Mexico where those were three strikes against most people," she told me in New York City, many months after Digna's murder. "Digna was working with few resources beyond her heart and sinew, and that was what she had going for her. It was all Digna."

We were chatting on a dappled spring day in a hotel room overlooking Central Park. Memories of Digna made us both laugh. She spoke about how much she liked her, admired her guts and tenacity, and understood her vulnerabilities. "In many ways, she was a study in contrasts," she told me. "She had this very sort of quiet, demure appearance and she spoke very softly, but she was as tough as they come. She wore clothing that was almost Victorian in how buttoned-up it was, but there was nothing stiff about her. She was full of warmth and love and openness and humanity."

When her book was published in 2000, Digna was included with Nobel Prize laureates Elie Wiesel, Desmond Tutu, and the Dalai Lama in a tribute to thirty-one rights leaders, her image captured in stark black and white by Pulitzer Prize winner Eddie Adams.

Ariel Dorfman (*Death and the Maiden*) adapted the material into a play, which debuted at the John F. Kennedy Center for the Performing Arts in Washington on September 19, 2000. It was a red-carpet affair, brimming with excitement, glamour, and an A-list of Hollywood actors onstage, among them John Malkovich, Kevin Kline, Julia Louis-Dreyfus, Alec Baldwin, Rita Moreno, Rubén Blades, Sigourney Weaver, John Callos Esposito, Glenn Close, and Edward James Olmos.

Alfre Woodard, lit by a single spot, spoke Digna's words:

"My name is Digna Ochoa. I am a nun, who started life as a lawyer. My father was a union leader in Veracruz, Mexico. . . ."[37] She told the story of a girl born into poverty, whose union leader father was tortured, and who went to law school to fight injustices she'd seen in the flesh.

From the audience, Digna beamed, especially delighting in the crowd's roar over her karate story:

"One time there was a guy who had been disappeared for twenty days. We knew he was in a military hospital, and we filed *habeas corpus* petitions on his behalf. But the authorities denied having him in custody. One night we were informed that he was being held in a particular state hospital. We went the next day. They denied us access. I spent the whole morning studying the comings and goings at the hospital to see how I could get in. During a change in shifts, I slipped by the guards. When I got to the room where this person was, the nurse at the door told me I could not go in . . . I told her that I would take care of myself; all I asked of her was that she take note of what I was going to do and that if they did something to me, she should call a certain number. I gave her my card. I took a deep breath, opened the door violently and yelled at the federal judicial police officers inside. I told them they had to leave immediately because I was the person's lawyer and needed to speak with him. They didn't know how to react, so they left. I had two minutes, but it was enough to explain who I was, that I had been in touch with his wife, and to get him to sign a piece of paper proving he was in the hospital. He signed. By then the police came back. . . . Their first reaction was to try to grab me. They didn't expect me to assume an attack position—the only position in karate I know, from movies, I suppose. Of course, I don't *really* know karate, but they thought I was going to attack. Trembling inside, I said sternly that if they laid a hand on me they'd see what would happen. And they drew back, saying, 'You're threatening us.' And I said, 'Take it any way you want.'"[38]

Digna looked luminous. Everyone said so. She posed with President Clinton for the photo that, the next spring in Mexico City, would prompt her boyfriend Juan José to ask: "Digna, *who are you?*"

That fall, she was the star of Kerry's book tour, occasionally accompanying her. Kerry remembers one particular moment at the National Press Club: "I told her story there and the audience, a rather sophisticated Washington audience, was just floored. I said, 'Here she is,' and Digna stood up and there was this standing ovation."

In the New York hotel room, we were both silent for a few moments. And then she added: "I have spoken to tens of thousands of people and hers is the story I always tell. I mix everybody else's up, but I always talk about Digna."[39]

Digna was the first person Kerry talked about when she was interviewed on *Larry King Live*, on CNN. "That's an incredible story," said King, about Mexico's karate-chopping nun.

"Yes, incredible, incredible," replied Kerry. "And I said to her, 'How do you get the nerve to confront them like that?' And I was expecting something about God or Jesus or love, because this is a nun,[40] and she said, 'I'm just so furious, I just muster all of my anger about all the terrible things they've done and it gives me this incredible sense of calm with which I can confront anyone.'"

"Wow!" said King. "Anger directed well."

That year, 2000, was a year of honors for Digna. She won a coveted MacArthur Foundation grant[41] to write about human rights and ABC news anchor Tom Brokaw (a network vice president) presented her with an American Bar Association award at a tony dinner at the Plaza Hotel in New York. Her client, Rodolfo Montiel, an impoverished campesino facing arms and drug charges in a Guerrero jail, won the U.S. environmental Goldman Prize for the fight against widespread logging in the western Sierra.

In Mexico, she received the Roque Dalton medal for her fight to prosecute soldiers on torture charges in a civilian court (the Montiel case). She knew she was balancing without a net. With fateful words, she accepted the award: "In Mexico, to defend human rights is to risk your life."

The year held one more glittering, star-studded affair, this time on the West Coast. Her achievements were celebrated in Hollywood.

On September 15, actor Martin Sheen presented Digna with Amnesty International's Enduring Spirit Award at the Beverly Wilshire Hotel in Los Angeles. Sheen was a fitting choice. He is known, of course, for roles in *Apocalypse Now* and on television's *The West Wing*, but he is at heart a scrapper, a veteran of social and political causes, who's been arrested more than once and thrown in jail for his beliefs. He, too, has been honored by Amnesty. It seemed appropriate that, on a glittering evening, the award was a glowing crystal globe, with an image of a candle burning through a coil of barbed wire. Digna's parents have it now.

"I really do love the symbol of Amnesty International," began Sheen's rich voice. "It embodies the old phrase that it's better to light a candle than curse the darkness. There's so much pain in the world. There's so much human misery. Unfortunately so much of it is inflicted, and we lose our humanity when we treat each other so badly. It's a reflection, I think, about how we really feel about ourselves, about who we really are. . . . We're all a part of that little candle, as long as we continue our efforts to keep it lit."

He praised Digna's courage and described how she was unflinching, despite having been kidnapped, beaten, and threatened with death. She stepped to the stage, wearing a simple black dress, her shiny hair tucked behind her ears. She seemed nervous, but once she began she spoke strongly, her words translated by an interpreter.

"Gracias. Buenas noches. Gracias . . . ," she said, as applause rolled over her. She began by praising her colleagues at the Miguel Agustín Pro Juárez Human Rights Center and described what life was really like in Mexico.

"I started my career in law with the dream of helping people, thinking that all it took to achieve this goal was to know the law," she said. "Later, I learned that, due to the rampant corruption and impunity in Mexico, it wasn't enough to be innocent, to be right and to have the law on your side. It was necessary to fight against an entire government structure that defends very specific political and economic interests."[42]

Digna was a universe away from the poverty and violence of Mexico. She told her Mexican stories in the Hollywood setting of the Beverly Wilshire Hotel, where Julia Roberts's dreams came true in *Pretty Woman*. Wilshire Boulevard is where Rodeo Drive begins, the street of dreams and the most expensive shopping venue in the world. The stars linger at Chanel and choose diamonds at Tiffany, Cartier, or Fred Leighton.

She told her stories where they weren't supposed to be told.

One can imagine the pique of Mexican consular officials, who day in, day out, polish a benevolent image in the City of Angels. Theirs is the Mexico of Spring Break, whitewash gleaming against blue seas, and romance—not tortured peasants and earth soaked in blood. One can image the fury of high officials back home in Mexico. This woman was really getting on people's nerves.

Digna accepted the award on behalf of her colleagues at the human rights center, PRO, and left the stage.

There was no hint of anything wrong in her relations with these colleagues. There was no sign she was going through the most difficult period in her life, or that she was crying herself to sleep at night.

She gave no sign of betrayal.

CHAPTER FIVE

Candle in the Wind

On Saturday afternoon, October 20, when mourners were filing under the green awning of the Gayoso Sullivan Funeral Home in Mexico City for a funeral mass for Digna Ochoa, President Fox was in a government jet, on his way back to Mexico City from business meetings of the Asia-Pacific Economic Cooperation in Shanghai. Already, protestors were pouring into the streets of the Mexican capital, carrying placards and chanting "Justice! Justice!" for the murdered human rights defender.

But, in China, before his departure, Fox said nothing. He failed to make the obvious pro forma comments—my government condemns the crime, mourns her death, we will see justice done, and so on. Over the next few days, his strange silence about the murder would become a political issue, offering the first clue that this president, greeted with such high hopes ten months earlier, might fail to live up to expectations.

His only comments that Saturday referred to Mexico's "new international role" under his leadership. The following year, in 2002, Mexico would host the APEC summit in the Baja California luxury resort town of Cabo San Lucas on the Baja Peninsula, and Fox expressed satisfaction with the week's planning sessions in Shanghai. Irony was piled upon irony. World leaders, Fox vowed, can count on Mexico's "impeccable democratic credentials which newly strengthen our voice among nations." He lauded his own "indefatigable promotion of democratic values and rigorous defense of human rights," without mentioning the murder of the country's foremost human rights defender.

Fox was traveling with his wife, Martha Sahagún, and it has been an emotional week for the newlyweds. Their world tour lasted twelve days, with stops in Prague, Hamburg, Toulouse, Madrid, Rome, and Shanghai. On Wednesday, they kissed for the cameras in front of St. Peter's Basilica in Rome after separate audiences with Pope John Paul II. Fox spent close to half an hour with the pontiff, while his wife had a few moments. Later, they declined to answer questions from Mexican reporters, who were interested only in whether Fox asked the Holy Father for an annulment of his first marriage. On July 2, Fox's fifty-ninth birthday and the anniversary of his election victory, he wed his former press secretary in a civil ceremony at the presidential mansion of Los Pinos. Despite rumors of romance, the wedding came as a surprise to the public.

Fox always maintained that, as a devout Catholic respectful of the laws of the Church, he would not seek a divorce from his first wife. "I declared publicly that I would never marry again," he said, in an interview with the *Toronto Star* in 1996. At the time, he was separated and the couple's four adopted children lived with him at the governor's mansion in Guanajuato. "I told the people that my commitment before God was for life. I think that has given me great protection in politics. Being with my kids, nobody asks about my wife."

But, in Rome, it was this new wife reporters were asking about, pushing hard for a tasty tidbit. Was she hoping to marry within the Church? Sahagún, holding tightly to her husband's hand, smiled and insisted such matters were "strictly personal."[1]

Fox speaks often of his faith, and the trip to Rome was personally important. He was only the second president of Mexico, after Ernesto Zedillo, to visit the pope. He had paused during his inaugural address the previous year at Los Pinos to bend down and accept a crucifix from his eldest daughter, Ana Cristina, then twenty-one. It was a significant gesture in a country where relations between church and state have been bloody, and presidents have been wary of Rome. Fox brought a cavalcade of dignitaries to the Vatican, including his progressive foreign secretary, Jorge Castañeda (soon to be replaced), and Guerrero governor Rene Juárez Cisneros, whose state would become significant as Digna's story unfolded. Fox was escorted into the private papal library by members of the Swiss Guard wearing, as they had for centuries, the red, blue, and yellow colors of the Medici family.

When the pope arrived, Fox bent to kiss the papal ring. "May God bless your country and all Mexico," he told Fox.

"Thank you very much for your time and the reflections you have shared with me, and thank you for your affection toward Mexico," replied Fox, before receiving the blessing of the Holy Father.[2]

The First Lady said she asked for Pope John Paul's blessing "for the women and children of Mexico. I asked him not to forget us ever in his prayers."

* * *

On Sunday, two days after the murder, Interior Secretary Santiago Creel was the first member of Fox's cabinet to comment. He was relaxed when reporters caught him in the capital as he stretched at the start of the Terry Fox "Run Against Cancer." Such informality with the media (let alone having a cabinet secretary participate in a foot race) would have been taboo even a few years earlier under the old-style PRI.

Creel, a lawyer in his forties who studied at the University of Michigan, had solid civic reform credentials. He was a co-founder of the respected newsmagazine *Este País*, and fought for free and fair elections. He was relaxed with reporters and, for years before his cabinet appointment, was on everybody's list for thoughtful opposition analysis. On this Sunday, he expressed his indignation over Digna's murder and promised his government would cooperate with Mexico City authorities in charge of the case. His commitment was important because there was no doubt the Interior Secretariat had valuable information about Digna's activities and, most certainly, about her enemies.

In Mexico, as in most Latin American countries, this ministry functions as the eyes and ears of the state. It controls a vast intelligence network that keeps watch on its citizens, including activists within the human rights movement. The Center for Investigation and National Security (CISEN) is by nature secretive. It's a spy agency and its files are plump with the intimate details of people's lives, gleaned by tapping phones, faxes, cell phones, and every other method of surveillance. Every twenty-four hours, this information is compiled into a report and four coded copies are made. They go to the president, the interior secretary, the director general of CISEN, and the head of the agency's analysis bureau. Each day, around 6 P.M., a messenger leaves the Interior Secretariat on Bucareli Street, en route to Los Pinos, with the president's copy.[3]

CISEN files would be a logical place to look for clues. Moreover, in the aftermath of the murder, human rights defender Adriana Corona told journalists she knew the agency had a file on Digna because she had seen it earlier in the year. She said that it linked Digna to guerrilla organizations.[4]

Corona's claim led to a Monty Python moment in a sad week. The People's Insurgent Revolutionary Army (known by its Spanish acronym, ERPI), felt it necessary to write a letter to Fox, which found its way into *La Jornada* and other media outlets. ERPI was relatively low profile, certainly in comparison to the publicity surrounding the Zapatistas, and its guerrillas were believed to be based in Guerrero, with cells in Mexico City. The letter from the rebels said that the murdered lawyer, Digna Ochoa y Plácido, was not—and never had been—a member of the People's Insurgent Revolutionary Army.

Fox had promised transparency in his inaugural address and Creel made the same commitment now. CISEN would cooperate. Mexico City officials "will have all the assistance—and I stress *all* the assistance—of agencies of the federal government in order to carry out the investigation and to punish those responsible," vowed Creel to a knot of reporters, before loping off to join the Terry Fox run. Later, he told CNN En Español that he "won't rest" until Digna's killers were brought to justice.

However, the president, back from Shanghai that day and apparently preoccupied with his own plans, said nothing. That night, British pop star Sir Elton John was set to perform at a gala to launch the First Lady's charity foundation, *Vamos México!* (Let's go, Mexico!), on the grounds of Chapultepec Castle. Sahagún founded the organization in September with the goal of raising $20 million for charity.[5]

There was something girlish about Martha Sahagún, an immensely capable woman in her fifties, always impeccably dressed and heavily made up, with layers of Pan-Cake, black eyeliner, and many coats of mascara. A Spanish verb for applying makeup is *pintar*, literally "to paint," and one could see why in the case of the First Lady. She was ultra-thin, lived in high heels, and could be coquettish with male reporters.

She appeared oblivious to increasing criticism about her lifestyle. Already, three months into the job of First Lady, she was being compared to Evita for her appetite for the trappings of power. Argentineans worshipped and adored Eva Perón, *Santa Evita*, but Mexicans apparently didn't share the sentiment for Sahagún. "Martita, that's enough," *Reforma*'s Guadalupe Loaeza tsk-tsked a week before, after the Spanish celebrity magazine *Hola!* splashed Fox and Sahagún smooching at the Vatican on the cover and devoted glossy inside pages to their most excellent European adventure.

Loaeza was a talented writer, with an unrelenting eye for the foibles of the rich. In her book, *Las Reinas de Polanco (The Queens of*

Polanco), she told delectable tales about the ladies who lived in the posh district of Polanco, with their vanity and bustling sense of entitlement. Polanco even looks down physically on the rest of Mexico City from its hillside perch in the north. It rises above the smog. Of Sahagún, Loaeza observed in *Reforma*: "It's good that she wants to do things that previous first ladies didn't, but I don't like the style. It's frivolous and affected."

Rumors had begun to circulate that Sahagún coveted the presidency in 2006, when her husband couldn't run by law. Already, appalled officials from the president's own party were slapping down the notion. (By 2004, the rumors would become such a drain on the Fox presidency—with endless cartoons depicting Sahagún as the real power—that Sahagún held a press conference to declare she wouldn't run, although "Mexico is ready for a woman president." It would do little to squelch the rumors and, by this time, Sahagún was fighting off congressional demands for an investigation into *Vamos México!* spending.)

Her gala on Sunday, October 21, proceeded according to plan. The castle of Chapultepec is one of Mexico City's most treasured landmarks. Built in 1785 for the Spanish viceroys on the hunting grounds of Aztec emperors, it was turned into a military college in the 1800s. It was the site where, according to national legend, brave young cadets known as the *niños héroes* (child heroes) defended themselves against American troops in 1847. This was sacred ground. The ill-fated Emperor Maximilian von Hapsburg, installed to rule Mexico by France's Napoleon III in 1864 and executed by a firing squad three years later, lived here with his wife, the Empress Carlotta.

It was a night of bejeweled opulence. Tickets, which started at $1,200, were delivered by special courier from Los Pinos, each with an electronic bar code and embossed table number for these VIPs and Super VIPs. The guest list was drawn from the country's political and moneyed elites, as well as foreign dignitaries. Among them was billionaire Carlos Slim Helú, one of the world's richest men (given an immense boost when his friend Salinas sold him the national phone company, Teléfonos de México), cabinet ministers Eduardo Sojo, Francisco Gil Díaz, and Sari Bermúdez, and the burly personage of U.S. ambassador Jeffrey Davidow.

Even some who declined the invitation felt the need to make a statement. Former Guanajuato governor Juan Carlos Romero Hicks, from Fox's home state, snubbed the gala, telling reporters: "I have other priorities. And, anyway, I like the Beatles."

"Not Mexican enough," sniffed Federal Deputy Elías Martínez Rufino, from the Democratic Revolutionary Party.

Fox arrived punctually, fresh from his whirlwind world tour, with Sahagún on his arm. His enormous frame was bundled into a tuxedo, while the petite First Lady was elegant in black. One almost expected her to come dressed as Marie Antoinette, in powdered wig and beauty mark. It was surreal. The gala site was fifteen minutes, depending on traffic, down the hill to the Zacatecas Street offices where Digna's body was found not forty-eight hours earlier, and neither the president, nor his wife, had even acknowledged her existence.

The extravaganza began with lobster marinated in a vinaigrette of fine herbs and lemon, followed by tuna sashimi in a ponzu sauce, foie gras with apple compote in port, and Canadian duckling salad with arugula and mixed greens in an *échalote* honey dressing. A choice of entrees offered beef medallions Armagnac, served *en brochette* with cherry tomatoes and asparagus spears, mushroom ragout, and duck marinated in herbs. The feast was washed down with bottles of Moët *&* Chandon and Louis Latour Pouilly-Fuissé, 1999.[6]

The tinkling of fine crystal floated through the night air.

Quite apart from the timing of the event, two days after Digna's murder, the gala had drawn criticism for being held at a national monument. The public had just spent $47 million renovating the castle and its critics said it was being used as a private fiefdom.

Officials from the National Institute for Anthropology and History filed a complaint about use of the venue, and cartoonists had a field day lampooning the Versailles-like extravagance of this increasingly royal couple.

A few hundred protestors blocked access to the castle's main entrance and a security cordon had to be set up to ensure that the First Lady's guests could be escorted safely inside without coming in actual contact with crowds milling outside.

"The country is dying from hunger," shouted demonstrators, as the concert began behind the castle's high stone walls. "*Foximiliano,* the castle is for the people."

Elton John sang "Your Song" to begin his concert, and ended, at 1:30 A.M., with the haunting "Candle in the Wind."[7]

He had written the song for Marilyn Monroe, and then performed it in September 1999, at the funeral of his friend Diana, Her Royal Highness, the Princess of Wales. It was about an actress who seemed far more wistful and vulnerable in life than Digna, but it still had resonance for her story.

For her legend burned on—and perhaps always will.

*   *   *

Monday dawned and from around the world messages of sympathy and support were flooding into Mexico. The European Community expressed official condolences and, in Washington, the State Department's Philip Reeker commented on behalf of the Bush administration: "The United States condemns the deplorable assassination of the lawyer Digna Ochoa. We're not going to contribute to speculation as to the perpetrators of this crime. But we expect certainly that the government of Mexico will fully investigate this murder and prosecute those found responsible."

The quick reaction from official Washington was significant, given the climate in the United States. Only a few weeks had passed since the terrorist attacks of September 11 and Americans were in shock, still holding funerals for firefighters and watching the gut-wrenching footage every day of earth-moving machines lifting the wreckage from the site of the World Trade Center in New York City. There was so much debris, it seemed as if it would never be removed. Psychically it probably never will be.

Less than two weeks before Digna's murder, President George W. Bush authorized the bombing campaign against the Taliban government in Afghanistan, accused of harboring Osama bin Laden and al-Qaeda terrorists responsible for 9/11. The White House, Pentagon, and State Department were focused on terrorism and war, and the ante had been upped by the anthrax scare in the capital. The United States had pulled up the drawbridge and turned inward, the president moving away from the Mexican administration he so warmly had championed only a few months earlier at the Cowboy Summit in Guanajuato.

Indeed, if one were to pick a perfect time to assassinate a high-profile human rights leader in Mexico, when the fewest number of people would be paying attention, it would be in the aftermath of September 11.

In this context, the administration's response, on the first business day after the murder, and before Fox had uttered a word, could be seen as a signal to Los Pinos that the White House had noticed and the murder of Digna Ochoa should not be ignored.

There were demonstrations in front of the Mexican embassy in Washington and petitions to President Bush. Nobel Peace Prize laureate Rigoberta Menchú, of Guatemala, warned that Digna's murder represented a "maximum alert" for the democratic transition in Mexico and the future of the Fox government.

Mary Robinson, human rights commissioner at the United Nations, called Digna's assassination even more tragic because it dashed the hope that the "intimidation and harassment of human rights defenders were finally being addressed seriously."

Still, Fox remained mute, leaving his press office to issue perfunctory comments a few hours after Reeker's remarks. It was difficult to imagine Vicente Fox of the election campaign—the boisterous debater with the common touch—failing to express his outrage or hurl himself into the debate over the murder of a human rights hero. Where was his passion?

For the first time, human rights activists began to speak out against him.

"Since Fox came to power, things have gone on the same. The disappearances and the injustices continue," Rosario Ibarra de Piedra told reporters at a protest outside the Interior Secretariat on Bucareli. She was well known in Mexico, the heart and soul of the human rights movement, and her comments were a blow to the Fox administration. A small woman dressed always in black, she had been fighting for justice since her son was "disappeared" in 1975 during Mexico's Dirty War against union leaders, teachers, social activists, politicians, and members of the clergy. Hundreds of leftists disappeared, among them Jesús Piedra Ibarra, a third-year medical student and political activist arrested by police and never seen again.

Already, there was a sense of gloom. The days passed, leads grew cold, the president was detached, and there were growing fears Digna's murder would not be solved. Respected historian Lorenzo Meyer told the Mexico City daily *Reforma*: "Someone did this knowing it would go straight to the heart of the new regime, and that nothing would happen."

Pilar Noriega, Digna's friend and veteran human rights investigator, looked terrible days after the murder, her voice hoarse and her eyes red from crying. "Whoever killed Digna acted with the conviction and the certainty that they could say, 'Look, I can do whatever I want, and nothing is going to happen,'" she told José Gil Olmos, of the newsmagazine *Proceso*. "They feel sufficiently protected that they are not threatened, even having committed a crime of such magnitude."

It took Fox until Tuesday, October 23, to personally acknowledge Digna's murder. After comments marking Doctor's Day in the republic, he paused and, as if in an afterthought to the medical theme, added: "If you will permit me, I do not want to end this speech without referring to a very lamentable event which has occurred in our country in the last few days: the murder of Digna Ochoa.

"With the assassination of Digna Ochoa, we all lose. Mexicans lose because they had in her a valiant defender of human rights. And the democratic state loses because it needs independent voices for all members of society."[8]

From the Lacandon jungle, Zapatista leader Marcos broke months of silence with a letter to *La Jornada*, published on Thursday's front page. He urged Mexicans "to shine a light to chase away these shadows and prevent the clocks from being turned back to the days of impunity, cynicism, and indifference."

He mocked Fox and Sahagún outright, ridiculing their evening with Sir Elton John at Chapultepec Castle. "When those who fight for social rights are being eliminated, the powers-that-be put on their best clothes, threw parties, and tossed a few coins to their charity in order to purchase indifference," Marcos wrote. "But there is no real change beyond the dictates of fashion."

* * *

From the beginning, clues pointed to the army and Digna's last trip to Guerrero—the all-terrain vehicle expedition—two weeks before her murder.

Digna was lead lawyer at PRO in the defense of two jailed campesinos, Rodolfo Montiel and Teodoro Cabrera, from a group called the Organization of Peasant Ecologists of the Sierra of Petatlán.[9] She had sought to prosecute two soldiers on charges of torture in the case, which centered on the lopsided battle between impoverished peasants and local power barons over preserving the forests. The environmental group was formed by villagers desperate to stop deforestation in the mountains, which had increased rapidly after the NAFTA agreement. The treaty, as well as constitutional changes to facilitate it, allowed companies to buy timber rights much more easily, directly from local forestry *ejidos*.[10] Digna wasn't working with PRO any longer and was supposed to be off the case. But she couldn't leave Guerrero alone; she kept shaking it like a dog with a bone. The murder investigation was awash in rumors of some big confrontation with soldiers during that final trek into the mountains.

"There are signs Digna Ochoa's murder came from the army. Members of the military were implicated in many of the cases she was handling," Emilio Álvarez Icaza, director of the Mexico City Human Rights Commission, told a press conference at the outset of his investigation. His organization was an arm's length government agency. He had been involved since the night of the murder, personally telephoning Attorney General Bernardo Bátiz and arriving at 31-A Zacatecas Street before Digna's body was removed. He was worried. He was all too familiar with the historic impunity of the military. (For its part, the army has never responded publicly to these allegations.)

Mexico City's PRD administration promised a full and open investigation. "We are going to get to the bottom of this," vowed Mexico City Mayor López Obrador. "These are the instructions I've given my attorney general. This shouldn't be happening anymore in our country. This belongs to Mexico's past."[11]

Attorney General Bátiz held daily press conferences and said his prosecutors were busy on several fronts: tracing the origin of the murder weapon, reconstructing the last forty-eight hours of Digna's life, and following several lines of investigation. Nobody had been ruled out, including Digna's friends, colleagues, and her lover, Juan José Vera.

They were investigating her professional life, from the Guerrero angle to her defense of three brothers jailed on terrorism charges after the August bombing of several branches of Banamex bank. She was supposed to visit them with Bárbara Zamora at Almoloya prison on Saturday afternoon, in preparation for a Monday morning court appearance.

"Personally," said Bátiz at a press conference, "I feel that this violent crime against a defender of human rights could be a sign of extreme right terrorism."

But he was blunt about where most clues were leading. While other lines of investigation couldn't be discarded, Bátiz soon told reporters, "The principal lines of inquiry are pointing toward the state of Guerrero and toward the conflicts of the campesino farmers with logging groups." He said her work and her relationship with the Guerrero peasant organization "placed Digna in a very delicate situation. . . . The campesinos [she defended] were interfering in huge investments."[12]

Guerrero was notorious for its drug-trafficking routes, marijuana and opium poppy fields, and political violence. The controversial Montiel/Cabrera case involved a disgraced Guerrero governor, local political bosses, killings in the high Sierra, soldiers from both the 19th and 40th Infantry Battalions, allegations of torture, and, in his role as former chief army prosecutor, General Rafael Macedo de la Concha, who now held the top civilian law enforcement job in the republic as Vicente Fox's attorney general.

Bátiz said his prosecutors were not afraid to investigate the military. That remained to be seen.

* * *

By the end of Week One, external pressure was mounting on Fox.

On Friday, October 26, the powerful *New York Times* weighed in with an editorial. The *Times* is the political bible of Latin America. Politicians study it to know what's what at the White House, State and Defense, the CIA and on Capitol Hill, reading between the lines when clues are subtle. There was no subtlety here. The editorial said Digna's murder bore "all the markings of a political execution, carried out by interest groups that are confident they can act with impunity, as they always have. The crime suggests a distressing continuity with an ugly past in a country that so hopefully greeted the election last year of President Vicente Fox and the end of the Institutional Revolutionary Party's 71-year rule."

The *Times* said Fox must ensure that "federal officials cooperate with the investigation, even if it leads to the army or police. Beyond the Ochoa case, Fox must act to rectify past injustices. To date, he has been far too timid in doing so. This timidity sends the wrong message—one of continuity—to groups eager to subvert the rule of law and obstruct the work of human rights lawyers like Digna Ochoa."

In the weeks to come, other news organizations weighed in against Fox. Just ten months earlier, he was the favored son, so full of promise, so richly praised in the American press. It felt like ten years. The honeymoon was over.

* * *

On Saturday morning, Fox recorded his weekly radio address, *Fox En Vivo (Fox Live)*, during a visit to San Cristóbal de las Casas in Chiapas. He promised "swift and urgent resolution" of Digna's murder and said that human rights activists were safe in Mexico. His office made a similar pitch in a series of full-page ads the government placed that weekend in newspapers across the country.

But back on his Guanajuato ranch Sunday, Fox made a telling comment.

"Look, this is a homicide—one more that has occurred in Mexico City," he said, adding that it was up to the city's prosecutors to solve it.[13]

The point was clear: Digna's case is just one more crime in the big city.

Reaction was immediate. Carlos Montemayor, a respected author and columnist, said that Fox "lacks the political maturity to understand social struggle." Mexico City Mayor López

Obrador told a press conference: "Maybe I'm not well informed, but we're talking about a crime against a prominent human rights defender. We haven't seen a crime of this magnitude for some time. So, I respectfully disagree."

When *Proceso,* the country's most influential newsmagazine, hit the newsstands Sunday, October 28, there could no longer be any doubt about the impact of Digna's murder on the young Fox administration.

The cover said it all: "Digna Ochoa: Fox's Aguas Blancas."

Proceso compared Digna's murder to one of the bloodiest events in recent Mexican history, one that stained the administration of Fox's predecessor, Ernesto Zedillo.

On June 28, 1995, state police ambushed seventeen peasant farmers on a remote mountain road in Guerrero, not far from the tiny community of Aguas Blancas (White Waters). They were all members of the Organization of Campesinos of the Southern Sierra, which was formed to fight for land and protest the policies of Guerrero governor Rubén Figueroa Alcocer. (It was a forerunner to the Petatlán environmental group.) Soon after forming, the organization's members began receiving death threats.

On this particular morning, they were en route to a protest when their truck was flagged down at a police roadblock. What happened has been documented by official reports and the Mexican courts: Guerrero police hid shooters in the brush and, after the men were ordered down off the trucks, they began firing and kept firing until every last man was dead. Then the police planted phony evidence, placing guns in the hands of corpses.

That night, Governor Figueroa insisted state police—*los judiciales* —fired in self-defense against guerrillas. He released a grainy tape, difficult to decipher, which purportedly showed one of the campesinos aiming at police from the truck. Newspaper reports quickly discredited his version of events. Acapulco's *El Sol* published crime scene photos showing one body—with and without a gun in the dead man's hand.

But the story didn't really break wide open until eight months later, when Televisa journalist Ricardo Roca aired a twenty-minute tape of the actual massacre on his Sunday show, *Detrás de las Noticias (Behind the News)*. It showed police opening fire on unarmed civilians and slaughtering them like pigs, before planting the weapons. President Zedillo told aides he was furious to learn the truth about Aguas Blancas on television.[14]

There was a judicial inquiry and the Mexican Supreme Court ruled that Figueroa, as well as other high-ranking officials, were responsible for the massacre.

The court described a "shocking and coarse attempt" by Figueroa to cover his tracks and said there was evidence to suggest a police provocateur among the campesinos. The report went on to warn: "Lies, manipulation, and dark political maneuverings will sink Mexico. . . . We must end this culture of lies and trickery. Only the truth will save Mexico."[15]

Human rights groups, including the PRO rights center, lauded the decision and, from Washington, the Inter-American Human Rights Commission urged the Mexican government to offer restitution to the families of the victims. Digna prepared evidence for the commission on behalf of the family of one murdered man.

Ultimately, however, President Zedillo let Figueroa off the hook. He stepped down as governor, and minor officials served jail time, but he was never charged with a crime. Instead, he boarded his private airplane and jetted off to his estates in Boca Raton, Florida. The lack of justice for the murdered campesinos haunted the Zedillo administration.

And now Fox faced his own Aguas Blancas.

In the Mexico City daily *Milenio*, political analyst Roberto Blancarte wrote: "The assassination takes us back several years to the most barbaric part of our political and social reality."

It was the beginning of the end of the bright dreams for human rights under Vicente Fox. Certainly, Fox had other burgeoning problems by this time, largely his early failure to deliver on the promise of jobs and better times. But, for the human rights community, for Mexicans expecting justice, and for a world waiting for Fox's new era to take root, his handling of the murder of Digna Ochoa was the first and most cutting disappointment.

"President Fox seems to think he has miraculously brought an end to human rights violations by expressions of goodwill," said a statement released by Amnesty International after Digna's death, and quoted in *Reforma*. "Everything indicates that the new government has achieved very few or no results in protecting human rights or investigating the violators of these rights. . . . Impunity has not been affected."

Similar views poured forth from activists who previously had held their tongues, reluctant to criticize Fox despite their growing misgivings. "When you ask President Fox whether he is in favor of ending torture, he says all the right things. But when it comes to stepping on people's toes and making things happen, he backs away," said Eric Olson of the Washington Office on Latin America (WOLA). "And it makes me wonder if he has a gut-level understanding of these issues."[16]

Curt Goering, deputy executive director of Amnesty International USA, called Digna's assassination "a horrible, tragic blow to human rights protection in Mexico. The rhetoric of the Fox administration indicated that he was prepared to deal with human rights issues differently than in the past. Well, in the aftermath of an event like this, the rhetoric rings hollow."[17]

An urgent petition was sent to President Fox and his attorney general, Macedo de la Concha, by eighty-three national and international rights groups, begging the Mexican government to live up to its legal commitments and fully investigate Digna's murder.[18] But the language of the petition revealed the deep pessimism of activists on the front lines of a struggle they felt was being lost in Mexico. "The harassments, threats, and execution [of Digna Ochoa], as well as the inefficiency and lack of will by the judicial apparatus to . . . penalize those responsible, makes the chances of democratization look increasingly bleak."

Alejandro Queral, from the Sierra Club, stated everyone's worst fear when he told the *New York Times:* "President Fox seems to be more concerned about keeping the military happy than he is about stopping their abuses."

* * *

There was a dark twist to the assassination of Digna Ochoa for Fox, one that, as the facts become known, would leave senior members of his government scrambling to explain the unexplainable. It was his government that succeeded in stripping Digna of her court-ordered bodyguards.

When Fox came to power in December 2000, Mexico was bound by an order of the Inter-American Court of Human Rights to protect Digna, an order that was given as a result of death threats and two kidnappings in 1999. Within weeks of his inauguration, however, Fox moved to withdraw that protection, over the objections (at least initially) of the human rights organizations involved in pursuing the case. His officials fought a complicated eight-month legal battle, and won.[19]

The protection order was lifted on August 28, 2001, five months after Digna returned to Mexico from exile and less than two months before her murder. She was alone and vulnerable on that October day precisely because the Fox government had convinced the court that her life was no longer in danger and she didn't need bodyguards.

To quickly backtrack: In its November 17, 1999, ruling, the court, based in San José, Costa Rica, ordered Ernesto Zedillo's government to "adopt without delay, all measures necessary" to protect Digna Ochoa, as well Edgar Cortez, Mario Patrón, and

Jorge Fernández, three of her colleagues at the Miguel Agustín Pro Juárez Human Rights Center. They were included in the protection order because death threats were arriving at the PRO offices and, on the October 1999 night that Digna was abducted and held overnight, the offices were broken into. Somebody erased the tape in the video surveillance camera before disabling it, ransacked the offices, and departed, leaving the door open and a note, with the words "SUICIDE POWER" in red ink.[20]

Digna believed the crimes were linked to PRO's involvement in the Montiel/Cabrera trial in Guerrero, a highly charged case because she was pushing to prosecute soldiers on torture charges. She also believed state agents were implicated in her kidnappings.[21]

It was an embarrassment for the Mexican government to be ordered to protect one of its citizens, especially because Mexico was highly sensitive about its sovereignty and bristled at the slightest hint of foreign interference. It was a card the government played often in dealing with foreign religious workers or rights activists who denounced unspeakable abuses: they were accused of meddling in the country's affairs and failing to understand the complexities of Mexico, sometimes being denounced as security threats and deported. But in this case, for the first time, Mexico had been brought before the international tribunal and, as a signatory to the American Convention on Human Rights in 1998, its government was legally obliged to abide by its ruling. The court also ordered Mexican authorities to fully investigate the crimes and submit a full report every two months.

The ruling hung over the bright new Fox administration like smog in the capital city, and officials rushed to appeal it. Federal lawyers argued that the crimes had been well and fully investigated.

But there was no evidence of that.

In fact, when the court first issued its ruling in 1999, Robert Varenik, director of the Washington-based Lawyers Committee for Human Rights, spoke for rights groups everywhere in pushing for that very thing: a serious investigation. "Mexican authorities have been promising for some time that threats and attacks would be fully investigated and the PRO staff protected," he said in a statement at the time. "Yet, we have still not seen any significant advances in the investigation and PRO staff is still in danger. We hope that the Court's order will prompt Mexican authorities to take effective steps to ensure the safety of the human rights defenders at PRO."

But, in the days after Digna's murder, *La Jornada* revealed there hadn't been much of an investigation at all. Mexico City prosecutors in charge of the kidnapping case handed it over to federal attorney general Antonio Lozano García in October 2000. His PRI government was in the last weeks of its administration, having already lost to Fox and the PAN in July. Lozano García did nothing with the case. His successor, General Rafael Macedo de la Concha, who was appointed by Fox, officially closed the file in May 2001, while his government was still before the San José court trying to have the protection order lifted.

La Jornada's story contradicted the government's position that there had been a serious investigation of the 1999 crimes. No arrests were made and the crimes were never solved—at least as far as the public ever knew. (I would soon develop my own theory as I continued to investigate Digna's murder.)

There were many unanswered questions. Why did Mexico City officials from the leftist Democratic Revolutionary Party cooperate with the right-wing PRI government, especially one in its last months of power before Vicente Fox took over? The PRD ran against a ruling party legacy of injustice, both in the Federal District and nationally, and yet, here they were, punting Digna's file, and those of her fellow human rights colleagues, over to those same PRI power brokers they had so roundly condemned for failing to take human rights abuses seriously.

And then, when Attorney General Macedo de la Concha, from the National Action Party, closed the case, the PRD said *nothing*. It made no sense.

Moreover, the death threats continued against Digna and the others even after they were placed under court-ordered protection. In January 2000, several threats were found in a drawer *inside* PRO's offices on Serapío Rendón Street.

The threats all shared the same crude style:

"Dear all. Have you had your breather? Because that was what it was. We let you rest. The next part is the most fun. Do you want to see, you sons-of-bitches, if your foreign accomplices still want to support you? Maybe yes, maybe no. Shall we see?

"Here goes the real thing, not only your goddamn lawyers, the others too will have a go. Weren't you all supposed to be real hotshots? Let's see who can stand the real thing."[22]

"We cannot with absolute certainty link the threats to the Center's involvement with any specific case, but many of the acts of aggression seem to be in response to [PRO's] defense of Rodolfo Montiel and Teodoro Cabrera," said a statement in early 2000 by the Washington-based Center for Justice and International Law. On several occasions, it continued, "Digna Ochoa was followed and persons pretending to be journalists approached her requesting inappropriate information."[23]

The Fox government simply ignored these incidents and pressed on before the court. It got more complicated. The San José court sought the advice of the Inter-American Human Rights Commission in Washington, where the case had originated with a joint petition for protection from PRO in Mexico City and CEJIL in the U.S. capital. The commission, in turn, went back to the same petitioners. All parties involved, including Digna herself, argued that the protective measures— so-called provisional measures—should remain in place.

But the Fox government persisted and, as spring turned to summer in 2001, there were further consultations until, in the end,

Digna gave up her objections. The court was obliged to accept the word of the Mexican government that the investigation had been full and complete and that no further threat existed against the Mexican rights lawyers.

Digna had done her best, but one can imagine her throwing up her hands. She was fighting alone, and for what? She didn't think much of the quality of her police bodyguards in the first place. She made her views known in an interview with *Reforma* in April 2001, shortly after her return from exile, telling the newspaper: "The only thing the government did was to assign me some inept judicial police. They didn't know how to drive, they were out of shape, they didn't know anything about security, and they weren't punctual."

Digna's American friend Tamryn Nelson felt she reached a point where she was simply exhausted with the struggle. Tamryn never forgot what Digna told her friends at her farewell party in Washington in March 2001, just before she returned home from exile. "Make sure you guys keep your eyes out for those provisional measures, okay?" said Digna. "Make sure you guys have got me covered."[24]

The words haunt Tamryn Nelson. She feels responsible, somehow. But there's "only so much you can do," she would tell me after Digna's murder. "You're helpless, you know."[25]

Digna expressed similar opinions about the quality of her bodyguards to her boyfriend, Juan José Vera. He was horrified when she told him about the death threats she found in her mailbox in August 2001. She found them just before the San José court lifted the protection order.

J.J. was alarmed and very frightened.

"We know very well where you are. . . . Did you think that you were free of us?"[26]

"You must go to the police immediately and report this," he told Digna.

"No, you don't understand," she replied wearily. "The Federal

District Attorney General's Offices will not protect you. They don't believe you."

Half-laughing, half-crying, Digna told him a story about her former police bodyguards. One day, she came out of her apartment, crossed the street, and, as she was getting into the patrol car, asked them: "Do you know anything about that car in front of my building? There are armed men in it."

But they were oblivious, completely and utterly oblivious.

"If they wanted to kill me," she told J.J., "they could have done it right in front of them."[27]

Usually, there were two or three police bodyguards. They had no cell phones, no radios, and, half the time, no gas. Digna was particularly worried about the safety of one officer who was pregnant.[28]

After the San José court's decision, even such bunglers as these were gone.

Digna was vulnerable in a way she hadn't been since the kidnappings in 1999, and she was scared, especially since she had plans to involve herself again in Guerrero and litigate another sensitive case.

She agreed to work with her friend, Bárbara Zamora, in the defense of three brothers[29] accused of planting homemade bombs at Banamex branches on August 8, 2001. The damage wasn't severe and Mexico City attorney general Bernardo Bátiz told *La Jornada* that "they just caused smoke and a fuss. It was more of a publicity stunt." But the case was politically volatile because of ongoing protests across Mexico over the bank's sale that August to the New York–based Citibank and efforts by President Fox's opposition in Congress to have the sale investigated. As the Associated Press wrote in August: "Banamex president Roberto Hernández, a friend and campaign donor of Vicente Fox, may have gotten as much as $3 billion for selling his stake in the bank, none of which he has had to pay back to taxpayers, who spent more than $3.4 billion to bail out his bank when it was drowning in bad loans."

Digna was excited about her chances in this case. She and Bárbara worked together over August and September and planned to interview the defendants in prison on Saturday, October 20, in preparation for a court hearing the following Monday. (Pilar Noriega had been involved in the case, but left her private practice when she accepted a position with the Mexico City Human Rights Commission.) The judge had thrown out the original charges police laid against the brothers and authorities had come back with blanket "terrorism" charges. "We are going to win this case," Digna told Juan José. "The prosecution can't sustain their evidence—we're going to win quickly."[30]

Still, she was nervous. On August 21, 2001, she wrote a letter to her sister Esthela in Veracruz. There can be no doubt that she felt she was being watched, that her telephone was tapped, and that her life was in danger.

Hola, Thelita,

You know, I want to write to you about this because it is less likely they would tamper with this message. I mentioned to you I have just accepted acting as defense lawyer for [National Autonomous University of Mexico] students who have been accused of belonging to the [People's Revolutionary Army][31] and planting explosives at Banamex branches. I am going to work with my friend Pilar on this case. It is a very delicate case, and it is better to take precautions. I would not mention any of this on the telephone, and I don't want to worry you, but it is better to take precautions. If anything were to happen to me, I want to remind you that you and Juan José are in my life insurance policy at Tepeyac Insurance and you already know I have included you in my bank account.

If anything were to happen to me, I request you and Juan José take care of my things. He should take what he needs, and you can see to whom the rest should be given. The only things I do not want is that your sister-in-law Patricia would have anything of mine, nor my mother.

If Agustín needs furniture, he can take what he needs. Everything in the apartment is mine, so you can decide what to do with it.

I don't want to say I am thinking about dying (weeds never die) but, because of my doubts, I would rather talk about it. I don't want you to get worked up or worry too much—I just want to clear up any doubts.

Love you heaps,

Digna

P.S. I suggest you print out this e-mail and keep it, and after that, delete it from your machine.

* * *

Now, with Digna dead, there was an unseemly official scramble to pass the buck. Who was responsible for having her bodyguards removed? *Nobody*, it would seem.

But there was an obvious and uncomfortable reality: Digna Ochoa was dead of a bullet to the brain, and an anonymous note at the scene threatened other human rights activists. How could this have happened if, as Mexico's new democratic government attested so vigorously before the human rights court in San José, her life was not in danger?

Even Marieclaire Acosta, appointed to the Fox cabinet with much fanfare as human rights ambassador and unprecedented cabinet status, dissembled about who started the ball rolling. Digna herself, it seemed. In March 2002, I met with Acosta in her offices in the Foreign Secretariat in Mexico City to talk about Digna's case and learn why the government fought to remove protection that she obviously needed.

"She went to Washington, D.C., and therefore, at one point, I think she had already requested that police protection be taken away," she told me. "It was her own opinion that she no longer needed those measures."[32]

Besides, she insisted, "the threats had stopped."

I was struck by her comments. A few months earlier, in the immediate aftermath of Digna's murder, Marieclaire Acosta stood out among the members of the Fox cabinet for her gutsiness, compassion, and determination to solve the crime. She alone, from the Fox government, attended the memorial service in Mexico City the day after the murder. She had joined the Fox cabinet with a solid reputation as a human rights defender, and she gave a stellar performance at a press conference at her ministry. She said that nothing less than the credibility of the young Fox government was at stake in the handling of the murder investigation. If it came up empty, she said, that credibility would be destroyed.

"Human rights defenders are the barometer of a democratic society. If we cannot protect them and the rule of law, then what are we talking about? People will say, 'What is the difference between democracy and what we had before?'" Acosta had declared.

This day she was different, agitated and defensive. I was puzzled at this change, but I chalked it up to a busy day. She was flying to United Nations human rights meetings in Geneva that week, and her in-box was full to the brim. She seemed reluctant to talk about Digna and when I pressed her, she rummaged in her bag for a Marlboro, lit up, and exhaled slowly.

"Yes, I was concerned," she began. "The assassination—or the death—of a human rights activist—well, of anybody—is of concern. Of course, I was concerned."

She assured me that the Digna Ochoa investigation would be complete and transparent, adding: "It is my role to ensure that this happens."

Furthermore, she said that the serious human rights situation in Mexico was the result of years of authoritarian government, and would take time to change. But she was optimistic. "We are laying down the foundation for a human rights policy—but it is going to be a long process."

Unfortunately, she wouldn't complete her role in that process for Fox. We didn't know it then, but some eighteen months later, in the summer of 2003, Fox would have her fired, abruptly and ignominiously, humiliating her as she was welcoming Amnesty International delegates from around the world to a conference in Mexico City. It's difficult to imagine a more insensitive sacking but it does serve to illustrate the government's utter disregard for human rights. Like a dilettante, Fox dabbled in human rights, but apparently he wasn't having fun anymore.

He didn't replace her, and the position evaporated. (Acosta wasn't the first loss on human rights issues in Fox's cabinet. His first foreign secretary, Jorge Castañeda—who accompanied Fox on his 2001 European tour—resigned in January 2003, rumored to have been a victim of cabinet hard-liners. Castañeda was a respected author and scholar who taught political science in the United States and Mexico, and wrote extensively about human rights. He was the creator of Acosta's position and was highly praised by international organizations for lifting the profile of human rights issues in Mexican foreign policy. His successor, Luis Ernesto Derbez, moved quickly to erase that legacy, including eliminating Acosta and her post.)

After she was fired, Acosta told the *New York Times:* "I see this as a sign that the more progressive elements of the Fox government have been pushed aside. The failure of the human rights agenda is part of the failure of the government to live up to its promises of real reform."[33]

Her words were fateful. The heady promises of the 2000 election campaign would gradually turn to dust.[34] Fox failed to appoint the "truth commission" he had promised to uncover the crimes of the past, and efforts to investigate former presidents for their roles in past massacres were thwarted by the Mexican courts. The Supreme Court, for example, ruled that former president Luis Echevarría could not be prosecuted for the massacre of student protestors by soldiers in 1971. "The blow to the quest for truth reveals what lies at the heart of the matter," wrote Mexican scholar Denise Dresser, in a commentary for the *Los Angeles Times* in 2005.[35] "Fox may not want crimes of the past to be punished or a former president to be imprisoned for them. Fox may say that he is committed to justice, but he would actually prefer that it not take place. That is because prosecuting the past would entail taking on the former ruling Institutional Revolutionary Party, and Fox has shown that he doesn't have the political will to do so.

"In Mexico," added Dresser, "the law is being used to hang up curtains instead of opening up windows. Meanwhile, justice is becoming the plaintive demand of a group of old men whose friends were killed in Tlatelolco Plaza in 1968, or who disappeared from the streets of Mexico City in 1971."

* * *

It didn't take long, in the fall and early winter of 2001, for opinion to harden against Fox outside of Mexico. The pessimism was clear by the time the U.S. Senate and House of Representatives held hearings in mid-November on Digna's murder, as well as on the plight of other Mexican rights defenders. The country's secrets were exposed and pressure was ratcheted up on Fox.

U.S. Senator Patrick Leahy, a Democrat, expresses his sadness and anger over the "senseless, cold-blooded murder of one of Mexico's most respected and courageous human rights lawyers." (He was probably unaware of his own link to Digna or that she was studying the law named after him in the weeks before her death.) He called her a "role model for all human rights defenders," and praised her "extraordinary courage, dedication, and commitment to some of the most disadvantaged members of Mexican society. . . . Ms. Ochoa frequently put the people she represented ahead of her own safety."

The veteran senator said her death could have been avoided,

and criticized Mexican authorities for failing to properly investigate the kidnappings and death threats of 1999. He made no effort to hide his frustration with the Fox administration. "It would be hard to overestimate the optimism I felt when Vicente Fox was elected Mexico's president after seventy years of misrule by the PRI," he said. "He promised to end the long history of abuses by the Mexican Army and police. No one expected miracles. . . . But it is the government's first duty to protect its citizens, and people did expect him to make justice a priority. . . . This has not happened."

Elisa Massimo, director of the Washington office of the Lawyers Committee for Human Rights, told a House committee that rights violations in Mexico were among the most serious in the Western Hemisphere. "Police, soldiers, and other state agents have long been implicated in extra-judicial killings, massacres, forced disappearances, torture, and other mistreatment," she said, explaining that those responsible were seldom investigated, let alone convicted of crimes. She too had welcomed Fox and his promise of a new era.

"But the murder of Digna Ochoa is a grim reminder that free elections, a new government, and good intentions alone are not enough to roll back decades of entrenched, official hostility toward human rights and those who advocate for them," she concluded.

A *Washington Post* editorial was grim. Fox was supposed to end a history of rights abuses by the army and security forces.

"But now, many Mexicans are wondering if he is serious about it," said the *Post*. "Despite the prose, Mr. Fox appointed an army general to the key position of attorney-general and has so far failed to create a truth commission to look into past crimes. While offering sympathetic words to human rights groups, he has not taken action in the cases of several prominent prisoners of conscience.

"Now a case has come up that should clearly establish whether

Mr. Fox's commitment to human rights is genuine. Mr. Fox has not pressed the investigation into who was attacking Ms. Ochoa [in 1999]. In fact, his government had dropped it, and had asked the Inter-American Court of Human Rights to withdraw protection orders it had issued for the attorney. Once Ms. Ochoa was murdered, Mr. Fox did not respond publicly for three days.[36] Finally, he met with human rights groups and set up a civilian commission to keep an eye on the investigation. But appointing an official commission is old-style Mexican politics. It won't help much if, as in the cases of other high-profile Mexican political murders in recent years, the investigation stalls as it begins to touch on powerful interests. If Mr. Fox is to change Mexico's culture of official impunity, he must ensure that federal officials and the military cooperate fully with the investigation, especially if the evidence points to official involvement."

* * *

By November, promises were fading in Mexico City as well.

President Fox and Interior Secretary Creel pledged full cooperation with Mexico City authorities. But police soon found they were on their own. The spy agency CISEN did send over a file on Digna, but it was disappointing to say the least. This exclusive file, supposedly culled from the deepest vaults of the best agents in Mexico, consisted of a few yellowing press clippings. Mexico City detectives, including the lead investigator, Alvaro Arceo Corcuera, were livid. He told reporters that the material "could have come from any newspaper library."

He didn't know it but relations with federal authorities were about to get much worse. His officials would soon find themselves staring into the barrels of army guns and praying for their lives.

But, by then, he would be off the case.

CHAPTER SIX

Los Papás, Mrs. Nobody, and the Fat Man

Digna was buried on Sunday, October 21, in Misántla, her hometown in Veracruz. The cemetery was on a few hectares of land, overlooking the misty mountains of the Eastern Sierra Madre and the valley below. The cemetery walls are purple and yellow and the mausoleums are ocher, turquoise, pink, white, and cerulean blue. Stone angels stand over the largest sepulchers and there were flowers everywhere, in pots and little cans, gathered into wreaths and wrapped in plastic, tied with ribbon and string. Occasionally, a green lizard darted across a tombstone. The sky was cloudless and, in the steamy afternoon heat, insects buzzed and tropical birds sang.

Above the gates to the cemetery hangs a little painted sign, perhaps for the benefit of those who might miss the true meaning of a setting so gay and festive:

> *Discover for yourself, Mortal,*
> *Your head bowed*
> *That worldly pride*
> *Here ends*

In a few days, Digna's family would return to this place alone, bringing food, drink, and gifts for the dead, for all their loved ones buried here, as they did each year on the first of November. The Day of the Dead is a tribute to life and to lives lived in Mexico, the most haunting, mysterious, and vibrant celebration among the country's many holidays. The cemeteries of Mexico are flooded with celebrants lighting candles, singing songs, and saying their prayers under the stars.

In Misántla that day, the Ochoa family was not alone. Hundreds of mourners accompanied them in a procession from the Church of the Ascension on the town square, where there was a funeral mass, to Digna's waiting grave. As they passed, men took off their hats and women made the sign of the cross.[1]

Many had come great distances to be here. Viviana Krsticevic was director of the Center for Justice and International Law in Washington. The day before, she had rushed to Washington-Dulles to catch United's 5:20 P.M. direct flight to Mexico City (the same flight Digna had taken home seven months earlier, in March), then rode two buses to reach Misántla. "We have to be there," she told everyone. "We have to show that this is something huge, that they can't just kill Digna and think nobody will notice, or that her friends, her colleagues, and the people who admire her won't do something."

Viviana stood with human rights activists from Mexico, Central and South America, the United States and Europe. She was a lawyer from Argentina, a slim, lovely woman who struggled to hold herself together. She thought about her friend's strong faith and smiled to herself at the memory of a lunch they once had in which Digna, at the time a novice with the Dominicans of the Incarnate Word, campaigned vigorously for Viviana to become a nun.

There were many happy memories, but Viviana couldn't stop fixating on the thought that Digna was in a box. She had seen her share of death but this was different. She couldn't seem to wrap her mind around the loss. "You know somebody and you remember her and her prissy white shirt and her little coat over her arm, and when you think that person is there, she's dead inside this box and somebody killed her, well, it's really a shocking thought," Viviana would say later.[2]

It was shocking, too, for Kerry Kennedy, who received the news too late to make it to Misántla. "Digna was so full of life and vitality, she was so alive, that for her to be gone was sort of incomprehensible," she said later. "And yet, one couldn't really claim to be shocked after all the threats and the fact that she continued to go into the line of fire."[3]

Viviana was welcomed by Digna's family: her mother, Irene Plácido, with her thick Coke-bottle glasses; her father, Eusebio, with his battered straw hat; and her brothers and sisters, aunts, uncles, nieces, nephews, and cousins. They were so familiar to Viviana, even though she was meeting Digna's family for the first time. She saw her friend in them, her smile, the shape of her face, the way she moved and talked. Esthela was the spitting image of her older sister and Viviana felt that Digna was here in spirit. The thought comforted her.

Sister Brigitte, with her kind face and sweet manner, delivered the benediction. She grew to love Digna when she lived with her Dominican order for eight years in Mexico City before deciding it was not her vocation. Sister Brigitte shared a birthday with Irene Plácido: October 20. She thought of that when she heard the news that Friday and her heart ached. What a terrible gift for a mother.

They lowered Digna into the ground to the sound of firecrackers announcing the arrival of a new soul in heaven.[4] She was only a few blocks away from the house on Obregón Street where she was born, and her father before her and his father before him, and where her aged parents would live out their lives grieving for their daughter.

But today, as was their custom, they looked out for everyone else.

"Eat, eat, you have to eat," Digna's mother told Viviana. "You have had such a long journey and you have to travel back. Come back home with us and eat."

"We're so glad you have traveled from so far away to be with us," said her father. "Yes, come—eat! Eat!"

And thus, dozens of Digna's friends and colleagues trooped back to the little house where platters of food awaited them and cool glasses of water and juice. They drank strong black coffee and talked well into the night. Viviana would remember their kindness, their composure, and how the large Ochoa family gathered everyone up like children and tried to soothe their tears.

Viviana needed this night. She felt vulnerable. They all did. They were afraid. Nobody really thought that Digna would get killed. She was so strong and courageous and they thought she was protected by all the international exposure.

Nobody thought they'd get her—not really.

* * *

In the days to come, fear enveloped the Ochoa family. The phone rang on Obregón Street, but there was nobody on the line, just muffled noises and heavy breathing. They felt they were being watched, especially Digna's oldest brother, Jesús, a teacher and PRD political organizer, who had assumed leadership of the family in crisis. He often spent his days now on the long bus ride from Jalapa to Mexico City, and his evenings shuffling around the capital, from one office to the next. The family had hired a lawyer to represent them and they were intent on doing their part to ensure justice was done on behalf of their slain daughter and sister.

On October 25, less than a week after Digna's murder, there was a grim replay of events. The Inter-American Court of Human Rights in San José issued another ruling for the Mexican government, this time ordering urgent measures to protect Digna's colleagues at PRO, targets of the death threat at the crime scene, as well as lawyers Pilar Noriega, Bárbara Zamora (who was the Ochoa family lawyer), and Leonel Rivero Rodríguez. The Fox government had to investigate and report back at two-month intervals. By the end of November, the court had extended that order to include Digna's parents and several of her siblings.[5]

The Mexican newspapers *Reforma* and *El Universal* received copies of a letter threatening several human rights defenders. *Reforma* decided not to publish but, on November 1—the Day of the Dead—*El Universal* printed the letter, which began: *"This is not a threat. It is a death sentence, and we will execute it to see who will be the next asshole who wants to play here."*

It was addressed to Mexico City human rights activists Miguel Sarre, Fernando Ruíz, and Antonio Vega, as well as Sergio Aguayo Quesada, whose book on Mexico's domestic intelligence agency had just been published,[6] and Edgar Cortez, director of PRO and Digna's friend.

"These five bloody busybodies are not going to be worth anything. We are going to fuck with them and we will see if the attorney general can do anything. Let's see how tough they are. They had better cover their asses if they don't want us to bump them off. The fucking life of each of these assholes is worth 6 million pesos. We want 30 million so that we won't bump them off. Here are your human rights and your democracy. You can shove them up your ass."[7]

This could be nothing more than a clumsy extortion attempt. Nobody knew, and that was the point. The mood in Mexico was crazed, as paranoid as in the days between the twin political assassinations of Luis Donaldo Colosio and José Francisco Ruíz Massieu in 1994, and everyone was jumpy and scared.

"Sometimes we pick up the phone and we hear a woman screaming," said Bárbara Zamora, who shared a law office downtown with Leonel Rivero Rodríguez. "Sometimes it's the sound of a machine gun. Once it was the theme from *The Godfather*. In any case, the message is clear."[8]

Meanwhile, Digna's killers were still out there while the case seemed to be stalled. The police investigation moved at a glacial pace, with no breakthroughs. Police stenographers worked long hours transcribing the testimony of witnesses, who were recalled two or three times or more, as the weeks dragged on. Interviews were grueling, often turning into marathon sessions. The paper file, which would grow to more than thirty thousand pages by the end, continued to build.

Bátiz held a press conference to announce he would make no more comments on the Digna Ochoa case until he had something to report. What he did have, he said, he wouldn't reveal for fear "it might alarm those behind the murder."

A lack of official comment didn't stop the case from leaking like a sieve. *El Universal* ran a police photo of Digna's body slumped over the couch at the crime scene and unnamed police sources—appropriately called *fuentes* in Spanish, for fountains—splashed and spilled endlessly.[9] The mill churned out gossip, rumor, and innuendo, each morsel more salacious than the last.

Digna's friends grew uneasy. Rafael Álvarez Icaza, from the Mexico City Human Rights Commission, believed investigators were sloppy and worried that the press was paying for confidential information. He was disgusted every time there was a story about the investigation leading to Digna's personal life. He had no doubt this was a political assassination and police should be concentrating on her enemies. She had enough of them. Ever since Pilar told him detectives asked her the first night if she was fighting with Digna over work, or if Digna thought she was being paid enough for taking on Pilar's cases, he's had a bad feeling in his gut.[10]

Journalist José Reveles, a reporter for the business daily *El Financiero* and one of the best investigative journalists in the country, had worked on the story from the beginning. He made his name breaking stories on the drug cartels and their ties to politicians and had a couple of books under his belt. Pepe, as his friends call him, was an unimposing man, with a salt-and-pepper beard, generous nature, and some of the best contacts in Mexico.

From his sources, he heard it all: Digna was killed by her jealous lesbian lover, by her male lover over another man/woman, by assorted participants in variations on the sex/lust theme; her boyfriend murdered her over the insurance money; she was a guerrilla leader taken out in a power struggle.

Police were also investigating Juan José for another reason. "Digna was a woman who looked like a nun. Of course, she had an exceptional inner beauty, but she didn't fit the profile of the bombshell," said Pepe. "Well, they met through the Internet and what I've heard is that the death threats were made with some sort of codes—by people with special computer knowledge—and that you would need to type certain letters to get them. Certain short-cuts that only some people knew about. So what this line of investigation leads to is that J.J. didn't just find Digna through a chat room but that he was planted there."

About the only scenario not considered (as far as anybody knew) was some kind of hit by the Dominican nuns, although prosecutors did have a strange question for Sister Brigitte when they brought her in to testify.

"Are you armed?" they asked, referring to the eleven nuns in the order, who lived in a pretty little house in the southern part of the city.

"*Armed?*" she replied. "No, of course not."

She did permit herself a secret smile.

With faith, she thought.[11]

* * *

Juan José Vera, Digna's boyfriend, knew he was a suspect and worried that the publicity would affect his teaching career. Police[12] keep asking him about the eight thousand pesos ($800) Digna left him in her life insurance policy. "For eight thousand pesos they think I took a human life, never mind that I loved her and she was my girlfriend," he told me in the spring after the murder, over lunch at an Italian restaurant on Miguel Angel de Quévedo Avenue. "They simply never considered that possibility."

Even his mother, Raquel Mendoza, was grilled by prosecutors. Digna had been a frequent weekend guest at the home J.J. shared with his mother, particularly over the summer months. "She came here in such a way, how can I put it? Well, she crept into my heart. She treated me better than any of my daughters-in-law," said Raquel, sitting on a pale brocade sofa in her perfectly appointed living room in May 2002. She looked like the school teacher she was, in a sparkling white blouse, plaid sweater, and discreet black pearl earrings. She had a weekly appointment to have her hair done and it was swept off her face in soft waves. She looked far younger than her seventy-five years. Digna never arrived empty-handed at her home. One weekend, she brought a bag filled with fresh jumbo shrimp, Raquel's favorite.

"Digna was always good-humored, always laughing. I remember the time my grandson—who was about three, he's four now—was standing here and singing to Digna, I don't know what, and Digna fell into a fit of giggles. And she said to J.J., 'How I adore Juan Carlos!' and we all shouted out, 'Digna, we'll lend him to you!'"

One November morning, officers surprised Raquel at her school and drove her to the Public Ministry at 100 Chimalpopoca Street, where they questioned her for six hours. When she told me about it months later, she was still flushed with anger at the memory. She recited large chunks of conversation verbatim and I wondered if her students could match her memory.

"They picked me up from work to take me to testify and I said to them, 'Didn't you stop to think of the damage you caused me? I need this job. You know how difficult it is to find a job, especially at my age, and you arrive at my work and take me away in a patrol car—and from a private school where the parents are so sensitive!' When we got to the station, I told them I wanted my lawyer and they shouted at me, 'No, no—no one else can come in.'"

"Why are you being so aggressive with me?" she asked the senior officer.

"You're making it hard," he replied. "You could make it easy on yourself."

"Well," she retorted, "maybe it's easy for you, but I am an elderly woman who has never been in a place like this and I'm frightened."

They took her to a large interrogation room and sat her down at a table with several police officers. She was the only woman, an old one at that, and felt overwhelmed and helpless. She must have looked faint because one of the officers asked if she was okay.

"Look here, mister, you are not being very nice to me. Tell me something—am I a suspect or a witness?"

"No, of course you're not a suspect. You're a witness," a young officer told her.

"But I don't know why I have been called to testify."

"We want to know if you know who killed Digna Ochoa," he said.

That was the last straw for Raquel. She was tired, she was hungry, her ankles were swollen, and her feet hurt. Besides, her interrogators had dirty fingernails. And they didn't speak proper Spanish: They made grammatical errors and used too much slang. *Señora* Mendoza was not impressed.

She threw back her gray head and practically shouted at them: "How am I supposed to know? Please tell me. If I knew, I would have come running here to tell you. And, furthermore, *you* know who killed Digna."

"No, we don't know," said one.

"Well, then, how come you don't? Weren't there other threats against human rights defenders? It was on television, you know, everybody knows. They said there were written threats against Digna. . . . You must know who sent these threats and they must be the same people who killed Digna because they *said* they were going to do it."

Raquel could not stop herself, she was so angry. But she was simply saying what most Mexicans were thinking.

"Look, I don't know anything about your work but, in spite of my old age, it seems perfectly logical to me that the people who killed Digna must be the same people who sent her those messages."[13]

Nobody answered and they never called her back to testify.

One day, not long after Digna's murder, a neighbor came by to tell her that two police officers had, that very day, removed the garbage from the neighbor's front lawn. It was out for collection that day, and police moved stealthily, creeping about and peeking over their shoulders to see if anybody was watching. They hurried up the street with the garbage bags. At the corner, they shoved them into the trunk of a patrol car, slammed down the lid, and roared off.

The two women collapsed with laughter. Obviously, police thought they were taking Raquel's garbage for clues. They went to all that stinky trouble for the wrong house.

* * *

Police pieced together the last hours of Digna's life. The coroner's office had estimated her time of death at between noon and 2 P.M. on Friday, October 19, and the schedule they found in her hand-bag at the Zacatecas Street offices contained two interesting final appointments. For Thursday evening, October 18, she'd written *"w/Papás"* (Parents) and police were able to reconstruct the evening.

At 6:30 P.M., Digna was to meet with six parents whose sons were students at the National Autonomous University of Mexico. The parents were themselves charged with disturbing the peace during the 1999 strike at the university, and faced prison sentences if convicted. It was a highly political strike, considered to be over the constitutional right to a free education in Mexico,[14] and Pilar Noriega had been involved in their defense. She handed the case over to

Digna when she took a position as a senior inspector with the Mexico City Human Rights Commission.

We know Digna was at her computer earlier that day because at 5:23 P.M. she fired off the e-mail advising Raquel about her will. She seemed to be in good spirits, judging by the merry tone and her *Shrek* joke at the end. She slipped out, possibly to get a bite to eat before the meeting. It looked like rain and it's likely she took her overcoat and umbrella.

Around 6 P.M., three women, Silvia Mariñelarena, Adriana Vidal, and Silvia Sánchez, arrived, rang the bell, and, when Digna didn't answer, waited at the front gate. It began to rain and, finding the outer door open, they sought shelter inside. There was a walk-through garage, which opened onto an inner courtyard. A curving staircase on the left led up to Digna's offices on the first floor.

Three men in suits were standing at the base of the stairs. One was talking into a cell phone, or a radio phone, and they heard him say: "We're here already, but there's nobody around."

He was about thirty, of medium height, with an athletic build and light skin. He looked like he'd just had a haircut; all three had short, military-style haircuts. He asked the women if there were any lawyers around. "He was very arrogant," Silvia Sánchez would later tell the police.[15] She asked him if he was looking for anyone in particular, and he replied brusquely, "Javier," without giving a surname.

The men stood around for about five minutes and then left. The women found it strange.

Around 6:30, Digna returned and they went up to her offices. A few moments later, other parents arrived and the meeting started. Digna told them her fee was 2,000 pesos (about $200) to cover the research, interviews, and court hearings. The first hearing was scheduled for the following Thursday, October 25, in 9th District Court in the capital, and she promised she would be there.

Digna was in high spirits[16] and joked around during the meeting. The group told her they had an appointment the next day at 5 P.M. with authorities at the university, and asked if she would go with them. She couldn't, telling them that Friday, Saturday, and Sunday were all extremely busy days for her. On Saturday, she had to go to Almoloya de Juárez maximum security prison with Bárbara Zamora, at least an hour's drive out of the city. She added that she had to leave Mexico City for a few days the next Tuesday, and they agreed to meet again on the following Thursday, the day of the hearing.

The meeting lasted until about 9:30 and Digna was left alone. She called J.J. and told him she was going home, joking that she had to catch him early, otherwise he would be too sleepy to comprehend a single word she said. She told him she loved him and would see him on the weekend.

* * *

There was another notation on page 147 of Digna's date book, *"09:30 w / Sra. Marisol Rodríguez."* Police set out to find Mrs. Marisol Rodríguez, but she turns out to be the mystery woman of the case. If no one knew her, and it was soon apparent that no one did, finding her was going to be a problem because the police had no second last name. (In Mexico, people go by two proper names, the first for the father and the second for the mother. If somebody is called Juan García Mendoza, for example, you know that his father is a García and his mother, a Mendoza.) They combed through official records from government agencies, police files, and such mundane tools as the phone book. On page 4,065 of the Mexico City phone book, for instance, they found Marisol Rodríguez Aguilar, but, alas, she didn't know anything about Digna Ochoa.

They located and questioned Marisol Rodríguez Sánchez, Marisol Rodríguez Porcayo, Marisol Rodríguez Rodríguez, Marisol Rodríguez Gutiérrez, Marisol Rodríguez González, Marisol

Rodríguez Galan, Marisol Rodríguez Caramazana, and Marisol Rodríguez Ambas, all without success.

Police interviewers filled pages of transcripts with the details of these women's lives: the names of their parents; their occupations; whether they knew Digna or her colleagues; what they thought of the human rights movement in Mexico; and what they were doing on Friday, October 19, 2001.

For the most part, as they informed the police in lengthy testimony, they were cleaning their homes, taking their kids to school and picking them up, buying tortillas, stopping at the butcher shop, eating dinner, washing up, doing homework with their kids, and retiring for the night. One woman reported that she took her daughter to the movies on Fridays. None admitted to knowing Digna, although several knew who she was.

The police concluded it was highly unlikely that this woman, this *Señora Marisol Rodríguez Nobody*, as she was dubbed, even existed. But Digna certainly appeared to believe she did. She wrote her name down in her agenda to mark an appointment at 9:30 A.M. on the day of her death.

Who was this person? And what did she—or he—have to do with Digna's murder?

* * *

The police were tracking another tantalizing lead. There was a witness to a noteworthy event at the law office at the time of Digna's death, a possible unsuspecting witness to a murderer.

Lawyer Lamberto González Ruíz hired a cleaning woman and had given her keys to the Zacatecas offices. Her name was Modesta Aguilera Mejía and she lived with her husband and baby daughter in the same apartment complex, one floor up on level B. On Friday, October 19, her husband went out around noon, leaving the door open. When she went to close it about five minutes later, she looked down and saw a man lurking outside Digna's offices and then, a few minutes later, saw him go inside. She described him as "a man of corpulence," as the police would put it, a fat man, with a dark complexion.[17] She told the police she'd never seen him before and she thought it odd that he hadn't knocked.

She had a bath and as she was drying herself off, about twenty minutes later, she heard two loud noises a few minutes apart. The walls shook slightly and she thought somebody was hammering, Pilar perhaps, hanging something on a wall below. She changed her baby's diaper and, beginning to think something untoward was happening downstairs, kept an eye out the window. A few moments later, she saw the same man going down the stairs.

She told prosecutors what she had witnessed. These events coincided with the time of Digna's murder and they would question her three more times in the weeks and months ahead. They would study the line of sight from her apartment to Digna's offices, measure the stairwell, conduct sound tests with the murder weapon, and question other neighbors about what they saw and heard over the noon hour at 31-A Zacatecas Street on the day Digna Ochoa died, as they connected the fat man to her murder.

CHAPTER SEVEN

The Train from New York City

I didn't learn about Digna until two days after her murder and, when I did, it felt like I couldn't breathe. It was early evening on Sunday, October 21, and I was on the Metroliner returning to Washington from New York City. I'd been posted back to Washington from Mexico City after the terrorist attacks of 9/11, working out of the same National Press Building where Digna was such a hit with Kerry Kennedy the year before. It had been intense working in the U.S. capital in the aftermath of the attacks and, on this particular weekend, I'd gone to New York City to meet with my managing editor, Mary Deanne Shears. It was a chance to talk about our coverage, but also to decompress, to have some dinner and see a play on Broadway, although Strindberg's *Dance of Death* may not have been the most upbeat choice.

This was my first opportunity to get up to New York from Washington, and I wanted to pay my respects at the site of the World Trade Center, to see close up what I'd been writing about for so many weeks. On this cold Sunday, slightly hungover, I stood across the street staring at the grotesque and naked girders silhouetted against the sky, as crews worked to remove debris. It was a sacred site, a holy place, and small knots of people on every corner were standing around, watching silently and shivering in the wind. We said our prayers and grieved for the dead and their families.

Now, on the train, I was reading the Sunday papers and there it was in the *Los Angeles Times*, a headline saying Digna had been assassinated. She'd been dead since Friday. I couldn't believe it. I'd known Digna for years. I met her right after moving to Mexico from Washington in February 1995. She knew how to get through to foreign journalists about rights issues she was investigating and her research and contacts were always solid. I liked her, I trusted her. She was a good lawyer and a savvy communicator, reason enough to be dangerous to the authorities. She was able to get coverage from the international press on stories that, without her, might not have made it into big foreign dailies.

The last time I saw her, she was wearing a pristine white blouse. I keep thinking about how she might have been wearing that same white blouse on the day she was murdered, how the blood would have soaked the front and ruined it. Silly, what you think about at such times. I was not the only one who remembered Digna's blouses. It's what Viviana Krsticevic talked about, Digna's prissy white blouses.

So many thoughts were racing through my mind. I thought about the last time I met with Digna in the offices of the Miguel Agustín Pro Juárez Human Rights Center in Mexico City. It was in January 2000, and she was telling me about the night she was kidnapped in 1999 and held in her apartment by armed men who left her tied to her bed beside an open gas tank. That's not even why I was there to see her. We were talking about a case she was working on in Guerrero and she referred to her own experience almost as an afterthought. She said she was terrified and the worst part was imagining what they were going to do to her. That is what I thought about now, as the train rushed through the darkness, taking me to Union Station. I looked out the window and I couldn't stop thinking about the last moments of her life, and imagining how utterly, utterly horrifying they must have been.

And I was angry. Digna was a small person. She couldn't have weighed much more than 110 pounds, and she had small hands and tiny wrists. Sure, she boasted to Kerry Kennedy about how she had intimidated judicial police officers with pseudo-karate moves. "They didn't expect me to assume the attack position—the only karate position I knew, from movies I suppose. Of course, I didn't *really* know karate, but they definitely thought I was going to attack," Digna had said.[1]

That image of Digna as kung fu master was amusing, but she would have been defenseless against her attackers. What courage it must have taken for them to overpower her and put a bullet in her brain. What strength. Did they laugh at her? Did they call her a bitch and say she was getting what she deserved? Probably. How pleased they must have been with themselves. This was what I was thinking about on the train, and about how Digna knew they might get her. The odds were against her; they always had been. She never really had a chance.

I was thinking too about how much I owed Digna. She had a big impact on my life. I learned to see Mexico through her eyes and care about the people she did. They were usually forgotten people. It was through her that I came to understand on a visceral level what it meant to abuse human rights in Mexico and what her work was about.

I had been to the southern state of Chiapas as early as 1993, before the beginning of the Zapatista war, and written about the conditions of Indian people in Lacandon jungle communities. Later, I would interview little kids in Chiapas who survived the massacre of forty-five people—seven men, twenty women, eighteen children—by a death squad in the Lacandon village of Acteal. Babies died, among them an infant of two months. It occurred as the villagers were going to Mass at a makeshift church on Sunday morning, December 22, 1997. Four of the murdered women were pregnant. This particular death squad was called *Máscara Roja* (Red Mask) and they opened fire with AK-47 assault weapons and then moved in, swinging their machetes at anything still moving. Mothers wrapped themselves around their children, offering up their own beating hearts to save their babies.

One little girl was found under her mother's bullet-ridden corpse. They called her the "miracle child." Her mother, father, brother and two sisters were all dead, and she was left blind and brain-damaged—but alive.

A small boy's arm was so badly mangled he would never be able to use it again. I didn't think doctors could save it. When I saw him, it was held together at the elbow by crude steel pegs and his fingers were gone, leaving a stump of a hand. His arm was grotesquely swollen and covered with deep gashes and his eyes were big and scared. They were full of pain. I see them still. This was what they did to a kid.[2]

The death squad was linked to local officials from the ruling PRI, intent on stamping out pockets of sympathy for the Zapatistas. Acteal lay in the municipality of Chenalhó, where some communities offered a support base for the rebels. In the days before the attack, federal and state officials ignored urgent warnings of impending violence from human rights groups based in Chiapas. Moreover, a high-ranking police officer told *Proceso* magazine that the death squad was accompanied by forty state police officers who "for three and a half hours were stationed at the entrance to the village while, scarcely 200 meters away, down the hillside, a massacre was committed."[3]

While President Zedillo sacked his interior secretary, only a few minor officials ever went to jail. In a report on Acteal a year after the massacre, a special federal investigator said that police armed the death squad and cited its links to local authorities. But the report failed to address the most important and obvious question of, as Amnesty International expressed it, "how high up official responsibility lies for these links."[4] And the Zedillo government failed to keep its pledge, made in the days after the massacre, to investigate the full scope of death squad activity in Chiapas.

How such atrocities could continue with seventy thousand federal troops blanketing the state, as they had been since the beginning of the Zapatista rebellion,[5] went unexplained. The perpetrators of these crimes (and Acteal was only the most shocking of many killings in Chiapas) were unpunished and the Dirty War raged on, with civilians dying by the truckload. The region was so soaked in the blood of innocents that Israeli prime minister Shimon Peres, visiting Mexico City from his own war-torn region not long after Acteal, pleaded for peace talks to resume in Chiapas. The European Parliament held hearings on the Acteal massacre, with a full airing of the failure of Mexico's leaders to take action. However, President Zedillo had his defenders, among them Canadian Prime Minister Jean Chrétien, who was asked about the Chiapas massacre. In that spring of 1998 he was in Santiago, Chile, attending another Summit of the Americas, with its focus on expanding the free trade zone and increasing commerce. He said the Mexican president was doing his best to stop the violence. "They made a lot of progress," said Chrétien. "You cannot claim that it's perfection, but perfection is difficult to attain."[6]

After Chiapas, Digna headed a group that filed legal complaints against sixteen paramilitary groups operating throughout Chiapas. But the government ignored these complaints, just as it had systematically ignored all others.

I wrote about seemingly unending massacres in the poorest and remotest regions—Acteal, Aguas Blancas, El Charco[7]—and I came to see the darkest and most savage side of Mexico. I also witnessed the awesome courage of Mexicans who, largely unheralded and at the risk of their own lives, fought to make a real and lasting change.

But it was in the Gulf of Mexico state of Veracruz, where Digna urged me to investigate a documented case of torture and murder by state police, that I had to look into the eyes of a mother whose seventeen-year-old son, Rolando Hernández, had been pulled from the river, lifeless, bloated, and bearing horrific marks of torture. Her name was María Rosa, she was only in her early thirties herself, and she had gone to the riverbank and looked upon the body of her firstborn child.

"I can say, truly, that I am sick with sadness," she told me.

They found her son on the morning of September 12, 1994, washed up on the banks of the Chiflón River in the Huasteca highlands of Veracruz. He had been missing for five days. I wrote about it for the *Toronto Star*: "He was naked, lying on his back, his arms thrust above his head. His feet had been tied and he had bullet holes in his head and heart. His genitals had been cut off and his tongue cut out. His eyes were gouged out, his intestines removed and one of his back teeth had been knocked out. His body was covered with welts and bruises."[8]

The back tooth was the clue. It was likely Rolando did not die quickly, and that the torture sessions had continued for hours, possibly days. Nobody knows for sure because there was no autopsy. A human being was found in this condition and *there was no serious investigation?* Moreover, Rolando was last seen alive, according to eye witnesses, in the custody of state police, who were taking him away.

On that trip to Veracruz, I saw for myself the pain and suffering of people treated as if they were less than human. María Rosa's love for her child was the same as any mother's love anywhere in our world and that was as plain as day to me.

It troubled me that there wasn't a huge outcry after her story was published, as it did when other stories passed under the radar, although I didn't quite know what I expected. It was disturbing on another occasion to research and write about the forced sterilization of seventeen Mixtec men, from three villages in Guerrero, by a state medical team called No. 3 Brigade. *Forced sterilization.* This was genocide, according to the definition of the United Nations Charter on Genocide. I'd kept a file with anecdotal evidence of forced sterilizations in southern Mexican states with a high indigenous population, without writing anything. (Imagine, there were enough press reports to open a separate file on the subject of sterilizing people against their will.) I chose to follow up on this particular case in 1999 because the verdict of forced sterilization, ethnic cleansing if you will, had been verified by the state's own human rights commission. Moreover, the money for No. 3 Brigade came from the World Bank, in a roundabout way, but World Bank money just the same.[9]

But my article came and went, without the public outcry I expected, and I felt somehow that I had failed. If I could have just made their humanity leap right off the page, perhaps people would have paid more attention to them. But I have come to believe that sometimes it is just too difficult to comprehend that these events happen in our modern world. It's beyond belief that people can be disemboweled and have their genitals cut off; that it is done by other human beings in positions of authority who ought to be protecting them; that people are sterilized against their will; that torture goes on all over Mexico; and that it is, just as all the human rights reports keep telling us, routine.

María Rosa's suffering was human enough for me. I met her and her family because of Digna. In the spring of 1995, she was trying to interest journalists in going to the region to report on the gruesome murders of young Rolando, from the hamlet of Cantollano in the Huasteca region, and another man, Atanasio Hernández (unrelated), twenty-seven, from the hamlet of El Mirador.

At the time, Digna was working on another case she thought we should cover. The year before, on January 7, 1994, in the first days of the Zapatista uprising, soldiers attacked the indigenous community of Ejido Morelia in Chiapas, destroying houses, looting, and dragging three men to the church sacristy where they were allegedly tortured, before being driven away in military vehicles to be summarily executed.[10] Their remains were found a few days later. She was helping to take the case, on behalf of the families, to the Inter-American Human Rights Commission in Washington.

I chose to go to Veracruz, where the nearest town to the hamlets of the murdered men was Ixhuatlán de Madero, located in one of the most inhospitable regions of the eastern coastal state. Digna was from Veracruz and understood very well what went on in her home state. Her father, a union leader, was tortured and imprisoned for a crime he didn't commit and, at twenty-three, she was kidnapped and raped by state police. But I didn't know about any of that when Petter Bolme and I began working on the Huasteca case.

Newspaper foreign bureaus are often lucky in hiring immensely talented staffers because of the quality of people who, but for personal circumstances, would never be available. Petter was no exception. He was a Swedish journalist and filmmaker whose marriage brought him to Mexico City and, eventually, a job as my editorial assistant. He was a smart, kind, and sensitive man. Once, after the massacre of Acteal, he could hardly bear it when I kept photographing the little blind girl, her head wrapped in bandages, after she began to cry. He asked me why I didn't stop immediately, and maybe I should have. "Because this is the photograph that will run," I told him, and I was right.

We journeyed together to Veracruz to investigate Digna's information about torture in the Huasteca. Getting there was difficult. The first time we tried, the April rains and swollen rivers cut off the mountain villages and drove us back to the capital, and we had to put it off until June. We drove to Poza Rica, a dingy industrial town on a brown river that flows into the Gulf of Mexico, and rented a jeep for a journey over a series of increasingly bad roads until, on the last portion heading up into the mountains above Ixhuatlán de Madero, we were on horseback. It was hot, well over 100 degrees Fahrenheit, and with each mile the land grew increasingly barren until our guides brought us to the remote village of Cantollano. There was no shade, no clean water, and I got sunstroke and was sick most of the way. Petter's fair skin was burned bright red. We rode scrawny horses with bad feet whose ribs stuck out. They were covered in sores and flies and they looked like they were about to fall down dead.

"Pretty bad," I told my mother later, when, listening to my account of the trip, she asked about the horses. My mother loves horses and it made her sick to picture these starving creatures. But how could one talk about the condition of their animals to villagers whose babies die of cholera and dengue fever and whose children are weak, with bellies swollen and hair turning orange from malnutrition in the Mexican Third World?

They were Otomi Indians and they lived in huts with dirt floors, in villages scattered throughout the high Huasteca. When they could, they descended to work in the lowland plantations of the big hacienda owners, returning to scratch out a living up in the clouds, where the corn grew stunted and brown. They used Stone Age tools of sticks, machetes, and crude hoes, and walked barefoot over rocky mountain trails. Once they used to live in the lowlands but they had been pushed farther and farther up onto the rocks by the hired guns of the plantation owners.

Their clothes were tattered, their faces gaunt, and their feet cracked and calloused. They had little and yet, when we arrived at sundown, they shared their rice and beans with us, welcomed us as esteemed visitors, and stacked garland after garland of fragrant flowers upon our heads. They gave speeches and sang songs to us in the cooling night air, and waited until morning, when we were rested, to recount how these two young men had been tortured and murdered nine months earlier.

Before I tell their stories, as they were told to us, I should put them in context. Rolando and Atanasio died in a land war of the sort that rages all over Mexico. Land is at the heart of the Zapatista Indian rebellion in Chiapas and behind long-simmering violence in states like Oaxaca, Guerrero, Tabasco, and Veracruz. These wars have not been settled. An uneasy peace is interrupted by sporadic fighting, various occupations, and marches to the capital by peasants in straw hats, carrying placards and sticks. One group from Chiapas calls itself *Las Hormigas* (The Ants) and the name describes very well how they creep along in their multitudes, bringing their grievances to the politicians in Mexico City.

Most of these disputes are over land claimed by indigenous people—but not all. In the Guerrero highlands, for example, where campesinos have run up against powerful local and international logging interests, and where Digna Ochoa got involved in the most famous case of her career, the Montiel/Cabrera torture case, the people involved are *mestizo*, or mixed race, like 80 percent of the Mexican population.

But they are all poor; that is the common denominator.

Land wars are an open wound on the body politic of Mexico and account for a majority of documented cases of massacres, torture, rapes, and extrajudicial killings reported by human rights organizations. These struggles have been going on for a long time but they intensified after Carlos Salinas amended the Constitution to allow communal land to be privatized and developed, whether through logging, factory farming, or other business enterprises. The amendment met the terms of the impending free trade deal and put one more weapon in the arsenal of big landowners and corporations with deep pockets. They use it to control larger and larger tracts of land, crushing peasants who stand in the way.

This is one of the biggest stories of the North American Free Trade Agreement (NAFTA) but it has gone largely untold because its victims have no power and, hence, no voice. Digna understood that and was sophisticated in her approach to changing it. Her promise during the last weeks of her life that she would give faces to the faceless peasants of Guerrero—by telling their stories in the United States and Europe—was not insignificant. She would humanize them. It was a powerful statement and her enemies understood its implications. By the fall of 2001, they'd had enough of her.

* * *

The specific conflict in these Huasteca highlands concerned one thousand hectares the villagers said was stolen from their grand-fathers by powerful men and their squads of *pistoleros* (gunmen) in the early part of the twentieth century. They had deeds and other legal documents to prove ownership, but it had made no difference.

And so, in August 1994, people representing forty-two families from the jungle villages of Plan del Encinal, Cantollano, and El Mirador simply moved in and began farming sections of the dis-puted land, which was owned by a wealthy *cacique* (from the Caribbean Indian word for "chieftain"). In rural Mexico, *caciques* are local political bosses who sit at the top of the social and eco-nomic pyramid. They are supported by the army and state police, often becoming friends with local military commanders who find it lucrative to cooperate with local power brokers. The biggest among them have their own militias, the savage death squads known as *guardias blancas* (white guards), who sweep into villages on horseback or in trucks, terrorizing people, stealing livestock, and leaving huts in flames.

The poorest regions of Mexico operate like feudal states. Peas-ants are modern-day serfs. The brutality of this medieval power structure is well-known within Mexico. "We consider the phe-nomenon of *caciquism* to be a violation of human rights," Jorge Madrazo, appointed director of Mexico's National Human Rights Commission by President Zedillo, told me when I was investigat-ing the Veracruz murders and the power of the political bosses. "These *caciques* are not public authorities; they just act as if they are." Madrazo identified the problem, but with no legal clout, his commission was powerless to do anything about it.

I'd seen it elsewhere in Mexico. During the first days of the

Zapatista rebellion in Chiapas, the army evicted thousands of Indians from their mountain communities, ostensibly to keep them safe but ultimately resulting, for many of them, in the loss of their land. They joined the ranks of the *expulsados*, drifting to cities and adding their numbers to outlying slums, aptly known as *cinturónes de miseria*, for the belts of misery they are.[11] I remember a conversation one day around that time with a group of wealthy young Mexicans whose fathers owned huge estates near the Chiapas town of Ocosingo. They'd pulled their four-wheel drive to the side of the road to check a tire, and I stopped to talk to them about the uprising, the growing number of refugees, and the land claims of the Indians.

"It's our land," said one. "We conquered them five hundred years ago, and they can go fuck themselves."

* * *

"We want you to know how we live," Jesús Rosas, from Plan del Encinal, told Petter and me in Cantollano. He and other leaders from surrounding villages journeyed to meet us, walking for days just for the opportunity to present their plea for justice to foreign reporters. "We don't accept that we are invading the land because it was stolen from our grandfathers," he began. "We are Mexicans, we are of this country. *They* are strangers in *our* land. You see the land of the *caciques*? You see that it's green and there is water. Our land is bad land. It is pure rock. It is worthless. We must organize ourselves. We must have land or we are going to die."

He told us that, for generations, people filed papers in the courts, despite long treks through mountains without roads and a language they didn't understand. Most villagers don't speak Spanish, let alone comprehend the complexities of the Mexican legal system. They couldn't afford lawyers. "We want justice," he said. "It is for the land that Rolando and Atanasio lost their lives."[12]

The occupation began in August at a hacienda called Las Tejas, near Plan del Encinal. It simmered for a few weeks until, late on

Wednesday, September 7, 1994, about eighty *pistoleros,* backed by state police under the command of Captain José Antonio Domínguez Martínez, encircled the hacienda. They waited until dawn and began shooting from all sides, while police dropped canisters of gas on the people from helicopters.

Two police officers and a six-year-old child were killed, while Rolando and Atanasio were among the wounded. Terrified survivors scattered to hide in the hills. One woman left her child, only days old and as yet unnamed, and the baby perished. Eyewitnesses said that when it was over, police took Rolando and Atanasio away. They were never seen alive again.[13]

For three weeks there was no word. María Rosa, her husband, Policarpo, and their four other children waited until, early on September 12, they were summoned to the banks of the river, where two bodies had washed up overnight. They had no trouble recognizing Rolando even though his body was badly decomposed.

"You see, he was my son," said Policarpo.[14]

I interviewed María Rosa in the little cemetery where a blue cross marked Rolando's grave. "We just want to know what kind of people would do such a thing to our children," she said.[15] She looked at me as if I had answers.

Atanasio had also been tortured. His body was full of bullet holes, his hands were tied behind his back, his tongue cut off, he had been disemboweled, and there was a gaping hole where his genitals had been. His eyes were gouged out. His father, Aurelio, and mother, Cecilia, walked three hours from El Mirador to claim his body and buried him that day, at midnight.

I met with his parents and asked them to tell me about him. They said he was a hard worker and loved playing soccer. He was quiet and kept mostly to himself. That changed, however, in the last months of his life, when he found someone he could talk to in Teresa, a young woman of twenty, who agreed to become his wife. She moved in with him and they planned to marry in the month he was murdered. "He was a serious person and he didn't talk to anyone," she said. "But with me, he talked. He used to call me *'Tere, mi amor.'*"

The rub is that Atanasio was the last person to be involved in a political struggle. He joined the occupation at Las Tejas because there was no other work and he could make a few pesos tilling the hacienda land. He rose at 3 A.M. the day of his death to pack a few belongings and left.

That day, his mother walked to Chomulco to buy corn.

"Why did your son get involved?" the corn-seller asked her. "Don't you know there are *pistoleros* and helicopters waiting at Las Tejas? He shouldn't have gone."[16]

When she saw her son again, he was three weeks dead.

Villagers from Plan del Encinal sent a courier to Mexico City to Miguel Cruz, a young Nahuatl organizer from a group called the Human Rights Committee of the Huasteca and the Eastern Sierra. They asked for his help in finding the missing men. He came as soon as he could, slipping through police and army road-blocks around the occupied land and arriving on the same day the bodies were discovered in the river.

He photographed the corpses. Digna had given us a copy of his photo of Rolando's remains. It was like a blow to the gut. His body lay half in the water, with a faded red plaid shirt thrown over his face and the ropes that bound him clearly visible around his ankles, which were swollen and mottled from the water. Three people, his father, mother, and grandmother, stood in a row at his feet. They were stiff, their hands at their sides, and their faces vacant and without emotion.

I know this look. I have seen it on the faces of survivors many times. It is not disregard or lack of feeling for the dead. It is merely that they are not surprised this has happened. They are beyond surprise.

The *Toronto Star* ran this photograph with my story, but not before a discussion among editors in the newsroom. Ultimately, it was up to weekend editor Joe Hall.[17] "It was not a difficult decision to publish this photograph," he would tell me later. "As a family newspaper, the *Toronto Star* has a policy against gratuitously showing dead bodies. There has to be an overriding and compelling public interest.

"In this case, I felt that, with all the denials and obfuscation by Mexican officials over the deaths of these—and other—murdered citizens, the documentary evidence [i.e., the photo] was an important element that added weight to [our] story. I considered the story and photograph of sufficient significance to run them on the front of the World news section."

The families of the victims of the Huasteca fought for justice for their murdered sons. Miguel Cruz brought them to the state attorney general, where they tried to give statements "denouncing" the crime—the *denuncia* of Mexican legal custom. But he was not allowed to translate for them, which rendered them voiceless. He also brought witnesses who wanted to testify that police had opened fire on unarmed women and children, and that the two officers died in their own crossfire. But police refused to take their statements. No police report was ever filed, not even to record the deaths of the two officers. There was no serious investigation and the families of the victims were later threatened by *pistoleros* for having spoken out.[18]

The Veracruz Human Rights Commission urged state officials to investigate these political murders. Digna and her colleagues at PRO appealed to President Zedillo, National Human Rights Commissioner Madrazo, Veracruz governor Patricio Chirinos, and state attorney general Rodolfo Duarte. They pleaded with authorities to end the practice of impunity and investigate the police, bringing the full weight of the law against those responsible. They pleaded in vain.

A report by PRO detailed how "torture is commonly used to investigate alleged crimes and to intimidate individuals or communities. Victims sometimes die as a result of extreme torture.

Those responsible for torture are not promptly or effectively investigated, prosecuted or sanctioned." It is also commonplace for judges to accept evidence elicited through torture.

Digna prepared evidence for the Inter-American Human Rights Commission in Washington, which reviewed the case and ruled that the police were undeniably involved, and recommended that the Mexican government compensate the families of the victims.[19] The commission also called for a full investigation into the murders and stronger constitutional protection against torture.

Nothing was done. The Mexican government failed to act on the recommendations of the commission and ignored all submissions from rights groups in Mexico. The families were never compensated, state officials ignored appeals from human rights groups to meet with them, and the crime remains unsolved.

It seems there were far more potent interests to protect than the rights of murdered peasants and their families, some of which appeared to go beyond the usual clout associated with money and power. In whispers and with furtive glances, even in the remotest sites, villagers told me about drug-trafficking in the region and the clandestine activities they witnessed on a regular basis. Like Guerrero, like so many other Mexican states, the narco trade infests Veracruz.

"Land is big business," I wrote in my 1995 story about the murders in Veracruz. "So is narco-trafficking. Deep in the jungle, there are cocaine-producing labs and small planes take off and land at all hours. The Indians know where they are, but nobody ever gets prosecuted. And nobody dares touch the political bosses who deliver votes to the ruling Institutional Revolutionary Party."

As I was trying to get to Cantollano in the spring of 1995, Veracruz state police brutally ended another occupation in the Huasteca. Human rights activist Teresa Jardi was appalled by the violence and, in a piece for the Mexico City daily *La Jornada*, accused the Zedillo government of "creating another Chiapas" in the mountains of Veracruz.

"Indians have lost land to narco-traffickers, to ranchers, and to public officials for a very long time," she told me. "There are no rights here; there is no justice; the *caciques* can do whatever they want."

In the end, she was right. There was no justice in the Huasteca.

But there was a ghoulish footnote to the bodies in the river.

Miguel Cruz and his organization pushed for autopsies and petitioned authorities to have the bodies exhumed, but they were refused. In December, however, agents came to El Mirador and did exhume Atanasio's body. They said they were from the Veracruz Attorney General's Office, and they had the army to back them up. His family protested but soldiers pushed them back. Before his horrified parents, they dug him up, sawed off the top of his head, cut through his rib cage, and removed ribs and various organs.

"We didn't like it, but we were afraid to say anything," his mother told me. "We thought they were doctors."

When I investigated further, lawyer Bernardo García from the Veracruz Attorney General's Office told me there was no record of any exhumation. The state was not involved.

I pressed him about the murders. Why hadn't there been a proper investigation? It looked to me like the case was dead.

"Of course, this case is still alive," he insisted. "But, you must understand, this is a very delicate situation. The zone is so isolated. The people don't speak Spanish. They are afraid of us. If they know something, they don't tell us. It is a difficult thing to investigate. What can we do?"

Not much, it would appear.

Atanasio's family never found who out carted away little pieces of their son.

* * *

I thought about the Huasteca and these long-ago events on my way back to Washington that Sunday evening, with the newspaper announcing Digna's murder folded in my lap. I remembered how she fought to find answers for María Rosa and the other parents, how it wasn't just a case to her and how deeply she cared about the people and their lives. She didn't give up. She kept the Huasteca file open, hoping to one day find a way to hold the torturers accountable for their most ignominious crimes.

I could see her bright face, and those damned prissy blouses, and, on the train from New York City, I promised her that I would do my best to find out what happened. Our lives had intersected and this was what I had to do.

CHAPTER EIGHT

The Bricklayer's Daughter

Digna had been dead almost four months when Petter and I traveled 230 miles northeast of Mexico City to Misántla. He had returned to Sweden three years earlier but had flown back to Mexico for a few weeks to assist me in investigating Digna's murder. We arrived by bus in the Veracruz state capital, Jalapa, with its steep streets and colonial architecture, and made arrangements with a cabdriver for the final 52 miles of bad mountain road. We were confident because he was from Misántla and said he knew the road by heart. Bad mistake. My stomach was in my mouth as he sped up and lurched around every tight curve, and then jammed his foot on the brakes to slow down. The brakes squealed, the gold cross hanging from the visor pitched wildly, and I was sure we were going to crash. There were crosses on the side of the road to mark where others had crashed and died. With each mile the air grew thinner, until at last, with me ashen and drenched in sweat, we climbed to 13,485 feet above sea level and arrived in Misántla at midday on a beautiful Saturday in February.

Esthela and Jesús were waiting for us in the town square. It was easy to recognize them. The noonday sun was high as they came toward us and Esthela looks so much like her sister that for a moment, squinting into the light, I almost believed Digna had come back. They took us to their parents' home on Obregón Street and I sat in the living room, holding the same notebook in which I wrote down their address and telephone number during my last interview with Digna, before she went into exile in Washington. She asked me to print only generalities about her family because she was worried about their safety. But she wanted me to say how much they understood and supported her work, and how much that meant to her. Her mother was a pillar of strength. "Don't let it stop you," her father had told her.

I never imagined I would meet her parents, or be here in this house on Obregón Street talking to them, under such painful circumstances.

I was surprised at how much I liked Irene Plácido. I thought she would be disagreeable but she wasn't at all. She was funny, with a dry sense of humor. I guess I made assumptions because Digna wrote Esthela in her August e-mail that she didn't want her mother to have her things if anything were to happen. And J.J. told me Digna was deeply hurt by her mother's negative reaction to their love affair. Señora Plácido was a devout Catholic, strict about matters of Church law, and there was nothing Digna could do or say to change her mind.

"She is not my mother! I don't have a mother anymore," Digna exclaimed one day, after a particularly bitter conversation.[1] J.J. recounted the incident and it did sound exactly like something an angry daughter would say. But I think the raw emotion of the outburst was testament to how much Digna loved her mother, and not the opposite.

There was no doubt, sitting here today in her living room, that Irene loved the daughter she lost on the day before her sixty-fifth birthday. It was the worst birthday of her life and the memory would shroud every birthday to come.

She was a woman toughened by hard times. I could see in both parents where Digna got her sinew. But later, as the family was leaving for the cemetery where a German TV crew was waiting to tape them for a documentary about Digna, I noticed that

Irene was crying, and she would dab at her eyes for the rest of the day.

Her face was Digna's face in old age. She was a small, rounded woman who viewed the world through thick glasses. She was soft-spoken and didn't waste words. She kept her hands clasped in front of her and twiddled her thumbs as she chatted. She had built a shrine to her murdered daughter in a corner of the living room, with bouquets of sunflowers and roses set before images of Digna and the patron saint of Mexico, the Virgin of Guadalupe.

"Was Digna like you?" I asked her.

"In her discipline, yes, she was," she replied. "She was so strong. She had such a strong character. . . . But she was also very cheerful, very happy, always joking and kidding around with her brothers and sisters."

Eusebio, also in his mid-sixties, was more animated than his wife. He took off his straw hat for the interview and looked me in the eye when he talked to me. It is worth dwelling on this point. I asked questions and he responded *to me*, even though Petter was sitting right beside me. This was most unusual, and I say this as a woman who has interviewed men all over Latin America. I am used to being a *gringa*[2] in a macho culture. I have done so many interviews with men and, if another male is with me—be it a photographer, a local fixer, or even a cabdriver—most will direct their answers to him, rather than me. Even highly educated and sophisticated men do this. It's as if they think the guy with me is a ventriloquist. It's comical really and if I am irritated enough, or if the situation is just too bizarre, I will point it out, although not usually. But Eusebio, a man of little formal education in this remote town, was different. Very good for his daughters, I think to myself, and his sons.

Irene and Eusebio had thirteen children, all anchored in a little house with dirt floors, where Eusebio grew up and where he brought his bride almost fifty years earlier. They were very poor, especially in the early years, and struggled to survive. They had a small grill for cooking and an outhouse in back. Sometimes the kids went to school without shoes. Digna was the fifth child and, by the time she was seven, she was out in the streets, a little barefoot Indian girl selling gum and candies to help her family.

Little kids can be seen working all over Mexico, on street corners in the capital and in towns a few hundred yards from the border with the United States. They scurry over to cars stopped at traffic lights and hoist up their trays filled with sweets and chewing gum, some of them so small one has to peer over the side to see them.

Digna was proud of her roots in Misántla and told her friends about her family, including Esthela, her kid sister who worked for the Bital Bank in nearby Martínez de la Torre; Ignacio, the younger brother who was studying law in Jalapa; and Jesús, the eldest boy, the hefty one, the schoolteacher who held various positions for the leftist Democratic Revolutionary Party (PRD) in Misántla. She loved to talk about her siblings, nieces, nephews, cousins, and each new addition to the Ochoa and related clans. She loved being an aunt and was anticipating the arrival of the baby girl her sister Elía was carrying. She never saw this baby, born five months after her murder.

Above all, Digna was her father's daughter. She had a special bond with Eusebio and his imprisonment was the single most influential event of her life and the reason she decided to study law. She always told people, "I have never forgotten that I am a bricklayer's daughter."[3] These were not just words, Juan José Vera told me once. "Digna was unaffected, an extremely unaffected person."

* * *

Her family was Totonaca and her ancestors lived in the mountains and green valleys of Veracruz long before the Spanish Conquest in the early 1500s. It is a beautiful land, full of myth and legend. Many years ago, in the time of the conquest, or so the story goes, a young man in the service of a knight wandered to this region and fell in love with a lovely Totonaca princess named Nacaquimia. He left to make his fortune in war, promising to come back to her, but was mortally wounded in battle. When the princess received the news, she broke down and the torrent of those tears became a spring that would flow forever and bear her name. To this day, people come from far and wide to Misántla to drink the refreshing waters of the spring of Nacaquimia.

The Totonaca civilization was almost destroyed by smallpox brought by the conquistador Hernán Cortés and his troops. "The unfortunate Totonacs, who had made themselves Cortés' first allies, were decimated," wrote Hugh Thomas in *The Conquest of Mexico,* his grand and authoritative study of the fall of the Aztec empire. They had no immunity against the disease, and whole households were wiped out.[4]

Thomas described the Totonacs as "a cultivated people, known for their embroideries. . . . [They were] tall and usually had good skin, with long heads. They were known for their embroidery and used fans against the heat, often looking at themselves in mirrors, and wore beautiful sandals."[5] It is believed the Totonacs migrated to the coastal lands around the time of Christ. They were industrious and artistic, shaping terra-cotta heads for burials and shrines at least as early as 700 A.D. It may have been the artistic Totonacs who introduced the art of sculpture to the Aztecs. According to another theory, they may have built the stunning Pyramids of the Sun and Moon at Teotihuacán, near Mexico City.[6] Although the pyramids' origins are still a mystery, excavation at the site has revealed many wonders, including a lower chamber painted with images of jaguars, and treasures that archaeologists are only beginning to study. Like the ancient Greeks, the Totonacs founded ceremonial games, building playing grounds at El Tajín where, to this day, tourists come to see the aerial skills of the *voladores* (flyers). Young men, festooned with gaily colored ribbons, swing from a high pole by ropes tied to their feet, moving in fifty-two expanding circles to mark the years of the Mexican century.[7]

The Totonacs proved to be invaluable allies for the Spaniards, teaching them about the land, providing a steady diet of beans, fish, maize, turkey, and fruit, and teaching them how to pan for gold. But their most vital contribution to Spain's future in the New World, indeed to the development of the Americas, was their willingness to lead Cortés to the capital of the Aztecs (also called the Mexica) at Tenochtitlán, where Mexico City now stands, its skyscrapers looming over ancient temples and palaces. The Aztecs had subjugated the Totonacs, forcing their chiefs to pay tribute, which was carried in convoys inland to Tenochtitlán. The Aztecs looked on the Totonacs as "the embodiment of the easy life," writes Thomas, "where women wore well-woven clothes with flair, and where sexual freedom was greater than it was in the austere highlands."

The historian Bernal Díaz, who traveled with Cortés, described one shipment consisting of "fine cotton clothing, two warriors costumes with shields, one necklace of greenstones, 400 quetzal feathers, two lip plugs of crystal with blue and gold mounts, 20 light amber lip plugs mounted on gold, one hair ornament of quetzal feathers and 480 pounds of cocoa beans,"[8] as well as an assortment of exotic birds.

The Totonacs took their revenge on the Aztecs through Cortés and his soldiers, who defeated the emperor, Montezuma. But in turn, they fell victim to smallpox and the gradual loss of their language, prestige, and power under the rule of the Spanish. By the middle of the twentieth century, even their land had begun to lose its richness.

Guadalupe Evangelista, Irene's mother, was the last of her line to speak the Totonac tongue. She was close to her grandchildren—they took turns living with her—and told stories about the countryside of her childhood, when fat shrimp rushed into the nets of the fishermen and deer and wild pigs roamed the forests in great numbers. Misántla is a Nahuatl word meaning "the place where the deer gather." Guadalupe Evangelista, dead these many years, lived to a very great age, although nobody knew exactly how old she was when she died. She was matriarch of a proud family and she taught her children and grandchildren to respect their Totonaca heritage even if, alas, she could not teach them to hold on to their language.

Jesús remembered that his grandmother's wisdom sometimes clashed with what he learned in school. Once, when he was around eight, a teacher was talking about "Mother Spain" and her great love for the colony of Mexico and its people.

"Spain is not our mother!" he burst out, echoing what he had heard from his grandmother. "She must be our stepmother because everybody knows that a stepmother hates her husband's children."[9]

* * *

Guadalupe Evangelista was wise to inure her grandchildren, as best she could, against what they would have to deal with in their lives. They needed self-respect in order to deal with ingrained, systemic racism in Mexico, and a brief digression seems in order to illustrate the breadth of this problem. It has a bearing on what Digna was able to achieve in her life, given, as Kerry Kennedy pointed out, she had three strikes against her, being a woman, an Indian, and a nun.

What I witnessed over many years in Mexico quite simply took my breath away. I knew that my Mexican friends and colleagues were as disgusted as I was and did their best to change a tradition that, instead of celebrating the original cultures of the republic, belittled them. It was the backbeat to daily life, and there are so many examples it's difficult to choose just a few. But here's what comes to mind.

A glossy women's magazine ran a supposedly tongue-in-cheek story about how to deal with one's Indian maid or *muchacha*, a word that means both girl and maid. The wise chatelaine must shower her *muchacha* with gifts, give her as much time off as she pleases, and, by all means (wink-wink), learn *her* language, in order to get a whit of work out of her. Otherwise, she will have an idle maid on her hands.

One felt watching Mexican TV that this was a Scandinavian country. Ads featured blond-haired moppets with blue eyes and pale skin, along with their equally Nordic-looking parents, selling everything from cars to baked goods. Petter did some work for an ad agency once and recalled actors being flown in from Texas.

A friend fretted over how he was supposed to teach his son respect when, on a family outing to a Polanco restaurant on a Sunday afternoon, their dark-skinned Indian housekeeper was denied entry. He was a professional man of means and, the next day, threw his weight around with the manager, but the damage had been done.

And, finally, one day, Petter came into work and talked about what his doctor had told him the day before. He had complimented Petter on his Spanish and said he was impressed that he spoke another language so well.

"But that's common in Mexico," replied Petter. "Most Indians speak Spanish and their own tongue."

"But that's not true," said the doctor. "They speak Spanish and they speak shit."

* * *

Irene and Eusebio were pleased they could send their children to school. "I wanted to study but I couldn't," Irene said, before quickly adding: "But I can write my name."

Her father died when she was seven and she had to stay home. She would have liked to become a teacher but it was out of the question. But she had a godmother who was childless and loved her like a daughter. This woman made sure little Irene got a solid religious education, taking her to Mass every Sunday, teaching her to say the rosary, and building the foundation of a faith that would remain unbroken throughout her life.

Eusebio couldn't go to school because he, too, had to work. He said he has had a good life, but one wonders what more he might have done with an education. His mind was quite extraordinary and he had a good memory for dates and numbers. Like many poor people, he could remember every peso he had held in his palm.

His father was a campesino who earned a few pesos a week toiling for local landowners. By the age of seven, even while trying to study, Eusebio was up at 4 A.M. to spend the day in the fields, planting, tilling, harvesting corn, and shooing away the wild pigs that ate the young stalks. He didn't get home until after 8 P.M. and, for his labor, he earned 40 centavos a day (less than 50 cents). He was expected to help support his family.

"Then, I went to work in the fields full-time and they paid me three pesos, while the men earned six pesos, because I was just a kid. That was in forty three. When I got older, they paid me ten pesos," he said. He married in 1956 and, soon after he "heard the call of the bricklayers who told me they made a lot of money. Thanks be to God, they gave me a job working at the school— right over there," and Eusebio gestured toward the front window. He learned his craft on the job and was earning 15 pesos after one year and 30 pesos after two. "Already my life was something else," he said. "I won't say it was better though, because I loved the countryside and missed it. My parents taught me how to plant corn and harvest, and so I was able to rent a little piece of land for my family."

Irene began having babies immediately, and her children arrived in the order of Carmen, Jesús, Luz María, Eusebio, Digna, Guadalupe, Elía, Ismael, Esthela, Roberto, Juan Carlos, Ignacio, and Agustín.

Each day, she rose at 3 A.M. to build a fire, make coffee, and cook tortillas on the grill, while her husband slept until five and her children until six. She took her hatchet into the mountains to the small tract rented by her husband to chop firewood, split it with her machete, and tie it in bundles. She chose hardwoods that burned well (although Mexican hardwoods are porous and burn quickly compared to solid, cold-climate trees), and she carried the bundles on her back, holding them by a leather porter's strap around her forehead.

Carrying firewood is quite literally back-breaking work and it's usually done by women in Mexico's indigenous cultures. Today in Chiapas, the descendants of the Maya still walk along the sides of the road, bent over, with huge bundles of kindling strapped to their backs and their babies tagging along behind, pulling on their skirts.

"Oh yes, I hurt very much," said Irene. "My muscles ache all the time. It feels like there is an elastic band across my back holding me so that I can't move."

She kept her children healthy. Oranges were cheap and she had home remedies for everything from diarrhea and sore throats to the flu. "My children never got sick with anything serious, thanks be to God," and she made the sign of the cross, "because I had no money to pay the doctor."

As a special treat, she made green banana tortillas.

"Umm, *muy sabroso* (very delicious)," Esthela said dreamily, from the floor where she's stretched out listening to her mother, along with Jesús, the very pregnant Elía, and Ignacio, home from law school in Jalapa.

Every morning, as if she didn't already have enough to do, Irene washed her family's clothes at the riverbank, lugging the laundry back and forth, and walked back to town to sell firewood in the streets until 4 P.M. She didn't get to bed until 10 or 11 o'clock. Her children, especially her daughters, were expected to help as they got older.

In the winter, when it was cold, the kids all slept together on a thin mattress on the floor, a tangled mass of arms and legs.

"It was hard, eh?" I said to Irene.

"*Pues sí,* but we did it. And now that I am very old I feel as if I didn't really do all that much at all. I don't know why because I certainly ran the course."

Her religion was her strength. "I have always said that Sunday is dedicated to the Lord and we always went to Mass on Sunday, always," she said. It was troubling to her that, in nearly half a century, she had failed to convince Eusebio to go to Mass every day like her. He only went on Sundays. She shrugged and threw up her hands. *"Uf!* What can you do with a husband?"

She lived her life without doubts and raised her children in the belief that Jesus Christ stands at the gates of Heaven, ready to welcome and reward those who have lived good Christian lives. "In order to live, one must die, and I believe we leave this life to go to a better life," she said. "I believe that my daughter is resurrected."

The room went silent and we thought about Digna. Soon, though, the mood broke and everyone was chatting about what it was like growing up in this household. Jesús remembered wrestling matches on the floor and practical jokes and calling each other names, which they still did. Jesús and Esthela jostled and poked each other like ten-year-olds, laughing so hard they had to gulp for air.

"You're an idiot!"

"No! *You're* the idiot."

Jesús and Esthela affectionately called each other *naco* and *naca,* slang for "Mexican" and derived from scrambling the last letters of *Mexicano/a.* Later, when I heard other, very different accounts from outsiders about the nature of this family, and Digna's place within it, I would think about this day, and the affection with which they treated each other.

Jesús recalled that Digna fell down a well at her grandmother's house when she was little. It was ten feet deep and half-filled with rainwater, but she was able to hang on to some sticks and keep her head above water. She cried until her aunt could pull her up with a rope. She was in the well about half an hour and badly shaken up, but otherwise uninjured. "Lucky the sticks were there," said Jesús. "Otherwise, she would have drowned for sure."

Little did I know how important this well was going to become in the murder investigation.

* * *

The defining moment in Digna's life came at sixteen, when her father was arrested, tortured, and imprisoned. It was 1980 and he was working at the Misántla sugar mill, Liberty Mill, and heavily involved in union politics.

Eusebio organized two marches to Mexico City after the government-owned mill closed in 1969. During the 1970 election campaign, President Luis Echeverría promised it would reopen and, when it didn't, the sugar workers marched to the gates of Los Pinos. The protests continued until the mill reopened in 1974. By then, José López Portillo was president and relations had turned sour between Misántla sugar workers and their national union, the giant Confederation of Mexican Workers (known by its Spanish acronym, CTM), with its six million members.

Eusebio wasn't surprised when the CTM supported plans to move the mill to a neighboring town, Martínez de la Torre. He believed the union there had better contacts with the party in power, the Institutional Revolutionary Party, or PRI. The Confederation portrayed itself as the defender of workers' rights in Mexico, but in reality it was a government-affiliated union that did what the government wanted. The Mexican Constitution guaranteed labor rights to a degree that put Canadian and American labor law to shame. But, in great Orwellian style, the fancy words were hollow and labor rights were routinely quashed. The army was called in whenever workers attempted to form independent unions.

For seven decades under PRI hegemony, which lasted until 2000, the CTM was controlled by union strongmen faithful to the government. For fifty-six of those years, that strongman was Fidel Velásquez, who was CTM secretary-general under ten successive PRI presidents, from 1941 until his death in 1997.

He was a legend in Mexico, a larger-than-life icon on par with Pancho Villa or Dolores del Río. He *was* labor in Mexico. I interviewed *Don* Fidel[10] in the union's downtown offices in Mexico City in 1995, two years before he died, supposedly at the age of ninety-seven, but possibly over one hundred. Cartoonists used to draw him dozing behind his trademark dark shades, or being lowered into place at PRI rallies by a complicated contraption of ropes and pulleys. When I saw him, he was sitting in a high-backed leather chair, belt buckle hiked to his breastbone, barely able to see across the most imposing desk I had ever seen. He was not wearing the shades, but his glasses were so thick his watery blue irises appeared to be oozing into the whites of his eyes. He'd had several strokes and was paralyzed on the right side and spoke with great effort. He was a tired old man reduced to making feeble jokes about being the world's oldest living labor leader. Given how weak labor was in Mexico, I thought he was the perfect symbol.

Even then, he was useful to the PRI. For more than five decades, *Don* Fidel ruled his union with an iron fist, signing a series of pacts with PRI presidents, keeping wages well below inflation, snuffing out attempts to form independent unions, and delivering the votes to the ruling party at election time. In the 1960s, he campaigned hard to keep Mexican workers from taking part in the protests that had begun on college campuses and swept across the nation. He didn't utter a peep when unarmed university students were gunned down by the army in the 1968 Tlatelolco massacre. *Don* Fidel even served two terms as a PRI senator, under presidents Echeverría and López Portillo.

Not surprisingly, he did nothing for Eusebio and his sugar mill workers. For years, rumors circulated that the mill was going to be relocated to Martínez de la Torre. Although it didn't happen, the threat was a club over the heads of the membership. Frustrated by the CTM's lack of support for their local, the Misántla workers formed their own labor coalition, a direct challenge to the authority of the umbrella organization in Mexico City and to the power of the PRI. They were getting dangerous.

Moreover, by this time, Eusebio was involved with grassroots protest groups fighting for political change in Mexico, including the Cárdenas Democratic Front (Frente Democrática Cárdenista) and the Democratic Current (Corriente Democrática). These organizations, springing up all over the country, were forerunners to the leftist Democratic Revolutionary Party (PRD), which nearly took down the PRI and Carlos Salinas in the elections of 1988. In Misántla, activism went beyond labor rights at the mill to include demands for decent roads, drinking water, land disputes, better health, and lower education costs. Eusebio's political activities got him suspended several times from Liberty Mill and then, in 1980, things got serious.

On the morning of July 1, state police showed up at the mill. They handcuffed and blindfolded him, threw him into the back of a police car, and drove off into the mountains. They were arresting him—if the euphemism applies—in connection with the murder of union rival José Luis Galán Rodíz, who was secretary-general of the sugar workers' union in Misántla. He was gunned down in front of his bodyguards, who did nothing. Police arrested a man by the name of Nicolás Cruz, who testified that Eusebio ordered the hit and paid him 40,000 pesos to kill the union boss.

Eusebio disappeared for forty-eight hours. His frantic family searched for him, while authorities insisted they had no idea of his whereabouts.

Eusebio remembers every moment of those two days. When they took off the blindfold, he was standing on a pathway in the bush, on the brink of a small gully about ten square feet. The officers, all burly men with big moustaches, aimed their guns at him and ordered him to run down into the gully.

When he refused, they said they were going to kill him.

"If you are going to kill me, then you have me tied up and ready," he said he told them. "If you are going to do it, do it now."

They laughed and, over the next two days and nights, held him without food or water, taking turns beating him up. They took him to the Misántla jail around 4 A.M. on July 3 and stuck him in a cell. When his family was able to see him, his arms and legs were bruised and swollen, one ankle was inflamed, and his left cheek was gashed and bleeding.

Authorities wouldn't allow a doctor to see him.

The entire Ochoa family, led by Jesús and including sixteen-year-old Digna, fought for his freedom. They sent a letter to Veracruz attorney general Francisco Portilla Bonilla urging him to guarantee Eusebio's safety and petitioning for his release,[11] formed a group they named Committee for Liberty and Justice, and fought in the courts. As the case dragged on, Eusebio languished in jail. It was soon established that the witness, this *Señor* Cruz, was tortured into naming Eusebio as the mastermind. He testified that state police officers threatened to kill him if he didn't sign a statement to that effect. They said they would let him go home, but they threw him in jail instead.[12]

"Your Honor, I would like to inform you that on the fifth of July, when I appeared in front of you, I was unable to admit that an agent from the Public Prosecutor's Office came to see me in my cell and threatened that if I didn't stick to the story which they obtained by beating me, I would be sentenced to fifteen years in jail, but if, on the contrary, I upheld my statement, I would be allowed to go free," he told the judge.

On January 5, 1981, six months after his "arrest," the court ruled in Eusebio's favor and ordered him released. The state appealed. It would take another six months before the charges were dropped and he was released.

Sitting in his living room so many years later, Eusebio says his ordeal was nothing compared to what he saw in prison. He witnessed police torturing innocent people into confessing crimes they hadn't committed.

"They club them, force water up the nose, and use hammers on the arms and legs. They keep on beating them. It is ugly and I saw it all going on. I know I would rather die than admit to something I didn't do, but I saw people in prison who were really innocent and they didn't know what to do. I saw grown men cry," he said, as his own eyes grew watery. "They were so desperate to get out that they would say anything. For me, the day finally came, thanks be to God, when I was returned to my wife and my children."

It is moving to see tears rolling down the old man's weathered cheeks. Jesús covered his eyes with his hand for a moment. "The thing about my father is that he fought for justice in Misántla. He never fought for himself," he says. "And that's what Digna did too. She was 16 when it happened and it made her reflect a great deal. It was something she carried with her all of her life. She told us that she was going to become a lawyer to defend against injustice."

Such was Digna's political education. Eusebio was her blood. She would make the point many years later when she told Kerry Kennedy she saw injustice "in the flesh with my father."[13]

Soon, however, she would live through her own harrowing experience with injustice.

* * *

Digna entered law school at the University of Veracruz in Xalapa[14] in 1984, when she was 20, and, in 1986, began working in the state Attorney General's Offices. She was on contract, continuing her courses and eventually completing her thesis on how the Mexican justice system deals with juvenile offenders in the justice system.[15]

At work, she had access to government records and came across evidence of a black list. It contents were chilling: Her father and brother were on it. She telephoned home immediately, warning Eusebio and Jesús that the authorities kept extensive files on them and others involved in the protest movement. (Digna's complete work history has vanished, beyond the few basics, including pay scale and the results of the pre-hire pregnancy test, which was against the law but still required in much of the republic. It was negative. "That's strange," a helpful official from the Veracruz Attorney General's Office confided to me in 2002, after failing to locate records she had assured me would be there. They were missing, which was unusual since nobody ever throws anything away in Mexico, a nation of packrats, where public and private business grinds along on the basis of duplicate and triplicate documents.)

Digna was frightened for her family. Eusebio was secretary-general of a group called the Democratic Current, as well as a member, along with Jesús, of the Civic Association for National Revolution. Their names were on a black list of so-called revolutionaries, who were purportedly eager to overthrow the legitimate power of the state.

"She told us to be careful. She said they had photographs, the names of the leaders of the membership, everything," said Jesús. "We weren't revolutionaries. We never thought the way to change things was with guns. We were trying to create a national dialogue and create change through the election process."

The times were extremely dangerous. Twenty years after 1968, another wave of protest was washing across the country, bringing with it violence and political assassinations. Carlos Salinas had won Los Pinos in 1988, in a vote everyone knew was stolen by the PRI, and the government felt vulnerable. Nobody was safe. Union leaders, teachers, priests, lawyers, and opposition politicians were being "disappeared" in crimes linked to the army, police, and death squads. The elections had ushered in a new era of repression and death, which would escalate over the decade to come.

By the time she was twenty-four, Digna was in the thick of it, following in her father's footsteps. While finishing her law school thesis, she became an outspoken activist, serving as legal adviser to the populist group the Democratic Current, working on land claims in Misántla and serving as a volunteer on cases with other bushy-tailed young lawyers, eager to change the world. She was trying to document a case on the torture of campesinos by state police, a subject close to her heart.

"We wanted to feel like lawyers, so we threw ourselves into it," she would later tell Kerry Kennedy. "Our mistake was to take on the case without any institutional support. I had managed to obtain substantial evidence against the police, so they started to harass me incessantly, until I was detained. First, they sent me telephone messages telling me to drop the case. Then by mail came threats that if I didn't drop it I would die, or members of my family would be killed. I kept working, and we even publicly reported what was happening. The intimidation made me so angry that I was motivated to work even harder. I was frightened too, but felt I couldn't show it. I always had to appear—at least publicly—like I was sure of myself, fearless. If I showed my fear, they would know how to dominate me. It was a defense mechanism."[16]

Irene Plácido worried about her daughter. Jesús warned her to be careful.

Maybe she was careful, in her way, but Digna was never one to hide. On August, 16, 1988, as a friend was driving her from work, a man jumped out of a white van, opened the door, grabbed Digna, and pulled her inside his vehicle, where three other men were waiting. They drove her to an abandoned farmhouse in Coatzalcolcos in the south of Veracruz, near the border with Tabasco, where they held her at gunpoint.[17]

It isn't clear how many men stayed with Digna, or whether they guarded her in shifts. What is clear is that they tied her up and beat and raped her.[18] They raped her more than once, but whether they gang-raped her, or took turns with what might be characterized as intermissions, was not entered into evidence at the time.

One of the gunmen got careless and put his pistol on the dresser. It's a good bet the men were drinking. Digna seized the gun and fired, shooting him in the leg.[19] She managed to escape, running half-naked to the road and hitching a ride, making it all the way to Mérida, the capital of Yucatan on the Caribbean Sea. She was a mess, terrified and utterly traumatized. She went to a priest, who took her to a women's shelter in a convent, where she registered under an assumed name and pretended to be a victim of domestic violence. Digna stayed in hiding for almost a month, before telling the nuns who she was and calling her family in Misántla.[20]

She told Jesús that her abductors were state police officers, and that for weeks she had been too scared to even pick up the phone. Before he could go and get her, Veracruz police arrived to pick her up. Jesús says they brought her back with her hands tied, in the back of a truck, under the broiling sun.

Jesús was scared that the police would torture her into making a confession. He begged human rights activist María del Rosario Huerta to insist on being present when Digna gave her official statement to the police. There had been a lot of publicity about Digna's disappearance—the family was getting good at this—and the prosecutor's office agreed. Digna was white and shaking. Señora Huerta observed that "she was very nervous and her trembling hands were noticeable during the interrogation."[21]

On September 17, 1988, Digna Ochoa gave a press conference

in Jalapa. She identified her kidnappers as Veracruz judicial police officers and urged the Attorney General's Office to investigate the crime and bring her assailants to justice. Privately, she named the officers.

Journalist Regina Martínez covered the press conference and filed a report to *La Jornada* in Mexico City.[22] She says it took courage for Digna to stand up and accuse her attackers. Even now, the stigma of rape intimidates and silences women. Back then, it was a forbidden topic in Mexico. Women were supposed to bear their shame in private. But in describing her kidnapping to the media, she did not leave out the fact that she was raped.

"Digna came from a family of fighters for social causes," Regina told me over lunch in Jalapa in 2002.[23] "She grew up with that and it gave her strength. She was courageous." Regina remembers the fear and paranoia that hung over Mexico and what it was like for political activists and rights defenders in that bleak time. She followed Digna's progress over the years and, on October 21, 2001, covered her funeral in Misántla.

Veracruz authorities in Jalapa didn't even begin an investigation into Digna's kidnapping.[24] Consequently, no charges were laid. Soon after, Digna left Jalapa and moved to Mexico City.

* * *

Over the years, she would tell only her closest friends and confidants what had happened to her. She would always feel a special kinship with women who were raped and, as a lawyer for PRO, would fight whenever she could to bring soldiers accused of rape to justice in civilian courts. Digna agonized over women she could help and those she couldn't, and talked about repression against women with her friends.[25] Stories were chillingly repetitive in Mexico: When women stepped forward with accounts of having being raped by soldiers or police officers, they were too often told they were crazy. Maybe they *were* crazy to think they could receive justice. They lived in a climate in which the constant for women,

191

most certainly women at the bottom of the social ladder, was the feeling of worthlessness.

There can be no greater indictment of the place of women in Mexican society than the unsolved cases of the murdered women of Ciudad Juárez, across the border from El Paso, Texas, who, for a decade, have been turning up dead in numbers now soaring over three hundred, their bodies found decomposing in the desert, with their breasts cut off or other horrible evidence of torture. Women come to the border towns of Mexico from all over the country to find jobs in the factories of the free-trade zone. Many of the Juárez victims remain anonymous, without faces. The case has become a shameful national embarrassment for the bumbling failure of the authorities to crack it—or even to take it seriously[26]—as national and international groups fight to raise public awareness and prod the national and state governments into action. (On the Day of the Dead in 2002, women from all over Mexico came together in protests for the murdered women of Juárez and the murdered Digna Ochoa.)

One of Mexico's most haunting and horrible cases of rape—sadly, an all-too-familiar story—involved a seventeen-year-old girl who was gang-raped by three soldiers in Durango in March 1997. Her name was Yéssica, and her mother took her to the Public Prosecutor's Office to file a complaint against the soldiers, but they told her to come back the next day. When she did, two of the rapists were waiting to taunt her. The case was not turned over to an investigator specializing in sex crimes for almost two months and, when it was, this expert told her she was crazy. He made her go for blood tests on eight separate occasions. She was told she had to "touch the rapist in order for the statement to be valid."[27]

Yéssica committed suicide on June 16, 1997. The Prosecutor's Office said the cause of death was exclusively medical, caused by an overdose.[28] Local authorities persisted in harassing the family, who had to leave the country. The ombudsperson for the city of Durango ruled that Yéssica had been raped by the soldiers, and denounced the handling of the case. He became the target of death threats himself and had to flee the state.

Digna fought one of her toughest battles on a rape case on behalf of three indigenous women who were allegedly gang-raped by soldiers in Chiapas in 1994. They said they were stopped at an army checkpoint in northern Chiapas, near the border with Tabasco (not all that far from where Digna herself was tied up and raped) and pulled onto the side of the road, where the soldiers attacked them. Digna went first to Mexico's National Human Rights Commission, an agency that depended on the federal government for its existence.

"She ran into a woman there, an official, who advised her to drop the case," remembered rights activist Rafael Álvarez,[29] who was working with her at PRO at the time. "She told Digna, 'Look, you don't know these women, this can take a really long time and, furthermore, Chiapas is very far away. Don't get involved in these problems.'

"Digna was furious. That reaction just made her want to work harder to find ways to put the issue on the national agenda."

She argued the case before the Inter-American Human Rights Commission in Washington, D.C., which investigated and recommended that the soldiers be tried in civilian court. The Mexican government refused to pursue the matter with the Mexican Army. Digna tried to do it on her own. But her petitions for justice were ignored by chief military prosecutor General Rafael Macedo de la Concha, in what would be the first of many times his life intersected with hers. Each time would prove to be more significant until, at the time of her murder, he was Vicente Fox's attorney general.

"Digna felt that this case showed the impunity of the army, and it made her even angrier because the national authorities [the human rights commission], which should have protected the rights of the women, were collaborating to create impunity," said Rafael. "She did not want to give up."

Digna was involved in another case in Guerrero, in which three women from Zopilotepec came forward to testify that they had been raped by two soldiers in December 1997. They said their husbands had been tied up and forced to watch, before being beaten with rifle butts. The men were taken to the state capital of Chilpancingo, where they were charged with drug-trafficking.

The rights commission sought to reach an "amicable agreement" between the victims and the soldiers.[30] PRO and other human rights organizations strongly opposed any kind of friendly settlement but, ultimately, there was no settlement. The soldiers disappeared into the shadows of military justice.

Digna was not deterred; she looked to the next case, and the next, and kept on fighting.

"She did not accept 'no' for an answer. She rebelled," said Rafael, in his office in the capital, some five months after Digna's murder.

"She had a very strong character. For a woman to reach where Digna did requires a lot of conviction and initiative. We would have discussions [at PRO] about whether to accept a case or not. You know, we would have to assess the consequences, the repercussions, how far we could go with it. Her attitude was not whether we would accept a case, but what would be the best way to handle the work. . . . She was very tough when she confronted the agents of the Public Ministry, and during trials. This is not common among women lawyers—among lawyers in general. They prefer not to get involved in confrontations. They don't want problems. They prefer to remain quiet.

"Digna was the opposite. She was very dedicated, very thorough when preparing for a case. She always arrived half an hour before. She was always respectful, but she never let anyone overlook her authority as a lawyer. We took this into account many times. When we had to decide who would be the best person to take on a case, very often we would choose Digna. We knew Digna's character."

He paused and a smile played at the corners of his mouth. Oh boy, did he remember Digna. She was more than a match for the authorities, he told me. "She had a different character. When Digna was afraid, she didn't like anyone to know. She always seemed fearless, always fearless . . ."

* * *

In the Ochoa living room in Misántla, the conversation with Digna's family wound down. Eusebio mentioned his last visit with Digna in Mexico City at the end of the summer, two months before her murder. They had talked about a land claims dispute in Misántla and he asked his daughter if she would do some work for a campesino organization. She agreed and they planned to talk more about it, which they never did.

"I never imagined that that they would kill her in such a cowardly manner. *Bueno*, I say it plainly—it is cowardly to kill a defenseless woman," said the old man.

"My daughter was a woman who felt very strongly for people who were weaker. If we passed people who were selling something and they were poor, she would see that they weren't well off and she would give them money as a present. That's more or less what she was like. She believed that it was better to give what she had to another person."

We left the house and walked through the narrow streets to Digna's grave. Irene carried a bouquet of flowers. Digna's tomb was painted a clear turquoise, the color known as *tropicana*, and there was a small mahogany placard.[31]

Srita. Digna Ochoa y Plácido
El 15 de Mayo de 1964
Falleció el 19 de octubre de 2001
Para mí morir es Resurrección (In My Death is Resurrection)

Esthela lingered at her sister's grave. She came here often to be with Digna; she talked to her and felt that Digna could hear. They used to speak every day by phone or e-mail. They talked after Digna sent the e-mail in August, talking about her work and giving precise instructions in the event of her death. Not that she would. "Weeds never die."

"Everybody supports you," Esthela told Digna. "Keep at it and fuck the government."

"That's exactly what I told her," she said to me, standing over the grave of her sister. "She said that it was wonderful I understood what she was doing. She told me to erase it, but I never did. I always kept that e-mail."

It was getting dark by the time we get back to the Ochoa home on Obregón Street and Petter and I were ready to leave. Irene met us at the door and led us to the kitchen where dinner was ready. There are plates of baked chicken and rice, vegetables and glasses of apple juice. "Eat, eat, please," said Irene. "You must eat before your journey. Please, we have enough for everyone."

CHAPTER NINE

Bad Breath, Bomb Threats, and War in Paradise

Digna Ochoa tore into her office, plopped her bag on a chair, and sat down, breathless and pushing her hair off her face, but ready for the interview. We were in her office at the Miguel Agustín Pro Juárez Human Rights Center in Colonia San Rafael, not far from the San Cosme Metro station, on a Tuesday morning in January 2000. She had gotten back the night before from Guerrero, where she had clients at the state prison in Iguala, and she was eager to tell me about the case. She didn't have much time but she clasped her hands in front of her and took a deep breath.

"Bueno, lista," she said. Ready. Her face was scrubbed and shining above her white blouse and her hair was still damp, as if she'd just stepped out of the shower. She was thirty-five, but sitting there at her desk, looked about fifteen. She grinned.

"What are all those papers?" I asked, about a stack on her desk that, even upside down and partially obscured, piqued my interest. I could see what look like headlines, all geegaw, with letters pasted in weird positions and black crosses lying on their sides.

"Oh, those," she said, blithely. "Death threats."

She pushed them over to show me, as if it was the most routine thing in the world to receive death threats. They were photocopied onto legal-size paper. She said these threats against her and her colleagues arrived here in PRO's cramped offices, some going back to 1995. But the pace had increased since the previous summer, when the center agreed to defend two campesinos from Guerrero, who she said were tortured into confessing on arms and drug charges. She said she would make copies for a story I was doing for the *Toronto Star*. I flipped through them for a quick taste.

"High Risk. . . . To celebrate, we are having two days of parties and you'll be our special guests. . . . Those who think themselves omnipotent also die. . . . You're next, you sons-of-bitches. . . . Eyes Shut Tight. . . . We'll Take a Raincheck. . . . Do you think you can mess with us? . . . You'll soon see what we can do. . . . You're all going to be fucked. . . . Today's the day. Why not? Do you want us to wait until tomorrow? Or the next day? Or the weekend?"

She handed me another page containing a single threat. On October 13, 1999, it was taped to PRO's front door: *"Careful. Bomb in the house. Just one. No big deal."*

It wasn't the first bomb threat, but everybody evacuated the building just the same. They were scared. A few years back, a death threat said Digna's plane would be blown out of the sky.

There was one more sheet, and Digna edged it slowly across the desk. It was a copy of her business card, with a black-marker drawing above her name of a tilted cross. Death foretold.

"My God, Digna, you could get killed," I told her, stating the obvious.

"Could be," she replied. "But it is very important that you don't feel alone, and I don't. My colleagues and I are in this together, and we must give each other support. We're a team. And when we succeed in getting someone out of prison, or securing justice for someone who has been tortured, it feels very good."[1]

I pressed her, asking if she was frightened. Yes, she told me, when she was kidnapped.

Kidnapped? I felt a chill.

She explained that she had been kidnapped twice in the previous six months. I hadn't known. The first incident occurred the August beore, when she was pulled into a car in broad daylight in Mexico City traffic. She knew it was premeditated.

198

There were three men and she could hear one shouting, "Is it her? Is it her?" They drove around for four hours, forcing her to withdraw 3,000 pesos (about $300) from two instant banking machines, using her bank card, before tossing her out into the street. They took her briefcase with her agenda and personal ID, including her voting card.

She was days away from her first court appearance in the Guerrero case, and she knew it was a warning to back off. Death threats arrived at the office in September and October, some by mail and others found at the receptionist's desk, in her drawer, and under plant pots. It was creepy: Somebody had been in the office.

And then, on October 5, something really unsettling happened.

Digna arrived home to find her stolen voting card sitting on a table. She had moved earlier in the year, leaving the Dominican convent in the south end where she'd lived for eight years. The voting card contained her old address. The message was obvious: *We know where you live.*

The next kidnapping was more brutal. Her voice was calm, but her hands were shaking as she recounted what happened.

It was Thursday night, October 28, and Digna was tired when she finished work. It was almost 10:30 when she got back to her apartment and went out onto the roof to bring in some laundry. She heard a rustling, felt something jammed over her mouth, and lost consciousness. When she came to, she was bound and tied to a chair, blindfolded, with a man sitting in front of her. She could feel her knees touching his and smelled his bad breath. She could sense the presence of another person in the room.

For the next ten hours, he interrogated her. He wanted to know what contacts she had with guerilla organizations, insisting that she name names. He focused on the Zapatista rebels in Chiapas and the People's Revolutionary Army (EPR), which operated mostly in Guerrero. Digna had spent her career dealing with Mexico's security forces and she was certain, by his terminology and interrogation techniques, that he was military, either from military intelligence (under National Defense), the federal judicial police (under the Attorney General's Office), or the Federal Preventive Police (under the Interior Ministry).

"Where do you get your guns?" he asked, calling her a bitch and accusing her and the rest of the PRO lawyers of being guerrillas. He said they were trying to overthrow the government, and deserved to be wiped out.

Digna was terrified, but tried to keep her voice steady. She was afraid of torture and her mind was spinning wildly, wondering what they were going to do to her. She had no doubt this would be the last night of her life.

She kept thinking she mustn't antagonize them.

"We are not against the government. We are not enemies of the state," she said.[2]

Throughout the night, the other individual tapped away on a laptop computer. She assumed it was a transcript and thought about the mountains of information stored away by government spies at CISEN.[3] Would this be added to her file? she wondered.

"We're not armed. We're not against the government," she kept insisting. "We're just lawyers who are trying to help people."

She had the wild idea that she might be able to win them over. She knew there was respect in the ranks of the military for General José Francisco Gallardo, who was in a military prison for having exposed human rights abuses and corruption in the army. She said she was working to free him. "You see, that shows we're not against the military," she said. But they just laughed at her.

After hours of interrogation, they dragged her to the bedroom, threw her on the bed, and tied her feet to the bed. She braced herself, waiting for an attack that never came.

She thought they were going to rape her.

Instead, there was silence and, after a few minutes, she could smell gas and struggled to free herself and remove the blindfold. When she opened her eyes, her abductors were gone. Next to her on the bed was a portable gas tank, its valve open and leaking gas.

She hadn't heard them carry it in, which made her think there had been a third assailant. They had closed the window in her bedroom.

She untied her feet and went into the living room to use the phone but it was dead. The front door to her apartment was wide open. She ran down the stairs to the street and called her colleagues at PRO from a pay phone. She was told their offices had been broken into overnight and the place ransacked. She didn't think her kidnappers wanted to kill her or they would have done so. She knew, however, that this time the warning was serious.

She waited for her colleagues in the street, where, the adrenaline dissipating from her system, she dissolved into tears and couldn't stop crying.

Later that morning, she gave a statement to investigating officers from the Mexico City Prosecutor's Office. She seethed with anger at the way they treated her. They didn't take fingerprints or search her apartment and spoke to her roughly, without respect. They acted as if it were her fault. She knew they didn't take the crime seriously and wouldn't do a serious investigation.

Digna had been talking with her head down, staring at her hands. Her story over, she looked up and made a final point. "I don't trust the police," she told me. "They don't understand our work. They have no respect for human rights. They don't understand psychological torture."

Her friend Pilar Noriega thought Digna relived her rape in Veracruz that night in her apartment in Mexico City. But they didn't talk about it, and Pilar never asked.

Digna and her colleagues began their own investigation. They met with officials from national defense, the federal Attorney General's Office, and the Interior Secretariat. Everywhere, the answer was the same: *"Mi gente no es."* ("It's not our guys.")

They took the case to the Inter-American Human Rights Commission in Washington, D.C., which forwarded it to the

Inter-American Court of Human Rights in San José, Costa Rica. The Mexican government was ordered to protect Digna and her colleagues, an order that remained in place until it was successfully overturned in the appeal by the Fox government in 2001. Digna followed up with the Mexico City Prosecutor's Office, pushing them for answers. A few weeks before our interview, an officer told her that she should buzz off and see a psychiatrist.

"That bothered me a lot," she said. "If this is the type of support you get from the authorities who are supposed to be carrying out the investigation, well . . . how lamentable!"

I followed the same trail in early 2000, telephoning these same government ministries (just as I would almost two years later when I investigate Digna's murder). Nobody had any information. Mexico City police apparently were working on the case but prosecutor Patricia Bulgarín (who would also investigate Digna's murder) was unavailable for an interview, despite many attempts to contact her. Digna had told friends that, whenever she called Bulgarín to ask about her case, the response was always the same: "Hey, *abogada* (lawyer), what's up? You got any news for me?"[4] as if it were Digna's responsibility to find her attackers.

No arrests were made—and they never would be. (I wondered then if I had pushed harder with police, if I had known then what I know now, whether it would have helped Digna. Certainly, she would have been interested to learn what Mexico City police were doing behind the scenes.)

Digna believed the kidnappings had to do with PRO's defense of the two jailed Guerrero campesinos, as did everyone at the center, including director Edgar Cortez. As senior litigator, she headed the defense team. The case was explosive because it involved allegations of torture by the army and because the jailed men were mucking around with the most powerful interests of the state of Guerrero and the people who ran it.

And so, of course, in January 2000, I made my way to Guerrero and the jail at Iguala to meet these prisoners for myself.

* * *

It was a minimum-security prison, or "readaptation" center, and Rodolfo Montiel, forty-four, and Teodoro Cabrera, forty-nine, were allowed to meet me in the interior courtyard, with armed guards observing from the watchtower. They both wore straw hats and *huaraches* and had moustaches. They were from Pizotla, an impoverished hamlet of about fifty people in the Petatlán mountains, about ten hours by foot from the nearest road.

Before they told me what happened, Rodolfo said I had to understand the real reason they were here. He said they were persecuted because he was a founding member in 1998 of the Organization of Peasant Ecologists of the Sierra of Petatlán and Coyuca of Catatlán, a group with a long-winded name and single purpose of stopping the deforestation of the Western Sierra. Their forerunner, the Organization of Campesinos of the Southern Sierra, lost seventeen members in the Aguas Blancas massacre.

Rodolfo had little formal education, maybe the equivalent of a year of grade school, but spoke with eloquence and passion. He was seen as a charismatic leader, capable of inspiring confidence. He had few teeth and had been feeling poorly since his imprisonment. He paused often to catch his breath. He said Teodoro wasn't a member of the peasant ecology group and shouldn't have been here. Teodoro was also ill, his one sighted eye rheumy and his chest sore from broken ribs.

Rodolfo explained that if logging continues at its current rampant pace in Guerrero, the mountains would soon turn to desert. "We had to fight back. If it doesn't stop, there will be no trees left in a decade," he said. "If nothing is done to save our trees, we Mexicans are going to die of drought. Our rivers will turn to streams, our streams to little trickles, and then dry up completely. If we don't fight now, what is going to happen to our children?"[5]

The peasants of Guerrero had always scraped out a living from the mountains, farming and cutting timber. The right to their communal lands, *ejidos*, was guaranteed by the Constitution written after the Mexican Revolution of 1910–1920. But after NAFTA (and the constitutional changes that preceded it), much of the land was privatized and big timber companies were able to buy rights directly from the forestry *ejidos*.[6] Clever men in positions of power in Mexico quickly saw an opportunity to make a great deal of money.

In 1995, U.S. lumber giant Boise Cascade Corporation acquired the exclusive rights over five years to harvest old-forest pine and fir over a vast section of land, known as the Costa Grande Forest, in the northern part of the state. The deal was signed by Idaho-based Boise Cascade's subsidiary in Mexico, Costa Grande Forest Products.[7]

Boise built a sawmill at Papanoa and the trees started to come down for shipment to the United States. The lumber trucks rolled through the mountain passes around the clock and the villagers began to organize. They launched their environmental organization with about fifty villagers and for two years they sent petitions, often signed with thumbprints and pictograms, to state and federal authorities, complaining of illegal shipments of timber and a complete lack of reforestation. They did everything by the book, amassing a huge stack of legal documents and petitions, all to no avail. They warned that, without the trees, the lakes and rivers were already starting to dry up and the land would soon be parched and worthless.

But what they didn't know was that the law was not on their side.

They were right, however, about the amount of deforestation. Satellite imagery obtained by the Mexican chapter of Greenpeace[8] would show that almost 40 percent of the forests in the area had been wiped out over the previous eight years. For a while, the Vicente Fox government would stop issuing logging permits in much of the Costa Grande forest, citing damage to the ecosystem.

By February 1998, the ecologists, frustrated with the lack of action, decided to take matters into their own hands by setting up roadblocks and preventing Boise Cascade lumber trucks from getting in or out of the area. The state government issued arrest warrants for Rodolfo and other members of the group, accusing them of being guerrillas and narco-traffickers. The army moved in and violence escalated, with soldiers raiding villages looking for members of the peasant organization and their sympathizers. Troops worked in tandem with police and with the hired guns of the local *caciques*.[9]

In a report on Guerrero, the U.S. rights group Global Exchange says: "Boise Cascade claims to have never cut down a tree in Guerrero—a true statement, as the [*ejido* union] contracted local laborers to fell and transport the trees. For this reason, Boise Cascade claims exemption from Mexican laws requiring that resources be replenished by parties responsible for their destruction."[10]

* * *

On the morning of Sunday, May 2, 1998, Rodolfo and Teodoro were relaxing after church in Pizotla. Their wives were related and the families were about to eat together, when some thirty soldiers from the 40th Infantry Battalion, stationed in the lowland city of Altamirano, descended on the village, firing AK-47s at the inhabitants. They killed Rodolfo's neighbor, Salomé Sánchez, with a bullet between the eyes.

Rodolfo and Teodoro escaped, hiding in the bush on the other side of the Pizotla River, but the soldiers set fire to the underbrush, flushing them out. They testified that the soldiers dragged them to the banks of the river, tied their hands behind their backs, and tortured them, beating them with fists and rifle butts, yanking their testicles until they pissed blood and holding their heads under water. This torture went on for two days, according to testimony before the Mexican courts, until a military helicopter arrived to take them to the base at Altamirano.

They were held incommunicado at the base for another three days, during which time they said they were beaten and given electric shocks. Teodoro says soldiers broke his ribs. They were photographed holding up rifles and marijuana plants—a rather slapstick touch—and signed confessions in which they admitted to possessing illegal weapons and being drug-traffickers.

"Sign or else," they reported being told. "Remember, we know where your families are."[11]

They were not brought before civil authorities in nearby Coyuca de Catatlán until May 6, four days after their arrest by the army. Nobody contests the fact that it took four days for the army to deliver them to proper civilian authorities. What was in question, however, was what happened to the hapless prisoners during that time. In those four days, they made unlikely statements, with Rodolfo claiming he was a drug trafficker and leading soldiers to his marijuana fields and Teodoro, weak, skinny, and one-eyed, admitting to being a guerrilla with the Zapatista Army of National Liberation.[12] That was a particularly absurd claim, given that the Zapatistas were based far away, in the Lacandon jungle of Chiapas and that, according to state interrogators, he also said he was a member of the People's Revolutionary Army (EPR).[13]

When they finally were brought before civilian authorities, they said they had been tortured into making false confessions. Teodoro said one soldier put a pistol in his mouth and threatened to shoot him. They identified two of the soldiers who beat them as Calixto Rodríguez Salmerón and Artemio Nazario Carballo, both from the 40th Battalion.

The military's version was that soldiers were investigating

reports of an armed band operating in the area and, when they arrived in Pizotla, five men ran out of a house and started shooting at them. They had no choice but to return fire, killing Sánchez, and capturing Rodolfo and Teodoro after an armed standoff. They found a plastic bag containing army fatigues, marijuana, and poppy seeds on the dead peasant. Teodoro then offered to lead them to his marijuana fields.

In June 1998, Rodolfo and Teodoro were sent to Iguala prison to await trial in federal court under presiding judge Maclovio Murillo Chávez.

Within two months of their imprisonment, Boise Cascade, headquartered in Boise, Idaho, pulled out of the region, to be replaced by other logging companies. Later, as the Montiel/Cabrera case became well known, the company posted a statement on its Web site about its three-year involvement in Mexico: "Throughout the time of our operations in Mexico—which permanently ended in April 1998—we had no information or awareness of the activities of Mr. Montiel or Mr. Cabrera, no personal acquaintance with them, and no contact. . . . We sincerely hope that no injustice or mistreatment has occurred."[14]

* * *

The following year, in 1999, the Miguel Agustín Pro Juárez Human Rights Center in Mexico City accepted the defense of Rodolfo Montiel and Teodoro Cabrera. By summer, Digna and her team of young lawyers, Jorge Fernández and Mario Patrón, waded into battle in one of the most violent and volatile states in the republic.

"Teodoro Cabrera and Rodolfo Montiel, two *campesinos ecologistas* from the Sierra of Petatlán Sierra of Guerrero, began to organize because there was an immoderate degree of logging in their woods from which the people had no benefit," Digna said once, describing the case to reporters.[15] "The water began to dry up and they began to have serious problems because the *caciques* tried to put the brakes on their organization. Above all, their protests were having an effect on their big economic interests. They began to threaten and persecute these campesinos to the point that . . . they fabricated crimes and fabricated their guilt. They intended to decapitate the movement by incarcerating Rodolfo, who is one of the leaders, and to this end, they used torture and they used the army to help them."

The case would soon explode nationally and internationally, bringing Ethel Kennedy to Mexico to fight on the side of the jailed campesinos, putting the new administration of Vicente Fox in the hot seat, and garnering honors and awards for Digna and Rodolfo. This battle would shape the rest of Digna's life, place her in the sights of powerful enemies, create jealousies among colleagues, and obsess her until her death two years later.

She fought for Teodoro and Rodolfo on two fronts: in the Mexican justice system and in the court of national and international public opinion. She understood how important it was to shape the battle as an ecological, as much as a human, struggle and in the months to come, Rodolfo and Teodoro would morph into the "campesino ecologists" or simply the *ecologistas* of future renown.

Two strong international movements—human rights and the environment—came together to support the prisoners.

This was a public relations coup, created in no small part by Digna's political astuteness. No case had caught the public's attention like this since Chico Mendes fought for the Amazon rubber tappers in the 1980s, paying with his life. Of course, Digna was lucky in the serendipitous timing of her interview with Kerry Kennedy in Mexico City in 1999, as PRO was working on the case. However, Digna made the most of her opportunity. She talked about Rodolfo and Teodoro every chance she got, in Washington, New York, and L.A., at the Kennedy Center and the

Beverly Wilshire Hotel. In winning Amnesty's Enduring Spirit Award in Los Angeles, Digna told her audience that people classified by the Mexican government as "criminal delinquents" were "being recognized by the U.S. foundations as leaders of genuine environmental movements and by Amnesty itself as prisoners of conscience."[16]

In December 1999, U.S. rights activist Laurie Freeman, who was then on a year's posting with PRO in Mexico City, accompanied Digna to Washington, where she spoke about Mexico's environmental defenders at a series of events for Amnesty International USA.

"She was amazing. I was impressed by her passion," she told me in an interview after Digna's murder. "She was a very smart lawyer. She was my first exposure to the criminal justice system in Mexico. She was very confident and the clarity with which she saw issues and could articulate them was unique."[17]

* * *

The army had a huge presence in Guerrero, estimated at up to forty-five thousand troops, although no official statistics are available.[18] Militarization had been increasing in Mexico since the early nineties, in response to the Zapatista uprising in Chiapas and isolated strikes by the EPR and ERPI (the People's Revolutionary Army and the People's Insurgent Revolutionary Army) in Guerrero and elsewhere. Always the justification for human rights abuses both in Guerrero and other states had been counter-insurgency and the need to crack down on rebels who threaten the republic.

The rebels had been convenient. If Subcomandante Marcos hadn't existed in Chiapas, so one theory went in Mexico, the Ernesto Zedillo government would have had to invent him. There was a persistent rumor in Mexico that the "Black Hand" of the shadowy Interior Ministry was behind Marcos and the

Zapatista uprising, and that it was the ultimate "black ops" tactic, orchestrated by government agents. The 1994 Zapatista uprising, disorganized and quickly suppressed, was the excuse for the army to send seventy thousand troops to Chiapas and never leave. Ramsay Clark, former U.S. attorney general, author, and social activist, had accused the Mexican Army of carrying out "a great occupation against its own people in Chiapas."[19]

Chiapas is one of the richest states in Mexico in terms of oil reserves, minerals, forests, and water, with one-third of the country's oil and 70 percent of its hydroelectric potential. It's on the border with Guatemala and a long-range plan for private sector development—championed by President Fox and called the Plan Puebla-Panama—called for a superhighway, bridges, ports, airports, and factories. The private sector needed the army in Chiapas in order to securely develop these resources.

Part of the conspiracy theory was the relative ease with which foreign journalists got through army roadblocks to interview Marcos during the shooting war, instead of being kept out. As well, the Zapatistas were a lightning rod for anger over indigenous rights, which otherwise might have moved like a brush fire across the republic. Instead, the issue had turned into a decade-long set of futile negotiations with the government, essentially going nowhere.

The same allegation was made against the EPR, which made its first appearance in Guerrero on June 28, 1996, at a memorial service on the first anniversary of the Aguas Blancas massacre. The federal government responded with a massive military deployment in Guerrero, unseen since the guerrilla uprising of the 1970s. People pointed to such clues of "black ops" as neatly pressed trousers found on dead rebels. However, distinguished author and historian Carlos Montemayor, for one, said that such notions were ridiculous and part of the fevered imagination of a country that loved to feed off rumors and spin conspiracy theories. He turned the theory upon itself, calling it a method of pretending that there were no rebellions in Mexico. Others had suggested that the government would have been foolish to try to keep journalists out of Chiapas, inviting even more accounts of repression.

* * *

The claim that the soldiers were on drug patrol in Pizotla that May morning in 1998 of the Montiel/Cabrera arrests was intrinsic to the military's version of events. After all, the war on drugs was the ostensible reason they were in Guerrero, above and beyond the guerrilla threat, which was covered off nicely with the military's added claim that Rodolfo and Teodoro had illegal weapons and Teodoro was a Zapatista/EPR warrior.

The government of Ernesto Zedillo gave the Mexican Army sweeping powers over civilians in a series of laws passed in 1995 and 1996. These laws were necessary, argued the government, in order to effectively fight the war against narco-traffickers.[20] Interior Secretary Francisco Labastida, who would later lose his bid for the presidency to Fox, authorized the army to participate in civilian police operations to an unprecedented degree, giving soldiers the right of arrest and detention of prisoners for ninety-six hours without charges (not that they weren't doing it already). The 40th Battalion had every right under the law to arrest villagers in Pizotla and to charge them with narcotics and weapons crimes, which were under federal jurisdiction.

Rights defenders were dismayed. They denounced Zedillo's new measures, warning that democratic reforms were being eroded by illegitimate laws and civic rights jeopardized as never before in Mexico. They said the army was being given omnipotence, turning civil institutions, including the presidency and federal and state attorneys general, into subordinates of the military. A new dynamic was being created in which the federal government handled external affairs and negotiated treaties, such as free trade, and the army was free to run the country. In many regions, the army effectively was the law, usually in conjunction with local *caciques*.

A trend began to put military officers in key civilian positions in the federal and state offices of the attorney general, culminating in 2000 with Vicente Fox's unprecedented choice of General Rafael Macedo de la Concha as the nation's chief lawmaker. It was a blow to the human rights community, which took it as a sign that, despite his lofty promises, nothing fundamentally would change in Mexico under Fox. People who had high hopes for his presidency were stunned by the move.

No president had ever interfered with the Mexican Army, or questioned its budget, but Fox was supposed to be different. Putting a general in charge of the law, however, seemed a clear message that there would be no serious judicial examination of security forces accused of abusing civilians, which, indeed, turned out to be the case, as a litany of rights abuses would attest in years to come. In the aftermath of Digna's murder, Mexico City attorney José Lavanderos pointed to the appointment of Macedo de la Concha as proof that Fox "doesn't have real power . . . [and] that he has ceded control of the attorney general's office to the army."[21] Under these circumstances, he had little hope that the murder of his friend and colleague would be investigated properly.

Fox failed to regain power from the military, according to his critics. "Now it is extremely difficult for the new administration to cut back these powers to the extent that there are very clear signs that, in reality, President Fox is not the supreme chief of the armed forces," human rights lawyer Mario Patrón, from PRO, would conclude in 2002, two years into the Fox presidency.

* * *

Pepe Reveles was not surprised by Fox's choice of Macedo de la Concha as attorney general. The seasoned journalist from *El Financiero* already had formed the opinion that Fox would not stand up to the army or the network of spies at the Interior

Ministry. He had the opportunity to ask Fox about the army's powers under the Labastida laws and was taken aback at the answer. The moment came one evening in November 2000, when a select group of journalists, Pepe among them, was invited to dine with Fox and Martha Sahagún (who was then press secretary) in the capital. Pepe described his dinner with Fox:

"Everybody started talking about the economy. You know, that was around the time people were thinking we wouldn't grow by 7 percent, or even 5 percent, as had been predicted. Now they were predicting 4.5 to 5 percent for 2001, and maybe even less. So everybody was talking about that, and Fox brought up the huge social security debt and how difficult it was going to be for his government to pay people's pensions. . . .

"And I spoke up. I said, 'Excuse me, I would like to ask a question that has nothing to do with what we are talking about, but I have other concerns. . . . You're going to assume power on the first of December, in less than two weeks' time, and you're going to have to govern within a framework [of army control] set up over the past few years by Francisco Labastida. These laws are unconstitutional, not to mention that you have all this domestic spying that is being run straight out of Bucareli [the Interior Secretariat],'" Pepe recalled telling Fox.

And then he posed a question to the president-elect.

"You will inherit all this in less than two weeks' time and so, I ask you, 'How are you going to handle it?'"

He said Fox stared at him and, without missing a beat and without the slightest hint of irony, replied: "Well, we'll keep the good and get rid of the bad."

It was all Pepe Reveles could do not to burst out laughing. Did Fox really think it would be as easy as that? Pepe believed that he did.

* * *

Digna was destined to clash with General Macedo de la Concha.

His role in the army (and, arguably, later as attorney general) was to protect his troops, and hers was to fight to prosecute soldiers accused of crimes against civilians. He became her nemesis in refusing to allow charges of torture in the Montiel/Cabrera case, verified by the country's own National Human Rights Commission, to be tried in a civilian court.

Macedo de la Concha was an elegant man, with impeccable tailoring, slicked back hair, and a striking resemblance to Paulie Walnuts on *The Sopranos*. He was the personification of military brio. The army was his life and his career was stellar. He attended both Mexico's Military College and the National Autonomous University of Mexico, where he earned his law degree. He was director of the military bank, Banjército, represented Mexico on arms and drug smuggling issues before the U.S. State Department, and, as a military prosecutor, rose to the position of First Magistrate of the Supreme Military Tribunal. He was in charge of the very system of military justice that Digna was trying to crack open, in Guerrero and elsewhere.

Rights lawyers argued that soldiers charged with torture and other crimes involving civilians should not be protected by *fuero militar*, or military justice. They pointed out that the Mexican Constitution says clearly that "if an offense affecting the military involves a civilian, the relevant civilian authority shall try the case."[22]

But that didn't happen in practice. While the military expanded its powers over civilians, the reverse did not occur. Civilian powers failed to enforce the state's constitutional rights over the military, and usually didn't even try.

Abuses by the military skyrocketed after the laws of the mid-1990s. Evidence contained in innumerable rights reports showed that, rather than focusing on narco-traffickers and real guerrillas, the army used its powers to target peasant organizations that threatened local economic interests, grassroots activists, and leftist politicians and organizers. The military cracked down in

Guerrero after the narrow February 1999 election of Governor Rene Juárez Cisneros over his PRD opponent, which was marred by allegations of vote-buying,[23] led to calls for an annulment of the vote.

In August 1996, Interior Ministry sources leaked a "black list" to the Mexican media,[24] evidence of a smear campaign against campesino organizations, including groups in Guerrero. There were close to three thousand people on the list and retribution for their social activism was swift, with arrests across the country and the deportation of foreign priests, nuns, and aid workers,[25] mostly from Chiapas, Guerrero, and Oaxaca. There were more forced disappearances and more incidents of torture. State governments looked the other way and judges routinely accepted evidence obtained through torture, a practice that continues unabated in Mexico, despite widespread calls for judicial reform.

One case in the files of the PRO Human Rights Center summed up the horror: a man recounted the escape of another prisoner being held in an adjoining room in a military torture chamber in Guerrero. The prisoner managed to get himself to a local hospital for treatment but military officials had him discharged and brought back to be tortured again. The man testifies to human rights workers that he heard the torturers boasting about how easy it had been for them to retrieve the prisoner "thanks to the power of the government."[26]

State authorities also like to blame atrocities on family feuds. Gonzalo Pastor, 29, a member of the Organization of Peasant Ecologists of the Southern Sierra (which lost 17 members at Aguas Blancas), was hacked to death in front of his family on Good Friday, 1996, by machete-wielding paramilitaries. When I later interviewed Sergio Pérez, a senior attorney in the state's Attorney General Offices about the case, he described the Pastor family, including eighty-six-year-old patriarch, Isidro, as "lazy, dirty animals who have been killing themselves for generations. That's how they do things here."

Digna was in the thick of it in Guerrero. "According to our statistics, Guerrero has been one of the states where human rights violations have been endemic," she told *La Jornada* in the fall of 1999.[27] The situation in Guerrero had gone from bad to worse.

"The Mexican Army continues to invade communities, illegally breaking into people's houses and robbing community members of what little they own. Some community leaders have been incarcerated, while others have simply been executed," she said, adding that soldiers have been "untouchable with regards to the law, and have acted with complete impunity, not only in Guerrero, but in other states."

Digna, coming from a poor Indian family, understood the impotence of barefoot villagers facing soldiers in tanks and Humvees. Her criticism, however, always involved individual soldiers accused of crimes or the army as an institution. She didn't attack the common grunt, who was usually from the lower classes, uneducated, and paid a miserable soldier's wage. Two of Digna's brothers were soldiers (although both left the army in disgust after her murder).

"The Mexican Army has taken over the functions of the police and public security forces although, according to the Constitution of Mexico, this is not their role to assume," she told *La Jornada*. "According to the Constitution, the army is responsible for national security, while the attorney general of the republic and the state police force are in charge of drug trafficking."

Time after time, said Digna, "those responsible [for crimes] are clearly identified as members of the Mexican Army and yet the attorney general of the republic hasn't looked into the accusations made against them. . . . Instead, he has declared the accusers incompetent and sent the cases to the military justice apparatus."

She gave an extensive interview to *La Jornada*. She attacked the power of local *caciques* and their hired *pistoleros*, arguing that "these groups also operate with impunity." She said there was no reason the soldiers accused of torturing Rodolfo and Teodoro should have been turned over to military justice under Macedo de la Concha.

"If the Mexican Army personnel are responsible for the systematic violation of human rights," she asked, "then how are they going to properly investigate themselves in regard to these cases?"[28]

* * *

Much later, in June 2002, I met with journalist Maribel Gutiérrez, in the cramped offices of *El Sur*, two blocks from the sea in the beach city of Acapulco, on Guerrero's Pacific coast. This city was the center of culture shock in Mexico for a foreigner. I often used Acapulco as a base for covering stories in Guerrero. The day would begin with a drive past Señor Frog's and Planet Hollywood, and by noon I would be interviewing peasants who lived in misery and repression. It was not uncommon to learn that someone I'd interviewed one week was in jail or dead the next, gunned down by soldiers or police. I interviewed people who, like the villagers of the Huasteca, walked days for a chance to tell their stories. They felt their only hope was the international media.

It seemed appropriate to pay special attention to Acapulco because it is such a tourist mecca. Every winter, sun-starved foreigners climb down from jumbo jets, blinking in the bright light and ready for their few days on the beach. Digna understood that. She told me once that she wasn't asking Canadians to give up trips to Mexico when it's -22 degrees Fahrenheit with the wind chill in the middle of winter, but rather to be aware of what's occurring and make their objections known to their government.

After the leftist PRD took the Acapulco municipal elections on October 3, 1999, the security crackdown entered a gruesome phase. That year, the San Francisco–based human rights group Global Exchange documented repression by soldiers and death squads that included, among many documented examples, an attack on a newly elected PRD city councilor, his wife and son by men with AK-47s. The boy was killed and the councilor was severely injured. The attack came as the family was on its way to a victory party in Acapulco. Although he later reported he could identify the shooters as PRI militiamen, Guerrero authorities refused to investigate, instead using the information as a pretext for arresting other PRD members and seeking to extract confessions through torture.

It was this world of impunity that Digna Ochoa was trying to change.

"If you examine every case of Digna's, be it Aguas Blancas, whatever, there is one constant—the army, the army, the army," Maribel Gutiérrez told me during our interview in Acapulco. "I remember when she took on the defense of the ecologists Rodolfo and Teodoro. She was very strong and she firmly accused the soldiers of torture. Now, look, all attorneys present the evidence when their clients have been tortured, but if the person under arrest is freed, if the case comes to a happy conclusion, they almost never insist on punishment for the torturers. No, they don't, I can tell you. They always stay on the surface of the problem; they are committed to defending their clients but they don't go after those who, through torture, which is a felony, made their clients confess to things they didn't do.

"Digna was different. She insisted very much on punishment for the torturers of Rodolfo Montiel and Teodoro Cabrera. She did the same thing when she took on the case of Barrio Nuevo San José, in the municipality of Tlacoachistlahuacan, she followed up and insisted on punishment for the soldiers who killed two campesinos and raped two women."[29]

Maribel said Digna didn't give up when those responsible for Barrio Nuevo San José or Aguas Blancas were not held accountable. She kept fighting.

It's wasn't the first time I'd heard about how Digna was different.

Maribel was a tiny, middle-aged woman, with the grace and tightly pulled-back bun of a ballerina. She was one of Mexico's most highly respected and admired journalists. She was also generous with information and she'd helped me on several occasions, as she had others. A political and social sciences graduate, she gave up a comfortable life in Mexico City to come to Guerrero with a few friends in 1992 to start up a newspaper, and not one that would gloss over killings and present Guerrero as a tourist paradise. Young, idealistic journalists were eager to work with her. "We thought that, in Guerrero, many things were happening and they were not being reported well," she said. *El Sur* and its handful of journalists had endured threats, political attempts to shut the paper down, and many brushes with bankruptcy in order to keep its voice alive. She had documented ties between the local *caciques* and the army.

"There's a pattern in Guerrero," she told me. "The *caciques* have the protection of the army for illicit operations, like drugs and illegal timber cutting, and, in turn, they become allies with the army to persecute supposedly armed groups. Everything gets more complicated when the army is involved. When the politics of counterinsurrection are involved, it's no longer just the fight between rich *caciques* and poor people; or the fight between the drug dealers who want to dominate and control the whole territory against the campesinos, who don't want to be under the thumb of the narcos; or the fight between the few who are getting rich from the woods versus the many who are affected by the logging and are fighting to protect the forests.

"No, the presence of the army complicates everything. The conflict isn't local anymore. It has become an issue of national security. . . . Those who denounce the *caciques* become part of armed groups to be persecuted, jailed, tortured, and sometimes killed."

She knew there were armed groups in the mountains. But in order to survive, she said, these rebels needed the support of the local population. Villagers repeatedly told her that they didn't need the army. They needed roads, hospitals, potable water, schools, support for their products, and a future for their children to end the despair. "If they got all those things, I think the armed groups would vanish."[30]

Maribel was another person who would resonate in Digna's life, and in the investigation into her murder.

* * *

While the military's legal clout over civilians was institutionalized under Zedillo, it would be misleading to suggest that the army hasn't always been a potent force in Mexico. There's even a saying that there are three untouchables: the president, the Virgin of Guadalupe, and the army. The strength of the military was particularly evident in Guerrero, where the crimes of the Dirty War reached savage proportions.

Hot and steamy Guerrero on the Pacific coast was one of the most woefully poor states in Mexico and, not surprisingly, had a history of revolutionary movements and insurrection. Pancho Villa took Guerrero during the Mexican Revolution almost a century ago, and it was the setting for Carlos Montemayor's classic *War in Paradise*,[31] a fictional account of the true exploits of rebel leader Lucio Cabañas in the early 1970s. He was a schoolteacher turned guerrilla, who captured the imagination of the country, a Mexican Che who led the army and intelligence forces on a merry chase through the mountains, pulling off audacious stunts and winning hearts and minds across Mexico. In 1974, Cabañas and his men kidnapped Guerrero governor Rubén Figueroa Figueroa (father of the intellectual author of the Aguas Blancas massacre and a scoundrel in his own right), and held him for one hundred days. But, in a moment when his captors left him unattended, Figueroa simply ran away. On December 2, 1974, soldiers shot and killed Cabañas. His rebel ranks had been infiltrated by moles.

The army took revenge for the uprising on poor villagers. Soldiers went up into the mountains, arresting entire communities and torturing and killing men and women alike. Accounts of abuses were documented by, among others, the National Human Rights Commission.

Journalist Pepe Reveles had tape recordings, made by a sociologist friend from the National Autonomous University of Mexico, of interviews in the mountains during the military sweeps of the Dirty War years. The statements of the people were horrifying. The men told how soldiers smeared honey over their bodies and buried them in ant hills. Women were tied by their legs and hung upside down to bake in the sun. In the village of Ajuchitlán, a woman testified that soldiers stripped her naked before they hung her by her feet and began to beat her. She was pregnant and they left her hanging there, taunting her and threatening to kill her.

"What struck me listening to those tapes is that I heard a man saying, 'My name is Teodoro Cabrera.' It was him, but when he was twenty-five years old. The tape is from March fourth, 1978, and the army is still up there today," said Pepe Reveles.

Listening to the tapes, these faint and quavering voices from the past, provided a singular framework within which to understand Guerrero. Villagers told of soldiers coming to the community of Llano Grande and rounding everyone up and taking them to the school. One woman said she was making lunch when the soldiers arrived. She rushed to the school with her tortillas in her hand and, when she arrived, she got a fright.

"I thought they were going to shoot us. They were everywhere with their guns. And they made us all line up outside and I was really frightened and then they dragged my husband over there to one side with my two sons. . . . They made the women line up in another place, each woman with her children. They kept us there in the sun. They told us we were going to be there all day in the sun, without food or water, and the children began crying with hunger and thirst and I had not even eaten and the man threatened to hit us in the face with the stick he was carrying."

She said the soldiers laughed when they beat the women. They herded the villagers into the school for the night and, when they left in the morning, they took her son and hanged him.

"So what you have now in Guerrero is simply a different stage of the same repression," said Pepe Reveles. "Now we have a sort of 'Dirty War Light.' But it is not that light at all. That was clear to me when I heard the voice of Teodoro Cabrera on the tape from twenty-five years ago, and thought about what is occurring now."

* * *

It's worth an aside to offer some flavor of the other world into which Digna stumbled in Guerrero, and that is the murky scene of drug lords and their ties to, among other authority figures, the military. Narco-trafficking is a constant in the state and it cannot be discounted that military repression against peasant organizations going all the way back to the 1960s and 1970s stems, at least in part, from the desire to protect the business of drugs as much as any other endeavor. It has been well documented in Mexico how the drug mafia has paid millions of dollars in protection money to military commanders including, in one embarrassing case, the very man appointed national antinarcotics chief by Ernesto Zedillo.[32] The state, whose drug trafficking is believed to be controlled by the Tijuana cartel, is a major transit point for drugs en route from South America, mainly Colombia, to Canada and the United States, as well as a significant marijuana and poppy producer in its own right. According to intelligence reports of the U.S. Drug Enforcement Agency (DEA), Guerrero is also becoming a growing source of street-ready heroin, processed in laboratories hidden throughout the state.[33]

There was no more infamous name in recent military history than Mario Acosta Chaparro, who was in charge of the military's operations in Guerrero during the Dirty War years, rose through the ranks to become a general, and went on to work with the state judicial police in the time of Governor Rubén Figueroa Alcocer. An investigation into his links to the drug world began in 1997 and, in 2003, a military tribunal convicted him of having ties to the Juárez cartel and sentenced him (along with another general) to fifteen years in prison.

Acosta Chaparro dealt with the underworld through the former head of the Juárez cartel, Amado "Lord of the Skies" Carrillo, who included the federal antinarcotics chief among his *amigos* in the military. Carrillo died in suspicious circumstances in 1997 in a private clinic in Mexico City after eight hours of plastic surgery for a nose job, face-lift, eye lift, chin implant, and liposuction to his stomach, sides, and chest.[34] His nickname came from the fleet of sleek 727s he used to transport his cocaine. He lived flamboyantly, widely recognized through photographs in glossy magazines, either at home with his family or with assorted beauties, and romanticized in *ranchero* songs that portrayed him as a modern Robin Hood. Apparently he was a religious man and was renowned for his contributions to the church, as well as to local charities. But he became too well known. It was believed he wanted a new face and body in order to go underground (another theory said he was merely vain) and that, while under anesthetic, he was betrayed by rivals who had arranged for a drug overdose. The burned corpse of one of the plastic surgeons who worked on him was later found in a barrel in the desert outside Ciudad Juárez, across the Río Grande from El Paso. When Carillo died, mourners left bouquets of flowers outside the gates of his mother's hacienda in the Pacific state of Sinaloa.

Acosta Chaparro was convicted because of his ties to Carrillo, a rare conviction by the military that, at face value, should be lauded. However, rights activists said that the military treated him with kid gloves and continued to urge authorities to bring him to justice in a civilian court for his alleged involvement in atrocities in Guerrero. He was also a member of the feared DFS—the Federal Security Directorate—which was the forerunner to the spy agency CISEN.[35] "In the DFS, he obtained so much information that he could be dangerous," said Pepe Reveles. "The DFS became associated with the narcos. Actually, they became the biggest *capos* of all the narco-traffickers." (Carillo's predecessor in the Juárez cartel died in a plane crash with a DFS commander.) He added: "I think Acosta Chaparro was jailed because of a settling of accounts in the military."

Acosta Chaparro was also tried by a military tribunal on charges of complicity in the deaths of twenty-two peasant activists in Guerrero, but was acquitted in 2003, leading to claims that the trial was a masquerade. The bodies of the Dirty War dead were often dumped out of airplanes over the Pacific Ocean, mimicking the actions of South American generals who pioneered the disposal technique. It's believed that hundreds of murdered campesinos met a similar fate during the Dirty War in the *vuelos de muerte* (death flights) over the ocean. Acosta Chaparro, who received extensive military training in the United States, including at the School of the Americas, also was implicated in the Aguas Blancas massacre in 1995, when he was a senior police adviser to the Rubén Figueroa Alcocer government.

During Acosta Chaparro's trial on complicity charges, relatives of Mexicans who disappeared in Guerrero carried signs that read: "Where are *Los Desaparecidos*?" Enrique González Ruíz, from one such group,[36] told the magazine *Vértigo* in 2005: "The Armed Forces were involved in the creation of clandestine chambers of horror and torture, in the kidnappings [of] people they considered to be subversive [and] in disappearances and extra-judicial killings. . . . The army does not have the capacity to have a complete and impartial trial. It consistently denies the responsibility of its senior officers in such crimes."[37]

* * *

In the summer of 1999 in Guerrero, Digna relished a court appearance on the Montiel/Cabrera case. The two men were facing the possibility of long prison terms on federal arms and weapons charges, and this particular hearing, literally called a face-to-face (*careo constitucional*), was her chance to question soldiers she was publicly accusing of torture. They were witnesses for the prosecution's case against her clients and, while they weren't on trial and she had to respect strict parameters (and a judge who kept telling her she was being tricky), it was a rare opportunity for a human rights lawyer to go up against soldiers in a civilian court.

Digna broke legal ground in Iguala that day. Its importance cannot be underestimated in Mexican human rights law. She interrogated soldiers in a judicial hearing. I asked many lawyers about this event and, if there was a precedent in Mexico, nobody could cite it. She pushed the soldiers as far as she could, the only time anyone from the Miguel Agustín Pro Juárez Human Rights Center would have a chance to do so in the Montiel/Cabrera case. It was the most critical legal hearing, a point I emphasize because of its later relevance in the investigation into Digna's murder.

Most likely Digna turned up half an hour early, as was her custom, at the Iguala courthouse on the afternoon of August 25, to appear before Judge José Martínez Guzmán, who presided over the hearing. Afterward, she was jubilant. She boasted to her friends that she had shredded the testimony of the two soldiers, Artemio Nazario Carballo and Calixto Rodríguez Salmerón, from the 40th Infantry Battalion, and left them sputtering.[38]

(Several friends remembered her descriptions of the day in court. She was cocky, there's no question. It's not the last time we would get a glimpse of this prideful, even foolhardy, dimension to Digna's personality. Next time, though, the stakes would be higher.)

Reading the testimony from Iguala, one can imagine her in court, soft-spoken and polite with each soldier, making her way meticulously through the long list of questions, which obviously were chosen with a great deal of forethought. They had months to prepare their stories. Still, under questioning, they couldn't get the basic facts straight. The two soldiers differed on where they captured Teodoro and Rodolfo, where they took them, how long they held them, how they questioned them, what they did to them, and why they delayed four days before handing them over to civilian authorities.

Rodolfo and Teodoro identified the soldiers and gave their versions of events.

"On Monday night, this man in front of me,"' Rodolfo began, pointing to Nazario Carballo, "shone a torch in my face and asked me where my [rebel] *compañeros* were. And he said, 'These hands will make you talk,' and he pulled at my privates.

"This is the man who beat up my wife, Ubalda Cortés Santana, and I heard him say to the other soldiers that he shot Salomé, and then he laughed and said, 'Now I have scored three. . . .'"[39]

Later, under Digna's questioning, Nazario Carballo managed to contradict himself in a single answer.

Q: Would the witness tell us what he did with Mr. Teodoro Cabrera when he was seized by the soldiers?

A: Disarmed him, arrested him, interrogated him, and then handed him over to my superior. Nothing more. Furthermore, I want to make it clear that there was no interrogation. Then, we transferred him to a secure place.

Digna allotted several questions to her clients' confessions about being guerrillas.

Q: Would the witness tell us when Mr. Teodoro Cabrera admitted he belonged to the Zapatista Army of National Liberation, as you mentioned in your statement?

A: They mentioned it themselves in conversation after they were detained.

Q: Would the witness tell us who else was present when the prisoners admitted they were with the Zapatista army?

A: The commander in charge of the base, Colonel José Arciniega Gómez, and myself and others who were near.

Later, she questioned the second soldier, Rodríguez Salmerón.

Q: Would the witness tell us when did Mr. Rodolfo Montiel admit that he was a member of the Zapatista army?

A: I don't remember the time but he told me that this gentleman whose name I don't remember [pointing at Teodoro] had a training field in the vicinity of Pizotla—he told us this after he was seized.

Q: Would the witness tell us who else was present when Teodoro Cabrera expressed what you have told us in your last answer?

A: He told me personally. There was him and me and no one else.

Q: Would the witness tell us when Teodoro Cabrera told him this—during interrogation or under some other circumstance?

A: It wasn't an interrogation—it was a chat and it came out that he belonged to the EZLN.

Q: Would the witness tell us where Mr. Rodolfo Montiel was at the moment you were chatting with Mr. Teodoro Cabrera?

A: At the location where we were detaining them so that they wouldn't escape. The two prisoners were in the same place and this conversation just came up.

Digna must have been amused. It's absurd to think that two villagers, run down and seized by soldiers, would simply begin chatting about being guerrillas.

Digna was dogged, raising objections on numerous occasions. For example, she wanted a previous statement amended, in which Rodolfo said he recognized his signature on a document he was forced to sign.

"I ask the court to certify that my client was behind a metallic grille, which prevented him from having a direct, clear sight of the document in which he recognized his signature, and that my client has vision problems and therefore would have problems clearly recognizing the statement put in front of him."

The judge didn't give Digna what she wanted.

Instead, the court certified: "The defendant, Rodolfo Montiel Flores, was behind a metallic grille—painted black, measuring two meters by one meter, with each opening in the grille measuring six centimeters by ten centimeters—when the documents were held against the grille, as close as possible, so that the defendant was fifteen centimeters from the documents and the signature in the document was in full view. . . . Furthermore, the area was illuminated by artificial lighting—two lights in the interior of the cell and four lights over the grille and four outside the cell."

Digna also objected when Rodolfo was questioned about a .45-caliber pistol supposedly found in his possession.

"I request that the question presented by the prosecution be dismissed because my client, in the amplification of his statement, says, on page 313, that he didn't know who gave him the pistol or the marijuana because they had his face covered."

The judge refused.

In her summation, she addressed the court:

"I request that the judge, in view of the torture suffered on the part of my clients at the hands of the army when they were seized—and based on Articles 3, 4, 5, 7, 8, 9, and 11 of the Federal Law to Prevent and Punish Torture, and in relation to Article 22 of our Constitution, and the guarantees made in Article 3, Sections I and II of Article 5 and Article 25 of the American Convention on Human Rights; I make the request of this honorable court, in accordance with Article 20 of the Constitution and Articles 88 and 89 of the Penal Code and Articles 3, 8, and 25 of the American Convention on Human Rights—[allow] that my clients, Rodolfo

Montiel Flores and Teodoro Cabrera García, be present in all the proceedings related to this case."

Digna had done what she set out to do. Not only did she enter the allegations of army torture into the official Mexican judicial record, she did so with each legal proclamation against torture landing like a slap against military impunity. It was a major achievement.

The judge granted her request. This, too, was important because Mexican legal proceedings were in camera.

The case dragged into 2000, while the judge continued to hear evidence. On May 6, a Mexican doctor, appointed by the court, found no signs of torture. However, Danish doctors from the international group Physicians for Human Rights examined Teodoro and Rodolfo and determined that they did bear marks "consistent with the allegations of the time and methods of torture suffered." They concluded that the two had been tortured.

In July, Mexico's National Human Rights Commission ruled that soldiers of the 40th Infantry Battalion committed human rights violations, including not handing Teodoro and Rodolfo over to civilian authorities. The commission requested further documentation from the army in relation to the allegations of torture and, when it was not forthcoming, made the legal presumption that the soldiers were guilty of torture.

They presumably faced military justice. It's hard to know since proceedings were secret. In the fall of 2001, however, it was determined by the military prosecutor that they had done nothing wrong and that charges were unnecessary.

On August 28, 2000, federal court judge Maclovio Murillo Chávez found the prisoners guilty, sentencing Rodolfo to six years and eight months and Teodoro to ten years, on drugs and weapons charges. He told an investigator from the New York–based Human Rights Watch that the army was given "the presumption of good faith" when accounts differed about what happened.[40]

"Despite serious contradictions in the self-incriminating

statements by the defendants, their confessions were given greater weight," noted Human Rights Watch in its examination of the case published shortly after Digna's murder.

"We dedicate this report to the memory of Digna Ochoa, a courageous lawyer who devoted her life to defending the victims of human rights abuses in Mexico," said Human Rights Watch. "Digna never shied away from taking on the most sensitive cases—including several of those documented in this report—even in the face of repeated harassment and threats against her life. When asked last April if she was afraid she might be killed, she responded, 'I knew from the outset that this line of work involved risks.' Asked if she ever considered quitting, she said no."

* * *

Rodolfo Montiel and Teodoro Cabrera learned of Digna's murder from the state penitentiary in Iguala. By this time, they were famous, particularly Rodolfo, one of the original protestors who began the roadblocks against Boise Cascade logging trucks in the Petatlán mountains in 1998. He was an Amnesty International prisoner of conscience and, in 2000, the recipient of the prestigious Goldman Environmental Prize, awarded by the San Francisco–based group of the same name.[41]

"Ever since I was a child, I asked God to give me leave to grow up and be a defender of the forests. If the forests care for us and give me life, then why shouldn't I give mine for them? And if the wild animals are my comrades and friends, why shouldn't I give my life for them and for all humanity, because today, there are many children like I was."

The Goldman prize carried a $125,000 purse—a lot of money anywhere, but a king's ransom in Mexico—but he couldn't leave prison to claim it. Not surprisingly, the story made a splash and Rodolfo found himself doing telephone interviews from prison.

In April 2000, the *New York Times* asked for a comment from Los Pinos on this Mexican who'd won such an acclaimed U.S. prize.

Press attaché David Nájera said that, lamentably, President Ernesto Zedillo hadn't been aware of the details of the Montiel/ Cabrera case. "But it worries us and we will focus on it now," he promised the newspaper.[42]

Nevertheless, it was a few months later, in August, that Judge Murillo delivered his guilty verdict and sentenced the two men to lengthy prison sentences.

Their supporters continued to fight for their release. Former Soviet president Mikhail Gorbachev and Ethel Kennedy wrote to President Fox soon after he took office in December 2000. Kennedy had clout. The widow of U.S. presidential candidate Bobby Kennedy (and Kerry's mother), she headed the Robert F. Kennedy Memorial Foundation, which focused on international cases of torture, illegal imprisonment, and murder.[43]

In February 2001, she visited Mexico to appeal personally to Fox. She journeyed to the penitentiary in Iguala, where she presented Rodolfo with the Sierra Club's Chico Mendes Environmental Award. Mrs. Kennedy was photographed with Rodolfo, reaching her hand through the bars to touch his face.

Still, nothing changed. The two remained behind bars.

And then, on October 19, 2001, Digna was assassinated and international anger rapidly coalesced into the battle over the peasant ecologists. On November 2, the Goldman Environmental Association turned up the heat with an ad in the *New York Times,* an open letter to Fox urging him to free them. Congress was gearing up for hearings on the murder of Digna Ochoa and the plight of other activists in Mexico, and reports of new death threats against rights defenders surfaced in the Mexican press.

The tension was palpable. Fox had to do something to relieve the pressure.

On November 8, 2001, less than three weeks after Digna's murder, the president ordered the release of Rodolfo Montiel and Teodoro Cabrera, after thirty months in jail. Fox said he had exercised his "legal authority" to act on humanitarian grounds.

The convictions stood, however.

From Misántla, Digna's family issued a statement of solidarity with the campesinos. Her father, Eusebio Ochoa, said he regretted that his daughter paid for their freedom with her life. He said Fox was trying to divert attention from the stalled murder investigation, adding that he wanted to see Digna's killers brought to justice.

Rodolfo Montiel and Teodoro Cabrera would never return to Guerrero. It was no longer safe for them there. Interior Secretary Santiago Creel promised that his government would ensure their protection in an undisclosed location in Mexico. Rodolfo would accept speaking engagements in the United States, his views taking on a new sophistication and global scope, as he reflected on the state of the planet beyond his mountains.

"I invite everybody to share the water we have to drink and the food produced by the earth. Let us look at it as if it were ours, not to destroy, but to build. Let us become aware, because it is for the good of our children, your grandchildren, and all the generations," he said, in other comments posted by Goldman.

"Since we are only passing through, at least we can leave them some pure air to breathe. This is the respectful wish of your friend."

Mexico City authorities, investigating Digna's murder, interviewed Rodolfo and Teodoro in Mexico City after their release and, in the weeks ahead, traveled to Petatlán to talk to witnesses about Digna's last trip into the mountains. Soon, these authorities would have trouble of their own with the Mexican Army.

Fox was hailed for his decision by Amnesty International USA, the Sierra Club, and other international organizations. Ethel Kennedy offered her praise.

"President Fox has made a courageous and just decision and I am happy beyond words," she told a reporter from the *Boston Globe*. "That Digna Ochoa . . . had to lose her life in order to let them resume theirs will forever be a blot on Mexico's history."

CHAPTER TEN

"Which One Is Digna?"

General José Francisco Gallardo was up early on Saturday, October 19, 2001, doing a little writing in his cell at El Bordo prison in Nezahualcoyotl, state of Mexico, about an hour's drive from the capital. He had been in prison for eight years.

It was just after 6 A.M. when he heard the news on another inmate's radio: *Digna Ochoa was assassinated last night.* He was devastated, immediately falling ill and taking to his bed. He saw her murder as yet more proof of the untouchable power of the army in Mexico.

A few weeks later, Gallardo did a radio interview from prison, in which he urged President Fox to subordinate the power of the army and take real control of the republic. "The army must be an institution of the state, and not an independent power," he told reporters.

He was in a unique position to understand the army. Once he had been the golden boy, shooting up through the ranks, his brilliant future assured as long as he played along. Had things gone differently for General Gallardo, he might have enjoyed the same success as Mexico's other famous general, Rafael Macedo de la Concha. Gallardo attended the U.S. military college at West Point as an exchange student, a coveted prize, and, in 1988, at age forty-two, became the youngest general ever appointed in the Mexican military. That year, he represented Mexico in the Seoul Summer Olympics, placing seventh in the demanding pentathlon, which required a five-thousand-meter horserace as part of the course. He was dashing, handsome, and highly intelligent. He married Leticia Enríquez and they had three sons, Alejandro, Marco Vinicio, and José Francisco. In 1993, the year he completed thirty years of service in the armed forces, Lettie learned that she was pregnant with her fourth child and they prayed for a daughter.

That year, however, their lives abruptly changed. His army career soured when he refused to participate in a military kickback scheme in which other officers were getting rich. Instead, he went on the public record to criticize corruption, narco-trafficking, and human rights abuses within the army and began what would evolve into a campaign for the creation of a military ombudsman. He stood up to be counted against the omnipotent army with spectacular style, writing an article on military injustice for the Mexican literary magazine *Forum*.

Such action was unprecedented in Mexico. He soon found himself facing trumped-up charges, including the theft of horse feed from army supplies. Military prosecutor Macedo de la Concha—his nemesis—directed the case against him. He was convicted and sentenced to twenty-eight years in a military prison. If there was a comical side, it's humorous to imagine this decorated cavalry officer creeping around under cover of darkness, heaving bags of animal feed into the back of a pickup truck and waving his accomplices off into the night. *Andale! Andale! . . . Go! Go!*

And so, as Macedo de la Concha rose to become chief military prosecutor and then attorney-general of the republic, Gallardo languished in prison. There, however, he took university courses, earning a master's degree in political science and working toward his doctorate in public administration (which he would finish after his release). He continued writing and speaking out against the military, urging reform and garnering international attention. Amnesty International and PEN Canada recognized him as an international prisoner of conscience and organized a campaign for his release.

Soon he was receiving death threats. His actions were highly dangerous and, essentially, he was a sitting duck. Death threats even appeared in his cell.

"Careful. . . . Don't Mess with Us. . . . There's a Bomb in the Gallardo Case. What Are We Going to Do about It?"

He found a single bullet on his bunk.

One day, he was wracked by uncontrollable vomiting and realized he'd been poisoned. He was taken to the infirmary, where he recovered and convinced authorities to transfer him to another prison. The death threats continued.

Lettie was scared too. Three months before her husband went to jail, she'd given birth to their daughter, Jessica. Once, in 1994, the phone rang in their apartment (she remained in their apartment in a military compound) and a man identified himself as an American Persian Gulf vet. He said a group of U.S. veterans had a system for detecting telephone surveillance and they knew her phone was tapped. He said the group wanted to warn her and the general. Gallardo began corresponding with the man, with whom he was still in contact (and wouldn't identify). Another time, Lettie picked up the phone and a voice said: "This is Agent Fulano, Military Judicial Police. . . ." She slammed down the receiver.

When Fox took office at the end of 2000, he promised to take up Gallardo's case. It was widely accepted that he had been convicted in a show trial. Before joining Fox's cabinet as human rights ambassador, activist Marieclaire Acosta had condemned Gallardo's treatment, telling the *Washington Post*: "Every time he went to a civilian court, the charges were dropped and he was pardoned, or he was found not guilty, so it's clearly a case of persecution by the army."

But Gallardo remained in prison.

His life was in danger. On December 18, 2001, the Inter-American Human Rights Commission urged the Mexican government to adopt protective measures to "avoid irreparable damage to the life and the physical, psychological, and moral well-being of General José Francisco Gallardo Rodríguez, and also his freedom of expression related to his life." The ruling also included his wife, three sons, and eight-year-old daughter.[1]

Furthermore, the commission reported that, in conjunction with the United Nations Working Group on Arbitrary Detention, it had studied Gallardo's case and concluded that the detention was illegal because it was the result of "arbitrary military procedures" that violated due process.

Still, Fox did nothing.

After Digna's murder, however, international pressure on Fox to free Gallardo had increased, as it had for the Guerrero environmentalists. To make matters worse for Fox, the Inter-American Human Rights Court in San José, Costa Rica, was set to rule on the Gallardo case in February. The Mexican government would likely be ordered to protect Gallardo by international law, which was going to be another embarrassing blow to the Fox government.

On February 7, 2002, just over three months after Digna's death and three days before the expected San José ruling, the Fox government released Gallardo. He was not pardoned. Rather, the president (through a general directive of military justice) simply canceled the last sixteen years of his sentence—on humanitarian grounds. Gallardo was put under twenty-four-hour police protection, including agents from the Federal Preventive Police.

Fox called him *Señor* Gallardo. Salt in the wounds of a military man.

(Macedo de la Concha later told reporters that, according to military protocol, Gallardo was demoted automatically when the military sentenced him to more than two years in prison.)

"Now we can hold our heads up high and face the world and say that protection and defense of human rights are promoted in Mexico," Interior Secretary Santiago Creel boasted to reporters.[2]

For General Gallardo, the fight to clear his name was just beginning.

* * *

I interviewed General Gallardo at his apartment, in a military complex in the south end of the city, in 2002, arriving with Swedish journalist Petter Bolme. Outside his apartment building, military plainclothes officers questioned us before we entered. But they wouldn't ask for our ID until we were on our way out.

Gallardo was going through files in his study when we entered. He'd been home only a couple of weeks and, as soon as she arrived with her mother, young Jessica leapt into his arms, where she stayed for the remainder of the interview. Husband and wife sat close, smiling and frequently touching hands, as if to reassure themselves that he was really home.

He told us that he doubted he would be here if Digna hadn't been assassinated.

"Digna's death lit up red lights all over the world and there was pressure on the Mexican government," he said. "Her case is the consequence of the impunity that we live in. If the president had done something concrete to end impunity, I don't think anything would have happened to Digna. But no action was taken. We have learned that there was no investigation into the threats against her, or into her kidnappings—never—on the part of the government. And Macedo de la Concha tells the media that he couldn't investigate her kidnappings because the case was closed (before he became attorney-general). Well, I don't buy it."

Gallardo used to speak often with Digna by telephone, beginning before she went into exile in the United States. She talked about the kidnappings and the threats against her life. He agreed with her that her abductions showed all the signs of military intelligence and they compared death threats. Both were warned: *"There's a bomb. . . ."* He served as unofficial consultant on the case of the peasant ecologists, telling her that he believed she had strong evidence against the soldiers accused of torture.

"All her cases were against soldiers—all of them," he said. "Digna had the courage, the astuteness, and the expertise, because she was a good lawyer, to do what was considered to be prohibited in Mexico. She was able to make the soldiers contradict each other and the result was we could easily see that, yes, they participated in acts of torture.

"Here's what happened," said General Gallardo. "The military in Mexico is very sensitive to being put on show. She was hitting at, and I put this in quotes, 'military honor.' She accumulated all this information on the case and she plunked it down in front of the Public Ministry. The military counselors had provided information that was so stupid and so clearly rotten—their so-called proof about the prisoners being guerrillas, etc.—that it caused tremendous anger. They looked like fools and they knew it."

It was a warm February afternoon, and I was gazing out the window as I listen to Gallardo. But I quickly snapped to attention when he mentioned certain plans Digna had at the time of her death. I hadn't known about them.

On April 13, 2001, a month after her return to Mexico from exile in Washington, she visited him in prison. It was their first face-to-face meeting after many telephone chats. She told him she'd just attended the spring sessions of the Inter-American Human Rights Commission in Washington, in which the status of his case was reviewed. She had extensive contacts in Washington and assured him she planned to use them to fight for his release.

Digna had an interesting idea. She had brought with her a copy of the U.S. Leahy Law, explaining that she believed they could use it, both to advance his case and to push for greater human rights protection in Mexico. Named after Vermont senator Patrick Leahy (who spoke with such eloquence on Capitol Hill after Digna's murder) and passed by the U.S. Congress in 1997, the law linked military aid and training to human rights, making it illegal for the United States to train or equip foreign individuals or groups (units, platoons, squads, brigades, etc.) convicted of gross human rights abuses.

Gallardo already had powerful U.S. rights groups in his corner, but Digna felt that more serious pressure could be applied for his release if they were able to use the Leahy Law to tighten the screws on the Mexican military. She'd spent her career focusing on rights abuses by the military and knew he was compiling data as well. They should work together; they'd be an effective team.

They talked about how human rights groups could launch a campaign, calling on Washington to cut off all aid to the Mexican military as long as it was tarnished by human rights violations. The campaign would center on evidence of abuses by the military that had been ignored. It was a simple strategy—essentially a public relations blitz—but one that could be extremely effective. The Mexican government was sensitive to bad publicity and if the United States started to pay attention to images of army abuses in Mexico, it would be both negative and hugely embarrassing.

It was a recurring theme in Digna's work. She was savvy about how to influence public opinion outside Mexico. She told Gallardo they could make use of the Leahy Law; she promised villagers in Guerrero she would "knock on doors" and make their stories resonate. It was the same strategy.

Human rights groups already were criticizing Washington for failing to enforce the Leahy Law with Mexico, with some of the best research on the subject coming from the Washington Office on Latin America (WOLA), which tracked American military spending on Mexico. In its reports, the group said the Leahy Law was being ignored.

The problem, according to expert Laurie Freeman from WOLA, was that nobody checked to see if the money was going to units involved in rights abuses. "If you don't have a good database, you can't catch potential matches," she said. "The spirit of the law is to hold people responsible. The United States isn't doing anything to encourage the Mexican government to be accountable for its abuses. And, in Mexico, the civilians sort of roll over and let the army do what it pleases. The Leahy Law is important now and it will become more important with Washington's increasing focus on terrorism."

Digna was aware of these efforts to hold the Mexican government accountable and she felt that, by combining efforts, they could make gains on specific cases, including General Gallardo's.

Digna felt the timing was good. Military ties between the United States and Mexico had strengthened since 1995, when Washington began stressing the need for increased security and greater Mexican cooperation in the war on drugs. That year, U.S. defense secretary William Perry visited Mexico to meet with President Ernesto Zedillo and his Mexican counterpart, General Enrique Cervantes. The Zedillo government brought in new laws that year and the next to give the Mexican Army a greater role in civilian justice, using the battle against narco-traffickers as justification, and the United States stepped up military aid, training, and shared intelligence with Mexico.

Mexico would soon become the largest recipient of U.S. military funding after Colombia. From 1996 to 1997, U.S. spending on military and police personnel went from $3.8 million to $79.4 million, which was separate from weapons and equipment sales, pegged at about $260 million annually.[3] (This covered reported spending. WOLA and other organizations did not have access to information about military spending that lay within restricted budgets. As well, there were informal links. During the Zapatista uprising in 1994, for example, I often saw U.S. military types coming off commercial flights at the airport at Tuxtla Gutierrez, as did other reporters. But it was all hush-hush.)

Over the next few years, the Mexican government took pains to buff up the image of its military. Foreign reporters were offered opportunities to cover the army, under tightly controlled conditions. A report in the *Wall Street Journal* painted a glowing picture of one General José Gómez Salazar, as he oversaw drug operations in Chenalhó, Chiapas. He was portrayed as a father figure, with the concerns of the people dear to his heart.

"In the jungles below, there are guerrillas to contain, drug traffickers to catch, heroin poppies to eradicate, millions of saplings to plant to fight erosion, roads to build, and even children to deflea and delouse," said the story, which began on page 1. "Here, on the scene of the violent and short-lived 1994 Marxist-led Zapatista Indian revolt, the army's mission is more than just winning hearts and minds. . . . It is assuming an increasingly high profile in Mexican society."[4]

* * *

My own opportunity to get up close and personal with the Mexican military didn't quite work out as smoothly. In April 1995 I received an invitation from President Ernesto Zedillo's press office to fly to Chiapas on an expedition with the Mexican military for foreign reporters. I'd been to Chiapas many times, pounding over dirt roads in a battered old Combi van for days to reach remote villages and, in the early days of the Zapatista rebellion, I had interviewed rebels, including *"el sup"* Marcos, villagers, and soldiers. These were the grunt soldiers, part of long convoys snaking along mountain roads as far as the eye could see. It seemed to me the invitation was a perfect opportunity to see the rebellion through the eyes of the military high command.

We were a tight little group, a couple of Chinese reporters, a Spanish film crew, a German bureau chief, and me, whisked off on a Friday morning on an air force jet from Mexico City, en route to the Tuxtla Gutiérrez airport in Chiapas. I believe we were the third or fourth group to be taken out. Naturally, I wrote about the adventure, describing the first-class service in the air—individual printed menus, sweet rolls, a variety of egg dishes, and good coffee—and the attentiveness of our gloved military attendants. They served champagne. We were told that we could speak directly to the people and see for ourselves what was going on. We traveled by helicopter to villages where the bellies of babies were swollen from malnutrition and mothers said there was no food.

That evening, as I was about to write my story, the bell rang at the front gate. It was a courier from the presidential palace at Los Pinos, bringing me my own personalized video of my day in Chiapas—me getting off choppers, staring at waterfalls, sitting in briefings, boarding the jet—looking about as important as I could be. I still have it.

After my report ran in the *Toronto Star*[5] I received a call from a perturbed press aide demanding to know why I had written the story. He told me "everybody knows" that certain parts of the day were "off the record." I was supposed to write about how well the army was keeping the peace in Chiapas and how soldiers acted like social workers. Needless to say, it was the last time Los Pinos offered me the deluxe treatment they like to lavish on the ladies and gentlemen of the world's press. (I did, however, get to go out on a few military drug busts, but that came from working my own contacts.)

* * *

Greater ties between the U.S. and Mexican military after 1995 meant greater problems. American nongovernmental organizations quickly focused on evidence of civil rights abuses, including murder and torture, by Mexican soldiers trained in the United States, notably at the U.S. Army School of the Americas. Located at Fort Benning, Georgia, the school was alma mater to the most brutal butchers of Latin America, beginning in 1946 when it was founded (in Panama) and spanning more than five decades.[6] Special Forces (known as the GAFE for its Spanish acronym) wearing black uniforms and ski masks[7] rounded up and tortured twenty civilians, one of whom died, during a mission in Jalisco. They were on drug patrol and the incident occurred over a lost pistol.

A survivor told the Jalisco Human Rights Commission that the soldiers made the men lie on their stomachs. "They tortured us by sticking some kind of needles in our feet and they also beat us with sticks." He said they put plastic bags over their heads, as the victims screamed for mercy. The dead man, Salvador Jiménez, was found bruised and battered in a shallow grave, covered with rocks and branches. A toenail had been pulled out.[8]

Human rights defenders applauded the Mexican Army for taking three soldiers to military court and handing down long sentences.

GAFE Special Forces were particularly active in Chiapas, which was not a major drug center, where they were used extensively in counterinsurgency operations, with regular Mexican troops. Their presence signified the importance the Mexican government placed on Chiapas. It was a literal powerhouse and many see reasons, beyond the hunt for guerrillas, for the blanket presence of the army. Chiapas had huge oil and hydroelectric potential and was at the heart of Plan Puebla-Panama, which was the private-sector development touted by President Vicente Fox to industrialize the southern zone of Mexico. The plan entailed the integration of nine Mexican states with Central America, forging greater economic ties and building a new superhighway to cut through the region.

Oil was vital to the Mexican government. According to Fabio Barbosa, a Mexican energy historian and social activist, it was the main collateral for the massive U.S. bailout that saved Mexico— and U.S. institutional investors—after the peso crashed in 1994. Barbosa's research revealed that the national oil company, PEMEX, guaranteed $7 billion in annual oil exports in order to cover the loan. There had also been a major oil discovery in Ocosingo, in the heart of rebel territory. The army often told reporters that the Zapatistas were under control in Chiapas. "I believe it when the army says the Zapatistas don't pose a military threat," Barbosa told me. "Instead, the army is in Chiapas for geopolitical reasons."[9]

*   *   *

Digna had something else up her sleeve. During her prison meeting with General Gallardo that April day in 2001, they agreed to pursue the idea of using the Leahy Law. Gallardo would include references to it in his articles, and she would investigate further.

He didn't know it would be the last time he would see her. With six months to live, Digna would not have the time to take on the Mexican Army on the scale she imagined.

After her death, rights activists would continue the battle, sadly including Digna among the victims of the human rights crimes she herself had denounced.

"In Mexico, it is widely assumed that government security forces are complicit in the assassination of Digna, either directly or at least through willful ignorance. It is long past time for the Bush Administration to end military aid, sales and training for these security forces," wrote Tom Hansen in the *San Diego Union-Tribune*, shortly after Digna's murder in October 2001. He was director of the Mexico Solidarity Network, a coalition of eighty organizations fighting to end human rights abuses in Mexico.

"Last year, our State Department licensed over $240 million to military sales to Mexico, and our tax dollars funded over $16 million in outright grants and training. These programs should be terminated immediately. The Bush Administration also should press for a full investigation, and for protection of other human rights activists."

One wonders what Digna might have been able to achieve, had she lived. In Guerrero, two weeks before her death, she talked with villagers in the Petatlán mountains about the sensitivity of the Mexican government to bad public relations. She was planning to see how effective she could be.

Her loss was painfully felt by activists who continue to urge the U.S. government to enforce the terms of the Leahy Law against Mexico. In the late spring of 2002, more than six months after Digna's murder, San Francisco–based Global Exchange sent a delegation to Guerrero where they met with representatives of small human rights groups and journeyed into the mountains. In several remote Tlapanec communities, they heard the testimonies of women who said they were raped by soldiers. One woman, only seventeen, claimed she was raped by Mexican soldiers on February 16, 2002. She recounted that she was washing her clothes at the river with her baby when she was surrounded by soldiers who hit her in the chest and stomach with rifles, and, holding her by her hair, asked her questions about guerrilla activity. She passed out and when she came to, she was being raped by two soldiers. She described their military patches. Her husband walked for eight hours and took several buses to the state capital at Chilpancingo to file an official complaint with the Public Ministry but the alleged crime was never investigated.[10]

"[She] gave her personal account of the rape to the female members of the delegation. . . . She did not receive medical attention after the crime, and continues to be depressed, cannot sleep or eat and is afraid to be alone."[11]

In another community, a woman testified that soldiers from the same battalion raped her on the dirt floor of her hut on March 22, 2002, while her children ran for help. They were looking for guerrillas but she couldn't understand their questions because she couldn't speak Spanish. She went to a doctor "who claimed that because she had given birth to four children there was no way to prove she had been raped."[12]

This delegation of human rights activists met with an official in the human rights section of the U.S. embassy in Mexico City. The person was in charge of supplying information to Washington for the implementation of the Leahy Law and they chronicled the charges, including official complaints to Mexican authorities in Guerrero, in the hope there would be an investigation under the terms of the law. They were disappointed. In their report they noted: "Human rights staff are unfamiliar with the Leahy Law in its totality and are therefore unable to enforce the law to its full extent."[13]

One does wonder what Digna, with her connections, might have accomplished.

* * *

In Petatlán, Eva Alarcón had a little restaurant, Los Chiquilitos, where she served beans, tortillas, chicken, rice, and succulent pork specialties of the Pacific coast. She was secretary of the Organization of the Peasant Ecologists of the Sierra of Petatlán, and was instrumental in setting up Digna's final excursion into the mountains in October 2001. I interviewed Eva in her restaurant in February 2002, a morning memorable because a cat on the thatched roof pissed through the straw onto our table, soaking my notes, clothes, and tape recorder (mangy creature, don't pretend this was an accident), and fire broke out in Eva's grill and has to be doused. Not good omens.

She was a big woman, descended from black slaves who were brought to the west coast in the nineteenth century, and had faced her share of hardship, which she seemed more than able to handle. However, she hadn't been able to secure justice for Sergio Cabrera González, a founder of the environmental organization, who was executed by armed thugs. She was at the wedding reception where he was shot in the back on September 20, 2000, by three men with AK-47s. He'd gone to get Cokes for everybody. Eva and a dozen witnesses went immediately to the police station nearby in Petatlán to file a complaint—*una denuncia*. Police took statements, had the body removed and, by 6 A.M., Eva believed arrest warrants were being processed. But authorities did not investigate the murder, nobody was ever charged, and the paperwork mysteriously vanished.

By the summer of 2001, fallout over the timber wars was continuing for the *ecologistas*. Rodolfo Montiel and Teodoro Cabrera were in prison in Iguala, several members were in hiding, with arrest warrants against them on assorted drug and weapons charges, and several others were in an Acapulco prison. "I told the *compañeros* that this fight is going to be very hard. I feel that they are going to go after us," the group's secretary-general, Felipe Arreaga, told them at the start.[14] Still, the pressure was taking its toll.

The group held a meeting and decided to contact Digna Ochoa, who'd been the original lead lawyer on the Montiel/Cabrera case. They wanted her to defend the fugitives, as they called the men in hiding, as well as several prisoners in Acapulco. But she'd been off the case since going into exile in August 2000 and they didn't know her whereabouts, or even that she had returned to Mexico that spring. Juan Bautista, president of the *ecologista* organization, went to see Rodolfo Montiel in Iguala and returned with Digna's new telephone number in Mexico City. He asked Eva to make contact.

Eva called her in mid-September and, three days later, Digna walked through the door of her restaurant in Petatlán. Eva was not overly impressed. Too naïve, she thought. As she recalled, "She was dressed in a little blouse with a round collar, pants, and little shoes and she looked like a schoolgirl. She seemed very sweet."[15]

When Digna left, Eva asked her husband, Pedro, "What do you think about the little schoolgirl?"

"Yeah, okay, but she seems pretty young and harmless," he replied.

"Well, she's the same kid who fought for Rodolfo's case and they say she's a very capable lawyer and she defended him with conviction," replied Eva.[16]

Digna told her that she was no longer with PRO.

"She got very serious and told us it was something she wanted to make very clear that she was not part of PRO because she didn't want PRO to think she was using their prestige or name. She said she was grateful that we had called her. She didn't have a lot of work, nor did she have much money. But really, all we were asking her was to be straight with us, and not lie to us, and she asked the same from us because she wasn't sure if she could trust us," Eva recalled in an interview months after the murder.

Digna said she would see what she could do and, a week later, called to say she had "landed a fish" for their cause. She was excited because Harald Ihmig, from the Hamburg chapter of FoodFirst Information and Action Network, an international agricultural aid group, would accompany her to Guerrero. (It is axiomatic in Mexico that foreigners have clout, whether they do or not.) Soon, Digna was back in Guerrero with her "big fish."

* * *

On October 1, they set out from Petatlán, an odd little band, with Digna on the back of an all-terrain vehicle driven by Felipe Arreaga, a man in his forties with a baseball cap pulled low over his eyes. There was Eva, a few other members of the group, and, bringing up the rear, Perfecto Bautista, an *ecologista* who would film seven hours over the next two days, making a permanent record of the last voyage of Digna Ochoa's life.

Harald, a theology professor from Hamburg, looked a sight on the back of his ATV, his bony knees sticking into the air and his long hair whipped by the wind. His boots were soaked through by the first night but they'd have to remain that way for the rest of the trip. Nobody wore his shoe size between the

Pacific Ocean and, say, Guanajuato, where they started growing men like Vicente Fox. Villagers couldn't stop staring at his feet.

Bouncing along on their four-wheelers over the rough terrain, they sweated through the intense heat of the Sierra Madre. In four villages over two days, Digna promised that she would "knock on doors" to raise money and support. She said she would make their faces known in the United States.

"Sometimes, we know about an organization but we don't know about the people behind it, or the conditions of their lives. We only know about such-and-such a village, or so-and-so. Therefore, it is important that people understand how you have to work from childhood, both men and women, and that you struggle throughout your lives," she said in La Pasión. "I don't know if you realize it, but the ecological organization, with Rodolfo, is already making some big waves since Rodolfo's imprisonment. . . . There has been a great deal of support.

"But there hasn't been support for you. My intention is to try to solicit that support, to knock on all kinds of doors and get what I can. I can promise nothing, absolutely nothing, but I will knock on doors and we will see if they open for us."

That night, sleeping next to Eva in the community of Banco Nuevo, she talked about her boyfriend, Juan José Vera, a mathematics teacher in Mexico City, as she would the next night in Eva's little house in Petatlán. In the darkness, she laughed as she said that J.J. really didn't understand how complicated her life was, or the true nature of her work. He said he did, she told Eva, but how could he? He lived a middle-class life in Mexico City and had never witnessed the abuses these people understood in their bones. She said, as she did over and over on this trip, that she loved Juan José deeply.

On the second day, there was a large military presence around the community of Banco Nuevo, which villagers found strange. Usually, when outsiders came to the highlands, the soldiers evaporated. "I have been to Banco Nuevo, and when I arrived, all the soldiers left the neighborhood as soon as word got out that I was there," Maribel Gutiérrez, from *El Sur*, recounted about her visit in August 1998. On that trip, she managed to photograph soldiers who were living on *cacique* Bernardino "Nino" Bautista's property.

"I went up there with a group of peasant ecologists because there was terrible persecution against them and they had had to abandon Banco Nuevo," she said. "They wanted to kill them, hang them from trees. They accused them of attacking Bautista's house and they said they were all EPR guerrillas. But when I got up there with my camera, they all left the house and started running away."

With Digna, the soldiers were bolder. They didn't run away; in fact, they seemed to be looking for Digna.

"Which one is Digna?" one soldier asked a group of villagers, according to witnesses.[17]

Nobody knew how the military had known her name.

Eva picked up the story.

"It's in Banco Nuevo on the second day. The soldiers are all beginning to come down from the mountains, which the people find odd because they always hide when there are foreigners around. I had arrived in town before Digna, and somebody comes running to say that soldiers are going in Digna's direction. So I jump out of the hammock and run to meet her.

"She was standing with a group of soldiers. Perfecto had stopped filming, so I grabbed the camera. It was I who filmed the confrontation between Digna and the soldiers."

The soldiers moved away when they saw the camera.

The video footage showed the incident, but Eva was too far away and there was no sound. Digna could be seen talking to the soldiers and gesturing broadly, as Filiberto Gómez, mayor of Banco Nuevo, looked on. They were standing by a stream.

Later, Digna told Eva that the soldiers demanded a stag (a

male deer) and Gómez said it would be very difficult for him to procure one.

"No, no, it's not difficult; you know how to find one. Get one for us," one soldier replied, according to Digna's account.

She got angry and leapt in, telling the soldier: "How can this be possible when there is a ban on deer hunting?"[18]

(By environmental law, communities are allowed to hunt one stag every six months, as well as one male iguana and other listed animals. Several bird species are completely banned.[19])

All afternoon, there were soldiers around. They circled the village in their tanks, while Digna did her interviews. Everyone was tense.

Later, Digna was sitting on the grass in front of the church, interviewing three people: Felipe Arreaga; Aurora Gómez, whose husband, Sergio Cabrera González, had been shot in the back by gunmen with AK-47s; and Sergio's stepbrother, Roberto Cabrera Torres, a fugitive with an arrest warrant against him. He became very nervous when soldiers showed up, afraid they were looking for him. Apparently they weren't.

Digna interviewed Aurora, who was in her thirties, with a worn face and thick hair that kept falling into her eyes. She asked about what happened to her husband and how she was surviving on her own. He was thirty-two when he was killed, leaving Aurora with four children, the oldest only eleven. She told Digna that everyone knew that the gunmen worked for Faustino Rodríguez, a local *cacique*. (Another brother, Jesús, was murdered, allegedly by *cacique* gunmen, in October 1998.[20])

At that moment, soldiers passed by in their jeeps. Digna leapt up, rushed over with her notebook, and began writing down the details of their convoy. The others eyed each other nervously.

She came back, sat down and picked up the interview with Aurora.

"*Bueno*, Aurora, did you denounce this crime of homicide to the authorities in Petatlán?"

"Yes, right away, but they never did anything."

Digna was in full legal mode. It was clear that this interview would be part of a future case.

"Am I to understand that you appealed to the Public Ministry to punish the guilty? Am I to understand that nothing was undertaken in this regard and there was never an investigation?"

"Yes, that is true," said Aurora, telling Digna that all the paperwork vanished. There is no record of anyone having made denunciations before the authorities. Included in the lost testimony were eyewitness accounts of the three gunmen.

"Do you want me to follow up in order to try to punish those responsible for the death of your husband?" asked Digna.

"Yes, I do," said Aurora.

Digna nodded, and continued.

"Tell me, for you, a woman of the countryside with four children to support, what has the death of your husband meant? How difficult is it for you to provide for your children?"

"We have nothing," said Aurora.

Digna asked if the widows of the community, Aurora among them, had ever had any help from the state.

She shook her head.

Harald also questioned her about her life. "I feel only sadness," she said. "It's just me and my children. I feel totally alone."

Digna turned to Roberto Cabrera Torres. He told her that he was on the run and unable to plant or harvest or support his family. He broke down sobbing and couldn't continue.

Felipe Arreaga began his story, explaining that he was born in Petatlán in 1949, and had been fighting to save the forests for most of his life, although the peasants didn't form an official organization until 1996. After free trade, the forests began to fall more rapidly. He said the peasants had always been persecuted in Guerrero, and remembered what it was like when he was young in the savage times of Governor Rubén Figueroa Figueroa. His mother and sister were killed by the death squads.

Digna asked him detailed questions about the Petatlán peasant ecologists' organization. He said that things got really bad for its members after journalist Maribel Gutiérrez, from *El Sur,* began to write about them in 1998. Everybody said, "Be careful, *Don* Bernardino is getting angry. But I never did anything to anybody in my life and my life's work is to save the woods and the water, so I kept fighting."

He had little formal education, but he was articulate and calm. He was also brave. He told Digna that it was important for their situation to be known beyond the mountains, and that he would help her in any way he could. He wouldn't pay the price for his involvement until well after Digna was dead.

Digna said she hadn't realized the extent to which the violence of the Sierra de Petatlán affected so many other *ecologistas,* telling them they had given her a good understanding of how things worked.

"It is very clear to me that you are affecting the interests of the *caciques* and, above all, the state. That's why you are being persecuted and why they are surrounding people, rounding them up, and killing them. I have no doubt that's it," she said.

"Now that I know how it works here, we will knock on doors. We know there are very powerful interests involved here, right up to the federal government—the state and municipal governments, all of them together. You are at the head of this movement, and I can see that despite having been imprisoned you are maintaining a strong spirit of survival. You are overcoming your obstacles."

When Harald mentioned that Digna would be working as a lawyer on their behalf, Felipe chuckled. "Yes," he said, "it is always hard to get lawyers to work on our behalf."

He was referring to PRO. The human rights center had been involved in some of these cases while Digna was in exile, but support was limited. Mario Patrón, from PRO, would later explain to me that it was a question of money and priorities for the center. Whatever happened, it was clear that the peasant ecologists felt abandoned by PRO. There were rumors that Mario was angry when he heard that Digna was going into the mountains in October 2001. Campesino leader Juan Bautista told several people that when he told Mario about Digna's plans, he snapped: "What's that old hag doing sticking her nose into our business?"

I was surprised at this, and later asked Mario. He said he didn't make the statement to Juan Bautista and that he always supported Digna. "If it had been my intention to impede [Digna's] access to Rodolfo and Teodoro, I could have done it," he said, "because if the defending lawyer says this person can't have access, they can't have access." Digna met with Rodolfo and Teodoro in jail before her trip to the mountains.

But when Petter Bolme and I interviewed Juan Bautista and his wife, Dionisia Wenses, in Petatlán, I asked him too about the "hag" comment. He looked surprised. His mouth falls open and he sputtered but no words come out. Meanwhile, his wife said yes, it was true.

It may seem to be an insignificant point—a discrepancy of how someone at PRO reacted to Digna's return to Guerrero—but I found it intriguing and would return to it.

Eva said that, beginning with her first trip to Petatlán, Digna asked many questions about whether the group was tied to the EPR or other rebels. It was what the government said, and the *caciques*. They assured her they weren't, and that they didn't grow marijuana. (There was no doubt that peasant farmers grew marijuana and poppy crops extensively in Guerrero, as elsewhere in Mexico. Sometimes it was the only cash crop and, from military drug helicopters, I have often looked down at fields of marijuana green as far as the eye could see. But everyone I spoke to about the peasants' organization swore to me that its members, and at the very least the core group, eschewed drugs and guns. They were devout Catholics and regarded narco-trafficking as a sin. Instead, the *caciques* were linked to drug production, even by the authorities themselves, as this account will show.)

"We told Digna that we weren't guerrillas, nor did we participate in kidnappings. On the contrary, the *ecologistas* didn't allow that kind of thing to go on in their zones, and if they heard of anything occurring, like a kidnapping, they were the first to denounce it," Eva told me.[21] "They didn't allow their members to plant marijuana, they were always going to Mass and saying the rosary, and, as Catholics, their consciences told them that drugs were wrong."

Before she left, Digna told Eva that she would be in touch. She was carrying documents pertaining to the fugitives and Acapulco prisoners, including a letter from the wife and daughter of one prisoner, Pilar Martínez Pérez, in which they attested that he was tortured by soldiers. She told Eva that she planned to investigate this case further, with the aim of taking it before the Inter-American Human Rights Commission in Washington.[22] And so, two weeks before her murder, Digna was up to her ears in the dark affairs of the remotest no-man's-land in the country. As José Reveles, from *El Financiero*, explained to me after her death, by taking on such sensitive cases, even talking to Eva about taking them to the Inter-American Human Rights Commission in Washington, Digna would become an enemy of the *caciques*, "and therefore an enemy of the military."

* * *

Digna and Harald met in Mexico City a week later to review the footage and make plans to release the video of their trip to show conditions in the Sierra Madre. Harald had to leave the capital for the southwestern state of Oaxaca and they agreed to meet again upon his return. On Monday, October 22, 2001, he got a lift out of the Mixtec village of Tlaxiaco and the driver told him: "This weekend, they killed Digna Ochoa."

Harald went white. The man didn't know that Harald knew Digna. "Look, take heart, *compañero*, that's the reality of how we live here. But the fight goes on."

Four years after Digna's murder, Harald couldn't read her e-mails without tearing up. Her last note said: "Have a wonderful weekend; a big, big hug."

* * *

Mexico City detectives followed the trail of Digna's murder to Guerrero, sending a team in December 2001, and again in January 2002. They were working with a scenario of how she died, apparently at the hands of professionals. It looked like the police believed these hit men could have originated in Guerrero.

On January 4, 2002, a second investigative team ruled it was a homicide and filed a report, a follow-up to the work of detectives on the scene the night of her murder. This second report, which also remained confidential (and which I wouldn't read until July 2003), was signed by detectives Manuel Laureles Pichardo, Jaime Álvarez Hernández, and Fidel Colín Beltrán. Behind the scenes, Renato Sales Heredia, a senior official in the offices of the Mexico City attorney general, had taken over the case from prosecutor Nicolás Chávez and its focus has shifted dramatically—but that wouldn't be known to the public for another two months.

Team No. 2 laid out its investigation, drawing a series of conclusions:

They began by saying that Digna was murdered between 12:30 and 12:40 P.M., Friday, October 19, 2001. The time of death was based on the testimony of the watchful upstairs neighbor, Modesta Aguilera Mejía, as well as the thanatological evidence of the body. There was some lividity, consistent with the position in which Digna's body was found, and the beginnings of rigor mortis, which, as Mexico City coroner Dr. Fernández had explained, sets in completely after about fifteen hours in Mexico City.

Digna's killers had studied her. (The report used "killer" and "killers" interchangeably.) They knew her daily routine, knew her customs, and had intimate knowledge of how she lived her life, both professionally and personally. The police figured this out because anonymous death threats were left *inside* her offices at the PRO human rights center, showing familiarity with the scene, and, in the last weeks of her life, threats turned up at her new address in the south end of the capital city. The psychological and physical damage she suffered as a human rights defender also were known to the killers. The report did not indicate whether this last conclusion was based on phone taps, conversations with friends and colleagues, or the presence of a mole close to Digna.

Her murder was calculated in advance by a group of people who carefully worked out the logistics. "We can state this fact categorically," said the police report, without revealing more.

In order for the crime to be pulled off, it had to have an intellectual author. Again, there can be little doubt that Team No. 2 knew more than they revealed in this written report. At the time of writing, they were following up leads in Guerrero.

Moments before Digna's murder, *Señora* Aguilera observed the "man of corpulence" (the fat man again), whose skin color she described as darker than the victim's (Digna had medium-brown skin), stopped outside Digna's offices. She saw him go inside. "We can attest with a high degree of probability that said individual was the same person who deprived Digna of her life."

There was no sign of a physical struggle between the killer and the victim, such as furniture thrown around, books strewn, tearing of clothes, or bruises on the face or head. That led police to believe that the killer was a person who was well aware of the tactics of submission and had absolutely no problem in overcoming his victim with stealth, rapidity, and efficiency. The killer easily overwhelmed her, physically and psychologically, and therefore had to be a person with a certain capacity for, and experience with, executing people.

So her killer was a professional—a hit man. Looking down at his friend's body on the first night, Digna's friend Dr. de León reached the same conclusion.

257

The crime scene was chosen because it met certain prerequisites of the killers. There was easy access from the street; in fact, all you had to do was lift the bar on the outside of the front gate. In contrast, Digna's apartment would have been a poor choice. At that hour, there would have been too many witnesses around. The time of day would have been carefully selected.

Another reason to carry out the crime in Colonia Roma was that the site offered many options for escape. Frontera Street, where there wasn't much traffic to delay a fast getaway, was only 130 feet to the east. Zacatecas Street also led directly into the major thoroughfare of Cuauhtemoc Street, where north-south traffic moved quickly (for Mexico City). The location, with so much traffic from these major streets, was the perfect place to cover the noise of a murder, and the killers must have counted on that.

Digna's apartment in Lomas de Platero would have presented problems. There were no offices on the ground floor in Digna's building, which consisted of twenty apartments over the five floors. One needed a key to get in and the door, operating on a motorized lock, closed quickly. The killers would have risked being seen by people inside, or having a neighbor pull the fire alarm. The access door to Digna's apartment had two security locks, a password, and a peephole.

The killer counted on easy access to Digna's office, being able to go through the main gates and climbing the outdoor spiral staircase. He could have been waiting outside and slipped in quickly past Digna (who might have gone out) or even had his own keys to the offices. The Police didn't elaborate on this tantalizing theory.

At around 12:30 P.M., *Señora* Aguilera heard the door open and close once and figured that Pilar Noriega had entered the office. She looked down and saw the fat man.

Between 12:35 and 12:40 P.M., she heard two loud sounds. She thought somebody was hammering. She didn't hear another

1. Digna's grin belies her aching body during her last trip into the Guerrero mountains shortly before her murder. *Ecologista* Felipe Arriaga drives the all-terrain vehicle.   **HARALD IHMIG**

2. Digna smiles at her boyfriend, Juan José Vera, on the beach at Acapulco in April 2001. She holds the black bag that was found at the crime scene.
   JUAN JOSÉ VERA

3. Digna celebrates a birthday at her parents' home in Misántla, Veracruz. It was one of her favorite photos (believed to be taken on her 36th birthday) and she gave it to Juan José.   **COURTESY OF JUAN JOSÉ VERA**

4. Digna and Juan José relax on holiday in Texas during their only summer together.   **COURTESY OF JUAN JOSÉ VERA**

5. Digna's body lies slumped over a couch in the law offices at 31-A Zacatecas Street in Mexico City, October 19, 2001. The caption reads "Location and Final Position." Her hands are under the couch. Toronto police inspector Gary Ellis cites the arc of powder on her buttock as a sign that she may have held the gun behind her back.

6. Digna's body was found wearing big red rubber gloves. Under the suicide theory, she shot herself twice—once in the thigh and once in the head—while wearing these gloves, switching the gun from one hand to the other.

7. One of the shells at the crime scene was flattened, presumably stepped on

8. Digna's headband was found just inside the door of the office where she died, leading the first two homicide teams to conclude it slipped off during the struggle with her killer(s).

9. There are two pails by the toilet in the Zacatecas Street office, a red plastic bucket and a small metal one behind. Digna may have used the red bucket for cleaning.

ALL PHOTOS ON THIS PAGE RELEASED BY MEXICO CITY PROSECUTOR'S OFFICE, JULY 2003

UBICACIÓN Y
POSICIÓN FINALES

5

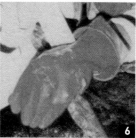

6

CASQUILLOS LOCALIZADOS EN
EL LUGAR DE LOS HECHOS

DEFORMADO

7

8

23

9

10. Digna's parents, Eusebio Ochoa and Irene Plácido, in their Misántla home four months after their daughter's death.
11. Digna's boyfriend, Juan José Vera, a few months after Digna's death.
12. Prosecutor Renato Sales defends the suicide theory during our first interview in his office in Mexico City in March 2002.

ALL PHOTOS ON THIS PAGE BY LINDA DIEBEL

13. Mexico City coroner Dr. José Ramón Fernández Cáceres says Digna's autopsy took one hour.
14. Digna's friend and colleague Bárbara Zamora had plans to visit prisoners with Digna on the day after her murder.
15. General José Francisco Gallardo, his arm around his wife, Leticia, in his Mexico City apartment a few days after his release from prison. He was an Amnesty International prisoner of conscience.   **ALL PHOTOS ON THIS PAGE BY LINDA DIEBEL**

16. Digna's friend Dr. Jorge Arturo de León pronounced Digna dead at the scene.
17. Lawyer Víctor Brenes overheard a PRO official saying Digna had committed suicide.
18. Denise Gilman, a Washington human rights lawyer and Digna's friend, is still angry at the way Digna was treated by her colleagues at the PRO centre.

16, 17 AND 18 BY LINDA DIEBEL

19. Carmen Herrera and Edgar Cortez, from PRO, failed to defend Digna at their press conference in Mexico City. **COURTESY OF MILENIO DIARIO, MEXICO CITY**

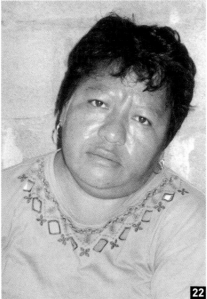

20. Sister Brigitte from the Dominicans of the Incarnate Word in Mexico City has good memories of Digna.
21. Former Jesuit priest Enrique Flota doubted Digna's account of her kidnappings in 1999.
22. Eva Alarcón helped arrange Digna's trip into the Guerrero mountains.

23. Guerrero journalist Maribel Gutiérrez wrote that hit men from Guerrero were hired to kill Digna.

24. International prisoners of conscience Teodoro Cabrera and Rodolfo Montiel, shown here in jail in Iguala, were freed by presidential decree one month after Digna's murder.

25. President Vicente Fox lost the support of national and international human rights communities over the death of Digna Ochoa.

26. Human Rights ambassador Marieclaire Acosta defended her government's push to take away Digna's bodyguards.   **ALL PHOTOS ON THIS PAGE BY LINDA DIEBEL**

27. Digna's family—(left to right) her father, Eusebio, and brothers Ignacio and Jesús—walks away from the cemetery in Misántla. PHOTO BY LINDA DIEBEL
28. Martin Sheen hugs Digna after presenting her with Amnesty International's Enduring Spirit Award at the Beverly Wilshire Hotel in Los Angeles in September 2000.   LUCY NICHOLSON/AFP/GETTY IMAGES
29. Celebrants at Pilar Noriega's birthday party, September 2001: (left to right) Juan José, Digna, Pilar, an unidentified guest and José Lavanderos.
        COURTESY OF JUAN JOSÉ VERA

sound. Police corroborated her testimony by performing sound tests with the same gun, which (apparently) was found to be in working order, and the two shots could be heard around the perimeter of the building. However, a third shot fired into the couch, with the barrel pressed against the cushion, wasn't heard.

The killer fired the first shots to intimidate Digna and the last to kill her. It was highly likely that the gun found at the scene was the same gun Digna showed to her brother. Ismael Ochoa Plácido, an army sergeant at the time of her death, described it to police and drew a picture. The detectives believed that she brought it to work in her bag. They didn't offer conjecture on why the killers would have used Digna's gun.

After the murder, the killer strewed starch around the office, put the red latex gloves on the hands of the deceased, and placed the black overcoat in her arms. Detectives had no doubt that he used the starch to mess up the crime scene in order to remove any clues to his identity.

He arrived at Digna's office with the gloves, the starch, and the death threat folded up. He was, they have no doubt, well acquainted with police procedure and methods, including finger-printing and handwriting analysis. There were no usable finger-prints; the death threat was a computer printout.

Robbery was never a motive. Digna's earrings, watch, money, and identification were found at the scene.

* * *

On January 15, 2002, a small team of about ten detectives from the Mexico City Prosecutor's Office arrived in Petatlán to investigate leads in Guerrero. They drove off on a sunny morning in a white Suburban van, and were flagged down in the main plaza by about fifty soldiers, their weapons raised and cocked. They were surrounded.

Eva Alarcón was watching, along with a crowd that had gathered to witness the commotion. "The police were all standing in the street with their cell phones, calling, calling, calling, and surrounded by soldiers who had blocked off the street and enclosed them," she said. "We were laughing, I have to tell you. Holy cow, you should have seen them, they were there for about three hours. They were practically in tears. I mean, they were pissing their pants they were so scared, standing out there in the sun."

The soldiers eventually took the police officers to their headquarters, located just off the highway, where they were held for some time longer. There was apparently a dispute over identification and their authority to carry guns in the state of Guerrero.

It was sorted out in the end. However, it did not bode well for an independent police investigation in Guerrero.

CHAPTER ELEVEN

Suicide?

In March, the jacaranda tree is in joyous purple bloom in my front garden in Coyoacán. I love spring in the capital, especially here in the south, in one of the city's oldest neighborhoods. Coyoacán is Mexico City's Latin Quarter, known for its artists, filmmakers, writers, and intellectuals. I rented my house on Alberto Zamora Street from Estéban García Brosseau, whose late father, Fernando García Ponce, was one of Mexico's most renowned modern artists. I worked in his old studio, a place full of energy and ideas. Next door lived Estéban's uncle, the celebrated writer Juan García Ponce. I'd never met him, but I'd heard often enough how grumpy and frustrated he was with this Canadian neighbor who, long starved for year-round greenery, refused to prune the jacaranda and ivy. Hummingbirds made their nests in the tangled thickness of the ivy, which delighted me, but the shade was choking the magnolia tree outside his bedroom window.

Up the street was the estate of *Señora* Figueroa, widow of cinematographer and muralist Gabriel Figueroa. He was a giant of postwar cinema, credited with creating a Mexican look in movies and influencing a generation of filmmakers. His friends included artists Diego Rivera and David Alfaro Siqueiros, actor Dolores del Río, and Spanish director Luis Buñuel, with whom he made seven films.[1] *La Señora*, now frail, was a kind woman, or at least that was the word among the street's maids and gardeners, who really knew what was going on.

In the spring, the outdoor cafés around Coyoacán's main square are filled with couples holding hands and old men in berets and woolen vests smoking Gitanes and arguing politics. Balloon and cotton candy sellers mingle with the crowds in the square, where venders set up booths every weekend to sell handicrafts, silver jewelry, leather goods, and T-shirts with images of Che, Marcos, and Jesus Christ, to Mexicans and foreigners alike. I was cocky on the weekends when I strolled through the crowds, knowing the tourists would be gone by Monday morning. They came to visit but I was *home*.

The weather was gorgeous, sunny and warm, frozen in these few perfect weeks before the rush of summer heat and the rainy season. The terrible smog, locked over the city all winter, had lifted and the city glistened. Soon, the whole country would slow to a halt for *Semana Santa* celebrations, the Holy Week rituals preceding Good Friday and Easter. The city's mood was contagious and I, too, was beginning to feel lighthearted. I believed my research into the murder case was almost over and I could begin to write about Digna's life and legacy. I hoped to put the importance of her work in the context of modern Mexico and lay out forces with a motive for murder.

I was about to see how wrong I was, and that my work was just beginning. I had no inkling on a morning full of promise how well I would come to appreciate the weight that Digna lived with every day—the suspicion, the paranoia, the listening on the phone lines, and privacy lost. It would happen to me on a much smaller scale, a trifle compared to what Digna Ochoa experienced, but enough to make me understand on a deeper level what life must have been like for her. By the time I left Mexico for good that summer, somebody would have broken into my office and the people who had been helping me with Digna's story would be nervous and afraid. We, too, would be engulfed in the dark stain that spread over her case.

It began on March 12, a warm spring morning. I picked up the newspapers pushed under my front gate and my jaw dropped at the headline in Mexico City's highest-circulation daily, *Reforma*.

"Aportan en caso Digna indicios sobre suicidio" (Evidence indicates suicide in Digna's case)

Suicide??!!

The report by Francisco Rodríguez was long and detailed, with a front-page diagram of the offices at 31-A Zacatecas Street and a sketched reenactment of Digna's death in three panels, like a cartoon strip. A woman in a skirt and high heels, hair nicely coiffed, held a gun and fired into her thigh, then knelt, holding the gun to her head and firing again. In the last frame, she was slumped over, dead. The gun blasts were illustrated with big comic book stars. Blam! Pow! Pow!

Quoting anonymous sources in the Mexico City Prosecutor's Office, the report said the suicide hypothesis was reinforced by new evidence uncovered during the investigation. This so-called new evidence included the particular characteristics of the gun, the trajectory of the bullets, and the small space in which Digna died. Police reports, backed by photographs of the crime scene, apparently suggested it would have been difficult for two or more people to have struggled in such a tight space without leaving evidence.

Instead, everything was essentially intact, said these sources, with no signs that Digna had had to defend herself. "That could signify that the lawyer offered no resistance, something that contradicts her character, considering that she was strong and experienced," said *Reforma*. It was a sick twist that Digna's own strong character was being used against her. These anonymous sources had informed the newspaper's correspondent that Digna Ochoa was an "aggressive person" who would have fought back against any assailant. And yet, without marks on her body to indicate resistance, the assumption was obvious: She must have killed herself.

Furthermore, police had learned that Digna apparently died in the clothes she'd worn the day before, based on descriptions from clients who'd met with her in her office on October 18. Investigators had concluded that she never left the building. Again, there was an inference to be drawn: Digna must have spent the night making preparations for her self-inflicted death.

Mexico City attorney general Bernardo Bátiz has previously said that there were three lines of inquiry into her death: Digna's work as a human rights lawyer, notably her last visit to the state of Guerrero; her love life; and her friends and family. Now a fourth hypothesis has been laid out in the pages of *Reforma,* the country's largest newspaper with its sister papers in Monterrey and Guadalajara.

Vanessa Bauche always knew this would happen. Many months later, the famed Mexican actor would reveal that a chilling thought crossed her mind the moment she heard Digna was dead. "They are going to say she committed suicide," she told journalist S. Lynne Walker, of Copley News Service.[2] *Señorita* Bauche, the lovely star of the Oscar-nominated *Amores Perros,* would play Digna in a documentary about her life by film director Felipe Cazals, which would make its debut at the 2004 Berlin Film Festival. Its title, *Digna: Hasta el último aliento,* plays on the meaning of Digna's name and can be translated: *"With Dignity: To the Last Breath."*

Of course, she knew. Vanessa Bauche had lived her life in Mexico. "There are many Dignas in our country," she told Walker. "She believed in justice and she believed in the Constitution. This faith, this innocent faith, is what took her to her death."

I, on the other hand, was stunned. I had been working on Digna's story for three months by then, and yet I didn't see it coming. I felt like I had been stopped dead in my tracks.

Digna was shot twice, in the left thigh and left temple. "She would have been sitting in one of the couches in the reception area and used her right hand to fire into her left thigh, looking for the femoral artery," said *Reforma.*

"Five minutes later, on her knees and biting into the overcoat that she was holding in her right hand, she shot herself in the left temple with her left hand."

That seems a bit strange since she was right-handed, but I read on. There were bloodstains where she was sitting and a bullet in the couch. There were more bloodstains on the floor where she apparently kneeled, gun in hand. The autopsy revealed that the second shot, the mortal bullet that remain lodged in her skull, was fired at point-blank range, which, as *Reforma* pointed out, was characteristic of what happens when a person kills herself with a gun. The force of the shot propelled her body forward into the other couch, which sat about three feet away.

But how could this suicide theory be possible, since police had twice ruled homicide in the death of Digna Ochoa? The story seemed to anticipate public skepticism. Sources had revealed a twist to *Reforma*. Investigators always worked with the homicide theory because there were no powder burns on the red rubber gloves pulled over Digna's hands, or on the exposed skin of her wrists and arms. Such traces would have indicated she fired the gun.

However, police ballistic testing had shown that this particular weapon—a semiautomatic .22-caliber pistol, made in Czechoslovakia and a collector's item—didn't leave powder burns on either rubber gloves or skin during repeated firings. Ballistics experts vouched for this theory, according to the report, which further informed readers that literature on the subject said many factors affect whether a gun leaves residue, from the type of gun involved to whether it was fired in a closed or open space.

Reforma also revealed that Digna Ochoa was killed with her own gun, a critical piece of evidence.

There was more, a tantalizing clue that was dropped into the story like a grenade. It said that investigators ordered a psychological profile of Digna Ochoa "in order to search for signs of suicidal behavior." There was no information about the report, other than the fact that it was compiled from interviews and video clips of Digna herself.

For the first time, it seemed that Digna herself was on trial.

It was obvious that journalist Francisco Rodríguez had good contacts within the Mexico City Prosecutor's Office. An accompanying chronology, titled "Sudden Death," listed the work they did as prosecutors came to discard the homicide theory. Many details of the case were revealed for the first time, exclusive to the newspaper.

To date, the leads appeared to point to Digna's work in Guerrero, particularly her work in the Montiel/Cabrera case and aggressive pursuit of soldiers on charges of torture. The Guerrero theory was nicely helped along by Attorney General Bátiz himself, who bluntly said that Digna was interfering with "huge investments" in Guerrero. *Reforma* therefore took pains to reveal that police questioned the soldiers accused of torturing the peasant ecologists and were satisfied that the Guerrero lead was a dead end.

Huh?

Police also questioned Rodolfo and Teodoro, who apparently testified that Digna Ochoa helped them only on the occasion she questioned the soldiers.

The point appeared to be that Digna wasn't important enough, or doing anything dangerous enough, to justify getting herself killed over Guerrero.

The story dutifully repeats the November 13 vow by Bátiz that every lead was being investigated. And very thoroughly, too, it would appear.

Furthermore, *Reforma* made mention of the fact that, on February 22, a special team, appointed by the Inter-American Human Rights Commission and headed by former Notre Dame law professor Pedro Díaz, arrived in Mexico City to investigate Digna's death. They stayed a week, relying on the cooperation of the Mexico City Prosecutor's Office. Then, on Thursday, March 7, lead prosecutor Renato Sales, who had taken over the case in December, testified before a special hearing into Digna's death at commission headquarters in Washington.

No secrets. The evidence appeared to be open to international scrutiny.

* * *

I am still reeling from the morning's news when I arrived at noon at the downtown offices of Mexico City lawyer Enrique Flota. His was an important interview, my link to his friend and colleague Renato Sales, who was in charge of Digna's case at the Prosecutor's Office. Sales had been ignoring my requests for an interview for weeks, and my hope in setting up the interview was that Flota could arrange it for me. He had powerful connections within the López Obrador government in Mexico City. He was a former Jesuit priest who left the order in 1995 to take on human rights cases, and eventually to serve as chief adviser to Rosario Robles, the first female mayor of Mexico City. She had taken over from her boss, Cuauhtémoc Cárdenas, when he resigned to accept the PRD nomination to run in the 2000 federal elections and lost to Vicente Fox.

Flota was an impressive man. He knew Digna, and as he talked about her, dates slipped easily off his tongue. He spoke about Digna's eight years with the Dominican nuns, telling me she joined the order on August 15, 1991, took her first vows on July 25, 1993, and renewed them on July 25, 1996. Sometimes he reeled off a date and said, "If I am not mistaken," but that seemed to be a formality. He either had a spectacular memory or had prepped fastidiously for this interview.

He was a sturdy man, not tall, but imposing, with a round face, large silver-rimmed glasses, and a neatly trimmed white beard and moustache. The top three buttons of his shirt were open, showing gold chains on his chest.

He had met Digna Ochoa in 1988, when both were involved in relief work for homeless victims of the 1985 Mexico City earthquake. She was only twenty-four, having just arrived in the capital from Jalapa, and glimpses of her youth from her friends were enchanting. She worked hard and took her work seriously. But she had fun too. She wore miniskirts and smoked cigarettes and loved the excitement of the city.[3]

Flota played an important role in her life, and those of several of her colleagues, because he coordinated their work on the 1995 case of the "presumed Zapatistas." Digna and Víctor Brenes, both lawyers with the Miguel Agustín Pro Juárez Human Rights Center, joined the team, along with Pilar Noriega, José Lavanderos, and Lamberto González Ruíz.

It was not surprising that these individuals—Pilar, Víctor, Lamberto, José, and Enrique—all rushed to 31-A Zacatecas Street on the evening of October 19. They were close to Digna, their bonds forged in this famous, groundbreaking case that made headlines in Mexico. It seems worthwhile to step back a moment from this interview with Enrique Flota to tell the story of the "presumed Zapatistas." It set legal precedent in Mexico and affected how Digna would practice law for the rest of her life.

The case arose from a military crackdown in early 1995, intended to capture Subcomandante Marcos (by then identified by authorities as former university philosophy professor Rafael Sebastién Guillen Vicente) and stamp out support for the Zapatista Army of National Liberation. On February 8, 1995, soldiers and state police launched an offensive in several regions, arresting union leaders, teachers, human rights workers, students, and farmers and charging them with terrorism, sedition, conspiracy, and other crimes. Marcos, of course, eluded them.

These army operations flew in the face of peace talks, which had begun the previous June, between the Zapatistas and the national government. President Ernesto Zedillo, who had taken office in December, went on television the day after army operations started in Chiapas to announce that arrest warrants had been issued for members of the top Zapatista command. They were linked by new evidence, said the president, to a multitude of serious federal crimes. Among those on the president's list were Marcos and architect Fernando Yáñez Muñoz, the alleged Comandante Germán. Human rights organizations were outraged, arguing that the arrest warrants contravened peace negotiations with the government. Many Mexicans believed that Zedillo bowed to pressure from an army that was trying to sabotage peace negotiations and put the neophyte president in his place for trying to broker peace with rebels. Later that spring, Zedillo signed a formal peace agreement, passed by the Mexican Congress, called the Law for Dialogue, Reconciliation, Peace, and Dignity in Chiapas. The agreement was just the beginning of the quest for autonomy and self-determination for the indigenous peoples of Chiapas, a process that was soon stymied by government inaction.

For Flota and PRO, the case of the "presumed Zapatistas" began slowly and snowballed. People were swept up all over the country, until there was a total of twenty-two political prisoners, in Chiapas, Veracruz, the State of Mexico and the Federal District. José Lavanderos knew one of the accused, Jorge Santiago, an adviser to the Diocese of San Cristóbal de las Casas in Chiapas. Santiago was sharing a cell in the notorious Cerro Hueco state prison in the Chiapas state capital of Tuxtla Gutierrez with Javier Elorriaga Bedegué, a video producer and journalist who had made a documentary about the Zapatistas. Elorriaga also needed a lawyer, both for himself and for his wife, Elisa Benevides, imprisoned in Mexico City and alleged to be another legendary Zapatista, Comandante Elisa.[4] Elorriaga later told La Jornada journalist Blanche Petrich that, in 1994, he'd served as a peace emissary delivering communiqués between Marcos and the office of then president-elect Zedillo. That, presumably, was why he was arrested.[5]

Víctor Brenes, now with the Mexico City Human Rights Commission, said that the case changed his life, as he believed it did the lives of the other lawyers involved, including Digna's. "It was something novel for us as well as for the government. The government was very surprised by what we did. It was the first time that a group of lawyers working in different areas got together with a human rights organization . . . and we took on the defense of all the alleged Zapatistas," he said. "It was a moment in which we could really use our training to advance the field of human rights law in Mexico."

They had prisoners in different states, little money, and a mountain of documents to analyze. José Lavanderos took the Chiapas cases, Digna and Víctor took those in Veracruz, and Pilar defended Elisa Benevides in Mexico City. Several of the accused in Cacalomacán in the State of Mexico, which surrounds the Federal District, appeared to have been beaten so badly in prison that Víctor and Digna began the process of bringing the case to the Inter-American Human Rights Commission on behalf of the PRO Human Rights Center. The prisoners said that "plastic bags were placed over their heads and they were forced to listen to a radio played continuously at high volume during their detention."[6]

Late at night, these young lawyers had serious discussions about the implications of this work and how it would impact on their lives and the lives of their families. It was dangerous, but they were not deterred. Digna, certainly, was well aware of what could happen to human rights defenders: she had been kidnapped and raped in Veracruz, and had named state police officers as her aggressors.

They had access to the files of all the accused, from Chiapas, Veracruz, the State of Mexico, and the Federal District. They developed a legal style that Víctor believed influenced Digna's work. "We analyzed each file, not just from the judicial perspective, but also in the distinct political context in the country. We immediately saw that there was a national theme to these cases, and that we were in the middle of it. We saw that our role was not just to be ordinary lawyers, but to assume a role in which we could try to find a solution to conflicts, as in Chiapas. That is not something we sought, but we were quickly thrust into the middle of it."

They discovered huge irregularities in the government's case, including fabricated witnesses and false statements by officials. In Mexico, under Napoleonic Code, trials are not public, and the judge reviews written evidence, including a statement by the accused. In reviewing written evidence for their cases, they discovered the government had been careless—completely and arrogantly careless. Several files named the same person as having witnessed the declaration of the accused—on the same day, in completely different cases, in different regions of the country. It would have been an impossible feat, even if the witness had existed in the first place.

Other times, the name of the investigating police officer was the same on disparate cases. "It was incredible," said Víctor. "We examined a case in Yanga, Veracruz, and found that the person from the Public Ministry who questioned the prisoners was exactly the same person who appeared as the witness on the file of Elisa Benevides in the Federal District."

He shook his head over the pompous stupidity of the authorities. "They never thought that anyone would put the files together. As far as they were concerned, the judge in Veracruz was never going to talk to the judge in the Federal District. Nobody would ever put two and two together. Imagine."

One day, he remembered, "there was a hearing in Toluca [in the State of Mexico] and José Lavanderos had to question a state police officer who had arrested the prisoners. . . . Digna and I went. Normally, we acted alone, but when there was a hearing, we went together. . . . One of the officers José was questioning was the same guy that I had questioned in Veracruz," he said, laughing. "The moment I saw him, I told José that he'd testified in Veracruz. José started to ask him questions about Veracruz, like how he could have been in two places at the same time. That's what it was like. And, of course, with this logic it was so clear that the government couldn't do anything else but set the prisoners free."

Víctor Brenes called these cases "a real parting of the waters in the defense of human rights cases in Mexico. We didn't just defend one case but we put into evidence the obvious abuse of justice in this country."

The government did not admit fault in any of the cases. But, across Mexico, the prisoners had been freed by the time the proceedings were finished in June 1996. Nobody had wanted to defend the "presumed Zapatistas." And now, as a result of this small coterie of lawyers, bonded together for life, the government had been forced to back down. It was a huge morale-booster for human rights law and the attorneys who practiced it with passion and a shoestring budget.

Of course, there was retribution.

Telephone death threats began to arrive at PRO, first against director David Fernández, then against Pilar and Digna.

Enrique Flota remembered the threats. "We knew we had to be careful because we were involved in very delicate matters in respect to the army and the federal government."

The threats were always very personal. *"David, you are going to be very sad because your mother is going to die in Guadalajara,"* said a note to David Fernández at the center. He was from Guadalajara. His mother still lived there.

Another was addressed to Víctor, José, Enrique, and David: *"How much longer are you going to have? The tragic hour is near. Ha! Ha! Ha!"* [7]

One day, there was a knock at Víctor's office door at PRO. He answered, but there was nobody there. He looked down and saw a couple of envelopes under the door. He opened one letter and read: *"Víctor, do you know where your children are? It's very easy for them to die between school and home."*

At that exact moment, he knew his kids were on their way home from school. He tried to call his wife, Lupita, but he couldn't reach her.

His fear was almost unendurable, until he was able to look upon his children with his own eyes.

Another time, in 1996, he had a meeting near the National Autonomous University of Mexico, off the *Periférico,* in the south end of the city. He called his wife, and she told him she was close by with one of the children, their baby. They arranged to meet. He drove to join Lupita and, as he approached her car, he saw that another car was following her. "I started to get very nervous. I could see there were three men. They were wearing suits, but they were military types. You could tell. There was a Metro station nearby and lots of people around. My wife was getting scared and she drove the car up on the sidewalk, in the middle of all the people, trying to get around them.

"The other car drove up right up beside her and the three men got out, leaving their car and obstructing traffic. I could see all this. I was about a block away. I got out and started to run to my wife. The men started banging on her car. I was running now and one of the men saw me. My wife was still inside the car, in her seat belt, with our baby girl. She was sitting in the front, and the baby in back. The guy looked at me, and then he took out his pistol and put it up against the windshield at my wife's face and held it there. He raised his other hand like a gun, looked me in the eyes, and said, 'Boom!'"

The men got back into their car and drove away.

That's what it was like for these defenders of human rights in Mexico. They were terrorized, and there was no protection.

Lawyers at PRO put together a case on the death threats and filed it with the Inter-American Human Rights Commission. Víctor remembered meetings with officials in the Mexico City Attorney General's Office. He remembered one incident in particular.

"I am very worried for you. What barbarism! But what can we do?" he said then attorney general José Antonio González Fernández told him.

That was the attitude of the PR attorney general.

"Nobody ever investigated. They never did anything," he said. "We asked the Mexican telephone company [Telmex] for help with the phone threats. We registered our phone numbers at PRO. We asked for phone taps. They did nothing. Nothing!

"And the authorities always told us, 'You have to give us some proof of who threatened you.' How the devil were we supposed to know who was threatening us? That's their job. They are supposed to investigate but they never did. The only thing they ever offered us were police bodyguards, but we had no confidence in them. I remember once being in a meeting with González Fernández and I asked him, 'Do you think I am going to put the lives of my wife and children at risk with a squad of judicial police?' And, he said, 'No, no, no, I am not talking about judicial police. I don't have any confidence in them either. My wife and I have protection from the presidential guard.' The attorney general was telling me that he didn't have any confidence in his own men either."

For Digna, too, the threats began in 1995.

One Saturday morning in 1995, a man put a death threat right into her hands. She was taking a theology course at the Archdiocese of Mexico on Durango Street in the capital. As she climbed the steps to her class, a man ran down toward her. She collided with him, and he pushed an envelope into her hand. It was a death threat.[8]

"They knew where we were, what we did, who we saw," said Víctor.

Why didn't the authorities do anything?

Víctor feared—and he admitted that he had no proof and that it was his opinion—that the threats were coming from the

Attorney General's Office itself. He echoed Digna's views about the threats against her, and the forces behind her kidnappings in 1999. Like Digna, Víctor believed there was a group of people who did the "dirty work of the Attorney General's Office. . . . They were not formally employed by the AG's office but they answered to them. . . . It is my feeling the threats against us were coming from this group. After all, we were all fighting to undo their work.

"I believe they were not acting alone . . . they were a group that was responding to political interests and they were working for the people whose interests were being affected. . . . I don't know if the attorney general himself knew that they were threatening us." Nevertheless, he did feel certain that the attorney general would have known about the existence of the group and that it would have been on his payroll.

The Inter-American Human Rights Commission would recommend to the Mexican government that the PRO lawyers be protected (the commission did not make any findings itself on who was responsible). It was the first of such rulings involving Digna and her colleagues but, over the years, they would all fall on deaf ears at Los Pinos, even as threats escalated into kidnappings and Digna Ochoa was forced to go into exile in the United States. And, when the government was ordered by the international court in San José to protect Digna, Fox's government had the order rescinded.

And why not? Mexican intelligence agents at CISEN certainly had a poor opinion of Digna and her activities. As with all intelligence reports, their suspicions would have been sent to the highest levels, including the presidential palace at Los Pinos. The spy agency kept files on her. A part of their records was leaked to Marcela Turati, from *Reforma,* six days after her murder.[9] It is a twenty-two-page report, opened on April 7, 2000, on Guerrero peasant ecologists Rodolfo Montiel and Teodoro

Cabrera, with a separate file on their lawyer, Digna Ochoa. A photo of Digna was clipped to the file, which was classified highly secret.

While it focused on Digna's work on the Montiel/Cabrera case against big logging interests, it also summarized her defense of the "presumed Zapatistas," including Comandante Germán and Comandante Elisa, as well as other cases going back to 1995. The real meat for CISEN, however, lay with her involvement with the army in Guerrero and her questioning of soldiers accused of human rights abuses.

The file underscored that Digna questioned these soldiers in a civilian court. She also asked to look at CISEN files. Undoubtedly, the request was denied.

According to CISEN, Digna was a PRD activist and supporter of Liberation Theology, a theological doctrine that holds that the Catholic Church cannot save souls as long as people are hungry, sick, and landless. Beginning in the late 1960s in Latin America,[10] priests, nuns, and laypersons who subscribed to Liberation Theology sought to help peasant groups organize themselves in order to better their lives, struggling along with the poor, and distancing themselves from the power structure of the Catholic Church. They were "the church from below." The Vatican went on the attack, particularly through the arguments of Cardinal Joseph Ratzinger, who discredited Liberation Theology as a "deviant" idea and Marxist in nature. Several priests involved with the movement were formally punished by the church. Throughout the 1970s, many left their orders and the church itself.

"She is anti-government," said the file. "She continues in the judicial defense on behalf of people identified as being members of subversive movements and dissident groups. . . . She has worked for the legal defense and liberation of indigenous prisoners tied to the EZLN and EPR.

"(She) has generated a favorable image of the Indians of Chiapas, Guerrero, and Oaxaca.

"She keeps criticizing the federal government, as part of her promotion of supposed repressive actions against civil society. She has focused her work on defending Indian rights. . . . She has litigated delicate cases, in which the constant is the supposed aggression by members of police forces and the Mexican Army [against civilians]. She is currently involved in the defense of Indians, and the peasant ecologist prisoners, who are accused of narco-trafficking and being members of guerrilla organizations.

"She was in charge of denouncing sixteen paramilitary groups operating in Chiapas," it said, describing Digna's struggle after the Acteal massacre of forty-five civilians, mostly women and children, in Chiapas. She fought to have the government rein in the death squads, to no avail.

Digna always believed that CISEN kept a file on her. She suspected that her phone was tapped and she was constantly being watched and followed. She was right.

* * *

I asked Enrique Flota if Digna ever spoke to him about being abducted in 1999, and if he knew how she was able to cope with the trauma.

At the time, he said, he was chief of staff for Rosario Robles, who took over as PRD mayor of Mexico City when Cuauhtémoc Cárdenas resigned to run for the presidency. He played a significant role, he said, in facilitating Digna's dealings with the government, and especially the Prosecutor's Office investigating the kidnappings.

"I helped to ease communication between Digna and the PRO and the Attorney General's Office which was, at the time, headed by Samuél de Villar. I especially helped her prepare for the statements she had to give [to the police]. I helped her by trying to smooth things out. At the time, there was mistrust on Digna's part toward the Attorney General's Office. She didn't trust them or the

[Mexico City] judicial police [who investigated]. She had to be really coaxed to give her version of events for the investigation."

I remembered what Digna had told me about the kidnappings. The police treated her roughly, with scorn, and didn't appear to take her seriously. She was cut to the quick when a cop told her to go see a psychiatrist. I ran over the facts in my mind: Her father was tortured by police and jailed on trumped-up charges; she was kidnapped and raped at twenty-four; she dealt with a steady diet of the most unspeakable torture by agents of the state in her work; and police treated her badly after she was kidnapped twice in Mexico City. I could understand why she might not have been eager to sit down with them. I said nothing to Enrique Flota, however.

"On the part of the Attorney General's Office there was also mistrust," he continued. "The personnel of the Attorney General's Office did not believe the chain of events she said happened in her house. For example, she said that when they left, they left her tied up beside an open tank of gas, and that she succeeded in freeing herself. This was one of the things they found strange—that her kidnappers didn't know how to tie a good knot and Digna was able to free herself. Also, if they left her with an open tank of gas as a way of killing her, one of the first symptoms was drowsiness."

His answer stunned me. I was already struggling with the suicide theory. Now there were doubts about Digna's kidnappings? And from a man who was one of Digna's closest confidants?

"The only thing I did at the time was to smooth things out so that she could go and give her statement without pressure, without hostility, and so that the Attorney General's Office could have her statement without mistrust. That was my intervention. Nothing else."

But what did you *think?* I asked him.

He pondered the question, fingering the gold chains around his neck, and said it is a difficult judgment to make. He wasn't directly involved in the investigation, after all. (He certainly seemed to be on top of it, and as the mayor's chief of staff he would have had access. That was clear from what he was saying.)

"My pure first impression, very subjective, with all reservations, is that I understand a little of both sides. Digna mistrusted the Prosecutor's Office. That's one thing. But it was the first PRD government we've had and [Attorney General de Villar] was my friend. . . . But I understand Digna's mistrust because, indeed, the history of the Prosecutor's Offices is that they have tortured people and been involved in crimes."[11]

Did you see the evidence?

Some, he said.

He lost contact with Digna when she left for Washington. He often met with his friend Renato Sales, who held a series of posts within the Mexico City Prosecutor's Office, including chief adviser to Samuél de Villar. And he was friends with Mexico City attorney general Bernardo Bátiz.

He looked at his watch. It was almost 1 P.M., and his time was running out. "If I can say just two things in relation to her death, and I am not going to reveal any secrets. It is a tough case and what the Attorney General's Office is saying is absolutely true—they have not discarded any hypotheses and there are also sub-hypotheses, which include the suicide theory and the theory it could have been a political crime. These are the two extremes and in between there are many variations—a forced suicide in connection with brutal threats, for example."

"Was she left-handed?" asked Swedish journalist Petter Bolme. He was my friend and had arrived from Stockholm a couple of weeks ago to help me with my research. He had been sitting quietly throughout the interview. The story this morning in *Reforma* said that Digna killed herself with her left hand.

"No, she was right-handed," he replied. "In the first days of the investigation, they discarded the possibility that it was suicide because generally when someone commits suicide there are powder burns on the firing hand and yet, in Digna's case, they didn't find any, either on the gloves or on her hand. . . . There are very precise tests to determine the presence of gunshot residue and tests on Digna's hands came back negative . . . same thing with the gloves. So they discarded the suicide theory because she didn't fire the gun."

But, he said, investigators realized that this particular gun, which belonged to Digna, did not leave gunshot residue when it fired. That turned the case on its ear. She could have fired the gun. He pulled out a piece of paper and, with his pen, sketched the outline of the gun, a .22-caliber pistol. His drawing showed the location of the cartridge at the front of the barrel. Shells were expelled upward and to the right, he explained, underscoring that it didn't leave powder burns on the hand of the shooter.

"That's what created the problems. . . . But tests showed, with gloves or without gloves, in every way possible, there were no traces."

"No residue whatsoever?" I asked.

"No," he replied.

"It's a tough case," he repeated.

"If it comes to the point that it was Digna who killed herself, it will be extremely painful. She is a myth, a symbol, but one has to arrive at the truth, whatever it is. And the same goes for the army. If it's found that they killed Digna, then we will go after them."

Attorney General Bátiz has made the same point. The army was not untouchable, not as far as his investigators were concerned. The little scenario in Petatlán, with the brave band of Mexico City investigators wetting their pants at the sight of army guns, played through my mind. I pursed my lips to keep from smiling.

"The truth is that I have resisted accepting this possibility. There are many facts that lean the investigation to this ultimate point; however, we still have to exhaust many things," said Enrique Flota.

We?

With that, the interview was over. He said he would contact Renato Sales on my behalf. I tucked his little drawing of the gun into my notebook, we shook hands, and Petter and I took our leave, heading out into midday traffic to find a taxi. Our heads were spinning.

When we arrived back in Coyoacán, there was a message that the Miguel Agustín Pro Juarez Human Rights Center would hold a press conference at 4 P.M. Digna worked for PRO for more than a decade and loved her colleagues. In the days after her death, PRO was named *coadyuvante* (coadjudicator, helper) in the investigation. It was a distinctly Mexican legal concept that gave another party a contributing role in a case. PRO had, for example, the right to examine all the evidence and make suggestions to the Prosecutor's Office. Boxes of police files on Digna's case already filled a back room at the center.

We could understand, with that morning's suicide bombshell in *Reforma*, why PRO would want to have a press conference. On our way over, I snapped on the car radio, and heard Bátiz, asked by reporters about the suicide theory at his morning press conference, confirming that the gun was Digna's.

"We have already corroborated this, and, in a certain way, it strengthens the theory [of suicide]," he said. "However, we have not reached any final conclusions."[12]

Was the whole world going mad?

Everything was going to be straightened out, I thought, as we once again headed north to PRO's offices on Serapío Rendón Street.

Who better to defend Digna Ochoa than her friends and colleagues?

* * *

There was a crowd outside the PRO offices. Media cars were parked willy-nilly. *Monitor, Sí,* said black lettering on bright yellow cars from one radio station. There were a couple of police cars, with officers standing around smoking, and journalists milling around. There was a sign on the sidewalk for a health food restaurant next door. "Try our Juices," it said. "For ulcers, carrot and potato. For good circulation, apple, celery, beet, and carrot." (Is there anything for mayhem and confusion? I wondered.)

Inside, the auditorium is packed, with cables snaking to microphones on a table at the front, and video cameras from the big TV networks, Televisa and TV Azteca.

Shortly after four, Edgar Cortez took a seat on the stage, flanked by PRO lawyers Mario Patrón and Carmen Herrera, who took over the judicial department from Digna.

They looked like deer caught in the headlights. Edgar, intense, with dark hair and beard, was dressed all in black. So was Carmen, her brow furrowed, chin in hands. Mario, the youngest at twenty-six, stared down at his crib sheet. And then it began.

First, Edgar read a brief statement, which said the Prosecutor's Office must base its conclusions on strict criteria and that their report must be reviewed by independent experts. He then threw the press conference open to questions, and there was a deafening roar from the assembled rabble.

What about suicide? Was she suicidal?

What about the gun? Did you know it was Digna's?

Edgar tried to step gently. "With respect to the gun, I believe that information is part of the official file, and I think that, for every point, it's the responsibility of the Prosecutor's Office to respond."

"But did you know about the gun or not?" asked another reporter. "Did you know or didn't you? The question is clear."

It was getting testy.

"The facts are in the file. Ask the Prosecutor's Office," responded Carmen.

And so it went.

"For us it's clear," said another. "You are *coadyuvantes*. Did the Miguel Agustín Pro Juárez Human Rights Center know that the gun belonged to the lawyer Digna Ochoa, who died on October 19?"

Mario leapt in to insist that PRO "cannot divulge the contents of the investigation."

Finally, after half a dozen similar questions, Edgar interjected: "We knew about the existence of the gun at the moment it was integrated into the investigation. That's the moment when we knew."

"Did you give the Prosecutor's Office a psychological profile of Digna?" asked Ernesto Osorio, from *Radio Red*.

"No," said Edgar.

Clearly, everybody had read today's *Reforma*.

Edgar denounced leaks in the Prosecutor's Office. Photos had run. Last fall, *El Universal* ran a photo of Digna's body. It would run again tomorrow.

Repeatedly, reporters asked, about the suicide theory.

"What we can say is that the parts of the file we have seen do not have enough evidence to make for a convincing conclusion," said Carmen. "There are still a lot of things that must be verified, including the investigation of the other hypotheses and a contextualization of the crime. There is still much to be done. We still have not seen enough information to consider the probability of this hypothesis. It is not a question of whether we believe it or not, it is a question of what the investigation shows. To ask what evidence there is, you will have to ask the Prosecutor's Office. We do not want to be responsible for leaking official information relating to the investigation, which the Attorney General's Office is guarding."

Petter and I exchanged looks. Was this the best PRO can do?

"It is not a question of whether we believe it or not"??!! For the second time today, I was in shock. Where was the angry, feisty defense of a fallen colleague? Why was nobody reminding everybody what Digna Ochoa achieved? The threats she faced? The courage she showed? Her abilities as a lawyer? Her tough, uncompromising

approach to the law? Her plans, her personality, her unstinting dedication?

Where was Digna?

What was going on here?

I was eager to ask my own questions. I found it so bizarre that this human rights center was not defending their fallen colleague and I wanted to know why. But I remained silent. I was trying to keep a low profile in Mexico while I investigated Digna's murder. More importantly, however, I knew that if I asked these questions—and it would be difficult not to push in follow-ups—I could forget about any chance of sitting down to do my own interview with Edgar Cortez. I had had a brief interview with him some time ago, but it was, in my view, merely our preliminary meeting. I sat on my hands, knowing I would get my chance.

Carmen acknowledged that the suicide theory was first raised at a hearing on March 7. (On that date, Renato Sales summarized the case before a meeting of the Inter-American Human Rights Commission in Washington, apparently mentioning suicide as one hypothesis, but now dwelling on it.)

At one point, Edgar said that prosecutors had been examining the suicide theory since early February.

"But isn't it a joke that after all these months it suddenly comes up that it was suicide?" asked one reporter. "Doesn't this seem like a big joke?"

Finally, I thought, a voice of reason.

Carmen responds patiently, speaking gently as if talking to a child.

"We have to say that we discussed with the Attorney General's Office the fact that they investigated the possibility of suicide three months after the event. The answer we got was that, due to omissions made by the first investigating team during the first stage of the investigation, they saw the need to rectify these omissions. They wanted to do so in that moment, and in that way. We accepted that answer. The investigation was oriented to that hypothesis."

Right. Clear as mud.

"Have you spoken to the prosecutor [Sales] today?" a reporter asked Edgar.

"No, not yet," he replied.

"But this morning, you called Renato Sales," the reporter shouted.

"Well, yes, but it was a telephone call," said Edgar. "I hope we can meet later."

There were shouts of laughter and derision.

"I have only one question," a woman said softly, from the back. "You who knew her personally, who worked with her, do you think she had reasons to kill herself ?"

I held my breath, waiting for the response.

Edgar began: "For us, the answer should come more from people who knew her. . . ."

Mario Patrón cut in, chopping Edgar off in mid-sentence. He would handle this.

"We aren't here to signal what we think. We are looking for the truth and the truth can't be based on convictions, much less personal ones, or based on personal relations. For that, we ask for proof in the investigations."

I didn't understand what was happening here. All I knew was that Edgar, Mario, and Carmen have done nothing to deflate the suicide theory, and I was going to find out why. I realized that my work was just beginning.

* * *

A final question, a statement really, came from another reporter at the back.

"I think that this case could end in impunity," he began. "I say that because there have been other cases that maintained the suicide theory and ended in impunity for the killers. I am thinking of Polo Uscanga. What do you think about the idea that the same thing could happen here?"

Judge Abraham Polo Uscanga, sixty, was shot execution-style in his office in Mexico City on June 19, 1995. Earlier that year, he had refused to issue arrest warrants on alleged corruption charges for several Mexico City transport union officials, who ran the bus company, Ruta-100. The charge was corruption, but the judge knew the real reason was the union's various affiliations, including inclusion on the list of "presumed Zapatistas." When the judge said there was no evidence to charge them with any crime, he was pressured to change his mind. He refused.

On the day of Uscanga's death, there'd been a blackout in his building, the elevator wasn't working, and he'd apparently had to walk up several stories to his office. His killers were very likely waiting there for him. Uscanga became the third person to be murdered in connection with the investigation into Ruta-100. In April, Mexico City transportation director Luis Miguel Moreno was found murdered in his office. His death was ruled a suicide by the Mexico City Prosecutor's Office, even though the body had taken two .38-caliber slugs to the heart. Police said he shot himself in the heart, then pulled himself into position and shot himself in the heart again. (One of the prosecutors in the case told me at the time he went for his heart because, as is well-known among suicide experts, he wanted to leave a pretty face.) Then, in June, assistant prosecutor Jesús Humberto Priego Chávez was shot to death in front of his home.

Judge Polo Uscanga told Mexico City prosecutors in early June that he was receiving death threats and had been kidnapped, tortured, and held prisoner for several days. He'd been threatened before, in 1994, when he released eight suspects charged in connection with a car bombing, supposedly in support of the Zapatistas. This time, he pleaded for protection. He blamed Federal

District Chief Justice Saturino Aguero Aguirre for the violence against him, telling *La Jornada:* "To me, it's not the threats that I have received that are at the heart of the problem. What really worries me is the situation in which the High Court of Justice finds itself when its president violates the autonomy and independence of the institution."

He was a judge, a man of power and privilege, a PRI veteran, and still there was nothing he could do. Mexico City authorities, federal authorities, President Ernesto Zedillo, ignored him. His was an execution waiting to happen. A few days later, he was found dead in his office, with a bullet in his brain.

The Mexico City Prosecutor's Office said it looked like suicide.

His office had been wiped clean of prints and a .38-caliber pistol, also apparently print-free, was found under his body, in roughly the same position as the weapon that would be found under Digna Ochoa's body six years later. Under pressure from the judge's family and human rights activists, a homicide investigation—of sorts—began into his death.

Two years later, in 1997, Deputy Attorney General Margarita Guerra y Tejada was appointed to head up an official investigation in the Judge Polo Uscanga case. She ordered the arrest of a left-wing activist.[13] She did so, as British scholar John Gledhill later observed, despite "abundant evidence that the case was profoundly 'political' and could involve high-ranking public figures [thereby] neatly exonerating Aguero Aguirre" and the PRI administration under which it had occurred.[14]

Her office later misplaced the evidence and the suspect was released. By then, like the fingerprints at the crime scene, the case had been wiped clean of political context. No other arrests were made and the esteemed judge's murder remains unsolved.

Margarita Guerra y Tejada.

Her name will come up again in these pages.

* * *

Edgar Cortez hadn't answered the reporter's question, and the man persisted.

The Federal District, indeed the republic, had a tradition of murders turning into suicides going beyond Digna's case, and he is not going to let his questions fade away.

"Does PRO believe that the suicide theory should be tossed out right now?" he asked.

Edgar stroked his short black beard.

"They have to verify the proof," he replied. "That's all I can tell you."

And, with that, we filed out of the room, most to work on stories for tonight and tomorrow, and two befuddled souls to wonder what else could possibly hit us this week.

We soon found out.

CHAPTER TWELVE

Saint Rosalie Talks to Jesus Christ in the Mirror

Enrique Flota was true to his word. The following day, Wednesday, March 13, I got a call to say *Licenciado* Sales Heredia would see me Friday, at 5:30 P.M., in the Mexico City Prosecutor's Offices on General Gabriel Hernández Street. A few minutes before our appointed time, Petter and I were escorted to the second floor, where Sales's office was located at the far end of a large space divided into cubicles for detectives. The air was blue with cigarette smoke and the loud comments of cops.

Two secretaries, in stilettos and big hair, were at their desks outside his door. One filed her nails and flirted with a tall officer who sported a droopy moustache and a pistol in a brown leather shoulder-strap holster. The other, wearing a sleeveless top in neon orange, beckoned for us to sit down, without taking her eyes from a TV in the corner. A hit soap opera, *Lo Que Callamos las Mujeres (What Women Don't Talk About)* was on, and she was mesmerized. The TV Azteca series was about the travails of women, mostly in finding true love.

(This secretary was watching the same soap the third time I visited Sales, on May 15. I notice that one of the characters was reading *La Jornada*, with a front-page headline quoting Defense Secretary Vega García. "Armed Forces Subject to Civilian Authorities: Vega García." I'd chuckled when I saw that edition of the newspaper back in February. Must one actually state that the army is subject to civilian power? In Mexico, apparently so. It was

February 20, I remembered, because that day I interviewed General Gallardo, who spent eight years in prison for daring to criticize the military. When I showed it to him, he laughed too, albeit bleakly.)

Petter and I waited outside Sales's office. A cleaning lady parked her cart in front of us, and sprayed the coffee table and three feet on either side of it with Mr. Clean. Finally, shortly after six, one of the secretaries answered her phone, looked up and motioned for us to go in. As we did, a short man with a round bald head bounded from behind a gigantic desk and pumped our hands. "Coffee? Tea? What would you like?" We asked for coffee and glasses of water, and the secretary bustled off.

Sales was charming, with the perfect manners of a senator's son. He was born in the colonial capital of Mérida to a fine old Yucatán family. His father, Renato Sales Gasque, had a distinguished career as a business professor, senator, judge, and, from 1985 to 1988, PRI attorney general of Mexico City, the same secretariat where his son now worked. (Unfortunately, he was forced to resign over a bungled case involving a murdered Mexico City journalist.) At thirty-eight, Sales is taking postgraduate political science courses to enhance an education that included law at the Jesuit-founded Ibero-American University in Mexico City, and graduate work in Mexico and Spain.

He was slim and elegantly dressed in shirt and tie. His habit of pushing up the bridge of his wire-rimmed spectacles gave him a studious air. My first thought was that his face resembled one of those masks of fair, bald-headed men worn by celebrants at festivals throughout Latin America. The masks represent the Spanish *conquistadores*, who landed in the New World more than five hundred years ago, carrying with them the baldness gene. Mask-wearers bob their heads goofily from side to side, drawing huge guffaws from crowds who like to mock them. Everybody knows who they're supposed to be.

Sales ushered us to a couch, lit up a Marlboro, and perched on the edge of a chair, ready to take questions.

I didn't know much about the forensics of the case at this point. I'd interviewed Mexico City coroner Dr. Fernández Cáceres, as well as Enrique Flota and Digna's friends and family members. I'd seen photos of the crime scene in the papers, illustrations of the gun, and, in *Universal*, a photograph of Digna's body slumped over the couch.

(I should remind readers that, at this point, I hadn't seen the two homicide reports on Digna's case, filed October 20, 2001, and January 4, 2002, by the investigating officers. They concluded that the killers stuffed Digna's dead hands into the gloves and littered the powder in order to mess up the crime scene and destroy evidence. I wouldn't see either of these reports for more than a year after my first interview with Sales.)

Today, I intended to show him the story in Tuesday's *Reforma*, which I had brought with me. I wasn't expecting much, given how close-lipped prosecutors could be, but I hoped he would shed some light on the investigation, especially now with the suicide theory floating around.

But Sales was open, surprisingly so.

He told us how difficult, how painful, this was for him. He, too, was a human rights advocate. Like Digna. He pulled out a book, *Legalized Injustice: Mexican Criminal Procedure and Human Rights*, and points to his name in the acknowledgments. The book, published in 2001, was a joint project of PRO and the Washington-based Lawyers Committee for Human Rights. A dedication had been added: *"In memory of Digna Ochoa y Plácido, murdered in her office on October 19, 2001, and to those who have fought courageously and persistently for the rights of all."*

Sales was deputy attorney general in charge of ongoing prosecutorial investigations. Until recently, his area had been legal affairs and human rights issues and he had worked with several rights groups, including the French-based Christian Action for the Abolition of Torture. "I have written articles for the press for a long time defending human rights," he told us.

He said he had no choice to include the suicide hypothesis in thye previous week's presentation to the Inter-American Human Rights Commission in Washington, and had done so reluctantly. José Cárdenas broke the news on his Mexico City radio show the next day, and the story ballooned from there. "José is a very astute and capable journalist with contacts in the Attorney General's Office," said Sales.

I pulled out the *Reforma* article and spread it out on the coffee table. "Is it true?" I asked him. He said the main premise was correct and that the theory, which had been discarded, was being investigated because of the murder weapon.

"But, of course, we are working on other hypotheses as well, because even though the weapon belonged to her we have to consider that it could have been removed from her house by a paramilitary group, or someone linked to a paramilitary group, and so we are continuing our investigation. We are not saying that it *was* suicide; we are only saying that it is a *hypothesis* that cannot be discarded."

He made a wry face. "But you know how sensationalist the press can be and that they have a very clear agenda in opposition to the interests of Mexico City's government," he said, explaining that the leftist PRD government of Mayor Andrés Manuel López Obrador had enemies. These interests, and he included the death squads, right-wing political groups, and the army, opposed the agenda of human rights defenders.

I told Sales I was impressed by the detail in the *Reforma* story. Clearly, somebody in his office was talking to the press. He concurred; however, he said he had no idea who leaked it and insisted his office was investigating. He said he'd love to know who it was.

Then he came up with the first surprise of one of the most surprising interviews of my career in journalism.

"Would you like to see the file?" he asked, and Petter and I nodded in unison.

He went to his desk and returned with a large binder of photographs and notes. He turned first to photos of a gun, which he said was the murder weapon. It was small, measuring eight inches on an accompanying scale, and I remarked that it looked like a plastic toy. (It was a remark that would strike me as strange when I listened to the tape recording of the interview much later, by which point I had the photo of the alleged murder weapon released by police in July 2003 as part of a massive file on the case. This gun didn't look like a toy at all and I would never have made such a comment about it. By then, I would have many questions about the gun that supposedly killed Digna.)

"We always knew the gun belonged to her, but all the initial tests carried out to see if she was the one who fired it came back negative," Sales said. His ballistics team did the Walker test to check for nitrates in gun propellant and a sodium rodizinate test for lead.

At the beginning of this year, however, his team carried out further tests, firing the gun and testing three times for gunshot residue, or GSR. They all came back negative. "It is a very unusual gun because it has its cartridge chamber very close to the barrel. Look, here," he said, pointing to a photo of the gun. The cartridge is in front of the trigger. "Usually the chamber is located by the butt of the gun," he said.

So, the lack of GSR on Digna's gloves and skin didn't prove she hadn't killed herself. Not with this weapon.

He slowly turned the pages and we looked at the police photos. They showed the offices at 31-A Zacatecas, interior and exterior shots, the gun, the powder on the floor, the headband found lying by the entrance, and Digna's body lying between two couches in the reception area. She was wearing that little white blouse with the black piping at the neck and her black trousers. She lay with her upper body against one couch, the left side of her head resting on the cushion and her legs splayed on the floor. Big red rubber gloves covered her hands, and there was white powder on her clothes, on the floor, and on the couches. It was even on her bag, which she'd left on a chair. Little red arrows indicated, among other evidence, blood spatter on a bookcase, the tracks of the powder, and three shells found in the reception area.

There were photographs of Digna taken before and during the autopsy. It was painful to see them, and I thought of what Gerardo González told me during our interview the previous week in Cuernavaca and how it had turned my stomach. He said police showed him photos of Digna naked. He found her body, and I could understand him viewing crime scene photos. But why did he have to see her naked? I wondered if others gawked at Digna's nude body.

We sat on Sales's couch, without words, trying to digest the information.

I pulled myself together and asked a question.

"Is it true there were no signs of a struggle?"

"Yes, true. There was nothing. A zero scenario of violence."

"But wasn't the body moved?"

"Well, the head," said Sales.

"That's all?"

"Yes. Only the head, and we think it was moved to check vital signs."

"By the doctor?"

"Probably," he replied. "The doctor says, 'No, I didn't,' but it was moved after she died."

He went on to say that Digna was moved at least an hour before the police arrived. She was found lying with the left side of her face on the couch, with the right side up. But the blood on her left cheek was dry, which meant that it had to have been exposed to air. Sales said that if her head had been in its final position from the beginning, the blood on her left cheek would not have been dry. He said the evidence suggested she fell differently, with the front of her face landing on the cushion. Somebody then turned her face to the left, apparently to check for a pulse.

Sales took the case in December. In January, he was promoted to deputy attorney general in charge of all prosecutorial investigations. This was his biggest case. He said the previous team of prosecutors showed "little sensitivity" to rights organizations. "To be specific, there was a wall up against human rights organizations and this lack of sensitivity was generating very intense friction" between the attorney general and the Mexico City Human Rights Commission, as well as the Miguel Agustín Pro Juárez Human Rights Center. He says PRO in particular pushed for another team.

"Attorney General Bátiz believed it was necessary that somebody who knew the case and had ties to these groups should be in charge of the investigation," he said. The case required the delicate touch of somebody human rights defenders could trust.

"You don't want to believe it was suicide?" I asked him.

"What I would wish for most in this world is for this hypothesis to be counterattacked," he told me. "I want to see a hole that would make it unsustainable. I don't want this hypothesis to stand up—but sometimes things are not as we would wish."

He paused. "And so, our responsibility—and I declare this now—is to tell the truth. If this hypothesis turns out to be true, we are going to tell the truth, even if it is not politically correct . . . Evidently, it wouldn't be very comfortable politically. I think that is obvious."

"Do you think it was suicide?" I asked.

"We haven't finished the investigation so we can't say it is one thing or the other. . . . We have to have provable facts," he responded.

I pressed, asking him again.

"I don't want to believe it, and we keep on working on many other things, but it appears to me that if it can be technically proven to us that it is, and that there is no possibility that it could have been any other way, then—well, *bueno,* you have to give up in the face of the evidence."

Petter let out his breath loudly.

"Look, on the basis of the published evidence, for us it's absurd to think that it was a suicide. I have never thought so. Something is missing here."

"That's precisely why we . . . okay, we don't want people thinking that this is an absurd possibility," Sales replied. "We won't be ready to announce it until it can be totally proven. We don't know if it is true or not; we are not totally convinced. There is a lot of evidence, and that's precisely why we have opened the door to the Inter-American Human Rights Commission."

He was referring to the investigative team, headed by former law professor Pedro Díaz, which recently spent a week in Mexico City.

He lit another cigarette and exhales slowly.

"This is slippery ground, tremendously slippery," he said. "We didn't want to get into it for the same reasons, because it *is* slippery ground." He stopped, sighed, and rather dreamily continued: "The human soul is very complicated. We don't know what transpires in a person's mind."

It was obvious what slippery ground meant. Here was Digna Ochoa, a human rights lawyer renowned for her courage and tenacity, admired and respected at home and abroad, notably in the United States where she had powerful friends. How could the Prosecutor's Office in Mexico City determine she took her own life and not be ridiculed? It was not as if Mexican authorities hadn't pulled this stunt before.

At this moment, I felt some sympathy for Sales. He was so earnest, he seemed sincere. Here was a man trying to do his best under difficult circumstances.

Petter, however, was unmoved.

"Based on the evidence, I can't see a conclusion," he said flatly. "So is there *more* evidence?"

"Of course," said Sales. "There is also the other evidence that *Reforma* mentions, although the newspaper story doesn't explain it clearly. One important clue to the position of the gun when it was fired is not the bullet, but where the shells landed." He explained that this particular weapon, with its cartridge chamber at the front, expelled shells upward and to the right. "To have fired the fatal shot, the gun would have had to have been here, at this height, and held inversely, for the shell to have fallen between the couch and the bookcase as it did." He demonstrated, turning his right hand upside down and using his index finger as the trigger. It would have been tough for the killer to maneuver himself into that position.

He explained: "That is a very difficult position in which to shoot someone. And, an even greater problem we can't get our heads around is how, given that another person had to fit into the tiny space, that other person could have done it."

"But shells can be moved," interjected Petter.

Sales said there were three shells, one found under Digna's legs, another under the south couch where she lay, and a third, believed to be from the fatal shot, found wedged into the corner between that couch and the bookshelf.

"Of course, the shells could have been moved, but well, there are other questions," he continued. "According to the autopsy report, death occurred between one and three in the afternoon. At one, a court clerk had gone by and knocked on the door. When there was no answer, he left papers in the door. The first person who opened the door saw the body and also observed that the papers fell. So this means the door had not been opened between one and six in the afternoon."

Dr. Fernández Cáceres said that Digna died between noon and 2 P.M. I had just interviewed him this morning. But I was not here to dispute the facts with the chief prosecutor on the case.

"Okay, we could say these papers could have been put back in place. Let's say they did all this. They moved the shells, they put the papers back in place, they put gloves on the victim, and they put powder on her hands. But if this powder was put on the hands of the victim before the murder, its distribution would have been different. There would have been powder everywhere and there would have been signs of resistance. The body showed no marks of violence or signs of resistance [to putting on the powder].

"Let's assume that the powder and the gloves were put on after she was shot in the head. Well, in that case, the distribution of blood on the blouse would have been different.

"But well, these are some of the pieces of evidence that allow us to think about this theory. Despite all this, however, there is still a possibility that they were very professional and designed this whole scene, which is precisely why we continue with the investigation, even though it is getting more and more difficult to think about the presence of another person at the scene of the crime."

I was not sure when my opinion of Sales began to change. Perhaps now, when it dawned on me that, despite his protestations, he had already made up his mind, and before our eyes had turned from undecided investigator to advocate of suicide.

We asked about the gloves. The photos showed the massive gloves dwarf Digna's small hands. They were thick, bulbous, and full of air.

"Were they put on properly?" Petter asked, although we could clearly see they weren't.

"No, they were not properly put on, but then, the hands contract. When the nervous system is affected, there is a contraction of the fingers," said Sales. "However, the hands were totally covered with the white powder," and he pointed to other photos. "So whoever killed her would have had to have completely covered her hands with powder."

"Of course," he added, "under the homicide theory, whoever killed her could have covered her hands with powder in order to put the gloves on easily."

"How do you know that she was moved?" asked Petter.

"Because the first people to see the body said it was like that, and moreover, we know because of the dried blood, that the head was the only part that was moved." He talked about the coat Digna had under her right arm and how it had blood on it, while one side of her mouth was clean of blood.

He described what I will come to call the "Chiclet theory."

He showed a picture of Digna's dark blue coat. "We are sure she had the coat here," he said, pointing to Digna's mouth. "There is a little piece of chewing gum on the collar. That means the coat was in contact with the chewing gum, which was in her mouth."

Sales thought that Digna might have stuffed her coat into her mouth to stop from crying out in pain after shooting herself in the thigh. The police thought blood on the floor between the couches indicated she kneeled for about five minutes before the fatal shot. (Sales didn't mention the chewed gum on the floor, which, at this time, I didn't know about.)

"So, the head was moved, as I have been telling you, because the coat has blood on it and the mouth doesn't. So, you have to move the head in your imagination in order to guess its original position. This is the only part that moved because, if any other part of the body had been moved, we would have had the presence of powder or other signs. Now, if the person who found the body says he found it like that, and the only thing that we know is that the head was moved, then perhaps he moved it."

Petter groaned.

"I don't understand anything," he said.

"It's basic," said Sales, sounding like Sherlock Holmes. One almost heard: "Elementary, my dear man, elementary."

Sales explained that Digna was kneeling when she was fatally shot. "The bullet is on the left side and the bloodstains on the bookcase are on this shelf," he said, with more pointing at photos. "If they had shot her standing, the bloodstain would be on a higher shelf and she would have fallen into a different position."

I am struggling to keep up with this barrage of information. I was taping the interview, but I knew I would have no way to review the forensic photographs later (or so I thought). I scribbled hurried observations in my notebook as Sales talked.

I asked about early rumors of two guns. He said there weren't two guns. I asked him about the bruising on Digna's body, indicating a struggle with her assailant. He said there was no bruising, other than a small bruise on her leg, and, of course, the two gunshot wounds.

At this point, he brought up another piece of evidence.

"There is a book, if you can see that," he said, pointing to a photograph of the bottom shelf in the bookcase. "It is called *Antología Poética de la Muerte [Poetic Anthology of Death]*."

Petter and I leaned in, squinting. We could just make out the lettering on the spine of a rather fat volume.

"The one that is out a little bit?" Petter asked. It stuck out slightly beyond the others. Only slightly, a fact that would have some importance for the Prosecutor's Office.

"Yes, it's the only book that was in that position," says Sales. "Inside this book there is a poem by Juan de Arriola, a sixteenth-century poet, a mystic. Here is a fragment of it."[1]

To our astonishment, Sales softly recited, emoting.

Look at this red purple
That is seeping from my veins
Onto white lilies
Turning them petal by petal into a carnation
In this unjust torment
Examine well whether
It is just that I am crucified
And you surrender to pleasure
Saint Rosalie talks to Jesus Christ
Jesus Christ talks to Saint Rosalie in the mirror.

There was silence. The air was electric. His reading had been so dramatic.

Sales told us the poem was called "Saint Rosalie Sees Jesus Christ in the Mirror."

Only later would I learn the significance of the poem and how it fit into the suicide theory. I would learn that Saint Rosalie—she was *Santa Rosalia* in Spanish—was born to a noble family in Sicily in 1130. Her father was Sinibad, Lord of Roses; her mother, Quisquina, descended from the French king Charlemagne. She was also known by her Italian name, *La Santuzza* (The Little Saint). As a young woman, she decided to live as a hermit and retired to a cave in order to dedicate her life to prayer and good deeds. On the cave wall she wrote: "I, Rosalita, daughter of Sinibad, Lord of Roses, and Quisquina, have taken the resolution to live in this cave for the love of my Lord, Jesus Christ."[2]

She lived in a cave until her death in 1166. Nearly five centuries later, her bones were discovered and, in 1624, she is said to have appeared in a vision to a hunter, telling him she would protect him and the city of Palermo, which was being devastated by the Black Plague. The plague lifted three days later, and Saint Rosalie was credited with saving the city. (She did not commit suicide but the poem is about yearning for martyrdom.)

I asked Sales if he had memorized the poem before. He said he learned it only after taking Digna's case.

"It's only a fragment," he said. "It's much longer. . . ." Abruptly, he changed the subject.

"We were talking about the powder," he said, flipping back to a photo showing powder stains on Digna's trousers. "If it had been applied after her death, it would have fallen over the creases. . . . We would have had a different distribution of the powder, but we don't have it here."

He began to talk about blood patterns, noting that blood from her fatal head wound soaked into the couch.

"It's impossible any other way?" I asked him.

"Than suicide?"

"Yes, that somebody else killed her and then moved her body."

"Well," he answered, "only if they moved it with the speed of light because, as you know, the bleeding from the head wound would have been immediate. Let's say the body had been moved—she was shot, they moved the body, they placed the body—there would have been a totally different pattern of blood droplets. It would have fallen on her blouse; it would have fallen in other places. They would have had to clean up the bloodstains and there would have been signs, but we keep searching for such clues that point toward murder. . . ."

He trailed off, and then picked up again. "Look, I am going to ask you to write 'NGOs' for me."

I was puzzled. I knew the initials stood for "Non-Governmental Organizations," or the civilian groups involved in advocacy work.

He wrote "NGOs" in my notebook, using capitals for the first three letters followed by a small "s." He drew big arrows to the word, and then circled it with a flourish, making a deep indentation in my notebook.

"Many people write it that way, especially people involved in the defense of human rights. We found something in the death threat that is just circumstantial evidence, as the presence of the book is. There is no direct link to the crime. But when there is no direct proof, investigators have to put together different circumstances to get circumstantial evidence. At the murder scene there was a message that said: *'PROs, you sons of bitches, if you keep it up we're going to screw another one of you too. We're warning you, this is no trick.'*

Oh, I got it. He was relying on the small "s" in the death threat left at the scene of the crime.

"It is hard to believe that a mercenary hired by the army or by paramilitaries would know how to use this terminology," explained Sales. "The people who use such abbreviations as, say,

'PCs' are IT people, computer systems people. They abbreviate using computer terminology. That is why we are continuing to investigate—because there are people who would write it this way among Digna's acquaintances.

"In my opinion, writing the little 's' in this way is a real give-away," asserted Sales. "I am not saying that she wrote the message herself but it could be someone who knew her and was hired by paramilitaries and betrayed her. That is why we are also investigating other people who knew her."

I asked him about the significance of the poem.

"Why this poem is significant to me is that it could have held significance for Digna Ochoa," he said. "Saint Rosalie is a martyr venerated by the Jesuits. . . . She was one of the first martyrs of Christianity. This is the martyr's cross." He pointed to a cross drawn on a death threat in the file. I recognized it. It was from an earlier death threat Digna received. "The cross that we observe in this threat, in many threats but especially in this one, is actually the Greek cross, or martyr's cross.

"What did this mean for Digna Ochoa? Well, Digna Ochoa was at the point of becoming a nun. She belonged to the sisters of the Incarnate Word, a Dominican order. Domingo de Guzmán was the founder of the Dominicans. There is a martyr's cross in the Church of Santo Domingo de Guzmán here in Mexico City and also in different churches in Santo Domingo. I am sure this cross had a lot of significance for her, being the religious person she was, someone who was shaped by a religious education."

Sales showed drawings of other crosses, including a small cross stamped into the metal of a nail file found in Digna's apartment.

"Isn't that just a nail file?" I asked. I was beginning to feel like I was in the Twilight Zone.

"It's a mold of a cross," he replied.

What was he saying? That the nail was the template to draw crosses on threats she sent to *herself*?

Sales shrugged and sais his office was investigating every possibility.

(Later, during one interview in April, sitting outside, he told me that it was significant that Digna was wearing a white blouse and had a red scarf. Red and white, he told me, are the colors of Christian martyrs. The red was for blood and the white was for purity.)

But now, in this first interview, he told Petter and me that authorities had copies of previous death threats sent to Digna, Pilar, and other members of PRO, as well as evidence from Digna's kidnappings in 1999. "They are linked as evidence to this investigation," he said, adding that the kidnapping case was sent to the federal Attorney General's Office by the Mexico City Prosecutor's Office under Attorney General Samuél de Villar.

He underscored the point. "These cases are linked, and we are accumulating proof."

As the minutes ticked by into the second hour, Sales was more relaxed and he was beginning to talk as if there was no doubt Digna killed herself. Moreover, he was suggesting, as Enrique Flota had earlier this week, that Digna had something to do with her own kidnappings in 1999.

Sales, too, found what he called "inconsistencies" in Digna's reconstruction of the kidnappings, particularly when she was overcome in her home, questioned overnight, and left tied to her bed beside a gas tank with an open valve. "I say this because it was revealed in previous investigations," he said, referring to the police reports on Digna's kidnappings. "There were facts that didn't coincide with what she was saying. She was saying that she was here but it was not possible for obvious reasons."

Digna said she was tied with bandages but, according to Sales, there were no marks on her arms and the bandages she said had been used to tie her feet were new.

"Is it possible that these two kidnappings and the last cell phone call were figments of her imagination?" I asked. I was referring to another incident before Digna went into exile in Washington. She said she received a threatening call on her cell phone and could hear her nieces in the background. She was terrified because she thought they had been kidnapped.

"That's *it*," said Sales.

"But nobody can say for sure what happened," I insisted.

"Well, I am telling you, there are a lot of facts that do not fit with her declarations."

I brought the interview back to Saint Rosalie. She intrigued me.

"The poem doesn't suggest a desire to commit suicide," I told Sales.

"No, no, you have to enter into the mind of the character," he said. "I'll recite more of it."

And he did, this time closing his eyes and swaying in his chair, as if in a trance. He emphasized various lines in this slightly different verse.[3]

Look at this red purple
That is seeping from my veins
Onto white lilies
Turning them petal by petal into a carnation
In this unjust torment
Look at this mortal anguish
Look at this unjust torment
And examine well whether it is just
Seek the fundamental message
That I am crucified
And you surrender to pleasure
Saint Rosalie talks to Jesus Christ
Jesus Christ talks to Saint Rosalie in the mirror

He slowly opened his eyes and stood up. He walked to his desk where he retrieved a small card with a picture of Saint Rosalie, a golden halo around her head, and passed it to me. (I would later spend weeks trying to find the same card in Mexico City stores selling religious articles, but shopkeepers said they were hard to come by because there was no demand for this particular saint.)

The suicide theory spun in my head. So he thought Digna wanted to be a martyr and staged everything to look like a murder?

But suicide seemed preposterous. Digna was a nun for eight years, her religion was important to her, and she often shared it with those close to her.

(This theme of her spirituality would run through several of my later interviews. Her friend Viviana Krsticevic still smiled at the memory of a lunch they had in San José, Costa Rica. "I remember her talking about being a nun and her calling, and the fact that you didn't have to be cloistered and secluded in a community any longer, and that you could have a very meaningful life and help change things," Viviana told me, during an interview in a Georgetown restaurant. She was Argentinian and remembered her childhood, including years with the nuns at Catholic school. "Digna thought I should become a nun. I used to be very Catholic and then my life and my beliefs changed, not so much my social commitment, but basically my beliefs about what the Church believed. But she had a different experience and she was really one of those people who felt very close to the Church." Viviana was fighting back tears. "Digna was a person who was very, very committed to giving her life to others. . . . She was an incredibly generous person and wanted to make things better for the oppressed. It was real. I never, ever doubted her calling or her generosity. Her religious beliefs made her strong and, at times when she was conflicted about different things, she was always—always—very trusting and had this incredible faith in God. That was where she found solace."

Digna's boyfriend, Juan José Vera, was blunter: "There is no way she would have killed herself. She would have never made a decision that would take her to Hell.")

* * *

In Sales's office, I was still holding the picture of Saint Rosalie.

"*Señor Sub-Procurador,* I don't know what went on in Digna's mind, but isn't suicide a *mortal sin?*" I asked him.

Sales answered quickly. "Yes, I know, it is a mortal sin," he said, as if he was talking about stepping on a crack in the sidewalk. "If somebody is a priest or a nun, it's difficult to commit suicide, but there are nuns and priests who have done so. Not only ordinary people commit suicide. Recently, I had an experience with a very religious person who committed suicide after confessing to a priest. First confessed, then committed suicide."

"All right, fine," I said. "But what is your evidence against suicide?"

Was there no other side to this case? I had learned of this suicide theory only three days earlier, on Tuesday; it was now Friday, and the verdict appeared to be in.

"Well, we thought that somebody could have organized the whole scene, precisely to make it very confusing," he said.

"I don't know how important this book is but, say it is, couldn't somebody else have placed it there?" I asked.

"Well, we thought about whether someone else put the book there and that someone designed this whole scene—someone who wanted to cause great confusion. But to have done all this, the person hired would have to have been a professional criminal, to have organized it all with so much professionalism, because it was an impeccable murder scene. To use powder with so much skill in a murder would mean the person was a professional killer. Contrary to what one might believe, it would be very difficult for an assassin to work with powder because it would leave fingerprints," he said, adding that there were no fingerprints.

No fingerprints? (But lots of people used that office, so there had to have been prints. I had been talking to the lawyers who regularly used the office, and nobody reported being fingerprinted. Blood tests, yes; saliva, check—but that's another story.)

Sales said there were fingerprint fragments, but nothing police could use.

No stone had been left unturned, he says. "We are investigating who would hire someone to do this and, in that vein, we are looking into Guerrero, the *caciques,* and others who might have been affected by her last trips to Guerrero. We organized a series of trips to the Petatlán region."

I knew about Guerrero from Eva Alarcón, from the peasant ecologists' group, and Acapulco journalist Maribel Gutiérrez. It sounded like a circus, what with Mexico City investigators being held at gunpoint by the army in Petatlán.

He insisted his office was tough, and that Attorney General Bernardo Bátiz called Defense Secretary Vega García personally to insist that it must not happen again.

"I received the call about Petatlán on January 15 around 11 A.M.," he began. "I was in my office. They told me that they had held [my detectives] at gunpoint for over three hours and were planning to bring them to their military base."

Sales said he told Captain Euripedes Martínez he wanted to speak to his superior immediately, and was passed to Colonel Jorge Cavillo.

"I told him, '*Señor Coronel,* if you have my people, we are going to go public right now. We are holding a press conference to say that the investigators in the Digna Ochoa case have been detained by the military.'

"He said, 'No, no, no, I don't know. Let me see. Don't worry. What happened is that they didn't have permits for all of the guns they were carrying.' . . . But they had permits signed by all the country's prosecuting offices, and as civil authorities, they weren't supposed to be detained by the military. . . . Precisely because of the fact they shouldn't have been detained, we thought it was an excess, and, at that moment, we had to stop that excess."

I asked the obvious: "Why didn't you call a press conference to say what had happened?"

I thought about what a spectacular story it would have been. Digna's career focused on uncovering abuses in the military, and now you had troops holding the police investigating her death at gunpoint? For three hours? With a whole town watching?

"We left it with Centro Miguel Agustín Pro because we felt it was up to them to manage it as they deemed necessary," he replied. He was referring to a press conference that PRO called a week after the incident, in which Edgar Cortez chided the military for a lack of full cooperation in the investigation. There was no mention of the Petatlán debacle.

The scope of the incident itself was not revealed.

I asked him why he didn't hold his own press conference. "Why didn't you make a big scene?"

"We did make a big scene," he said.

He said Bátiz spoke to Defense Secretary Vega García, telling him, "It had better not happen again. [He told him] they had to [cooperate] with our investigation, and that it was not acceptable that the army should obstruct the investigation. If there is anything clear, it is that this Attorney General's Office does not depend on the federal government. It depends on the Mexico City government. We have no relationship with the Mexican Army. We are not subordinate to the army. I want to make it very clear: We will not make deals with the Mexican Army."

* * *

We turned back to ballistics and the angle of the bullets.

There were three shots. He said one bullet was fired into the south couch. Police dug out the bullet and believed that it was the first shot fired, either to test the gun or as a warning shot. The shell apparently ricocheted off the wall and landed on the floor in front of the couch.

Another bullet, fired into Digna's thigh, was recovered from the second couch, the so-called north couch. The shell was found under Digna's legs. Sales said this bullet entered Digna's leg from right to left. "The medical examiner says that it was from left to right because he had the body on the examining table and he didn't realize it," said Sales. "But ballistics experts are the only ones who can appreciate the precise trajectory of the bullet. . . . Whoever fired the gun, or if she fired the gun, it had to be from right to left because of how the bullet was found and where it was found."

There was a lot of powder where Digna sat on the north couch (she was found lying against the south couch) supposedly to put on the gloves. "If someone handled the powder, or if she did it, this was the spot."

He discussed the shells, noting that somebody stepped on one of them, squashing it. He said that the shell from the fatal shot landed in the corner between the couch and the bookcase. He reiterated that the chamber was in front and shells were ejected upward and to the right, he reminded us, so the gun had to have been inverted.

"The gun was upside down?" asked Petter.

"Well, this is the hypothesis. She is right-handed, and this is difficult to do, so she has to be like this. . . ."

He jumped up. He was about to ask his secretary to bring him a gun so he could show us how Digna Ochoa would have shot herself. He changed his mind. He would use a stapler instead. He took it in his right hand, crossed it in front of his face to the left side of his head, turned it upside down and pressed it against his temple. *Pow!*

He was absolutely clear. Digna killed herself with her right hand.

"Maybe they made her do it," said Petter.

"Well, if somebody did that, then they told her, 'Shoot your leg, and, now, shoot yourself in the head.'"

"You don't know if it was her," insisted Petter.

"Okay. Or they shot her. Let's suppose that somebody forced her and they said, 'Shoot yourself!' and then they shot her with the same gun . . . they turned her hand around and shot her in the head, and, as you said, they placed the shells. Well, all the hypotheses are *possible*, I guess . . ." and he trailed off.

It's getting late, almost 7:30, and Sales had been generous with his time. I ask him about Digna's final hours.

He told us she ate her last meal "between nine and ten in the morning," although tests were unable to tell what it was. "We assume she ate in her office because we found a small plastic bag with a clean food dish with a spoon, a glass, and a label without anything on it, and a little sponge in another bag that was still wet. We thought that she brought the food with her."

It sounded like Digna. So tidy, so organized.

Why would she eat and then kill herself? I wondered.

I asked him if any of Digna's friends testified that she was depressed.

"Yes," he answered quickly. He said some of her last clients on Thursday evening described her as "very withdrawn."

Before we wrapped up, I asked Sales one more time if he thought Digna Ochoa killed herself.

He sighed. "Unfortunately, there is so much information pointing to this line. And I say 'unfortunately' because that's the last thing we want . . . it's the most difficult hypothesis because it suits the extremists."

Digna may have killed herself for very unconventional reasons, he said. He spoke ponderously. It reminded me of the "church voices" I heard as a child, when adults spoke with strained piety at Sunday service. Children have good ears.

"If a person decides to give their life for their ideals, they are still fighting for their ideals, still fighting for what they consider just, still fighting for what they consider valuable," he said. "If that was the case with *Licenciada* Digna Ochoa y Plácido, she would have given her life for her ideals. So, in that case, she would have to be applauded and it would be absolutely respectable. I don't think that we should fall into the taboo of condemning it in itself, just for the idea of suicide. People are very complicated. They have many reasons. So, at the end of her story—I insist that if we confirm that hypothesis of suicide—she would have given her life for her cause."

Again, he emphasized his difficulties with the case.

"It is a terrible position because we are walking a tightrope. On one side we have the extreme right and on the other we have the extreme left, and these extremes touch. . . . The extreme right wants to use the case to denigrate the human rights movement. And the extreme left wants to use this investigation as a launching pad to dig into the intestines of the army, or the government forces, to denigrate the army and the state."

Caught in this web was the poor fly, Renato Sales Heredia.

What about PRO? I thought about Jesús, Digna's brother, and J.J., her boyfriend, and others who had told me about her break with the human rights center while she was in exile in Washington. I felt this was the missing piece somehow. I thought about the press conference and the lukewarm defense of a friend and colleague. What happened? Did it have something to do with Digna's kidnappings in 1999? Did Digna's colleagues think she made it all up?

"Why does PRO have *coadyuvante* status in this case?" I asked Sales.

"Their position is difficult," said Sales. "But they decided to be *coadyuvantes* because of a reason I can perfectly understand. The message at the crime scene says, '*PROs, you sons of bitches*' . . . Everybody started from the basis that it was a homicide. Nobody at the beginning, except maybe some people who knew the *licenciada* very closely, thought about suicide. So evidently because the threat was addressed to PRO, and because PRO was threatened, they felt the need to be *coadyuvantes* in the investigation. Then, as the facts had come out, they have unfortunately led us to this other line of inquiry that, I insist, was not conclusive.

"However, at this time, the line that prevails, the stronger line, according to her personal and professional history and her recent life experience, is suicide."

We thanked the chief prosecutor for his time. We shook hands, and said our good-byes.

Petter and I headed down into the street to hail a cab and make our way to the other end of the city, and our interview with Dr. Jorge Arturo de León, who did not believe for a second that his friend killed herself. He would spend many hours with us that night, telling us why. He was sick about the fact that PRO had such important status in the case. He felt it was a mistake and didn't believe Digna was being well served.

"When I remember Digna I want to cry," he said. "Okay, we were close. And I had a lot of admiration and respect for her and I miss her. As for PRO, I do not see those same feelings at all and it grieves me."

* * *

It was very late when the taxi dropped me off on Alberto Zamora Street. I was exhausted, but I knew I had to get down my thoughts about this incredible day. I wrote about the interview, about Sales's charm, about the *Poetic Anthology of Death* and the horrible images, now burned into my brain, of Digna in the crime photos.

"It is clear that he has made up his mind," I wrote from my desk, which overlooks a garden planted a quarter century ago by the painter Fernando García Ponce. "He believes that Digna killed herself and left clues, that she wrote the threats herself and that it was all directed at PRO."

Sales told me he spent a lot of time at the computer, researching Saint Rosalie and suicide by nuns, among other subjects. He said there was a Uruguayan poet, Delmira Agustini, who committed suicide in the early 1900s. He believed she held a clue to Digna's case.

(I would discover that Sales was wrong. The Uruguayan poet Delmira Agustini died at the age of twenty-seven—shot by her ex-husband of two months. She was a murder victim, not a suicide.)

He took my notebook and wrote, "red gloves homicide suicide"—giving me his own Google search terms—and I hurriedly tapped out the words. Most of what came up was pornographic and I imagined Sales, late at night, in his office, chain-smoking and carrying out his weird quest to uncover the dark secrets of Digna and the nuns.

"I feel like I am talking to an adolescent about girls menstruating, or some other forbidden topic," I wrote. "Sales is a Catholic and there is such a sense of mystery, of darkness, of nuns behind closed doors, of passion, of blood, etc. He shows me a crime photo of a nail file from Digna's apartment with a cross carved into the end. He believes, I realize, that she sent the death threats to herself. There is not enough time and I am going to have to go back to him, but I have no doubt that he has made up his mind. He is a good salesman."

I kept writing, unable to stop, even though it was now well after midnight.

"I realize that he is talking to me because he is looking at the longer-term public relations battle. When he comes out with a suicide ruling, he is going to need allies to defend the conclusion outside the country. Maybe that's me. . . .

"I thought my book would be an exploration of her life and death and a description of the enemies around her. I never thought those enemies could include people who were supposed to be on her side. I never thought I would have to deal with the assertion that she wasn't murdered, that she killed herself. I felt the case building. I feared that the conclusion was going to be suicide.

"I have taken on far more than I knew."

* * *

I should add a point here that I believe is important.

I did not dismiss the suicide theory out of hand. I knew Digna, yes, and I respected her. She had an impact on my life. But I wasn't in a position to know one way or the other what happened in the last moments of her life, and I hadn't done enough research yet to put those moments in context. And here's something I'm not proud to admit: I knew I could write a good book if the suicide premise turned out to be true—perhaps even a better book.

Imagine: a story of a split personality, a hardworking human rights lawyer by day and a lunatic by night. Imagine a woman who led a double life, covering up her passions and harming herself and others in devious ways. Imagine the final tragic outcome of death by her own hand. I thought about it from the moment I read the *Reforma* article—until I met with Sales three days later and he would, with his certainty, rein in my raging imagination.

It would take more than three years to chronicle what I would come to see as a cover-up and many more pieces of the puzzle would have to fall into place before I did. I would see the absurdity of the suicide hypothesis and uncover the half-truths, spin, and frenzied fantasies of those who toiled within the offices of the Federal District attorney general. I would see the larger pattern of the web. Sales, in that first interview, made me think something was wrong. But he was over the top. As they say, he protested too much.

I watched the cover-up unfold from the beginning. I would watch as a charade of justice played itself out over following months, knowing the end of the story had already been written.

Why? Why would millions of dollars and the might of Mexican authorities—hundreds upon hundreds of person hours by the time it was finished—be dedicated to destroying the memory of a woman who, when alive, weighed almost nothing at all?

She was not even here to defend herself. Hardly a fair match.

* * *

I would interview Sales on two more occasions, and each time he would emphasize his personal difficulty with the suicide theory.

"It is extremely difficult and the truth is that, for me, my political career is at stake. I know that," he told me, on April 8. "For me, it would be unbelievably better if this suicide theory would just go away."

He was always sincere. He brought a tear to his own eye.

Digna had apparently broken with PRO—or PRO with her— a year before she died.

"I feel that she was in a very difficult existential position because of her break with PRO, and for not having been invited to join the commission of human rights," he told me in April, tossing a new element into the mix. Digna was supposed to have been angry and jealous because her friend, Pilar Noriega, was appointed to the Mexico City Human Rights Commission?

"She no longer belonged to any group. Some say it is hard to accept this hypothesis because she was full of a great inner joy; she was full of life. But that is such a subjective argument. We all know that there are people who, shortly before they kill themselves, are full of inner joy because they have already made their decision about what they are going to do. They have made up their mind."

Each time he began by saying how unbiased he was. Each time, however, it was as if a switch had turned on and he could not stop building his case for suicide. I wondered who he was trying to convince.

He did offer me one intriguing piece of information. He said that Dr. Pedro Estrada, head of special investigative services for the Mexico City Prosecutor's Office, didn't agree with the suicide theory. Dr. Estrada's experts removed Digna's body from the scene, did the examination before the autopsy, and carried out all fingerprinting, bloodwork, fiber analysis, and ballistics.

I practically jumped out of my chair. *"De verdad?"* ("Really?")

Well, not quite. He said that Dr. Estrada *initially* didn't agree with the theory, but that he had changed his mind. (When I later interviewed Dr. Estrada, he was charming and affable, but a brick wall. He wouldn't tell me anything about Digna's case, and especially not his opinion.)

In April, too, Sales told me: "The first things we asked ourselves, assuming that it was a murder, is 'How did they kill her?' and 'Who killed her?' and that is where the problems began. Because if she was murdered, then the killer would have had to perform almost impossible stunts. They would have had to position themselves in a certain way, turn the weapon in a very special way, place some kind of plastic sheeting on her blouse so that it wouldn't get stained, place the papers back under the door, place the cartridges where they were.

"Therefore, at that time, we said whoever killed her was not just an ordinary assassin but a perfect professional. We also said that it was very difficult to imagine how she could have been killed and therefore there must be another explanation. . . . And we feel that the most logical explanation is suicide. All the evidence we have points in this direction. However, I insist that, even though this is the strongest line, this does not mean we have reached a conclusion. If something comes up that allows us to say her killer was a professional, we will. If any detail comes up that will allow us to link the gun, or the people she knew, or her friendships, to a professional killer, we will immediately discard this hypothesis and begin to look into it."

Such evidence did arise, as you will see in the pages ahead.

But Sales, and those who followed him on the case, didn't take it seriously.

* * *

A few months later, I read a report in which the take on Sales rang true. It was written by Greg Adair of the San Francisco–based human rights group Global Exchange. Posted in Mexico City, he led a delegation that visited Mexico that spring to investigate Digna's death.

The delegation met with Sales in his office in Mexico City two weeks after my first meeting with him, and filed this report:

"Mr. Sales took over the investigation in December 2001, as a result of the ineffectiveness of the first investigative team, including numerous leaks of sensitive information, causing setbacks in the investigation.

"Mr. Sales's introductory remarks included a lengthy explanation about his impartiality and distance from political interests in the case. He spent the first half-hour of the conversation explaining that, as a member of the PRD (Party of the Democratic Revolution), promoting the suicide theory would be contrary to his political motives, then spent the next hour and a half trying to convince us of the theory, without a single reference to other possible lines of investigation. He also described the pressure he feels from the international human rights community. Mr. Sales emphasized that he believes he will face strong criticism if he concludes that Digna Ochoa's death was, in fact, a suicide.

"Mr. Sales explained that, although much of the evidence certainly appeared to indicate an assassination, Digna's death was more likely a suicide intended to (falsely) implicate the Mexican Army and allow her to die a 'martyr,'" said the report.

"Mr. Sales then described a complex, unsubstantiated theory of Digna's allegedly troubled mental state, her desire for revenge against the government and her former colleagues at the PRODH, and her quest for martyrdom. Despite the extent to which Mr. Sales is counting on psychological theory to wrap up the case, he failed to indicate that he has ever placed a psychiatrist or psychologist on the investigative team, or that he had ever sought out the services of a forensic psychologist to review evidence or report on Digna's *personal* history.

"During the meeting, Mr. Sales insinuated knowledge of Digna's personal life that casts doubt on previous death threats she received. . . . Mr. Sales went on to great lengths to convince us of what appears to be his personal conviction—that Digna committed suicide. While none of the members of the delegation are trained investigators, some members of the delegation left the presentation questioning the viability of the suicide theory."

The report laid out its conclusions:

"The investigation of the assassination of Digna Ochoa is plagued by political posturing and is not a serious criminal investigation.

"The discussion with Mr. Sales confirmed that the investigators are focusing almost exclusively on a suicide theory and that the overwhelming bulk of their work, including interviewing Digna's family members and co-workers, has targeted her mental health and her personal and professional relationships, rather than suspects related to previous death threats and kidnappings, such as persons linked to the Mexican Army.

"The delegation feels that any competent investigation must first focus on the persons, institutions, and interests most threatened by Digna's life's work in human rights—which had for over six years resulted in death threats, abductions, torture and attempts on her life—before turning to more complex theories. The delegation is equally convinced that, beginning with a conclusion, and then searching for evidence to support it, is simply bad police science."[4]

* * *

There was, however, something Greg Adair and his delegation didn't know. Sales spoke with such authority about psychological theory for a reason. A confidential psychological profile had been compiled on Digna—two years earlier.

This is what I was about to find out.

CHAPTER THIRTEEN

She Doesn't Wear Makeup, Does She?

My last interview with Sales was on Wednesday, May 15, 2002. Today was Digna's birthday. She would have been thirty-eight. I didn't know if Sales was aware of the significance of the date, and I didn't mention it.

He hadn't allowed me to use my tape recorder since our first interview, in which Petter Bolme was present. This interview began badly when he challenged me about comments he said I made criticizing his investigation. It was untrue, and I told him so. I had not discussed my opinions. In any case, he was fishing. I have lived in Mexico long enough to know better than to reveal what I was learning, even though this reticence by this time had earned me the mistrust of Digna's brother, Jesús, and loss of contact with the Ochoa family. It was sad because I felt a special connection with Esthela, but there was nothing I could do. I know that anything I revealed about my findings will be reported in Mexico, and I didn't want to see a campaign to discredit them before I even had a chance to write.

We discussed the case for about half an hour, during which time Sales told me his office was pursuing leads about Digna's early life in Veracruz. I mentioned I'd had trouble getting official documents in Jalapa but he didn't let me finish, jumping in to say his people were having the same problem. (I didn't offer that I procured the documents I sought from the state Attorney General's

Office in Jalapa.) He gave me a copy of a short article in *El País* from August 1988 about Digna's disappearance,[1] adding that his investigators had located someone who could discredit her story. He said, however, they could't use it because they couldn't disclose this person's identity, which I found curious because the police either had a reliable witness or they didn't.

Then, as he had before, he asked me if I would like to see something. He handed me a file, which he said was a psychological profile of Digna Ochoa, entered into evidence on March 10, 2000, as part of the Mexico City prosecutor's investigation into her kidnappings in 1999. She gave statements to police and an investigation was launched into the August incident, in which she was pulled into a car, and the October abduction, when she was held overnight by unknown assailants and left, tied to her bed, beside an open gas tank.

His secretary rang to say his next appointment had arrived, and he allowed me to use an adjoining office to study the file, closing the door behind me. I flipped through to the end and saw it was signed by psychiatrist Lucia Bustos Montes de Orca and psychologist Jovita Guadalupe Bravo Montes. To create a record of my own, I began to dictate:

Psychological Profile
No. 0007832
March 10, 2000

The purpose, according to the authors, is to "establish the principal characteristics of the personality of Digna Ochoa y Plácido." It was written "in accordance with the prerequisites of clinical forensic psychology," and was based on three sources:

a) Two files from the Mexico City Prosecutor's Office on the kidnappings, which were reported by Digna Ochoa or, as she is called, "the person being evaluated."

b) Observation and analysis of a VHS video of Digna's testimony to police about the October 28, 1999, kidnapping in her home "based on the psychological interpretation of her body and verbal language."

c) Psychological profiles of the various anonymous threats sent to the Miguel Agustín Pro Juárez Human Rights Center, first by psychiatrist Lucia Bustos Montes de Orca on October 19, 1999, and then, by Bustos Montes de Orca and psychologist Jovita Guadalupe Bravo Montes, on February 24, 2000."

I was nervous. I didn't know how much time I had and I returned to dictating the profile into my tape recorder, careful to note numerous uses of bold type (shown here as plain type) for emphasis:

"The following results show personality characteristics of Digna Ochoa y Plácido with a high degree of probability, according to the parameters of clinical psychiatry:

A) Identification card. Digna Ochoa y Plácido, 35, single, Catholic, originally from Veracruz state, lawyer, works in judicial area of Miguel Agustín Pro Juárez Human Rights Center, hereafter known as 'the Center.'

B) Mental exam: At the moment of the evaluation, we were not able to find signs to indicate alterations in her superior mental processes *of memory, language, orientation, attention, concentration, or social perception.*

C) Perception: No indications of any organic cerebral damage. Good visual coordination. Strong and rapid movements and, on some occasions, rudeness.

D) Intellectual capacity: She impressed us as normal or average. She possesses normal anticipatory capacities—planning, observation, analysis, and synthesis. She can go to extremes to get, or distort, or change information as she finds it necessary, but if she is wrong, or she doesn't have anything to say, she is capable of refusing to answer. She is incapable of admitting she made a mistake, on occasion looking for justification and blaming others. She thinks she's the boss, which is incongruous (she is divorced from reality), and she lacks deduction or logic. We found her cultural level to be average.

E) Family antecedents: It is known that she originally comes from the state of Veracruz and she lives alone in Mexico City. It is probable that her family's social economic stratum is lower middle class or middle class. There is no information about the family and she never mentions her parents, brothers, or other family members, by which we can deduce that her relations with members of her large, original family are not close or deep. It tells us that there is a communications

323

problem with her family. Her need for affection, protection, and guidance were not adequately satisfied, and that is why Licenciada Ochoa reflects a state of general dissatisfaction.

F) Work and educational background: Primary and secondary school, B.A., law degree. According to the first time her name appears in an investigation, October 7, 1996, it can be deduced that, from that time, her only job has been in the judicial area of the Center.

G) Interpersonal relations: She is an insecure woman, who appears not to have been well treated early in her life and is hugely susceptible *to feeling rejected. That is why she doesn't like to be criticized or hurt. Also, she* misinterprets *other people's intentions, feeling easily attacked, above all by individuals who represent authority and can indicate to her whether she is behaving well or not. She rebels against that which* she considers unjust *and, as a defense mechanism to avoid feeling attacked, she lashes out and, as a professional, she sublimates her own aggression into the 'Defense of Human Rights' of those whom she considers mistreated.*

Although she pretends to be respectful of human rights, the reality is that, due to her nature, she cannot adhere to the norms, transgressing them when she feels it is necessary. For instance, she devalues and doesn't follow the guidelines of the authorities who are in charge of the investigation. This reflects her conflict with authority and elements of an antisocial nature.

Others don't understand her mood changes and this situation makes it very difficult to relate to her in a profound, lasting, and harmonious manner. She prefers to isolate herself emotionally from those around her. She doesn't talk about friends, acquaintances, or family members. She makes references only to those colleagues who were working at the Center Pro, and these references don't reflect positive or friendly sentiments. The declarations of her colleagues certainly show that they are concerned about what she has been through and that this is due to their fear that the same thing could also happen to them.

H) Sexual and sentimental relations: Apart from her difficulties with interpersonal relations, it is known she is single. There is no reference to whether she has a boyfriend or a partner. She doesn't take any care in her personal appearance and she doesn't wear makeup. She wears only little earrings, a ring, and a necklace, which could be a religious image. Also, observing her posture and clothing, it's worth noting that she is slightly hunched. She wears informal clothing, mainly dark colors and low-heeled shoes, a high neckline (as you can see from her credential of a voter registration card, as well as in the video).

In her apartment, there is the minimal furniture necessary to live. There are only two floral arrangements and a religious icon on the living-room wall. There are four religious crosses: in the dining room, on the staircase, in the bedroom, and on one door. Everything reflects a masculine image, probably denoting difficulties in her process of psychosexual identification and/or in the management of her sexuality.

I) Mood and impulse control: According to the statements of those close to her during the investigation of the denounced events, she is unstable and has a changeable character, sometimes swinging from tranquillity and good manners to anger and despotism. Her behavior is egocentric and she is susceptible to criticism, feeling as if she has been rejected or attacked. Her control of impulses is diminished. If things don't go as she says, or plans, she is angry and verbally attacks. She feels like the victim and looks for those responsible, without accepting her own responsibility. Also, in her declarations, she affirms that nothing is being done for her or for the Center Pro. This way of thinking caught people's attention and Licenciada Ochoa observed this and tried to take advantage of it, feeling more secure of herself being recognized in some way—recognized and exercising more power and control over those she feels are attacking her.

J) Clinical diagnostic impression: Her personality traits indicate to us the personality upheaval known as schizoparanoia, with strong narcissistic signs, aggressive and therefore antisocial. *This means that her insecurity drove her to misinterpret reality, perceiving ideas of damage and persecution, preferring to emotionally isolate herself from others in order to avoid feeling attacked. She is not direct in showing her lack of approval for those she thinks are guilty of attacking her. In her way of defending herself and defending others who are unjustly attacked, it is possible for her to break the rules and show no respect for authority, above all if it is male. Thanks to her profession in defense of human rights, she obtains gratitude, recognition, power, and control.*

K) Psychological forensic impression of her testimony: Due to the previously described psychological forensic traits, as well as her testimony, we find that there are incongruities in her declarations, in her behavior, and in the verbal descriptions contained in her denunciations.

This tells us there is a low probability that her declarations are true. It means there is a high degree of probability that she is hiding information, distorting, lying, or making it up. She is a victim with little credibility.

The following is an analysis of the dynamics of her personality, related to the events that were investigated.

CONCLUSIONS:

1. *That Digna Ochoa y Plácido does not present any signs of alterations of a psychiatric kind (madness) in her higher mental processes.*
2. *There are no indications of any organic brain damage capable of altering her behavior and visual and motor coordination. She has rapid and strong movements and, on some occasions, rudeness.*
3. *She has normal or average intellectual capacity, trying to present a good image of herself without accepting that she can make mistakes. She justifies her behavior and looks for guilt elsewhere.*
4. *She belongs to a family that didn't adequately satisfy her needs for affection, guidance, and protection and she feels mistreated. She has little communication with her family and she reflects a state of general dissatisfaction.*
5. *She has been an average student and worker, developing a great interest and energy in her work as a lawyer in the judicial area of Center Pro.*
6. *She presents a problem with her personality called schizoparanoia, with strong narcissistic signs; she's passive-aggressive and has an antisocial nature. All this behavior is characterized by a basic insecurity that has made her emotionally isolated from other people. She misinterprets reality because she feels she is a victim of damage and she feels persecuted, unjustly treated and attacked. She does not show her lack of approval in a direct way; she justifies herself and blames others for what she herself creates. She is rebellious and has conflicts with authority, especially with masculine authority; she has mood swings and problems with her interpersonal relations. If things aren't done as she wants them, her diminished capacity of slowing down, tolerance, and frustration in controlling her impulses can lead her to transgress the normal level of anxiety in her search for attention, recognition, power, and control.*
7. *As a defensive mechanism she sublimates her own aggression in the defense of human rights.*

8. *There is a high probability that she has conflict with her psychosexual identity and/or the management of her sexuality. She has no partner and faces difficulty in establishing a lasting, deep, and harmonious relationship with a partner.*

9. *From the standard of forensic psychology, as well as from her testimony, she is considered to be a* witness and victim with little credibility in her denunciations. That is because she can make up, distort, hide, and/or lie regarding the information she is offering, *without assuming her own responsibility.*

10. *In addition to the preceding, and according to the nature of the working hypothesis, it is important to point out that there are similarities between the personality characteristics found in the author of the threats and Citizen Digna Ochoa y Plácido, which leads us to think that it's possible that these denounced crimes were made up. Or, if they really happened, they were distorted and/or magnified by Digna Ochoa.*

It is necessary to investigate in order to corroborate or discard this hypothesis with a psychological and/or polygraphic evaluation to determine her degree of participation in the crimes that she herself denounces.

Lucia Bustos Montes de Orca   Jovita Guadalupe Bravo Montes

There was an annex but I stopped reading. I needed a break before I dictated the rest. I couldn't believe what I'd already read—or that Sales gave it to me. What was he thinking? He must have figured I would agree with its conclusions and be convinced of the suicide theory.

But I was quite taken aback. This profile had been written without Digna being interviewed by a health professional in a clinical setting. As stated at the outset, it was put together using transcripts of her statements to Mexico City police about the kidnappings; video footage of her testimony about the second kidnapping; and psychological profiles of those who wrote some of the death threats, profiles that these two medical professionals themselves authored. There was no indication of how much time they were able to observe Digna on camera, and no attached transcripts.

This did not look like any clinical profile I had ever seen, although I intended to check.

Setting aside this obvious problem, the profile's overwhelming, stifling sexism leapt off the page. This was the dark side of *machismo,* and it made no difference that it was written by two professional women.

She didn't wear makeup. She didn't dress up. She wore *flat* shoes. *Imagine!* She doesn't decorate her apartment. Could this woman make a proper home for any man?

There was no man in her life so she must have had problems with her sexuality. She must have been a lesbian. José Reveles, from *El Financiero,* told me that rumor had flown through police ranks months ago.

She didn't show proper respect for authority, particularly *male* authority. She thought she was the boss. I remembered what Veracruz journalist Regina Martínez had told me over lunch in Jalapa after Digna's murder about the political and social history of Veracruz. "Digna grew up in a tradition of social struggle," she said, referring to her family, particularly her father, who was a union leader and political prisoner. "Here, there are rich and there are poor. If you are poor, it's not your place to fight. . . . Digna did not know her place."

I could almost hear the profile's authors tsk-tsking over Digna's vocabulary and verbal inflections as they watched her on video. She spoke the language of her impoverished childhood, often using *pues* or *este*—the Mexican equivalent of *um*—and allowing her voice to rise tentatively at the end of a sentence. She did not speak like *las reinas de Polanco* (the queens of Polanco), as author Guadalupe Loaeza called the rich ladies who lunched in the capital city.

Perhaps the deepest cut was to her work. These experts said

Digna used her career merely to sublimate aggression. It was clear that they had no comprehension of what the defense of human rights meant. They were unclear on the concept. Theirs was a different universe, in which there was really no need for human rights defenders. Digna's story was stripped of its very real political and social context.

I thought about a story human rights lawyer Denise Gilman told me in Washington. She was working on a project in Mexico in 1999 when Digna's case (and that of other PRO lawyers) was forwarded to the Inter-American Human Rights Commission. Digna had been threatened and kidnapped, and the commission was considering whether to recommend protective measures to the Mexican government. Denise spoke to several investigators in the Mexico City Prosecutor's Office (who were working on Digna's case) and she remembered that prosecutor Patricia Bulgarín "thought the threats were coming from inside the PRO. At one point, I asked her about the Federal Preventive Police because they were kind of new on the scene and it was really unclear what they were up to at the time."

"And she said, 'Oh, they're great. We're working with them closely.'

"And I said, 'No! I mean, are you *investigating* them?'"

It hadn't occurred to Bulgarín that police could be responsible, even though Digna kept saying she believed the threats came from the authorities themselves.

In a similar vein, I wrote a story in 1999 about the murder of Jorge Aguirre Meza, a rights activist from the west coast state of Sinaloa. He'd been a federal drug agent until he realized that the only reason his superiors wanted his information was so they could demand bigger bribes of the drug lords. When he cracked a case on the Arizona border, linking suspects on both sides of the border with huge shipments of cocaine, he was recalled to Mexico City and told to keep quiet. The case was never investigated. So he left the federal agency in disgust, returned to his home state, and threw himself into human rights work. I talked to him often; he was a great source. When he was mowed down in his front yard by men with AK-47s, I wrote about his heroism, and his cornball jokes, and about how he kissed his little red-haired daughter as we talked in his kitchen. I cried when they killed him.

The day my story ran in the *Toronto Star*, I got a call from one of President Ernesto Zedillo's communications people. He wanted to pass on his condolences, and he was very sweet. But he treated it as my personal sorrow. He seemed to have no idea that the loss was Mexico's, as much as mine (more than mine!), and that, as press aide, he should have been using the phone call to inform me of the president's vow to track down his killers. That vow never came and Jorge's murder is unsolved.

* * *

I could hear the mumble of voices in the adjoining office. I considered some of the profile's obviously false assumptions, including the portrait of Digna as essentially friendless and unable to communicate with her family.

Digna didn't want to talk to the police about her kidnappings. Enrique Flota had to coax her into it; he acted as an intermediary. She was afraid for herself, for her friends, and for her family. Moreover, she believed that the authorities themselves—whether CISEN, Federal Preventive Police, Federal Judicial Police—were behind her kidnapping. Why would she share details of her personal life with the police?

During our last interview, in January 2000, she gave me the address and telephone number of her parents in Misántla. She talked about her family, particularly about her sister Esthela. "Please don't use their names in your story," she asked me. It was vital to her that her family be shielded from publicity for their own safety.

Digna dressed simply. She was with the nuns for eight years. She left her Dominican order in early 1999, just a few months before the first kidnapping. She dressed for her work. One wouldn't apply eye makeup for a trek into the jungle, or to visit one's clients in a prison in Iguala.

Mexican authorities disagreed, however. A police report on Digna released in 2003 made a comment, based on observing the video footage shot during her last trip into the mountains two weeks before her death.

"In one of the videos, we see her in the mountains of Petatlán in a sleeveless blouse, but still without makeup and scruffy."

I laughed out loud, thinking about how *scruffy* I've looked in the jungles of Mexico and elsewhere. Would I be deemed to have a gender identification problem? Or be thought slovenly and depressed? Heaven help me.

The terrain in the Guerrero highlands or Veracruz is rough and unforgiving. The heat is oppressive, soaring to 115 degrees fahrenheit. Two things, and only two things, are important to survival—water and shade.

And perhaps eyeliner.

* * *

Later, in Toronto, I took this profile to Dr. Peter Collins, an expert on violent crime and, with a lifetime of experience, one of Canada's most renowned forensic scientists. He was manager of the forensic psychiatry unit, behavioral sciences section, investigative support bureau, of the Ontario Provincial Police (OPP). He served as consultant psychiatrist to the behavioral sciences branch of the Royal Canadian Mounted Police (RCMP). He was a staff psychiatrist at the Center for Addiction and Mental Health in Toronto, and headed the center's police liaison program. He was an associate professor of psychiatry in the faculty of medicine at the University of Toronto. I had to wait two months to get an appointment with Dr. Collins because his schedule was so busy and he traveled often to testify in criminal cases, both in Canada and around the world. He worked with international criminal justice agencies, including the FBI, Interpol, and Europol.

Before our interview, I sent him a copy of the report. Now, in my opening question, I asked what he thought. He didn't hesitate. In his professional opinion, based upon Canadian psychiatric standards, the report was "psychobabble."

Dr. Collins continued: "These people are making observations, and coming to conclusions, on things that would be ludicrous for any psychiatrist to do. They are coming up with conclusions that are irresponsible because they are attributing a diagnosis to someone whom they have not assessed—and you cannot do that."

He withdrew his copy of the profile from his briefcase. On the first page, I could see notations in small, neat script.

"My notes in the margin are things like 'not possible.' You know, right at the beginning, where, 'with a high degree of probability,' they come up with personality characteristics? Well, you can't do that, not based on the information they have. In their diagnosis, the authors have stressed that their work is based on the standards of 'clinical forensic psychiatry,'" and he paused before making his next point.

"Well, there was no interview. There was no mental exam. What they are doing is they're taking nonclinical situations and attributing clinical syndromes and diagnoses—some of which I've never even heard of. I mean, this whole thing of schizoparanoia. No such thing!"

Dr. Collins relied on the *Diagnostic and Statistical Manual of Mental Disorders*, published by the American Psychiatric Association. "It's not a bible, but it's a guideline," he explained. It allowed him to have a common language with other psychiatrists and psychologists. "There are certain inclusion criteria and certain excluding criteria for a wide variety of diagnoses and conditions." The other touchstone text was the *International Classification of Diseases*, published by the National Center for Health Statistics in the United

States. Says Dr. Collins: "There is no such thing as *schizoparanoia* in either one."

We were in his offices at the Centre for Addiction and Mental Health on Queen Street in Toronto, and he pulled the texts from his bookcase to show me. He was an energetic man (as his C.V. attests) and he talked fast, even faster as he expressed his annoyance.

"What they're doing is taking a snapshot, a still frame, and filling in what the movie was before [and] after that still frame. . . . Instead of describing what they are seeing in the frame, they are now attributing an entire life, and characteristics and personality and problems, to the woman prior to that frame being taken. . . . They're giving us the ending when they only have that one still frame."

I asked him about the references to Digna's so-called problems with authority.

"That's ridiculous," he snorted. "I couldn't do that. As a police psychiatrist, could I say someone has trouble with authority based on one interview? *No!* They're extrapolating above and beyond the interview and attributing personality. I look at tapes all the time, but I am very careful what I say about them."

He had an opinion about Digna's behavior.

"If she's been mistrustful of the police, and she's being interviewed by the police, she's going to respond in a different way than she responds normally to the rest of the world. So if the police are her enemy, she's obviously going to respond differently. You cannot attribute a psychological state to someone based on a specific response to an authority. It may just be the way she reacts to the police.

"Does that make her narcissistic, antisocial, or passive-aggressive? No, of course not! If she's paranoid about the police, and somewhat hesitant and paranoid when interviewed by the police, does that mean she has a paranoid disorder? Again, of course not! She's responding appropriately to her circumstances.

What they're doing is attributing pathology to someone who is responding in a guarded manner."

Dr. Collins emphasized that the report could not be called a psychiatric profile, "not from a police perspective, using the police definition of a profile, which is a criminal investigative analysis. Anyone can use the term 'profile,' but in Canadian policing, we would not consider this a profile."

* * *

Back in Renato Sales's adjoining office in May 2002, expecting him to walk through the door at any moment, I still had the profile's fat annex before me. I dictated as fast as I could. The annexed material appeared to combine police reports with psychiatric analysis and made the most serious allegations against Digna Ochoa—allegations that, as I learn, would change the course of her life. It set out to show "according to the standards of forensic psychology and the testimony" that Digna was not a credible witness and concluded that she hadn't told the truth about the kidnappings, particularly the October 28/29 assault in her apartment, in which she was tied up and questioned. Nor could she be believed about the death threats that appeared in the offices of the Miguel Agustín Pro Juárez Human Rights Center around the same time.

Its premise was clear: Digna Ochoa was never kidnapped. Instead, she fabricated threats in order to gain attention. She was sending death threats to herself, and to her colleagues, even as she was faxing out bulletins to national and international human rights organizations in which she criticized Mexican authorities for failing to find the perpetrators of the physical and psychological attacks. She didn't really believe in human rights work; it was her sick little way to get some attention.

It was problematic to follow the evidence presented in the annex. Supposedly, Digna's testimony was riddled with lies, omissions, and far-fetched scenarios. She was portrayed as uncooperative and rude. The authors shredded her testimony, going so far as to present a graph presenting Digna's version of events as well as statements by her colleagues (or by Digna herself) purportedly contradicting her. Observations considered to be particularly significant were emphasized with bold type—sometimes in the oddest places. According to the annex: Digna told police that abductors stole her watch when they held her in a car on August 9, 1999. And yet she was wearing an identical watch during a meeting with the police. No proof, such as make of watch, color, etc., was offered. She said her abductors took her wallet, containing her voter's card, in August. And yet the card subsequently showed up in her apartment in October. Digna said she was frightened because the card's reappearance proved that her enemies knew where she lived, even though she had moved and only her old address was on the card. That doesn't make sense, said the authors of the annexed report. Why didn't it make sense? They didn't explain.

It was as if the entire modern history of Mexico—of brutality against rights defenders and campesino organizations—was nonexistent. The political dimension of Digna's work was erased, as surely as special prosecutor Margarita Guerra y Tejada stripped the assassination of Judge Polo Uscanga of its political context.

There are several other so-called inconsistencies in Digna's testimony, all of which appeared readily explainable.

The annex noted that, on October 13, 1999, Digna and PRO lawyer Jorge Fernández discovered an anonymous threat at the PRO offices. *"Careful. Bomb in the house. Just one. No big deal."* Digna handled the threat, apparently against the instructions of police who were looking for fingerprints. Since the psychological profile of the author of the threats pointed to somebody within PRO, Digna's actions made the police believe she was the culprit. But it seemed a moot point, given that police did not carry out proper fingerprinting of the threats that, four years later, still sat in a box at the offices of the federal attorney general. The police became doubly suspicious when Digna stalwartly defended herself and her colleagues, saying that nobody at PRO could be responsible for the death threats and refusing a polygraph test. One could see her, seething inside at the refusal of police to grasp the notion that Mexico's own security forces could be involved, and growing more reserved and skeptical.

Digna said she was grabbed on her terrace by a man who stuffed her mouth with something that made her lose consciousness; however, police found no evidence of a toxic substance. That didn't prove anything.

When she regained consciousness, Digna said somebody was in front of her wearing dark pants, socks, and no shoes. She couldn't see more because her eyes were covered. But the police said the person was right in front of her and she should have been able to observe more than feet, which seemed to be conjecture.

She freed herself and called her colleague Alfredo Castillo, at PRO. But there was no phone line. How could she have done that? Digna said she called from her cell phone, in the street.

And she omitted to tell police that Pilar Noriega was at her home the evening of October 28, which apparently negated her entire story. Later, Pilar would tell me that she wasn't at Digna's home that night and didn't tell the police that she was. (If that basic piece of information was wrong, I wondered, what else may the police have fabricated?)

Repeatedly, the authors of the annex stressed that, in her testimony: "Digna seemed unsure of herself, and changed her mind when describing events. 'I guess, I think, I'm not sure,' were spontaneous statements. Compared to the statements of *real* victims, according to the psychological standard of the testimony, she is not considered a reliable victim or witness. . . . She doesn't interrupt because she doesn't want to lose the sequence of what she is narrating. She takes a long time to answer, she has to think about her answers, she doesn't know what to answer, and she mimics suggestions offered by the police.

"Example:
"Digna felt something.
"Police: Like a leg?
"Digna: Yes, a leg."
The police quibbled over picayune points that were recounted by a witness so shaken that she broke down and wept in the street after her ordeal and couldn't stop weeping.

"Digna describes how she was taken to the location where they put her on her bed and how they laid her down on the bed to tie her hands, feet, and mouth. She modifies how she previously described the location. There is no similarity. First, she describes how she was held by her left arm to take her to the bedroom [but] when she talked to the Prosecutor's Office, she says her assailants took her right arm.

"First, she says that they sat her down and pushed her backward, raised her feet, and taped her mouth, while in her other declaration to the Prosecutor's Office, she points out that she was sat down and pushed backward, held by her feet and put in a sitting position. As she was sitting, they proceeded to tape her mouth and this is how she justified her final position. . . . Neighbors heard nothing except for one woman's account of a breaking sound. But Digna mentions nothing about anything being broken."

The same day, the report said, PRO officials found their office ransacked. The police believed the perpetrator was someone who knew the office. "Digna Ochoa is the common factor in the receipt of the threats."

The arc of the report rose to the statement that, as a result of her actions, "the Digna Ochoa case becomes the most important case of all."

It was a theme I would hear repeated, in similar language to this report, in the months, even years ahead, as well as from someone very close to Digna. By the end of my investigation, I came to believe I could trace this sentiment back to its source in the March 2000 psychiatric report, assess the emotions behind it, and review the damage it caused.

It was the venom in the veins.

"From now on, the Center and *Licenciada* Ochoa are known, where before they were not known, either on the national or international level," the annex said. It listed all thirty-nine organizations that were advised of the kidnappings, either by Digna herself or by others at the Miguel Agustín Pro Juárez Center, including the president of Mexico, federal cabinet ministers, Mexico City authorities, human rights officials, journalists, and international political and human rights organizations. They were brought up to date and informed of failings by Mexican police to "protect and solve the different physical and psychological attacks against Digna Ochoa and others." (At the time, PRO, in conjunction with the Center for Justice and International Rights in Washington, also began the process to have Digna and her colleagues placed under international court-ordered protection.)

"The working hypothesis in observing Digna Ochoa is that she shows personality traits similar to those found in the psychological profile of the author of the last threats," it said. "This leads us to believe that it is feasible that it was she who really instigated the aggressions or that they were distorted and magnified by Citizen Digna Ochoa y Plácido. . . . She was trying to obtain the benefits of more recognition, power, control, and prestige because now she is known. Where before she was never recognized as a lawyer, her case is known at the national and international level as the case of DIGNA OCHOA, and others. Therefore, it is possible that there will not be any more threats (the Center is busy with the defense of parasites). But once this defense is finished, (there is) more time and, closer to another event related to human rights, it is very probable that there will be other threats."

* * *

The authors were disdainful of Digna Ochoa for publicizing the death threats and kidnappings, both nationally and internationally. At the time of this report in early 2000, the Mexican government was under a court order to protect Digna Ochoa, PRO director Edgar Cortez, and lawyers Mario Patrón and Jorge Fernández.

However, there was no comprehension of the purpose of human rights organizations. It was routine to set up mailing lists (which include the offices of presidents and prime ministers) and send mailings about alleged abuses, campaigns, areas for special concern, upcoming events, etc. It was the same the world over. Communicating information to raise awareness was their raison d'être, whether it was in launching a campaign to free Nelson Mandela or to focus on systemic torture in Mexico.

Since its inception in the late 1980s, PRO had grown into one of Mexico's most effective rights organizations, sending out denunciations of death threats and appealing for action by the Inter-American Human Rights Commission.

But police didn't see it that way. They saw people helping "parasites."

They concentrated on deconstructing Digna. What they didn't do was conduct a serious investigation into the crimes against her.

* * *

I dictated a last line that the report bore the seal of the attorney general of the Federal District, deputy director of prosecutorial investigations, homicide division #10. I packed up my stuff and knocked softly on Sales's door.

"What do you think?" he asked me.

"Incredible," I replied. It was an honest response.

I asked him if anyone else had seen this report, and he told me that it had been shown to Edgar Cortez at PRO, when it was completed in March 2000. PRO was an adviser (*coadyuvante*) to the police on that case, as they were on the current investigation into Digna's death. Sales explained that PRO had been involved then because its lawyers took the threats and kidnappings to the Inter-American Human Rights Commission in Washington. He had known Edgar Cortez for years, through his own human rights involvement. (Both attended the Jesuit-founded Ibero-American University in Mexico City.)

Once again, I was surprised. *Edgar knew?* He knew that the police didn't believe Digna Ochoa in March 2000? He knew that they suspected her of sending the death threats and staging her own kidnappings?

I knew that this was an important missing piece.

So, for insiders, Digna's reputation was destroyed back in March 2000. Who else knew? It looked like Enrique Flota had been aware of its existence. He was close to the previous attorney general, Samuél de Villar, as well as to Edgar and others at PRO. The file went to the federal attorney general. Is that why the Fox government sought to have the protection order lifted at the San José court?

But Digna didn't know; of that I would become convinced.

Digna Ochoa had been tainted by a flimsy psychological profile, without ever having had the chance to defend herself. A chain of events began with the creation of that profile, a chain that led to Digna's exile in Washington, her break with PRO, her return to Mexico, her decision to continue her work in Guerrero without a national organization to back her, and, eventually, to her death.

There was one more incident before Digna left for Washington. On July 24, 2000, she received a threatening call on her cell phone, with voices in the background, and believed her nieces have been kidnapped in Misántla.

She panicked and rushes to Edgar's office. Edgar would tell the Prosecutor's Office that "she started to cry and then she fainted."

This threat was never reported to the Inter-American Human Rights Commission, or the court in San José. By August, Edgar insisted that Digna leave Mexico for exile in Washington. He later informed me: "It was my decision and my decision alone."

* * *

The spy agency CISEN, operating out of the Interior Ministry, knew all about the police investigation into Digna's kidnappings, which began in 1999 and continued into 2000. There was more in the CISEN file on Digna, leaked to the Mexico City newspaper *Reforma* five days after her murder.

"The first investigation carried out by the Mexico City Attorney General's Office found that her denunciations and statements contained inconsistencies, contradictions, and, apparently, fabricated proof. Already, police work has shown us that one of the threats [left at the PRO offices] didn't have any wrinkles or tears in the paper on which it was written. . . . Astonishingly, she affirmed that her voting card [was] returned to her and still she didn't want to accept being under . . . the protection of the authorities."

Digna, it said, claimed she was interrogated overnight for nine hours on October 28/29 about the activities of the PRO human rights center and her ties with EPR and ERPI rebels. Other rights leaders adopted her view that the authorities were behind the crimes. CISEN said: "On November 9, 1999, Adrián Ramírez, president of the League for the Defense of Human Rights, declared that the [kidnappings] could have been the work of [security forces], the Federal Preventive Police, Military Intelligence, or National Defense Intelligence."

CISEN agents obviously thought Digna was an EPR guerrilla. Their file on Digna emphasized that, on December 15, 1999, EPR leaders sent out a communiqué on the detention of *Comandante* Antonio and *Coronel* Aurora, calling these arrests "an expression of a neo-liberal counterinsurgency offensive, carried out by the government on behalf of big national and international capital. . . . These arrests are supposedly part of a plan of attack against political and social organizations, including human rights groups, as is the supposed aggression against Digna Ochoa, from the center."

It was not particularly surprising that CISEN thought Digna was a guerrilla. That is their mind set. However, Digna defended people accused of crimes against the state and it would be naïve to believe there were no rebels among those she helped. But it's worth pointing out that, in the early years of PRO, she and other lawyers spent many hours discussing how they would be perceived. Víctor Brenes remembered they decided not to go to a Zapatista conference—a huge event held at Aguacalientes in the Lacandon jungle in 1995—because they did not want to be seen as Marcos groupies. They didn't want to be seen as crossing a line, and gave great weight to matters of ethics and professional objectivity.

The CISEN file on Digna added an interesting tidbit, saying that, on December 9, 1999, Edgar Cortez met with Interior Secretary Diódoro Carrasco to discuss the investigation into the threats and kidnappings. The secretary, at the helm of one of the most powerful and secretive ministries in Mexico, promised to support the investigation and assist in any way he could. Edgar's meeting with him appeared somewhat irregular, given that Mexico City police were in charge of the case; however, the CISEN file, at least according to *Reforma,* offered no further details. What Diódoro Carrasco did was unknown—but, in any case, the investigation would soon be turned over to federal officials.

In the fall of 2000, six months after a confidential psychological profile—which had never been publicly released[2]—said Digna was not credible, Mexico City police forwarded the case to the offices of the federal attorney general. There, it was mothballed.

After Digna's murder, Edgar told reporters he was aware that federal officials archived the investigation in 2000, but he added that, as far as he knew, there were no more death threats against Digna Ochoa.

* * *

Digna's brother, Jesús, was uncomfortable with PRO's role as *coadyuvantes*, an "assistant" role that gave them access to all the evidence, including sworn statements, as it was gathered. He didn't like Edgar Cortez[3] and began to voice his concerns publicly shortly after Digna's murder. It was Jesús Ochoa who told reporters that Digna was no longer with the Miguel Agustín Pro Juárez Human Rights Center, later revealing that she left on bad terms almost a full year before her death.

Juan José Vera, Digna's boyfriend, felt Edgar Cortez took advantage of Digna.[4] "Even in August and September 2001, after Digna had already left PRO, they were still using her image for their benefit. They would talk about Digna in very ambitious ways, giving the impression that Digna was still part of their projects," he told me once. "Someone in Washington wrote to Digna about it. She never told me who it was, but she said to me, 'Can you believe it?' Digna had gained personal prestige beyond PRO and so they continued to use her name. I told her, 'You've got to draw the line. You have to send out a release saying that you no longer work for them.' But she would just say, 'I respect the work of PRO too much and, if I do that, it will damage their image.'"

There are several versions of how PRO gained this special *coadyuvante* status in the police investigation. Prosecutor Renato Sales said it was routine, given the death threat against the center at the crime scene. But Juan Carlos Plácido, Digna's cousin, told me he signed the necessary papers for PRO. He said that lawyer Carmen Herrera approached him at Digna's funeral in Misántla and urged him to give permission on the part of the family, promising that PRO lawyers would "watchdog" the investigation and ensure Digna's killers were brought to justice. He agreed, without consulting other family members. When they found out, Jesús and Digna's other siblings were angry with him.

By the spring of 2002, many people were concerned about PRO, including Digna's friend Dr. Jorge Arturo de León. At our March interview at his home, the first of several discussions, he sat in his living room, his big frame hunched over, his hands clasped in front of him, his face anguished as he talks about his misgivings with PRO's official role as a party to the police investigation. He had many reasons for thinking it was a mistake: He didn't think PRO should be involved in an investigation that concerned them, or that the center had the money or technical expertise to do proper police work. And he was disgusted with the failure of Edgar Cortez, Carmen Herrera, and Mario Patrón to defend Digna at the press conference earlier that week.

He let out a sigh with his entire body. He believed Digna was being betrayed and he felt powerless to do anything about it.

CHAPTER FOURTEEN

The Shunning

In August 2000, Digna Ochoa was a reluctant exile to Washington. She would never warm up to the American capital. She was living in one of the most beautiful cities in the United States, but she pined for Mexico and home. She felt isolated, even though she was making friends. She took an English course, but felt comfortable only in Spanish and resisted when friends pushed her to practice. "You're as stubborn as a mule," Tamryn Nelson would laugh and tell Digna.[1]

Human rights organizations pulled together, especially when lives were in jeopardy. People scrambled to accommodate Digna. When she arrived in late August 2000, she began work with the Center for Justice and International Law. The center, headed by Argentinean lawyer Viviana Krsticevic, litigated cases before the Inter-American Human Rights Commission in Washington, as well as the Inter-American Human Rights Court in San José, Costa Rica. Viviana had supervised Digna's case the year before, first in Washington, and then in San José, where they successfully obtained the court's protection order against the Mexican government.

Digna threw herself into her work, investigating several Peruvian cases and coordinating a hearing for human rights defenders before the Inter-American commission. She felt good about this hearing because it led to the appointment of a special "rapporteur" to study the problems of human rights defenders, including issues of well-being and security. When she heard about Digna's death a year later, Viviana remembered that particular hearing. How sad and ironic, she thought, that in the end there was no help for Digna.

She worked in a cheery space, overlooking the rooftops of Washington. The center was on Connecticut Avenue NW, half a block from the Q Street exit of the Dupont Circle Metro station. Dupont Circle is an area of nineteenth-century stone mansions, cafés, bookstores, restaurants, and the requisite Starbucks a few steps from the office. At the clubs along Connecticut, there was live music, including the *ranchero* ballads of lost love and heartache that were Digna's favorites.

Digna and Tamryn, who worked as a researcher at CEJIL, became friends. Digna liked corny lines. Tamryn recalled how she would introduce herself, by playing with her name, which meant "worthy of respect, deserving, dignified." Lifting her chin and trying to look regal, she would declare: *"Soy Digna, Dignissima, Dignitaria."*

She was always clowning around and playing tricks on her colleagues, just as she had with her many brothers and sisters growing up in the little house in Misántla, Veracruz. Soon, she would need all the dignity, strength, and humor she could muster.

As August turned to September, the days were warm and balmy, with little rain, and Tamryn and Digna often ate their lunch together in the park. They talked about politics, their lives, and Digna's yearning for home.

For the first few months, she lived with Denise Gilman and her husband, Ariel Dulitzky, in their home near Capitol Hill. Ariel, an Argentinean lawyer with a master's degree in law from Harvard,[2] worked for the Inter-American Human Rights Commission, while Denise, an American, was with the Washington Lawyers Committee for Civil Rights.[3]

Denise was friends with both Digna and lawyer Pilar Noriega, and they'd often traveled together in Mexico for their work. "I remember eating *pozole* in the basement of a church in Taxco with

Digna and Pilar. It was so much fun," Denise would tell me later, saying she could almost taste the delicious soup. "Pilar is just such a total character. It's hard to describe, but I remember sitting there and Pilar got it into her head that I was Jewish so she wouldn't let me eat the pork *pozole* because I wasn't allowed to eat pork. Well, my dad's Jewish, but I eat what I like. Digna stuck up for me, telling Pilar, 'She can eat whatever she wants.' You know, we just did silly things."

By the time I interviewed Denise Gilman, Digna had been dead for six months. It was the spring of 2002 and we were having lunch al fresco in a little café in Washington, just as she had often done with Digna. Denise was a lovely woman, in her thirties, with an oval face, delicate features, and large blue eyes that were, as she spoke, filling with tears.

"Ah, we were so silly. Once, in Cuernavaca, Pilar decided we should buy these little airplane bottles of tequila so that we could go back to the PRO and say we'd each drunk a bottle of tequila over the weekend. So we hung out at Pilar's house and then she decided she couldn't drink because she was taking antibiotics, so Digna and I shared one of these bottles of airplane tequila and went back and told everybody we drank a bottle together. Just normal hanging-out stuff. . . ."

Denise told me Digna called a few weeks before her arrival in Washington to ask if she could stay with the couple. She also inquired if Ariel would become her adviser on her MacArthur Foundation grant. When Edgar ordered Digna into exile, she'd had to change her idea for the project from Mexico to the United States. She'd been planning to focus on the Montiel/Cabrera case, but she now intended to analyze the effectiveness of the human rights political infrastructure (the Inter-American Commission, etc.) for defenders. She thought she could write a workshop manual on how best to make use of the system, illustrating it with cases, including the Guerrero environmentalists, to show failures as well as successes.

Denise and Ariel loved Digna and were delighted to welcome her. They had lots of room in their airy home near the Capitol Dome. But there was something troubling about Digna's phone call, and they talked about it afterward.

"It's weird," Denise told her husband. The phone call had come out of the blue, but, according to Digna, her boss, Edgar Cortez, was supposed to already have made all the arrangements. Digna was surprised to learn that he hadn't.[4]

Denise thought it strange Edgar hadn't called to make sure Digna was looked after, but put it out of her mind. So did Ariel. A slim, wiry man, with an infectious sense of humor and a busy schedule, he tried to make time to talk to Digna in the evenings.

A few weeks after she arrived, Digna pulled Denise aside.

"I am feeling kind of guilty," she said. "We never talked about how long I was going to stay here, or anything. How do you guys feel about it?"

"We're happy to have you. Stay as long as you like," replied Denise, giving Digna a hug and doing her best to ease her friend's obvious discomfort.

Digna explained she could pay $50 a week in grocery money. She apologized for not having more money.

Denise knew Digna had no source of income at this time, other than her MacArthur Foundation grant (which usually awards around $25,000 a year).[5] Denise wondered why PRO wasn't providing her with any money; after all, it was Edgar who had sent Digna into exile in an expensive city, and she was running out of funds.

And then, in September, Edgar called Denise and Ariel to talk about Digna. He reached them separately, at their offices.

" 'You know, we don't believe her most recent threats,' " Denise said he told her. " 'We don't think they really happened.' "

The couple was shocked. Nothing made sense to them.

Here was Digna living in their home, in political exile, and now, suddenly, her director was saying there was a problem with her account of a phone threat in July. If Digna wasn't telling the truth about the threats, then why had Edgar sent her into exile for her safety, as well as that of her colleagues at the Miguel Agustín Pro Juárez Human Rights Center in Mexico City? And why hadn't he reported this new development in the case to the Inter-American Human Rights Commission and the San José court? It was a grave matter for the international court to have ordered the Mexican government to protect one of its citizens. The court needed to have all relevant information.

Edgar apparently didn't believe that Digna had received a phone threat on July 24, the one in which Digna feared for her nieces' lives. It seems the call hadn't shown up in either Digna's phone records or in her cell phone's memory.

Edgar wanted them to convince Digna to see a therapist, which Denise thought was a good idea anyway, given what Digna had been through over the past year.[6] There were more phone calls back and forth between Washington and Mexico City. It seemed to Denise that Edgar Cortez was expressing his opinions to everybody but Digna, and she was becoming increasingly angry over this treatment of Digna, as was Ariel and other Washington friends they consulted.

Ariel felt that Edgar and PRO were putting them in an extremely difficult position with Digna, given that they knew he didn't believe her.[7]

A few days later, there was a conference call between Edgar in Mexico City and Denise, Ariel, Viviana from CEJIL, and a couple of Digna's other friends in the United States.

"Please, you really have to talk to Digna about this," Denise told Edgar. "You are putting us in an impossible situation. We are living with this person and you are asking us to take actions based on your decisions. You don't believe her but you're not telling her. In any case, it makes no sense. You sent her up here because you say you feared for her life, and now you are saying you don't even believe her. What is going on?"

Denise would never forget that phone call. Six months after Digna's murder, she was still seething.

"I am pissed at them," she told me over lunch. "I'll be honest, I am just overwhelmingly pissed at PRO—just the way the whole thing came down."

She was never satisfied with Edgar's explanations for his actions.

Denise brooded. Should she tell Digna? She waited.

* * *

Despite her problems with PRO, September 2000 was an exciting month for Digna. Two gala events were coming up and she tried to put aside her anxiety over Edgar.

She flew to Los Angeles for the Amnesty International dinner at the Beverly Wilshire Hotel on Monday, September 16, where Martin Sheen was to present her with Amnesty's Enduring Spirit Award. The RFK Memorial Center, which works on international human rights cases, nominated Digna for the honor.

Digna was to make an acceptance speech and, for days before her flight, she e-mailed Edgar, asking for his advice about what she should say. She telephoned and left messages for him.

But there was no response.

The night the award was given, nobody but Digna's closest friends had any inkling something was wrong. In her speech, she shared the award with her colleagues at PRO, praising their strength, courage, and dedication.

Before she left for L.A., Tamryn Nelson teased Digna about Antonio Banderas. Someone from Amnesty apparently told her she would meet the actor at an event in L.A. and Digna had to admit to Tamryn she didn't know who he was. That gave everybody a big giggle.

Tamryn was excited. Sweet-faced, in her twenties, and agog over the handsome Spanish actor, she kept telling Digna how great it was. "*Imagine!* You're going to meet *Antonio Banderas.*"

"Well, I guess he is kind of cute," said Digna upon her return.

"That's Digna," thought Tamryn. "She just doesn't care about any of that stuff."[8]

On Thursday, September 19, Ariel Dorfman's play, *Speak Truth to Power: Voices from Beyond the Dark,* adapted from Kerry Kennedy's book on human rights leaders, debuted at the Kennedy Center for the Performing Arts in Washington. President Bill Clinton opened the play and actor Alfre Woodard read Digna's part.

Digna went shopping with Viviana and purchased a new suit for the occasion. Her choice was simple, dark and a little austere, or so Viviana thought, and completely different from the white suit she'd worn a few days before in Los Angeles.

"It was really something for her to go and buy a suit because she really wasn't into clothes," Viviana said later. "She looked very beautiful, just radiant. And it was a wonderful, wonderful moment when the crowd at the Kennedy Center recognized her. It was a luminous moment because she had been through so much, and I saw that night how she had been able to overcome so many things. She was very strong. She had that rock, which was God."[9]

The days passed, and still no word from Edgar. Digna wanted to report the last threatening phone call in July to the Inter-American Human Rights Commission. She felt that it should be included in her file, especially since the case had been forwarded to the San José court, which slapped "protective measures" on the Mexican government. Apart from her own anguish, she felt it was improper to withhold information from the commission.

But, inexplicably to Digna, Edgar had vetoed the idea.

Digna didn't understand what was happening.

"What's going on?" she asked Denise. "What's going on?" she asked Ariel. They could hear her on the telephone with other friends. The bleak question reverberated through their home: *"What's going on???!!!"*[10]

Finally, one evening, Denise and Digna were alone in the living room. "What's going on?" Digna wanted to know.

Denise couldn't stand it anymore. No longer able to pretend, she told Digna the whole story. She told her about Edgar's phone calls, the conference call, and his belief that Digna made up the whole scenario of the threats involving her nieces.

Digna looked stunned, and then collapsed in tears.

"So that's it. So that's it," she repeated in a shaky, almost inaudible voice. "I would have never guessed that was it."

Of course, there was more—much more.

Neither Denise nor Digna knew about the psychiatric report from the spring of 2000, which alleged that she'd lied about everything. They had no idea that Edgar—and possibly some of Digna's colleagues at PRO—had seen this police file, in which it was suggested that Digna herself was the perpetrator, not just of death threats against herself and her colleagues, but of her own kidnapping, and that she couldn't be trusted.

That night, Digna told Denise there had been a case at PRO years earlier in which someone was suspected of being an infiltrator. They later found out it wasn't true and everyone felt terrible about what they'd done to this person. Digna thought they had learned their lesson and would never do it again. She thought they would all be supportive of one another, no matter what.

(There apparently was, at another time, a CISEN mole at PRO. He was working as a volunteer in the legal department and, once his cover was blown in 1997, he simply evaporated. PRO lawyer Mario Patrón told me about this during an interview in Mexico City after Digna was murdered.[11] He said somebody from CISEN admitted it directly to PRO director David Fernández during a showdown they were having about threats to the rights agency at that time. Mario wouldn't tell me anything else, and I found it curious that CISEN would have offered up the information to PRO.)

Digna didn't want to believe that Edgar thought she was lying about the calls, especially given their shared experience. How easy it would be to erase any record of a phone call, she told Denise. Edgar should have known that from their case work. Denise agreed. "It's not as if cell phones don't have weird records," she would tell me later.

(The call would not necessarily have shown on Digna's cell phone. For example, calls from blocked numbers are not listed under incoming or missed calls. And, while all calls are recorded by the network provider,[12] it's not clear how deep the official investigation to determine what happened went in Mexico City. If the investigation by Mexico City prosecutors into Digna's kidnappings could be taken as the standard, it didn't go very deep at all.)

Digna and her colleagues at PRO were well aware of the established liaison between intelligence agencies and the Mexican phone company. "Telephone espionage has always counted on the collaboration of . . . Teléfonos de México," wrote Sergio Aguayo in his book about CISEN, *La Charola.* "Three fiber optic cables go from [CISEN] to three Telmex centers. . . . A few years ago, a Telmex employee was in charge of looking after (CISEN). There was a legendary *Señor* Prado to whom they sent a card with the numbers they wanted tapped, without any formality whatsoever (nobody handed over, or even asked for, a judge's order). . . . That same official was in charge of arranging for the president to have direct telephone lines with members of his cabinet during trips in Mexico and abroad."[13]

PRO lawyers had their own history of bad experiences with Telmex. When the death threats against the center began in 1995, Víctor Brenes was angry that telephone company officials wouldn't lift a finger to help.

In Washington, Digna's pain was overwhelming. While her friends watched her suffer, Edgar remained unavailable and inscrutable to her in Mexico City, shunning her by failing to respond to her numerous, and increasingly plaintive, e-mails.

* * *

I was ushered into the office of Edgar Cortez at PRO on April 30, 2002. It was my second interview with him, the first having come three months earlier, in January. At that time, he told me he was born in Tlaxcala, Mexico's smallest state, the son of merchants, grew up in a middle-class home, studied law in college, joined the Society of Jesus, studied philosophy, social sciences, and theology, and became a Jesuit priest. He worked with street children in Tijuana before coming to Mexico City and accepting a position with PRO, where he succeeded David Fernández, also a Jesuit priest, as director in 1996.

We had a brief, uneventful interview in January because the suicide theory hadn't broken yet. This day, however, having been to Washington, I had many more questions.

Edgar was a slight man, handsome, with black hair, a moustache, and neatly trimmed beard. There was an intensity about him, even when he was silent, almost a brooding quality. He was watchful, but perhaps I felt that because he was not comfortable with me and wouldn't look me in the eye.

"Digna was kidnapped twice in 1999, and there was that call in 2000 when she thought her nieces were threatened," I stated, a few minutes into our interview. "Do you have any problems with Digna's factual version of these events?"

"No, I had no problem with her version," he replied.

"You had no doubts at all?"

"No. If I had had doubts, I would not have asked her to leave the country. If I took such a sensitive decision as to tell her to leave the country, it was because it seemed to me that she was under threat."

"I have done a lot of work on this," I told him. "I have spoken to people in Washington, at the commission, etc., who told me you telephoned them to say you had doubts about Digna's version, and that it would be a good idea to get medical, psychological attention for her."

"Well, we made this suggestion to her a long time back to seek therapy because I believe when one is living with threats, it always affects a person's health and integrity, and so that wasn't the first time we had proposed it. It was always a suggestion, though, made with the clear understanding that it was a decision only she could make—to get therapy or not, and when."

He said Digna didn't agree to see a psychiatrist.

(Digna was not here to respond. However, I remember her telling me how outraged she was at being brushed off by Mexico City police after her kidnappings. One officer told her to go see a psychiatrist. "That bothered me a lot," she told me. "If this is the type of support you get from the authorities who are supposed to be carrying out the investigation, well . . . how lamentable!")

I kept returning to the same issue of whether Edgar believed Digna.

"You didn't telephone people in Washington to say you had doubts about Digna's version of events? I am not saying you are lying, but there it is."

"Well, they're confused," he replied.

Later, I tried again.

"Did you have doubts about whether, in reality, Digna was kidnapped?"

"No, no, no, no, if I had . . ."

"Because this is really important."

"Yes, but if I had had doubts, I wouldn't have presented the denunciations, all the denunciations," he says, referring to PRO's denunciations of death threats and kidnappings to authorities in Mexico City, as well as the launch of formal proceedings before the Inter-American Human Rights Commission and the Inter-American Court of Human Rights in San José, Costa Rica. "If I had had doubts I wouldn't have done it. Each time something happened, we made denunciations before the authorities. I tell you that, if I had had any doubts, I wouldn't have presented these denunciations to the authorities."

"Do you feel satisfied that, in all your relations with Digna—your conversations, your actions—you acted in a proper manner?" I asked him.

"Yes, in my opinion, yes," he says. "My actions at the time seem to me to have been more than adequate."

I tried one more time.

"Just to be clear, there was no confusion about what Digna said happened in the two kidnappings and the last threatening telephone call?"

"I repeat again—I never doubted her. If I had ever doubted her, we would not have made the denunciations at the time."

"Well, there are people now who think it was suicide."

"That," said Edgar, "is a question for the Prosecutor's Office to answer. They are the ones doing the investigation."

I asked him what he thought.

"Our opinion was that Digna's death was a consequence of her work as a human rights lawyer," he said.

"So murder?" I asked.

"It is the responsibility of the authorities to say if it was a murder or suicide."

On another point, he said PRO did not have problems with Renato Sales's handling of the investigation. "The problem we had with the first investigative team was that they thought the role of *coadyuvantes*—something that has only recently been incorporated into the law—was to provide information and evidence to the Attorney General's Office, and not to have direct access to the file."

I asked: "As far as your role as *coadyuvantes*, given your history with Digna and the fact that you knew her, isn't there a conflict of interest in PRO being *coadyuvantes*? Isn't this a problem for you?"

"No, quite the contrary. The fact that we knew her, and had a history with her, seems to us to be a benefit," he replied.

When I reminded him that many thought that PRO had let

Digna down by not defending her against the suicide theory, he said that people misunderstood the role of *coadyuvante*. PRO wanted to be close to the investigation and the only way to do so was by assuming the responsibility. But he stressed that "it is not our responsibility to investigate. That is the responsibility of the authorities. Our role, rather, is to follow the investigation and be vigilant about it."

PRO must be "respectful" of the work the police are doing, he said. Several times he complimented Attorney General Bernardo Bátiz for his oversight of the case, beginning with the night of Digna's death.

That evening, Edgar got a voice message on his cell. He telephoned his office and "they just told me that Digna was found dead in her office. That was all the information I was given. My first thought was to get to the scene to learn the details."

"And when you arrived, what did you think of the police investigation that was under way?" I asked him.

"The authorities got there immediately, police, the special agents of the Public Ministry," he began. "Later, the attorney general himself arrived. He did a tour of the scene. He gave instructions to the people who were there, telling them what things they should give the most attention, and what should come first. He asked us if we had any special requests to make, and he assured us that he was being very careful to look after and protect the integrity of the evidence."

He said he had no special request for Attorney General Bátiz.

* * *

Meanwhile, to return to Washington in the autumn of 2000, Digna Ochoa poured her heart out in e-mails to Edgar Cortez, her boss; to her longtime friend, Jesús "Chuche" Maldonado, also a Jesuit priest and her mentor; and to others at PRO. Denise had told her that Edgar doesn't believe her and one can picture her, alone at her computer, tapping out her heartbreak into the void.

To Michel Maza, a friend at PRO, she wrote: "At this moment, I feel so lost and distanced from everyone with whom I shared so much and everything I invested in. I never thought I would be in such circumstances."[14]

To Edgar and Chuche, she sent an e-mail marked "urgent—at least to me."

"To Chuche and Edgar: To me, the time spent at PRO was a gift. There were difficult moments, but also good and lovely ones. I was always convinced that it was worth the pain. . . . The time I spent in the [Dominican] Congregation enriched me and helped me to give much more profound feeling to my work at PRO.

"Professionally, I learned a great deal. I have grown as a person, my faith has grown stronger, and I thought I had found friends with whom I fell in love, little by little, certainly some more than others, but I think that's normal. . . . I think I did what I could for my work. Perhaps I could have given more, but I don't know how.

"You know how much it cost me to leave Mexico. I accepted because you made me believe it was for the best. (If only you knew how silly and stupid I feel now for having believed it.) Maybe it was better—for you.

"If you wanted me out of PRO, it wasn't necessary to throw me out of Mexico. You simply could have told me that you saw it as more suitable, and that I was too heavy a burden to carry. I could have accepted that with less pain than all this.

"I thought you knew me, and you, Chuche, all these years, and now this. You don't know how it hurts me, but I refuse to accept it because you have given me so much and I love you sincerely. I thought you knew me.

"I can assure you that it doesn't hurt to lose my job as much as to lose those whom I have considered my friends and loved so dearly. I have spent hours thinking about all this and still I can't believe it is real. I wish it were a nightmare.

"Perhaps I should tell you that this situation hurts me far more than all the annoying threats, and all that has happened to me. Just yesterday, I found out that you think what happened on July 24 is not true. Now I understand your shortness and your distance with me. What a shame you didn't have the honesty and confidence to tell me directly. I wouldn't have had to find out from others, especially when other people knew too, and the last one to find out was me—and not from you, but from other people here. I can't imagine what more could happen to me—but, *whatever*. It can't hurt me as much as this doubt about me and the things you have done in this way.

"Yesterday, people from Amnesty London talked to me about financial support for my stay here in Washington. . . . There aren't any support programs but they are going to see what they can do for me. I didn't know what to say because I was surprised. I didn't know anything about it.

"Don't worry about my expenses. Starting today, consider yourselves free of any responsibility for me. Thank you for all those years at PRO, and for all the support. I believe I know now what you were waiting for, but you didn't know how to tell me. I know how to make it easy for you: I ask you to remove me from PRO. Edgar, when you come to Washington next time, it would be useful to bring whatever I am supposed to sign. . . .

"Don't worry, I won't tell anyone and I will look after my affairs myself. Thus, I free you from any responsibility for me and, likewise, I will feel free to do what I want. I don't know if I will stay or return to Mexico, but that won't be your problem. I assume the responsibility. Edgar, I hope I can speak with you when you are here. Let's hope you can dedicate a little time to talk with me, face-to-face. I sincerely need it, and I think that I deserve an explanation. Adios, Digna."[15]

Her e-mails were achingly human. She seemed to be on an emotional roller-coaster, with her attitude shifting from bravado to anger to regret.

Edgar was due to fly to Washington for meetings of the Inter-American Human Rights Commission, which were set to begin on October 20.

She implored Jesús Maldonado, her old friend and mentor.

"*Hola*, Chuche, I confess to you sincerely that your silence to my letter hurts me deeply. I don't understand the little importance you give to me," she wrote.

* * *

Chuche Maldonado held tremendous importance in Digna's life. He was a founder of PRO and served as its executive director from 1988 to 1995.

"Look, we're just setting up the center and we need a lawyer. Work with us," he told Digna when she arrived in Mexico City.[16] She'd fled Veracruz where, as she recounted in a press conference in Jalapa, she was kidnapped by police, raped, and tortured.

Digna's friends say Jesús Maldonado urged her to join the Dominicans of the Incarnate Word. Víctor Brenes thought he was unduly influencing her life and spoke to Digna about it.

"Digna, please take care when you talk with Chuche," Víctor told her. "You know, he's going to invite you to become a nun. I'm not so sure that's a good idea."

Digna roared with laughter and entered the Dominican convent anyway. She began her studies in 1991, leaving eight years later without taking her final vows.

Jesús "Chuche" Maldonado held the secrets of Digna's heart and soul. He knew her weaknesses and her most profound fears. He knew her like a psalm.

From Washington, Digna begged him to tell her what is going on, and why Edgar wouldn't talk to her.

"I thought you knew me," she wrote. "I believe you do know me, and have for such a long time. You have meant so much to me, and that is why I have wept and suffered as I have.

"Chuche, for the affection of all those years, I beg you to understand what this means to me. . . . If I didn't love you, it wouldn't hurt so much. . . . You, especially, have surprised me. . . . I wish I could have spoken to you. A hug, Digna."[17]

And still he ignored her.

* * *

I don't know if Digna ever spoke to Chuche Maldonado again. He grieved Digna's passing very publicly in October 2001, as did Edgar Cortez. In an interview the next year with Mexican documentary filmmaker Felipe Cazals for his film about Digna, *Digna: Until the Last Breath,* in a segment called "The Silence of Jesus," he seemed to distance himself from her.

He said that he didn't think Digna ever understood why she had to go into exile or how he and the others had felt that "it was very important for all of us given the pressure" and best for Digna herself. "Since she didn't understand this, she started to exert pressure when she was up there to say that we . . . I don't remember how she said it, but something like we kicked her out, or tried to, when that wasn't it. When she took that sort of aggressive stance, I told her, 'That was not my intention, and if you don't understand that, what can I do?'"

* * *

At last, Edgar arrived in Washington and met Denise and Ariel for dinner in a Chinese restaurant in Dupont Circle. He told them again that he didn't believe Digna's account of having received a threatening phone call in July.

"Are you sure?" Denise asked him.

"Yes," she said he replies, insisting that there was no record of the phone threats. There can be no other explanation.

They urged him to talk to Digna.

"She has to have a chance to defend herself," Denise insisted.[18]

He kept promising he would speak to her, but delayed. Eight days passed before he finally called her.

On a late October Sunday, Edgar met with Digna for coffee at a Starbucks near her office. They spoke privately and when the meeting was over Digna was no longer with the organization where she had spent the last twelve years of her life. It may be that Digna initiated the break, but Edgar did not invite her to stay. She must have felt she had been masterfully manipulated by those who knew her best.

A few days later, Digna sent another e-mail to Edgar:

"I wanted to write these lines to express my feelings after our conversation last Sunday," she said. "You left me with great sadness and pain for all that has passed, and how things have gone, above all for what you think. . . . Edgar, you have given me pause to think and, just supposing you had been right and I was ill, I don't believe that sending me away was the best way to help me, especially given that, if I had been ill, it would have been due to my work for the center.

"How did my actions convince you that, as you said, I probably was affected psychologically by what happened? . . . Even if you don't share this opinion, I repeat to you once again, the events of July 24 are true. Your doubt floors me and hurts so much.

"If, in the future, you realize that you are wrong, and that it was an unjust error, I merely ask that you take that into consideration and never repeat it with any other colleague because it is too deeply damaging.

"I leave with much good I found in you and others at PRO. I want only to say thank you to all of you for having given me this opportunity to spend these years with you. They have been the best for me to date. I hold no rancor or resentment because that would only damage me, and I already have enough pain to last me."

Digna's friends in Washington rallied to support her. She met often with Tamryn and one day told her why the threatening phone call in July frightened her so deeply. "I have no children of my own, and my family, my brothers and sisters, and especially my nieces and nephews, are very dear to me. If they go after me, that is one thing. But if they go after my family, that's another matter entirely."[19]

Digna spent hours trying to figure out what happened. She felt totally betrayed.[20] She was frustrated because she always felt there was something more to it with Edgar Cortez, and the others, than the July phone threats.

(I believe she never knew the full extent of it. Till the day she died, there would be no sign that Digna realized how precarious her position was with PRO. She never learned about the pseudopsychological report of March 2000.

Depressed, Digna began to see a therapist in Washington and was pleased with the results. She felt she needed somebody else to tell her she wasn't crazy. She told Denise Gilman that her therapist said she was having a completely normal reaction to the terrible things she had endured.

She was sad, but she continued to work. She remained full of life and energy, still enjoying good jokes and cooking for Ariel and Denise. A specialty was *pollo en jitomate* (tomato chicken). And she found solace in her religion.[21] Her Washington hosts saw that she wasn't the type of person to just give up and go to bed.

But Digna still brooded, and so did Denise and Ariel. Denise began to think that perhaps PRO itself, as an organization, may have become unglued by the years of constant death threats, tension, paranoia, and danger. She wondered whether maybe, as a defensive action, the center didn't want to believe anymore that it was under threat.[22] She had worked with political asylum cases and she'd seen people reach the point where their minds didn't want to process information anymore. The pressure was simply too great.

She even raised that possibility with Edgar, trying to be as delicate as she could. That night, she told her husband what she had done and he laughed at her for a week.

"You basically told Edgar that PRO is insane!" said Ariel,[23] and Denise laughed too, a release in grim times.

Digna again wrote to Chuche:

"Above all, why weren't you sincere and honest in speaking clearly to me from the very beginning? You know I love you so much, and that, for me, you have been a special person who helped me in a very difficult time. I don't know why you don't do the same now. . . .

"I am thankful for having the opportunity to have been with all of you. But it is painful because I didn't succeed in building relationships solid enough really to sustain a difficult moment. I thought I had, but perhaps I imagined it because I wanted it to be so. It hurts too much to think I had friends, and for so long, and, suddenly, it's over. I don't understand and it is difficult for me to accept. You knew everything that was going on and that hurts me the most, and will take me longer to absorb. With the help of God and some new friends, I will do it."[24]

In November, unable to let go of the pain, Digna wrote a long farewell to all her friends at PRO. She was still chewing over every detail, struggling to figure out what happened, obsessing. Her letter was directed to everyone.

"I said this to Edgar and now, I say it to you that, really, what hurt me the most in all of this is to have lost all of you, whom I love and considered to be my friends," she wrote.

"Never did I imagine leaving PRO in these circumstances, but, *bueno*, things are thus and can't be changed. I don't really know what you think, but I want to give you my version of why I left the center. When I agreed to come to Washington, it was because you convinced me that it was for the best and the truth is that I believed it. Since then, I have discovered that it was for the best, but for PRO. It hurts me very much that there wasn't enough sincerity, honesty, and confidence to simply ask for my resignation, and not provoke so much pain. This whole situation has almost succeeded where threats and aggression could not."

Digna urged Edgar to reconsider his decision not to inform the Inter-American Human Rights Commission, as well as the San José court, of the July threat. Several of her colleagues in Washington also were uncomfortable with this decision, she wrote. The court's order of "provisional measures" to protect Digna and her PRO colleagues was a serious matter for Mexico, and Digna felt that everyone should be kept up to date. It was an active case and these new threats were part of it.

She wrote of the pain of waiting eight days to see Edgar in Washington, and then of learning of his doubts. "And here it was: The last threats were doubted because the telephone company didn't register the calls. (I can't believe you'd give them more credence than me when you know how they manipulate things.)

"I tell you, it's true what happened July 24. I didn't imagine it, I didn't dream it, I didn't invent it. . . . It's true that I didn't react in the best manner that day. But I ask you, who can program themselves to react in such and such a way? Many times, I have told myself how I wish to react in a circumstance, but my reactions are so spontaneous that I have no time to think, 'How should I react?'

"Moreover, the worst is that if you and Edgar thought that I was unwell, I think it was very unjust to send me away, alone, and without any real support at a time when I certainly needed it the most. It was more serious in light of the work I have done for PRO, although I assure you that I feel fine and I am totally certain that I am fine. I confirm it.

"All of this has caused me great pain and great sadness and, I repeat, where all the threats have failed—Edgar and you have almost succeeded. . . ."[25]

When one considers what Digna Ochoa had endured in her life, this was a singularly powerful and heartbreaking statement.

The break with PRO was life-changing for Digna. She had risked her life for the Miguel Agustín Pro Juárez Human Rights Center, and now she realized that, to them, she was just another lawyer.[26]

For a long time, Digna didn't see any light at the end of the tunnel. At her lowest point, despite her cheeriness with Ariel and Denise, she came to believe that her past has been destroyed and her future didn't exist.

* * *

When I interviewed Edgar Cortez at the end of April 2002, I was not aware of the existence of Digna's e-mails from Washington. Nor did I know about the psychological report prepared by the Mexico City police; Renato Sales wouldn't give that to me for another couple of weeks.

However, in his office in 2002, I did ask him about other issues. To slip back to that afternoon for a moment, I was with Edgar Cortez in Mexico City, my tape recorder still running and more questions on my mind.

I was curious about the exact circumstances under which Digna left Mexico City to go into exile in 2000, and asked him about it.

"It was not an easy decision to make," he said. "But the threats were continuing to come and so the decision was taken that she should leave the country. If you want me to be precise, it was not a group decision. It was my decision. I am the director. I am responsible for the security of the people who work here."

"Was the plan that she would continue working for PRO?" I asked.

"The idea was she would spend some time out of the country for the sake of her safety. And because the idea was to protect her safety, she was supposed to be discreet and not give public statements, to keep a low profile," he said. "She would continue in her work with human rights by receiving training in the Inter-American system, she would continue to help PRO from Washington in the cases we had before the Inter-American Commission. During that time she would continue being part of the PRO team, and receive her salary, and after a while we would evaluate the situation and she would return to the country and resume her activities."

However, he explained, after a few weeks, Digna began to make public statements. I mentally calculated the time frame and realized he was talking about such public statements as her acceptance speech when she won Amnesty International's Enduring Spirit Award, in September 2000. Digna desperately sought his advice on her acceptance speech but he ignored her.

"Her statements appeared in Mexican newspapers at the time," he told me. "I mean, these were statements she made while she was out of the country and she'd had to leave the country because her safety could not be guaranteed. I would have preferred that she'd consulted with me directly on any declarations she made. They appeared in *La Jornada* and *El Universal*. I mean, this was an event that was in, ah, yes, California, which was organized by Mrs. Kerry Kennedy, who published that book about human rights defenders, about all of that."

(It is interesting that he thought Kerry Kennedy organized an event by Amnesty International. In any case, it was clear he thought Digna received the award because of her.)

"Was that a problem?" I asked. "Was it a problem that Digna won the award?"

"Oh no, no, no, the problem was that the whole point was discretion. What we were trying to achieve was her safety and it was a signal that she was not complying with the way in which we agreed to manage things."

I was beginning to wonder if this had as much to do with professional jealousy over Digna's recognition as with her security.

I asked him what happened when he met with Digna in

Washington but he was tight-lipped, saying that they came to an understanding, and: "I have nothing more to say."

What did he hope to see achieved in the investigation?

"Of course, we want to see justice in relation to Digna, but also in relation to other defenders of human rights. Digna was not an isolated person," he said. "You see, Digna didn't work as an individual as a human rights defender, but always as part of an institution, always as one associate among many other lawyers. . . . Digna was a human rights defender among hundreds of others, and [there] must be justice for all of them. It seems to me that you cannot think that this is just about Digna. She was not alone. She was part of a team and that is my concern—that it be understood that she was part of a team."

One among *hundreds*? Over the course of our interview, he returned several times, without prompting, to this theme. Digna seemed to fade before my eyes, until she became lost in a crowd. (Edgar's words would stick in my mind. I would think of them when, in the near future, I read the psychological report on Digna in Sales's office. *"Where before she was never recognized as a lawyer, her case is known at the national and international level as the case of* DIGNA OCHOA, *and others."*)

At one point, I asked Edgar to describe Digna's contribution. What made her good?

He shook his head, and paused before responding:

"I find that very difficult to answer because, in reality, although people talk a lot about Digna's cases, all the cases she worked on, she really worked as part of a team with other lawyers. Yes, she worked on the case of the 'presumed Zapatistas,' but as a member of a team that was coordinated by someone else. She was part of the team and the strategy was defined by the lawyer who was coordinating the team."

(He was referring to Enrique Flota, the former Jesuit priest who first floated the suicide theory with me and put me in contact with prosecutor Sales.)

He continued: "I think one of Digna's contributions was that she was always open to the idea of being a team player. Decisions of strategy on how to approach the case of the prisoners was never taken by just one person. They were always taken collectively."

"Well, working on a team," I began, "Digna still won the Amnesty International Award, she was involved in the book by Kerry Kennedy, and she won a MacArthur Foundation grant. How did that happen?"

"*Bueno*, what happened was that there were various threats and she became very well known on an international level because of these threats, the kidnappings," he replied. "But when they give these awards, there is always a big campaign and a lot of solidarity among many organizations [working for a nominee] and Digna's case was already well known. You know, she gave the interview to Kerry Kennedy, and her case became public, she was internationally recognized because of the book . . . But, again, I would say that Digna's disposition was always to be part of a team [and] the political and judicial strategies of her cases were always defined by a much larger group."

I can't let it go.

"But she received the attention. . . ."

"Yes, because we denounced what happened to her," he said. "But she was always part of the Center. It was always said that these threats were against Digna but they were threats against the entire team."

* * *

At the beginning of December 2000, Digna moved into an efficiency apartment in the Park Plaza on Columbia Road in the neighborhood of Adams Morgan, not far from the CEJIL office. She loved being on her own and her spirits lifted. Christmas was coming and she was excited about plans to fly home to Mexico to spend it with her family in Misántla. She'd been back briefly in

November for a meeting of the MacArthur fellows, but this time she will be able to relax.

She flew back to Washington in January, relieved that 2000 was finally over and looking forward to the new year of 2001. Things would be better, she told her friends. For the first time, she was coming to grips with the idea of a future after PRO and she began to make plans to return to Mexico City in March. She couldn't wait to get home. She'd never given serious thought to her boast to Edgar Cortez that she might remain in the United States. She was *mexicana* to the bone, and her country called for her return.

It was an exciting time for her and there was a bounce in her step. She had met Juan José Vera in an online chat room and, as February turns to March, their relationship intensified. She was beginning to fall in love with a man she had only seen in a photo, and it excited her. She was writing to him two and three times a day, including him in her plans and telling him she believed their relationship could work out.

She asked her cousin Juan Carlos to look for an apartment for her in the south end of Mexico City, where rents were affordable on her grant money from the MacArthur Foundation. She didn't have a job and didn't know when she would be able to earn more. She told friends that she was looking forward to getting back into litigation in private practice.

The weeks went by quickly. Digna was busy with the upcoming spring hearings of the Inter-American Human Rights Commission. She was the guest of honor at a small going-away party on Friday, March 2, two days before her flight to Mexico City from Dulles International Airport in nearby Virginia.

Tamryn Nelson would never forget her final words that night.

"Make sure you guys keep your eyes out for those provisional measures, okay?" she said, about her court-ordered protection. "Make sure you guys have got me covered."[27]

* * *

Digna returned to Mexico, friends kept in touch by e-mail, months passed and lives moved on.

Soon it was another autumn in the U.S. capital and Ariel and Denise had an addition to their family. Their first child, Leo, was two weeks old and they were looking forward to showing him off to the grandparents. On Saturday morning, October 20, Ariel was on his way home after picking up his parents at Dulles. They arrived on a flight from Buenos Aires that morning, eager to see their new grandchild. Denise was at home with the baby.

Digna followed Denise's pregnancy long distance. "It must be almost time, no?" she e-mailed Ariel on September 16, sending them both a big hug. "I can just imagine how happy you are about your first *pimpollo* (cherub)."[28] She said she was claiming the baby as her own "little nephew," and that was all there was to it.

She told Ariel she was working hard on the MacArthur project and sent part of her work, apologizing for being late. She estimated she could forward more in about three weeks and told him about the cases she had taken over from Pilar Noriega, who was now with the Federal District Human Rights Commission. She mentioned that she was supporting the Guerrero peasant ecologists, without going into detail or mentioning that it would involve an expedition into the mountains.

"You know, I have been very well since I came back from Washington," she wrote. "Everything has started to go well, I am working on different cases, very happy, and things are great with *mi compañero,* Juan José. We understand each other and it's just super."

But she was frightened. "The problem is that, in August, two letters arrived at the mailbox in my apartment," she wrote. "They were just like the ones we got at PRO. Threats. The first one made me so mad, my first reaction was to throw it in the garbage, as a way of denying it. But I calmed down and kept it, without saying anything to anybody, not even Juan José. But, a few days later, another arrived and I started to get worried. Still, I didn't tell anyone, but after all the tension it caused me, I spoke first to Juan José, and then to three friends. Just now, we've decided to investigate using private detectives to see what happens. If they don't get anything, we'll go to the police.

"I spoke to Edgar to ask him if anything arrived at PRO, and he said no. I took advantage of the conversation to ask him, once again, if he had anything more to tell me about what happened before, but he said there was nothing to say. So I didn't even show him the letters. I have taken certain precautions, and the investigation has begun. Let's hope they can give me some indication of who is sending these damned letters. *Bueno,* I will keep you posted."

(Besides Juan José, Digna confided in Dr. de León, Pilar Noriega, and German theologian Harald Ihmig about the death threats. After sending the e-mail to Ariel, she also told General José Francisco Gallardo, who was then in prison. I asked Edgar Cortez about them during our interview.

"I did not know about the threats until the day of her death. That's when I was told about them," he told me. However, he said Digna had mentioned the previous threats against her, which were kept at the PRO offices in Mexico City.

"When I saw Digna in August, she asked me if I had photocopies of the threats and if I would give her a copy. I said yes, and some days later she sent someone to pick them up. I asked her why she needed the copies and she said she wanted to send them off to be studied.")

Ariel e-mailed a birth announcement to Digna on October 5.

On the tenth, Digna sent her congratulations, adding: "I have just returned from Guerrero and things are much clearer to me."

Ariel was alarmed.

"Digna, what were you doing in Guerrero?" Then, half-joking, he added: "Be careful. We can't look after you because we have a baby to care for now."

It was their last communication. He never found out what she was doing in Guerrero, or that she had promised to work for the peasant ecologists, those who were in hiding with arrest warrants against them, and several others who were imprisoned in Acapulco.

* * *

Ariel was over the moon about Leo. He had already posted the baby's photo as the screensaver on his computer at the Inter-American Human Rights Commission. In the car on the way home from Dulles, he was telling his parents about him. They were about halfway home when Ariel's cell phone rang.

It was Denise. She told him Pilar had just called to say that Digna was dead. His first thought, after the shock, was for his wife, who had just given birth and was struggling with the news without him. He slammed his foot down on the gas, pushing to get home.

When Denise heard Pilar's voice, she thought she was calling with congratulations about the baby. She could hardly believe what Pilar was telling her.

She was flooded with guilt.

"Oh God," she told Pilar. "We all really fucked up."[29]

Denise was haunted by should-haves and might-have-beens. She should have pressed the Mexican authorities, she should have dealt differently with Edgar Cortez and PRO, she should have convinced Digna not to return to Mexico.

But she knew nothing could have kept Digna from going home.

CHAPTER FIFTEEN

The Hit Man from Guerrero

By early June 2002, it looked like Renato Sales had all but tied the case up with a bow. Mexican authorities were getting ready to declare that Digna killed herself. The yellow police tape had been removed long ago from the Zacatecas Street offices, the carpet vacuumed, and couches and bookcases wiped clean of blood.[1] Boxes of evidence sat in Sales's office at the *Procuduría General de Justicia* in Mexico City; he has amassed thousands of documents and his experts were working on a video production to show that Digna committed suicide.

He gave an interview to Ginger Thompson, Mexico correspondent for the *New York Times,*[2] in which he described Digna as a woman "full of serious emotional conflicts." He said that leaders at the Miguel Agustín Pro Juárez Human Rights Center doubted the veracity of death threats against Digna and that she staged the suicide in order to make herself a martyr. She was alienated from PRO, depressed, cut from off from her family, friends, and boyfriend, and she saw her death as "a way to keep fighting, to recover a place in the world of human rights that she did not have anymore."

According to the story, "Edgar Cortez, the director of the Pro Center, did not cast any doubt on the threats Ms. Ochoa received during the early part of her career there. In an interview, though, he suggested that he began to doubt threats Ms. Ochoa reported to him in 2000. When pressed, Mr. Cortez said the group believed that Ms. Ochoa was 'worn out' and had decided to look for ways to help her 'remake herself.'"

This is about a month after my interview with Edgar, in which in response to my repeated questions, he always said he didn't doubt Digna and had not told anyone in Washington he did.

The story underscored the value of Digna's case for Mexican justice and President Vicente Fox. "Her case is very important for us," Fox told the *Times*. "We must ensure that justice is done." He insisted that the military had given its full cooperation to investigators at all times.

Mexico City Mayor Andrés Manuel López Obrador continued to leave the handling of the case to his attorney general, Bernardo Bátiz. However, in the *Times* article, Sales had become the official voice of the capital's PRD government. Everybody appeared to be on the bus, heading to the station marked *Digna Ochoa: Suicide.*

There was, however, one niggling problem for Mexican authorities. It was the pending report on the murder investigation by Pedro Díaz and other experts from the Inter-American Human Rights Commission who have been working on the case. The Díaz team was constricted by tight guidelines, which were designed to protect the sovereignty of the Mexican state and were worked out through haggling among the commission's political bosses at the Organization of American States.[3]

President Fox could not be embarrassed by any review that concluded justice was not being done in Mexico. That would muddy the claims of a robust and burgeoning democracy under the first opposition president in seven decades. There were diplomatic realities at stake. What was once envisioned as a no-holds-barred investigation into the murder of Digna Ochoa (which I had been hearing about through sources for months) had been whittled down to a scrawnier, albeit talented, team from the Inter-American Human Rights Commission, composed of former law professor Díaz; Sergeant Al Voth, a ballistics expert with the Royal

Canadian Mounted Police; and forensic specialist Dr. María Dolores Morcillo Méndez, from Colombia. Original police work was not part of their mandate and they were restricted to a review of the evidence.

Still, nobody knew what they would report, and Mexican authorities didn't want to be broadsided. Staffers from the Mexico City Prosecutor's Office burned up the phone lines to Washington. "You show us your report and we'll show you ours," they essentially said. They wanted a preview of the Díaz report so that they could release their verdict without worrying about being publicly contradicted. They were told it didn't work that way and that the timing of the Inter-American Human Rights Commission report did not depend on what was being announced in Mexico City.

Washington officials pulled their hair out each time they read about the high regard in which Díaz reportedly holded the Sales investigation. I often spoke to sources in the United States on days when a Mexico City newspaper suggested that Pedro Díaz was very pleased with the work being done by Renato Sales and his investigators, only to hear laughter on the other end of the line. I was told that either no such thing was said or that a comment was stretched out of context. In Washington, there was frustration over never-ending leaks in a police investigation that was supposed to be confidential. *Reforma*'s breaking of the suicide theory, with its rich detail and inside information, was a good example. It was believed that the leaks were coming from Renato Sales and his team. They called it "amateur hour" in the Mexican capital. The report wouldn't be finished for some weeks and, upon completion, it would be kept confidential by the Inter-American Human Rights Commission. (It has never been released. PRO, however, as one of the official recipients of the report, makes copies widely available to human rights defenders, both nationally and internationally.)

Still, in June, Sales appeared ready to release his findings, when all hell broke loose. A series of newspaper articles exploded on the scene, taking the Digna Ochoa investigation in the very direction discounted by Mexico City officials—linking it to narco-violence in Guerrero.

On June 5—just two days after the Sales interview appeared in the *New York Times*—Maribel Gutiérrez published the first in a series of articles on Digna's murder in the Acapulco-based *El Sur*.

"A Hit Man from the Petatlán Mountains Killed Digna Ochoa: Informant," said the headline. The story was picked up by *La Jornada* in Mexico City, and Sales and his team were left scrambling to react.

Since October, this investigative reporter, backed by a team at her newspaper, had broken story after story, including the news that Digna was in the Guerrero mountains two weeks before her murder.

Now, her most recent report created controversy by offering up suspects, albeit murdered ones, who were reportedly hired by a local *cacique* to murder Digna. Her accounts detailed a sorry history of bungling by Mexico City police in the Guerrero investigation—the timeline suggesting it occurred after Sales took over the team—and suggested there was no serious intention of doing a real investigation. In fact, according to *El Sur*, police had other motives in mind when they went to Guerrero to interview people.

According to the report, Guerrero hit man Nicolas Martínez Sánchez, with accomplice Gustavo Zarate Martínez, traveled to Mexico City, where they shot Digna in the Zacatecas office. Martínez Sánchez was a police officer who'd had various jobs in Guerrero and was, according to sources, "very prepared for this type of work." He was a "professional," and would know not to leave fingerprints. A third man accompanied them, but they apparently killed him before returning to Petatlán.

The killers, in turn, were murdered, both executed in gangland-style slayings in two separate ambushes in the mountains. At the time, police characterized the slayings as "revenge killings among local families."

Zarate Martínez was gunned down in an ambush twelve days after Digna's murder, his body riddled with bullets and left at the side of the road. A few months later, on March 4, Martínez Sánchez was driving his beat-up Dodge pickup truck at 7 A.M., with his son, his brother-in-law, and his nephew, when unidentified men opened fire with AK-47s, killing everyone inside. There were more than eighty bullet holes in the truck.

Martínez Sánchez had lived in fear since the murder of his alleged accomplice, according to *El Sur*'s sources, knowing he could be next. "I'm scared they're going to kill me because I was involved in that thing with Digna Ochoa, and it's a big problem for me," he reportedly confessed to the newspaper's informants who, not surprisingly, insisted on anonymity. He said that the first order to kill Digna came when she was up in the Sierra for two days at the beginning of October, but that the decision was changed. He does not know why. They were told to watch Digna, follow her to the capital, and keep her under surveillance. Then, on October 19, the order came to kill her.

Everybody in the mountains knew Martínez Sánchez. His nickname was *El Cuarterón*—a person who's square-shaped. Later, reading through massive documentation released by Mexico City police, I found that he was described more fully. It was a part of the report in which police were trying to show that Digna's murder had nothing to do with Guerrero and that the hit man theory was erroneous. Martínez Sánchez, said several witnesses, was so heavy they couldn't imagine him being able to travel to Mexico City.[4]

Was this the fat man?

* * *

There were several reports on alleged links between Digna's death and the lucrative drug routes through the Sierra Madre, an area reportedly controlled by the Arrellano Félix brothers of the Tijuana drug cartel. Soon after Digna's murder, Televisa journalists Carmen Aristegui and Javier Solórzano aired a hard-hitting report on *Círculo Rojo* (Red Circle), about the "Guerrero connection." They told the story of the *campesinos ecologistas* of Guerrero, suggesting that there was collaboration between the army and the Rubén Figueroa Alcocer government to suppress the movement under the cloak of "counterinsurgency operations." Their report covered the 1996 Aguas Blancas massacre of seventeen peasants by state police at Aguas Blancas, after which Figueroa Alcocer was forced to resign as governor. British scholar John Gledhill praised the Televisa report for putting the environmental struggle in the context of a long history of regional dominance by the Figueroa family and the tradition of *caciquism* "through which power was reproduced. . . . They also presented the case that Montiel and Cabrera had been victims of wrongful arrest and torture at the hands of the military."[5]

In *La Jornada*, Alberto Nájar traced the Guerrero *narco* trail shortly after Digna's murder. He wrote: "Here, in Guerrero, *caciques*, soldiers, *narcos*—they're all one." It was in the wake of these reports on Televisa, as well as increasing international pressure, that President Fox announced the release from prison of Rodolfo Montiel and Teodoro Cabrera.

* * *

In interviews with Maribel Gutiérrez, informants attributed Digna's murder to a *cacique* from Guerrero, claiming that the killers were hired by Rogaciano Alba Álvarez, a rancher and former PRI mayor of Petatlán. He had his fingers in many pies and had clashed with villagers, including the peasant environmentalists, many times. He reportedly had close ties to former governor Figueroa Alcocer, as one would expect of a PRI heavyweight, as well as to the army. He was a founding member of one of Figueroa Alcocer's regional organizations.

"That's his official curriculum vitae," Nájar wrote in *La Jornada*.[6]

Witnesses declared before a judicial hearing in Guerrero, in February 2000, that Alba Álvarez headed a group of armed civilians and soldiers from the 40th Battalion that killed a campesino and his pregnant wife in 1999, and left their bodies in a dump.[7]

Alba Álvarez reportedly didn't want Digna Ochoa in his mountains, asking questions about old murders and making his life difficult. The *caciques* already had seen one deal go sour, when the U.S. giant Boise Cascade Corporation pulled out after the *ecologistas* began their campaign, and they didn't want to see the whole issue stirred up again. (According to reports in several Mexican newspapers, the three most feared *caciques* in the mountains were Alba Álvarez, Bernardino "Nino" Bautista, and Faustino Rodríguez.)

British academic John Gledhill said that Digna "gathered extensive information about the violence and intimidation that the communities suffered at his hands and those of lower-ranking local bosses under his leadership. Enjoying the close support of the military, which also protected the trucks transporting his processed cocaine and locally grown opium poppies and marijuana, this *cacique* had even been accused of burning alive one of the past victims of his wrath."[8]

* * *

Alba Álvarez denied having ordered the assassination of Digna Ochoa to journalists at *El Sur* and Mexico City prosecutors.[9]

In fact, it turned out that the Mexico City police knew all about the allegations against him. A prisoner in jail in Acapulco, Alfredo Torres, made the same claims shortly after Digna's death. In December 2001, a political committee of prisoners in the state capital of Chilpancingo, Guerrero, sent petitions to the authorities, accusing Alba Álvarez of involvement in execution-style killings, narco-trafficking, and illegal cutting and shipping of timber, a development that was reported by the Mexican press. They urged President Vicente Fox, Attorney General Rafael Macedo de la Concha, and Mexico City Attorney General Bernardo Bátiz to investigate the allegations, including those concerning Digna.

The Police took statements from Alba Álvarez on December 21, 2001, and on January 18, 2002, in connection with Digna's murder.

"How good for me that you have called me in," he told Mexico City detectives.[10] "I am happy to give my statement in order to rid the air of all these falsehoods and lies that are floating around out there about me. They are absolutely untrue."

He testified that he didn't have any weapons, didn't know anybody who belonged to the army in any capacity, and didn't know Digna Ochoa, although he knew who she was. "I have never had the pleasure of making her acquaintance," he said.[11] The day that Digna was murdered he said he was storing corn at his ranch in the Sierra.

Alba Álvarez, a *priísta*, later told reporters that the leftist PRD government of Mayor López Obrador in Mexico City wanted him served up as a "scapegoat" for the murder of Digna Ochoa. "For political reasons, they want me involved in the assassination of this lawyer because the mayor of Mexico City is PRD. I rescued Petatlán in 1993, when it was in the hands of the PRD."[12]

The reports by Maribel Gutiérrez (which ran as a series) also claimed that Mexico City investigators, headed by Franz Borges, didn't handle the investigation into Digna's case in a professional manner in Guerrero, notably during interviews with prisoners in Acapulco.

For Borges, apparently, it was personal. He was stationed in Acapulco during the 1990s, part of a joint police-military operations team, and personally knew seven state police officers killed in a shootout in March 1999, in the village of Rancho Nuevo.[13] Instead of asking the prisoners what they knew about the Ochoa case, he spent his time grilling them for information about the death of his friends.

The police also interviewed Faustino Rodríguez. He was the *cacique* allegedly involved in the case of peasant leader Sergio Cabrera González, who was murdered at a wedding reception. Several people made statements to police implicating him in the murder, but the files disappeared. His widow, Aurora Gómez, talked to Digna, and his was among several cases that she documented and planned to take before international authorities.

Rodríguez told police that he had problems with the Cabrera brothers, who were "delinquents" and stole cattle and killed people, including two of his sons. But he said he didn't know Digna Ochoa and didn't even know she had visited the mountains.

(Roberto Cabrera Torres, Sergio's brother, was a member of the ecologists' group and the only Cabrera brother still alive. He was a fugitive, facing a charge of murder as well as weapons and drugs charges. According to his interview with Digna in the mountains, as well as previous statements by other witnesses to the crime, he was far from the site where Faustino Rodríguez's son was killed in a shootout in 1999.[14])

The police couldn't find Nino Bautista, and therefore didn't interview him. He was a legend in the mountains of Petatlán. A story was told about him by the villagers. It seemed that a new military commander once arrived to take over the area.

"Who is the most violent man around here?" the commander wanted to know.

And the people all said, "Nino, it's Nino."

So the commander ordered them to distribute a wanted poster: *Se busca Bernardino "Nino" Bautista.*

When Nino saw the poster, he went up to the military commander and presented himself, bold as brass, and asked, "You looking for me?"

From that moment, Bautista and the commander became the best of friends, eventually setting up a lumber business together.[15]

According to *El Sur* (and later told to me by Eva Alarcón), Mexico City prosecutors conducted their investigations in Guerrero without much consideration for how to get information from those who might have it. They arrived in mountain communities, where people were scared of the military, in armored jeeps, protected by soldiers. They held meetings in public, demanding that people step forward if they knew anything about Digna Ochoa. They wrote up statements for people to sign, in which they swore they had never been harassed by police officers or soldiers.

Before returning to Mexico City on January 23, 2002, Borges told *El Sur* that Digna's death couldn't have had anything to do with Guerrero because she did nothing to support the peasant ecologists and had not harmed the interests of the *caciques.*

It was significant that prosecutor Borges made this statement to Maribel Gutiérrez. He was just wrapping up his fieldwork and yet, it appeared, his mind was made up. This argument, that Digna's murder had nothing to do with Guerrero, remains a constant theme throughout the investigation.

* * *

When the stories broke in *El Sur*, Mexico City Attorney General Bernardo Bátiz responded by saying the that police were looking into it.

"This information from the newspaper, *El Sur*, gives us new data and sheds new light on the case," he said at a press conference on June 6. "Police are already in Guerrero investigating."[16]

He added: "We interviewed Rogaciano Alba twice, and the other people mentioned, and nobody knows anything and the two hit men are dead. We are investigating with our own people in Guerrero, and we will get more information. But this is just a hypothesis that went public. We even interviewed the journalist, Maribel Gutiérrez, and we are analyzing whether there is anything new."[17]

At the press conference, Bátiz was asked about the three

shadowy men who reportedly were staking out Digna's building on Zacatecas Street the night before her murder.

"Yes, we did a very thorough investigation," he replied. Building 31-A Zacatecas is "an old building, with a few apartments and offices, and anybody can open the front lock and walk in." He said, without elaborating, that the men were there to see another lawyer.

Maribel Gutiérrez was interviewed by the police after her stories appeared. A lawyer for *El Sur* cut off her testimony when questions became aggressive about her own whereabouts on October 19, 2001—almost as if she was supposed to be a suspect in Digna's murder. The questions appeared to be tailored to gain more information about her sources and about the peasant political movement in Petatlán. She didn't believe the police were serious. She did not reveal the names of her informants.

* * *

Her stories landed at a sensitive time for Sales, who had been under fire by the Ochoa family and the activists from the national and international rights community for the suicide theory. On June 21, 2002, he resigned in a letter to Bátiz.

The investigation was going down in flames and the scandal threatened to envelop the government of Mayor Andrés Manuel López Obrador. The mayor held a press conference the next day to discuss the Sales resignation and the Digna Ochoa case.

"[Sales] believes a lot of controversy has been generated over this point and that it would be best to leave it aside so that the investigation can continue until we arrive at the truth," López Obrador told reporters at City Hall.

However, in his letter of resignation, Sales underscored the suicide theory. His boss, Attorney General Bátiz, accepted his withdrawal from Digna's case, but refused to accept his resignation as deputy attorney general, instead expressing his full confidence in him. Sales remained on the job—an ominous sign to those hoping for a verdict other than suicide.

His team of detectives—Team No. 3—filed a report on June 28, a week after his resignation. It was not released publicly and I wouldn't get a look at it until its contents were included in documents posted to the Internet by the Prosecutor's Office more than a year later.

There's nothing different from what Sales told me during our three interviews—with one significant exception. It had now been established that Digna was holding the gun upside down in her left hand, rather than her right, for the mortal shot. The dramatic contortions Sales performed for me with a stapler appeared to have been for naught.

The Sales team failed to explain why a right-handed person would shoot herself with her left hand, but it covered the omission.

"It is not the role of the criminal expert to demonstrate the behavior of the victim," said the police report. "It is a concrete fact that [she] had the gun in her right hand [to shoot herself in the thigh] and changed the gun to her left hand. . . . It is up to the criminal expert only to show conclusively in which hand she had the gun at the time of the shooting."

According to this version of events, Digna fired a shot into the sofa to test the gun. Then she shot herself in her left thigh, "with the high probability that she was aiming to hit her femoral artery."

She fired the third shot into her left temporal region, wearing the red rubber gloves. This was proven by a bit of brain matter lodged inside the glove on Digna's left hand. There was also a "high degree of probability" that the gun fell off Digna's gloved hand when her body was lifted by police at the crime scene.

Nobody heard the shots being fired. Police later proved this point by conducting tests with the gun at 31-A Zacatecas Street. "Nobody could have heard anything."

This report said that, while sitting on the north sofa, Digna put the powder on her hands before pulling on the gloves. This was demonstrated by the pattern in which the powder stained her pants—it didn't fall into the creases made by someone in a sitting position. (The Sales report wasn't clear about whether the powder was in the gloves when Digna pulled them on, or whether she somehow put on the powder and then pulled on the gloves. If the latter were true, then where was the container for the powder?)

The bloodstains on the sofa indicated that Digna sat there (presumably waiting to die) for about five minutes after shooting herself in the thigh. She bit her overcoat in order to muzzle the sounds of her pain, which was shown by the piece of gum (the Sales Chiclet theory) found by police on her overcoat. (There is no mention of the gum on the floor, which investigators mentioned right after Digna's death.)

Only her head was moved after her death.

Digna was wearing the same clothes she wore the night before, which showed that she spent the night in the office. The police established that she was "predisposed to committing suicide."

The team laid out the most likely scenario of Digna's death:

She found herself alone in her office on October 19, 2001. She went to her bag and withdrew the gloves. She also took out the anonymous threat, which she had prepared, and placed it in plain view, on the desk in the reception area. She placed her hair band near the door to simulate a struggle. She put the glove on her right hand, and with that hand, fired a test shot into the south sofa. She listened to see if anyone had heard. She then went back to her bag, took out the other glove, and, sitting on the north couch, put it on.

During these movements, Digna left a trail of powder all over the floor.

She then shot herself in the thigh, waited, stood up, and took a step forward, placed the gun in her left hand, placed it at her left temple, and fired point-blank.

The team had consulted a forensic psychiatrist, Pedro Arturo Mendoza, who determined that a tumble Digna took into a well as a child caused mental damage. She had had a history of convulsions, including an episode in July 2000, when Edgar Cortez, director of PRO, reported that she began to cry in his office (over the threat to her nieces) and then fell into a faint before him.

She was a woman of average intelligence who threatened suicide in letters to her sister Carmen and to a boyfriend, Adrian, in 1987 over problems they were having. She had conflicts with her mother. It was significant that she killed herself the day before her mother's birthday.

"This coincidence is very significant because many suicides choose a date to coincide with a familiar anniversary," said the report, adding that Sister Brigitte, a Dominican nun who was close to Digna, also celebrated her birthday on October 20.

The report then discussed a range of psychiatric conditions (which contained the familiar language of the 2000 police report filed during the kidnapping investigation, although it was not cited.) She was an obsessive-compulsive, with signs of depression.

She claimed to have been kidnapped by police in Jalapa in 1988, although the police discounted the incident and said she made it up.

Through all the threats against her, she became a well-known person. Unfortunately, once she was sent to Washington, she was asked for her resignation. She felt "abandoned, unprotected and rejected, she had nobody to support her, and those she felt were her friends were lost to her."

She told people that the threats weren't threats of death, but of resurrection. (Digna was actually repeating an attitude about death expressed to her by another Dominican nun, one in which she took great comfort.) The team added that it was not known for sure if Digna had the book of poetry with the poem about Saint Rosalie in her hands, "but it was sticking out, almost falling out."

Digna wrote to her sister Esthela in August 2001 to say that she was not thinking about death, which, according to psychiatrists, meant just the opposite.

In an almost blasé manner, the report said that, on August 20, 2002, forensic doctors Sergio Ubando López and Marna G. García determined that "based on the signs of the body at the time of the autopsy, which was generalized muscular flaccidity, the time of death occurred between sixteen and sixteen [sic] hours before the autopsy." It does not make any attempt to explain the process by which forensic specialists are filing this report—ten months to the day after Digna's death. She was buried on October 21, 2001, two days after an autopsy that lasted only one hour.

* * *

At the end of June, Attorney General Bátiz signalled where he stood on the case.

"I Resist Accepting It," said the headline to a story in *La Jornada.*

However, the story presented an attorney general who appeared, in fact, to be laying the groundwork for suicide. Whichever theory was true, he said, "we must defend Digna Ochoa. Be it suicide or homicide, what she did for human rights, those she defended, what she left, how she lived, is still here. If she died defending those human rights, certainly her death has a higher significance. But, if she died by her own hand—and this could be the outcome of her case—her sacrifice still ought to have a high value."

Moreover, he emphasized, human rights defenders in Mexico were safe.

"In general terms, at least in the Federal District, human rights defenders are working tranquilly—except Digna Ochoa, who died."

* * *

I left Mexico in the middle of July 2002. I had done extensive interviews over almost seven months, watching the case unfold from the inside, and I was growing increasingly nervous about my own investigation. I had been working with two assistants,

Leticia Flores, a former accountant from Mexico City, and Reem Algharabali, a British-educated journalist from Kuwait. Both had thrown themselves into the story with spirit and energy, working long hours listening to interviews and transcribing tapes.

In early June, however, during a visit to Canada, I got a panicked call from Lety. She was standing with Reem at a pay phone a block away from the office, and she told me they were afraid to go back. They were working in the office, which was the top floor of my house in Coyoacán, when they heard voices and movement below. At first, they sat stunned, whispering to each other, then began thumping the floor and talking loudly to try to scare the intruders away. (Thinking about it now, they might have been more prudent to get out over the roof, and it scares me to think what could have happened to them.) They didn't call police, but that was totally understandable in Mexico City.

When they went downstairs, there was nobody in the house and no sign of forced entry. For weeks, there had been strange phone calls with nobody on the line, or muffled and crackling sounds. It was an old story in Mexico City. We were sure the phones were tapped and a general air of paranoia settled over the once breezy office on Alberto Zamora. Despite their fears, Reem and Lety went back to work the next day, jumpy and unable to concentrate. I returned a few days after that and, until my departure, there was no further disturbance. But they were convinced somebody had entered the house, either looking for files and getting a surprise that people were there (since I was in Canada) or attempting to scare them. Both were relieved to finish their work for me.

In July, a Canadian friend, Mark Trensch, flew down from Canada to drive back with me. Frankly, he was the biggest and toughest-looking friend I had—which was the point. Mark was tall, bearded, with long hair and broad shoulders, and it was comforting to have him along for the ride. With my files in the trunk and a long drive ahead of us, we set off from my home of seven years.

I made it all the way to the border city of Nuevo Laredo, a stone's throw from the United States, without incident. And then I hit a pickup truck at an intersection.

Three men jump out of the truck. There was no damage to their vehicle, whereas the front end of my Honda was bashed in. There was no doubt in anybody's mind whose fault it was, and I looked over to see a couple of police officers lounging against a building. I was shaking inside, thinking about my files in the trunk. A crowd gathers and my car was boxed in. I couldn't drive away, even if I want to.

I was lucky though. The driver looked at me, looked at Mark standing there, big as a house, calm, his arms crossed, and decided to let me off with paying him sixty bucks. He didn't bring in the authorities. The outcome for me could have been bad. I shuddered to think about the police going through my files on Digna Ochoa—the tapes, transcripts, newspaper clippings, court documents, and more. The officers, who weren't traffic police anyway, showed no interest in crossing the street and the crowd began to melt away.

I got back into my car and, with my heart in my mouth, turned the key. The engine started and we limped to the frontier and cross to the United States. The American customs officer looked at my car with surprise and recommended a garage a few blocks away. My car made it there and then the engine died. I felt that somebody was watching out for me.

CHAPTER SIXTEEN

Margarita Guerra y Tejada

On August 1, 2002, Attorney General Bernardo Bátiz announced a new prosecutor in charge of the Digna Ochoa case—the third after Nicolás Chávez (working under Deputy Attorney General Alvaro Arceo Corcuera) and Renato Sales. It was the third prosecutor but the expected report would actually be the fourth, since, in the eight months after Digna's murder, three separate teams of detectives had filed their findings about the crime—in October, January, and June. The first two called it homicide, while the third, under Sales, ruled suicide. The latest choice for prosecutor was former federal judge Margarita Guerra y Tejada, who rose to prominence as special prosecutor in the shooting death of Judge Polo Uscanga, whose case still hung in suicidal limbo.

Bárbara Zamora, the Ochoa family's lawyer, was horrified, pointing to Guerra's handling of the Uscanga case, but she was ignored. Guerra was appointed on the advice of a special committee of *Reforma* columnist Miguel Angel Granado Chapa, lawyer Magdalena Gómez, and human rights crusader Rosario Ibarra, whose son disappeared during the Dirty War. But Ibarra later told reporters she didn't endorse Guerra.

She began her work on August 1 and, on October 17, gave an interview to Blanche Petrich from *La Jornada*, who had done extensive reporting on the case, beginning with her poignant coverage of the funeral in Misántla. In one article, Petrich described a series of problems with the suicide theory, including the fact that the gun was found under Digna's legs and the *Antología Poética de la Muerte* (*Poetic Anthology of Death*), with its poem about St. Rosalie and Jesus Christ, didn't belong to Digna, which destroyed its relevance as a supposed road map of Digna's innermost heart. Petrich also revealed that male DNA was found on Digna's last death threats, in the saliva used to seal the envelopes.[1] But this first interview with a new prosecutor was not the time to raise these specific issues.

Guerra was a short, round woman with a pixie cut, who wore her glasses on a jeweled chain around her neck. Her October interview with Blanche Petrich ran with a photograph of her in her office, poring over some of the case's voluminous documentation. She began by saying that errors were made, some of which were pointed out earlier in the year in a preliminary report by Pedro Díaz from the Inter-American Human Rights Commission, including the comment that the Mexico City Prosecutor's Office wasn't following up leads properly.

"I am not going to make anything up," she assured Petrich. "I am not going to rush or delay this investigation. I am looking for the truth, and when I find it, I am going to show it perfectly, backed by proof. I have not discarded any line of investigation. I am not inclined toward any particular hypothesis, either of homicide or suicide. I am looking for what I call irrefutable proof."[2]

Guerra said Mayor López Obrador called her personally and asked her to take the case. She said she had a team that included six agents from the Public Ministry working for her, as well as three Mexico City detectives and five agents, one of whom was a woman. The woman was likely Patricia Bulgarín from the Prosecutor's Office, who expressed such faith in the Federal Preventive Police to American rights defender Denise Gilman during the investigation into Digna's kidnappings in 2000. She didn't say, however.

Guerra boasted that she was an old hand at the job, beginning as an investigator in 1975. For this investigation, she had more than two thousand statements to go through, fifty of which she considers important, and work done by 108 detectives since Digna died, one year ago almost to the day.

The errors of previous teams, she said, were not made through malice but through a lack of experience. She, on the other hand, would apply "a scientist's mind." There would be no more examination of the import of Saint Rosalie, and the psychological profile put together by the Sales team in recent months would be discarded.

"With all due respect," she said, "it's just not good police work. It was done by a single psychiatrist, reviewed by one detective, and signed by [Sales]. In the opinion of a judge, it doesn't have much value."

While the March 2000 psychological profiled handed to me by Sales obviously figured into the work done by his team, there had been no reference to it publicly. Nor would there be anything other than a passing reference in Guerra's final report.

There was a discordant note in the interview. Justice Guerra noted that, despite the advice of her friends and colleagues, Digna failed to see a psychiatrist and there was no clinical evaluation available. She apparently did not know that Digna did see a psychiatrist in Washington and felt enormous support.[3] However, she told Blanche Petrich that even without a psychiatrist's report her new investigating team would be able to form an opinion based on postmortem analysis, thanks to videos, recordings, interviews, and letters.

Her aim was to write a history of Digna Ochoa (and in a year's time, she would entitle her final report "La Historia de Digna Ochoa y Plácido"). She would approach her work logically and sequentially, she told Petrich, although she had to stress that the last three months of Digna's life are the most critical in the murder investigation, especially her final trip to Guerrero.

This was an interesting statement, given that her final report on July 18, 2003, devoted its most intense analysis to a microscopic examination of Digna's early life. Once, in the middle of the night, my eyes glazing over as I plowed through a mountain of papers, I was taken aback by a line about her time in primary school.

* * *

In April 2003, Canadian lawyer Leo McGrady, Q.C., flew to Mexico City for meetings on Digna's case, part of a small team from Lawyers' Rights Watch Canada and the Bar Human Rights Committee of England and Wales.[4] They had been following the investigation for some time, focusing on whether it complied with international legal obligations that bound the Mexican government. He had practiced law in Canada since 1969, mostly in British Columbia (he lived in Vancouver), the Yukon and Northwest Territories, Ontario and Alberta, and had handled hundreds of criminal cases.

He met with Guerra in her offices, along with two British colleagues, in a building not far from the Mexico City Prosecutor's Office, where, in fluent English, she discussed the case and allowed them to examine evidence. Although her report wouldn't be released for another three months, she said she had no doubt that Digna Ochoa committed suicide, and painted the same picture of the paranoid, delusional, and troubled woman that appeared in her final report some months later.

I didn't speak to Leo McGrady until the spring of 2005, but he remembered the impact of Guerra's comments on that April afternoon two years earlier.

"The thing that hit me most dramatically was the amount of time she spent slandering this woman, which was in itself a revelation to us where the focus of this investigation was," he said. "Much of what she was discussing of Digna's life, with much obvious distaste and disapproval, was nothing more to me than different experiences of a young woman growing up in a difficult home, if indeed they were true. She went on about how she grew up in a large, poor, dysfunctional family, had left a convent, had failed in love. I thought that we mere mortals fail in love and it's not evidence of some moral failing. . . . She saw her as a wacko."[5]

McGrady and his colleagues didn't express their view to Guerra. "We were careful not to, but by this time our skepticism was growing," he said.

Justice Guerra talked about the travel she'd done personally on the case, including to Digna's home state of Veracruz. McGrady asked her several times if she had been to Guerrero, without getting an answer. She finally admitted that she hadn't.

* * *

It seemed appropriate that her report was leaked to the media ahead of time. Her office scheduled a press conference for Thursday, July 18, 2003, and then changed it to Saturday morning. On Thursday, several news agencies posted bulletins on their Web sites that Guerra had ruled suicide. She actually ruled "probable suicide."

Reforma reminded its readers that the newspaper had the story back on March 12, 2002, before Guerra's investigation began. This was quite correct; I remembered my own shock. All these months later, the investigation essentially embellished a story in *Reforma*, whose source was likely Sales himself.

By the time Guerra, with Bátiz at her side, held her press conference on Saturday morning, her findings had been leaked and press aide Marcos Ramírez spent his time denying accusations from Mexican reporters that Guerra's mind had been made up from the beginning.[6]

There didn't appear to be much original police work, other than an exhaustive examination of the minutiae of Digna's life, including the observation that she hit her head when she fell down a well as a child, apparently causing brain damage.

It was considered significant by a police psychologist—well, *probably* significant at any rate. "From a hypothetical standpoint, we point out that *Licenciada* Digna Ochoa y Plácido *probably presents neurological deterioration*,"[7] said a study by police psychologist Arturo Mendoza Vega, the last four words marked in bold type in Guerra's "Story of Digna Ochoa." The tumble down the well figured prominently in establishing his hypothesis. "According to her mother, Digna lost consciousness, although she added that she wasn't injured (apparently) but she was very frightened." He cited the childhood accident as the origin of later problems. Here Edgar Cortez had been very helpful, telling the police how Digna, as an adult, broke down in tears and suffered some kind of spell in his office on the day she believed her nieces had been kidnapped.

However, Irene Plácido told me a very different story about her daughter's fall when I interviewed her in Misántla a few months after Digna's death. She said Digna wasn't knocked out and was able to keep herself above the water in the old well by holding on to branches. If she had been unconscious, she likely would have drowned. Jesús recalled the fall when I asked about events from Digna's childhood—What did she like? Who were her friends? Any mishaps?—and everyone remembered the afternoon it happened. She was very little and very scared, but that was all. She was not examined by a doctor.

The Guerra report noted primly that in April 2003, Irene Plácido and other members of Digna's family *refused to make statements*"[8] (again, emphasis theirs) to authorities, having withdrawn their cooperation from the police investigation into their daughter's death. It was not hard to see why when Digna's own mother had become the source of information used to paint her as a deranged and suicidal woman whose mind was altered by a fall down a well. By April 2003, with Guerra's report still three months away, the well story was the subject of much speculation in the Mexican media about the source of Digna's alleged imbalance.

Guerra concluded, as did Sales, that Digna had deep psychological problems and satisfied her need for attention through human rights work. She sent the death threats to herself and others at PRO, and killed herself in a scene staged to look like murder. She left a death threat to further wound her former colleagues at PRO. (This terrain must seem like familiar ground to readers who recall the psychological profile prepared by the Mexico City's Prosecutor's Office in March 2000.)

There were two new pieces of evidence, however.

Guerra's investigators resealed the premises at 31-A Zacatecas Street at the beginning of 2003—more than a year after the lawyers had resumed using their offices. There, in a storage room on February 26, 2003, they found a little plastic bag marked *"polvo para manos"* (hand powder). It had apparently been overlooked for sixteen months. The handwriting was Digna's, according to the Guerra team, and the powder matched the substance found on Digna's hands, the couches, her bag, and strewn all over the carpet on the day of her death, October 19, 2001.

They also found, on these same premises, forty-nine words cut from newspapers and, according to Guerra's experts, similar to the ones used in death threats against Digna and PRO lawyers. No samples were provided.

Bárbara Zamora was so distraught over the "finding" of the powder, which she learned about in February, that she resigned as lawyer for the Ochoa family, along with a colleague. Whether or not they were correct in their view of the discovery (and I would come to a different conclusion), "they felt this finding was blatant fabrication and that they could no longer work with the Office of the Special Prosecutor under such circumstances," said a report in 2005 by Lawyers' Rights Watch Canada. "Zamora claims that Guerra was uncooperative with the Ochoa family [which had *coadyuvante* (special assistant) status in the case] and did not respond to petitions she filed requesting that Guerra get testimonies from certain people and exhume the bodies of two men cited [in *El Sur*] as being linked to Ochoa's death."[9]

Zamora had requested that Guerra interview witnesses and exhume the bodies of the Guerrero hit men. Digna's brother, Jesús, using the family's *coadyuvante* status, had been fighting to have this done since Maribel Gutiérrez broke the story of these alleged assassins in *El Sur* in June 2002.

Guerra's report contained three psychological reports she commissioned on Digna Ochoa (again, only a passing reference to the March 2000 profile), two of which concluded that she had a suicidal personality. The third determined that she didn't, and instead showed healthy human attributes.

"[Guerra] said that she was considering treating the psychiatric report which argued against a suicidal nature as an obstruction of justice case," Canadian lawyer Leo McGrady said of his April interview with Margarita Guerra. "I was very surprised by that— that she would do that simply because she disagreed with the report." (In the end, she took no such action and she referred to the dissenting opinion briefly in her final report.)

The report from Guerra went over familiar ground: There was no forced entry, the murder weapon was Digna's own gun, this particular gun leaves no GSR (gun shot residue), and a bruise on Digna's leg was eight days old. No mention was made of earlier police reports that two guns were found at the scene, or that Digna suffered physical abuse before being shot, including a blow to the back of her head. (In March 2002, Sales told me these reports were inaccurate.)

Digna likely committed suicide and staged the murder scene out of desperation, according to Guerra. "Digna Ochoa had fantasies, obsessive neuroses, and suffered from long periods of depression," she told the press conference, adding that Digna "shut herself off to the world" over conflicts with her lover, financial worries, and her "abrupt departure" from PRO and the convent.[10] Guerra added: "There wasn't one thing that could lead us to conclude that someone was interested in taking Digna's life, or even harming her."[11]

There were thick indexes, separate files, some two hundred crime photographs, various diagrams of how Digna killed herself, and a video presentation using computer-generated imagery to show a simulated Digna Ochoa killing herself. It includes 282 sworn statements, 260 judicial proceedings, 269 examinations by police experts, and 595 reports by Judicial Police and other authorities.

The Mexico City Prosecutor's Office posted the file on its Web site, but removed it two weeks later, noting that the Ochoa family objected to the material. While the information was substantial, it was selective. Interviews were summarized, medical reports were jumbled and blended together, and the findings appeared to be a repackaging of Sales's conclusions a year earlier.

There was no sequence to the photographs, which were not dated or numbered. It was impossible to determine which photos of the office and other evidence (apart from Digna's own body) were taken in the aftermath of her murder and the ensuing months, and which were taken as late as 2003.

There was almost a sweet naïveté to the report, if one thought the judge and her team believed what they were presenting. Leo McGrady believed she did. "The one thing that struck me in spending time with her was that she seemed, indeed, to be an honest person," he told me. "I think that the level of corruption surrounding her was so disturbing, however, that even if she was honest, it would be very difficult to investigate properly because there was so much skewed evidence in the first place."

Within the Guerra team's report, one section was called the "Military Line."

It stressed that soldiers would have had no reason to kill Digna because she didn't threaten them. It treated the power of the military in Mexico as if it rested in the hands of a few individual soldiers in Mexico, whether from the 19th Infantry Battalion (the Montiel/Cabrera case) or the 40th (Digna's trip into the mountains).

Teodoro Cabrera, the peasant ecologist whom Digna defended, was quoted as saying that Digna wasn't the main lawyer on the case. He said that Digna merely passed by the prison in Iguala in September 2001 to say hello to him and Rodolfo Montiel. Strange then that later, in his declaration, he said she spent four hours with them. It seemed to have been a long hello.

Various military commanders stressed that Digna had no problems with soldiers or *caciques* in the region. Said the report: "It is certain that some of Digna's activities were tied to the members of the military, in particular the 40th Infantry Battalion with its base in Altamirano, Guerrero, but investigations into those activities in no way lead us to suppose the existence of any problem, altercation, or action, which would denote animosity on the part of the soldiers involved toward Digna Ochoa. We cannot determine the existence of any fundamental reason that [her work in Guerrero] led to her death. In no way whatsoever can we suppose that any elements of the Mexican Army had any motive sufficiently powerful to want to take her life."

Digna accused two soldiers, Artemio Nazario Carballo and Calixto Rodríguez Salmerón, of torturing Rodolfo and Teodoro in the Petatlán mountains. But the report said they had nothing to do with her death, even boasting that, having investigated allegations of torture, military prosecutors found no reason to charge them with anything. (It's worth noting again that the national human rights commission determined that the pair were tortured based on their testimony and the absolute refusal of the military to cooperate in any way or even respond to civilian authorities.)

On her final trip into the mountains, said the report, her relations with the military were casual and pleasant. It was true that a few soldiers asked Banco Nuevo mayor Filiberto Gómez to procure a stag for them, but when he said it wasn't possible, they withdrew politely, asking him to let them know if he was able to come up with anything. There was no mention of the fact that Digna jumped into the middle of the encounter.

The report made it clear that Digna could offer no support to the peasants of Petatlán. All she could do—and she said this repeatedly—was knock on doors, which, the report emphasized, probably wouldn't be opened in any case. So how could anyone assume that her visit represented any kind of threat?

Another separate section, called the "Guerrero Line," discounted the hit man theory.

Cacique Rogaciano Alba Álvarez, former mayor of Petatlán, "never had the pleasure of making her acquaintance." He had no dealings with the peasant ecologists and had nothing to do with Digna's murder. He knew former Guerrero governor Rubén Figueroa Alcocer only in passing, and treated him in a familiar manner because they were fellow *priístas*. He called him *"compadre"* but "it's just a way of speaking, the same way as I talk about my *compadre* Ernesto Zedillo."

Asked about press claims that he hired *Señor* Nicolas Martínez Sánchez, *"El Cuarterón,"* to go to Mexico City to kill Digna, he said he knew nothing about it. "The little I know of Nico, I wouldn't say he was the kind of guy to commit murder, and on such a scale."

As for his murder? "He never told me he had any enemies."

Cacique Faustino Rodríguez also had nothing to do with Digna's death, according to the report of Special Prosecutor Margarita Guerra. The only weapon he owned was a .22-caliber rifle, which he occasionally took out to shoot birds when he walked his land. He was busy cutting wood on October 19, 2001, and heard about Digna's death later, on the radio. He hadn't even known she was in the mountains.

* * *

At the joint press conference with Guerra, on July 20, 2003, Bátiz said his office was "not necessarily" closing the case.

"Nor are we saying that this is the absolute truth," he added. "We are saying it's the legal truth. . . . We arrived at it with the intention of finding out what happened, and we did so in good faith."

Whatever kind of truth Mexico City officials believed this to be, it was the verdict that would cling to the case of Digna Ochoa, smearing her life and staining the human rights movement in Mexico. The day before Guerra's press conference, *El Universal* columnist Óscar Herrera mocked Digna, seemingly pleased at seeing her brought low: "The myth of Digna Ochoa originates in the shadows of human rights organizations. . . . The rumor [of her suicide] is official."

Already, the tables had been turned and human rights organizations had become the dark forces lurking in the shadows of events in Mexico. There would be more fallout in the days to come.

A few voices were raised in protest, including activist Rosario Ibarra, who declared, "I don't believe it was a suicide. I believe she was going to attack economic interests, and that is why she was killed."[12]

From Vancouver, Lawyers' Rights Watch Canada sent a letter to Attorney General Bátiz: "The recent announcement by Special Prosecutor Margarita Guerra . . . that Ms. Ochoa died by her own hand is more indicative of persistent problems with the investigation than of the cause of Digna Ochoa's death. Gratuitous, derogatory statements made by the Special Prosecutor's Office about Ms. Ochoa served to further discredit the integrity of the investigation."[13]

The letter continued: "At the time of Ochoa's death, three factors emerged: It was widely accepted that she had been 'assassinated' (in the words of the Inter-American Human Rights Commission) because of her work as a lawyer, and the involvement of government agents was suspected. Digna Ochoa had expressed the opinion that the military was involved in the attacks and threats against her. These critical factors have yet to be properly investigated."

The letter, which reviewed international agreements and codes that bound the Mexican government to fully investigate Digna's death, was copied to President Fox, Justice Guerra, and national and international rights agencies.

At the press conference, Guerra praised the Fox government, including Attorney General Rafael Macedo de la Concha, for delivering full cooperation. In her report, she said she asked for, and received, the full support of Mexico's attorney general, secretary of defense, interior secretary, and others.

She ignored, however—as did her boss, Bátiz—pointed criticism of a lack of military cooperation by Pedro Díaz, in his report for the Inter-American Human Rights Commission. The report said that it was impossible to conclude either suicide or homicide from the ballistic evidence that the commission was allowed to review and identified shortcomings in the investigation. However, other than the frustration with the military, it generally pointed to systemic problems in the Mexican justice system as the reason for inadequacies in the investigation.

"Despite continuous requests to the Secretary of Defense, we were not able to get any of the information we sought," said Díaz.[14] "This is deplorable from the point of view that it involves a criminal investigation in which all entities of the State have an obligation to collaborate . . . without diluting or omitting anything. . . . That we have to depend on information obtained from archives and press reports in relation to the case of Digna Ochoa is absurd."

(I wrote letters, as instructed, to the office of Mexican defense secretary Gerardo Clemente Vega García, requesting an interview on the case of Digna Ochoa. I did not receive a reply. Requests for interviews with Attorney General Macedo de la Concha and Interior Secretary Santiago Creel were declined.)

In Misántla, Digna's family reacted coldly to the Guerra report.

"They are certainly trying to hide something," Jesús Ochoa said, at a press conference. "We will continue to believe it was murder."[15]

He told the *Washington Post*, "I'm disillusioned and angry. This is a terrible blow to the family. It is a result of my country's terrible justice system."

* * *

On the Sunday after her verdict, Guerra gave another interview to Blanche Petrich. She insisted that she had based everything on objective evidence, just as she promised when she began the investigation one year earlier, in the summer of 2002.

However, she made an interesting suggestion about how she came to reach her conclusions. The key to the case, she said, was "a Jesuit priest who worked very closely with Digna and who described her as a woman with a personality full of light and shadows."[16]

She didn't identify the priest. The statement, though, echoed remarks former PRO director David Fernández made in Felipe Cazals's film about Digna, titled *Digna: Until the Last Breath*. "I think Digna always had a contradictory personality," he told Cazals. "She could be very sweet and close and affectionate. But she could also be very aloof, aggressive, and hard—not just with adversaries but also in her relations with the PRO Center and her friends. I think this attitude changed over time and, at the end, there was more trouble."

Guerra's insights could have come from Fernández. From my own interviews, however, the statement about light and shadows rang true to me as something any number of Jesuits and former Jesuits associated with PRO might have said about Digna Ochoa. I wondered if it was her former mentor Chuche Maldonado; Enrique Flota, who directed the defense of the "presumed Zapatistas"; or Edgar Cortez.

I didn't think it mattered who said it anyway, since it seems to reflect the view of all these men. To me, Digna was judged and found guilty. I was just not sure what her crime was—other than becoming famous.

"I am not going to permit Digna to become a martyr," David Fernández reportedly told police.[17]

He had more to say to Cazals, darkening Digna's reputation with the sly, "I heard complaints later, toward the end of her life, that she didn't fulfill certain responsibilities or make reports—a little laziness, or maybe distance from the cases."

He stepped back from such gossip to add that "when I was director, she was always an efficient collaborator."[18]

* * *

There was one more curious fact that had hung over Digna's case like a shroud since her murder.

On October 19, 2001, as people milled about in the darkness of the courtyard at 31-A Zacatecas Street, PRO employee Alfredo Castillo asksed Víctor Brenes if he could borrow his cell phone. Víctor, Digna's close friend and fellow lawyer, was on autopilot, and handed the phone to him wordlessly.

Alfredo took the phone and made a call.

"Edgar," he said, "Digna has committed suicide."

Víctor snapped to attention, angry and confused.

"You can't say that," he exclaimed.[19]

But there it was. The idea of suicide was articulated on the very first night, even though it would not be exposed as a police theory for months to come.

Within a few days, PRO would be named as *coadyuvantes* in the case, working to assist police every step of the way. They would remain in this role until October 18, 2002, when Edgar Cortez announced their withdrawal, ostensibly over problems with the Prosecutor's Office.

CHAPTER SEVENTEEN

The Experts: The Coroner, the Scientist, and the Cop

Dr. James Young was an extremely busy man. One might not think so, walking into his Grosvenor Street offices in downtown Toronto, to be greeted by a short, affable man with a big grin and an office as neat as the proverbial pin. The focus here was on comfort. He had a plush sofa, a couple of easy chairs, no clutter, and, amazingly, no computer. He didn't use one. It drove his staff crazy; they couldn't even send him e-mails. Computers weren't the style of a former sports reporter and small-town doctor who had a photographic memory and no problem keeping a dozen balls in the air.

His primary focus was his job as commissioner of emergency management for Ontario, a new post that evolved from the tragedy of 9/11 and that eventually meant he had to give up the post of chief coroner, which he'd held for fourteen years.[1] Days after al-Qaeda terrorists slammed two hijacked planes into the World Trade Center, Dr. Young found himself in New York City, coordinating efforts to identify Canadians among the dead.[2] He had never seen a city in shock like that.[3] "The minute I watched the second plane hit the World Trade Center, I realized that we had entered an unfortunate and different era in North America," he would say later.[4] "Gone forever is our ability to point to terrorism in the rest of the world and reassure ourselves that this is someone else's problem." It became his job to help figure out the implications of 9/11 for Ontario, Canada's largest and most populous province, and work with the federal government to improve intelligence gathering and emergency measures. He was also responsible in Ontario for the Office of the Fire Marshal and the Centre of Forensic Sciences, where labs processed evidence for crimes occurring across the province.

The last few years had seen him shuttling between domestic crises and foreign attacks. It was Dr. Young who, as a nation grieved, arranged and oversaw the autopsies of four Canadian peacekeepers killed by a U.S. bomb in a "friendly fire" incident in Afghanistan. It was a sensitive and highly political assignment that could have harmed already frayed relations between Canada and the United States over the deaths. That October, he flew to Bali to help with forensic autopsies in the carnage that followed the al-Qaeda nightclub bombing. His life was even more complicated in 2004, when Ontario went through two of its worst crises in modern times: the SARS outbreak, which practically shut down the province in the spring, and the massive blackout that turned out the lights in August.

Clearly, his plate was full. But Dr. Young still couldn't resist a good crime story. I tweaked his interest in the Digna Ochoa case on the telephone and, from the moment I walked into his office in late summer, 2002, he was hooked. We met just after Special Prosecutor Margarita Guerra took over the case. It was well before Mexico City authorities flooded their Web site in July 2003 with more than three thousand pages of evidence and two hundred crime scene photographs.

From the beginning, Dr. Young was suspicious of the theory that Digna shot herself in the head after failing to hit her femoral artery. I also mentioned the test shot into the couch. "It doesn't make sense," he said. "People who are going to commit suicide with a gun generally shoot themselves in the head. They don't try to maim themselves in a limb and bleed to death. If you are going to commit suicide, you want to end things quickly, relatively painlessly. It's also not my experience you see a test fire."[5]

He found many things bizarre. I tried to show him how Sales, in his office the year before, demonstrated how Digna worked her arm around to shoot herself in her left temple with her right hand, holding the gun upside down. I had trouble because it was so awkward to do (and as we would later discover, in a final report that concluded Digna died by her left hand, not true). "Generally, a right-handed person would commit suicide on the right side of the head, not reach around and shoot upside down on the left side."

He focused on the test shot, the thigh wound, and the awkward way the mortal blow was fired. "If I was dealing with something somebody told me was a suicide and I walked in and saw those three things, I would start to ask myself questions as to whether it was a suicide because it doesn't fit an overwhelming pattern of what you see in suicides," he said. "All three would raise flags with me. . . . There are lots of red flags on this."

"I don't think I've ever seen anyone put gloves on to commit suicide. I don't know why they would. But if you had a rubber glove on and you fired a gun to commit suicide, the chances of that gun falling off [your hand] is low. You've got bulk and you've got rubber." (The gun was found under Digna's legs, apparently having slipped off her firing hand.)

He kept shaking his head. "Boy, you should be asking a lot of questions."

I had brought the photo from *El Universal.* And he kept seeing something: "There's something about the position of her legs which bothers me. I don't like it," he said. He was unaware that this was also the first reaction of Dr. de León, Digna's friend, who was among the first to see her body. He felt it had been arranged.

Once Mexico City authorities posted their reports on the Internet in the summer of 2003, I had actual photographs and forensic information to take to Canadian experts.

* * *

In March 2004, I prepared for an upcoming interview with

Dr. Young. Dealing with huge amounts of research in Spanish, I was laboriously copying sections from the Mexican police file, trying to trace the autopsy findings through various incarnations signed by different doctors, and I saw that the first description of Digna's body said that the temperature hwas at room temperature—*igual* (equal).

But in a later description the temperature had been changed to *"inferior"*—below room temperature.

How could that be? There was a myriad of problems with the forensic findings, going from one report to the next, but to see a word actually changed, thereby changing a medical fact, showed me how the evidence was altered.

They were trying to support a theory that Digna died earlier than between noon and 2 P.M., which would invalidate the eyewitness evidence of the upstairs cleaning lady who saw a fat man at the office at the time of Digna's death.

In his office, Dr. Young shook his head.

"That's a detail that is surprising to change because you would expect that what you wrote down at the time is correct," he began. "It's really not that reliable a factor anyway, but if you are going to make the comparison, you must record the body temperature and the ambient temperature. Did they actually take the temperature?"

I told him they didn't. I also tell him that Digna's body was described at one point as showing the first signs of rigor mortis and, later, as being flaccid. It was not clear how much time elapsed between the two descriptions.

"I think that what they are trying to do is add detail to support a time of death," he said, underscoring once again the unreliability of depending on rigor mortis or body temperature to determine time of death in the first place.

I explained that further investigation by a forensic team in August 2002 came to a different conclusion on the time of death, putting it between 10 A.M. and noon.

"You can't add these details by looking at a photo afterwards. It's not going to tell you temperature or [a feel for] rigor mortis— really, all those kinds of things should be done by one person. I've never heard it done by committee."

His point was that everything had to be clear. "The tradition in writing a pathology report . . . is that it is written by the pathologist who did the examination, and if . . . we have a second autopsy, there would generally be an addendum or a second report. You don't blend three into one, or three people's reports into one, because that's the whole problem. Does it represent one report or does it represent a blending of different people's viewpoints? It's not a consensus document; it's a legal document.

"I might review photos," he continued, "but it would never involve merging my observations at a later date in with someone else's who was there at the time. . . . That's not the way. It should be very clear that different reports are written, what they're based on—I mean, after the first one."

He said you couldn't change the facts without the laying of hands upon the body.

"The assumption in a pathology report is, okay, the body is there, and that's what it's based on. As you review it, and you're reviewing it only from photos and other reports, it becomes increasingly important to make it clear to the reader what it is you've relied on in order to make those determinations, because there are some real limits around it. You don't have the ability to lay your hands on and feel temperature and feel postmortem rigor mortis, and the observations—the colors—may be a little bit different because it's photographs. You may see something someone else hasn't seen, and you may be able to draw some stronger conclusion based on your experience, but the downside is that you're not there, and you're not actually seeing it at the time, and that carries some weight as well. You'd have to set the parameters because that, quite fairly, sets the limits—how much, how reliable the thing is and what it's based on."

* * *

The report by Pedro Díaz and his team from the Inter-American Human Rights Commission was also highly critical of the forensic handling of the case. It said that usual medical procedures weren't followed from the time Digna's body was removed from her office. No temperature was taken and the characteristics of the body were not adequately noted.

"This is necessary information in order to know if a body has been moved," said the report.

* * *

Robert Warburton was a gangly Aussie who'd been working as a ballistics expert for more than a quarter of a century. He was a forensics officer with the Western Australian Police Service, participated on study tours with, among others, the Royal Hong Kong Police, the Northern Illinois Police Crime Laboratory in Chicago, and the National Institute of Forensic Science, in Victoria, B.C. He had taught forensics at the university level and authored training and procedures manuals on firearm identification, as well as bullet and cartridge casing comparison.

When I interviewed him in Toronto, beginning in the summer of 2003, he was Section Head, Firearm and Toolmark Section, Ontario Centre of Forensic Sciences. I brought him a copy of the ballistic report prepared for the Inter-American Human Rights Commission, and various documents from the Mexico City Prosecutor's Office.

The ballistics evidence was reviewed for the Inter-American Commission by Al Voth of the Royal Canadian Mounted Police. I had what was obviously a translated copy of his English report, which was problematic, especially given the technical language. I contacted Al Voth in Alberta and he agreed to an interview as long as RCMP headquarters agreed—which they didn't. The Inter-American Human Rights Commission also declined interviews on the Pedro Díaz report—which had never been officially released.

Voth's report said that no conclusion of homicide or suicide could be made from the ballistics evidence provided. It identified several problems with the investigation, saying there was no professional chain of custody of the evidence (the gun was damaged while with police), the shells could have been moved, and the various investigating teams disagreed over the trajectories of the bullets.

In Toronto, Robert Warburton made another point: All guns leave gunshot residue (GSR) in a radius of about four feet around the firearm. He further explained that it specifically comes from the muzzle but that semiautomatic firearms such as the FOI (Firearm Of Interest, which we were discussing from police photos and Voth's report) discharge gunshot residue in high quantities from the open breech during the extraction and ejection process. These elements consist of the unique heavy metal elements from the cartridge primers and ignition compounds, generally lead, barium, and antimony. It is a fact, he asserted, and it doesn't matter what type of weapon is used. Therefore, he poked holes in the theory that Digna's particular gun, a .22-caliber pistol, would not have left GSR on the gloves—which apparently was the very reason that the Sales team began to consider the theory that Digna might have killed herself. According to Warburton, if Digna fired the gun, there should have been GSR on the gloves.

"It's invisible to the naked eye," he said.

On this point the Voth report (without an interview) was confusing to me. He said he had no reason to doubt the conclusion of Mexican police regarding the absence of GSR on the gloves.[6] But then he pointed out that Mexican police conducted only a sodium rodizinate test, which was "not as sensitive or as specific" as tests with a dispersion scanning electronic microscope "which were not done even though police had one of these in their lab."[7]

One would think that if Mexican police were going to launch a suicide theory on the characteristics of the FOI, as Warburton described it, they might at least have carried out every imaginable test to determine if there was GSR on the red rubber gloves worn by the victim.

Four police teams filed ballistic reports. Two said it was homicide and two, suicide. They all came up with different and contradictory reports. Warburton said that when reports differ, he leans to the team at the crime scene. "One would think that the first team had evidence in its pristine state, with the least alternation and the best opportunity to arrive at the most accurate conclusions." It was an opinion shared by experienced cops and forensic experts everywhere. In fact, Mexico City deputy attorney general Alvaro Arceo Corcuera expressed exactly the same view in a letter to *La Jornada* in early 2002—just as Sales was getting under way—saying he would hope that the hard work of the previous investigative teams would not be ignored. Under Arceo Corcuera, Nicolás Chávez was lead investigator. That letter—a minor mutiny—should have been a clue that senior officials within the Attorney General's Office knew all about the Sales suicide theory and had serious misgivings. Furthermore, Sales had told me that chief forensics expert Dr. Pedro Estrada didn't agree *initially* with the suicide version. Unfortunately, none of these insiders talked frankly to me and I could hardly fault them for their prudence, given what was at stake here and what could happen to dissenters in Mexico. Why should they gamble with their lives? Consider what happened to dissenting judge Abraham Polo Uscanga, or any of the other victims of political murders in Mexico.

Robert Warburton had another question. What exactly *was* the gun found at the crime scene?

From the beginning, Mexican police identified it as a .22-caliber DUO pistol, manufactured in Czechoslovakia. But his research showed that DUO made only a .25-caliber weapon. To Warburton's eye, the handgun appeared to be a cutdown and altered .22-caliber rifle, fitted onto a DUO grip. It would seem important that Mexico City investigators make a proper identification of the weapon.

The gun was old and its configuration, with its notably short barrel, would have made firing difficult, he said. He wondered whether—if indeed, this was the murder weapon and this was a question that had intrigued me—the shooter would have been able to fire three shots. He also noted that the police appeared to have failed to note whether there was a bullet in the chamber, since the spring action of a semi-automatic would have pushed one into firing position. There were five bullets left in the magazine.

The gun was dropped while in police custody. When Canadian lawyer Leo McGrady looked at it in Margarita Guerra's office in Mexico City, he had one reaction: *"This thing fires?"*

* * *

I worked with one more expert in Canada.

Inspector Gary Ellis was chief of homicide for the Toronto Police Service when I interviewed him for the first time, in July 2003.[8] A month before, his officers solved a crime that shocked the city, the abduction, rape, and murder of a ten-year-old girl. He used DNA evidence, from a discarded Coke can on the street, to make an arrest. The suspect confessed and pleaded guilty before a judge, sparing the family a lengthy trial.

Inspector Ellis had worked as a staff inspector at the FBI National Academy in Quantico, Virginia, for a year and participated in several joint investigations with the RCMP. Now he was finishing a Ph.D. at the University of Toronto in his spare time.

Looking at two hundred crime scene photos from Mexican police, he seemed puzzled. We were in his office in police headquarters in downtown Toronto, and he was staring at the photos of Digna's body, of the trail of powder, her purse on the white plastic chair, the gun, the death threat, and the red rubber gloves on her hands. There were photos from the crime scene and the autopsy.

"I don't like the arrangement of her feet," he told me, after flipping through the pages of photos for the first time. It was a gut instinct.

"No, fingerprints, eh?" he said. "That's very strange."

"Did they fingerprint the bullets?"

I didn't know.

He was also having trouble with the theory that Digna was aiming for her femoral artery.

"It's in the groin, you know," he said. "That's clearly an inaccurate conclusion."

Inspector Ellis was still staring at the photos, but now he was gone back to the beginning. I wanted him to move on, past the mundane photographs of corridors, entrances, and a bathroom, to what I believed were more important shots.

But he kept looking at photo #20. The bathroom.

"Is it possible she was cleaning her office?" he asked. He pointed to a red bucket by the toilet. A woman couldn't sit comfortably on the toilet with it there.

He pointed to a red cleaning brush on top of a desk, and boxes, some full of files, others folded up, the way people do as they finish with boxes after a move.

A light went on for me. Digna was a neat freak, fastidious in her work and in her personal life. I remember seeing in one of her declarations that Pilar Noriega talked about how Digna once looked at her watch, gasped, and said she had to get home. Her boyfriend Juan José Vera would soon be at her apartment, letting himself in with his key, and she hadn't made her bed. She couldn't leave her apartment messy. She had to fly.[9]

I thought about Digna's e-mails to Juan José after she returned to Mexico City from exile, and how they were full of details about making her apartment just so.

I had wracked my brain going through all the theories about

how, and why, the killers pulled the gloves over Digna's dead hands. I read the rumors of death squads in Guerrero leaving red gloves on their victims but now I wondered if this was myth. Could it be as simple as this?

Digna began work in her new office on Tuesday, October 16, and had been very busy, including at least one late night. Other lawyers used the office, including a couple of guys, and the cleaning lady was part-time. It probably wasn't clean enough to suit Digna, and Friday was the first chance she had to go at it.

Right! Of course. This made sense to me and this was what I believed.

Digna was cleaning the office when the killer or killers came to the door. She would have put on the powder herself before putting on the gloves. It was a common practice in Mexico to use powder (starch) with cleaning gloves. They slip on more easily and they don't chafe the skin of your hands.

I couldn't say with certainty that Digna was using the red bucket in the bathroom for cleaning that day, or whether it was a waste basket. (There did appear in photos to be another bucket for waste paper, sanitary pads, etc., tucked into the corner behind the first bucket.) I also couldn't confirm that the cardboard boxes were Digna's. But I was convinced, thanks to my interview with Toronto police inspector Gary Ellis, that Digna put the gloves on either to clean the office or to wash the containers that had held her breakfast that morning. Mexican police at the crime scene found a Tupperware-like container and utensils that had been washed—for me, a significant point that had been in the back of my mind since Digna's murder. She had breakfast that morning, but too early for forensic specialists to determine the contents of her stomach.

I think the little plastic bag of powder found in the office in 2003 might actually have been Digna's. Police said its contents were identical to that found at the crime scene. Everybody thought it was preposterous for evidence to materialize out of thin air, sixteen months after the fact. But it was not hard to believe that the police overlooked it. Or it may have been that it was planted later, but that didn't change the fact that Digna really could have been cleaning her office or washing up.

There was powder littered throughout the office. But if Digna was wearing these gloves, with the powder on her hands, when her killers grabbed her, wouldn't there be a trail through the office as she struggled? There was powder by her headband inside the door, which was where I think they grabbed her.

Inspector Ellis wasn't finished with the photos.

"What's that there?" he asked, pointing to a photo of Digna's body. On top of her right leg, just below her buttock, was an arc of white powder.

"That stain is where you would hold a gun if you put it behind your back," he said.

If, for example, Digna got her gun from her bag when she heard a knock at the door, she would have held it behind her back at precisely that spot.

This made sense too.

"Why else would the powder be on her purse?" he asked. It sat on the chair, gaping open.

Digna's killers probably brought weapons, and then used Digna's own gun. One could imagine them laughing at such a prospect. *"Bitch, you think you can shoot us?"*

It was possible they didn't intend to kill her *there*, says Inspector Ellis, which explained why she had her coat in her arm. Maybe they were about to take her somewhere else.

He had to rush off to a meeting. As he got up, he made an observation about police work, and life: "Never divert the truth by what you would like to believe."

He had another truism from thirty-five years of slogging through police trenches.

"The weaker your case, the bigger the boxes."

CHAPTER EIGHTEEN

Cover-up?

There were differing accounts about how much paperwork was accumulated in the investigation into the death of Digna Ochoa y Plácido. Some said the Mexico City Prosecutor's Office had compiled fifty thousand pages. Others said, no, that was too high, there were only thirty thousand. But we can safely assume that, placed end-to-end, these pages probably would encircle the great city of the Aztecs and perhaps even begin a slow march north toward Monterrey.

Furthermore, a goodly sum of money had been spent on this one case by the government of Mexico City. Special Prosecutor Margarita Guerra y Tejada told visiting Canadian lawyer Leo McGrady she was spending 400,000 pesos a month (roughly $40,000). Over a year, that's almost half a million dollars, and she represented only one of four teams of detectives,[1] plus outside consultants. The final sum to prove that one human rights lawyer committed suicide totaled well into the millions.

And now, dossier complete, what were we being asked to believe? Here's how Digna Ochoa was supposed to have killed herself:

She put on big rubber gloves and, with her right hand, shot herself in the left thigh. She was aiming for her femoral artery. She was wildly off-base, the bullet coming nowhere near her groin. The gloves were bulky on her hands. Still, bleeding and in pain, she switched the gun from one hand to the other, pulling her gloved right index finger out of the little trigger hole and squeezing her left index finger into that same hole, ready to fire the mortal shot. She was not left-handed.

Holding the gun upside down in her left hand, she shot herself in the head, well above her left temple. She shot herself on such an angle that the bullet traveled from up to down and from back to front. A police sketch tilted Digna's head to match the trajectory of the bullet. Her head was similarly cocked in police video reenactments of the crime.

She killed herself, staging it to look like murder, because she yearned for the glory of martyrdom. And yet she used her own gun. It was found under her legs, having magically slid off these same big, red rubber gloves.

Gloves or no gloves—it looked to me like the emperor had no clothes.

* * *

It was not difficult to find holes in the case. Inconsistencies showed that Mexico City prosecutors Renato Sales and Margarita Guerra pushed aside information that did not fit easily with their suicide theory.

Silvia Mariñelarnea, for example, who met with Digna in her office the night before her murder, did not tell police that Digna was depressed or unusually quiet, as Sales claimed. Neither did other parents from the National Autonomous University of Mexico who were at that meeting. They said just the opposite, that as usual she was full of life, jokes, and energy.

"We told all that to the Prosecutor's Office," she told Blanche Petrich, from *La Jornada*. "We now see that our declarations were not even taken into account."

Before the meeting, Digna appeared to be in good spirits. She dashed off an e-mail to her boyfriend, Juan José Vera, for his mother who was preparing her will. "*Hola, amor*, please pass this on to your mom. Thanks. I love you," she wrote, labeling the note a colloquial *"pa-tu mamá"* (for your mom), and ending with word play on a favorite movie, *Shrek.* Juan José showed this e-mail to the police, but it wasn't included in the massive documentation released by the Special Prosecutor's Office in July 2003.[2]

Nobody claimed that, the night before her death, Digna was wearing the clothes she was found in. According to Mariñelarnea, "We said that she was dressed in a white blouse and dark suit, not that it was the same clothes. We can't attest to that."[3]

Should we be surprised that Digna, of the white blouses, the prissy white blouses, her standard uniform that made her friends chuckle, was wearing a white blouse and dark pants on the day of her death? And yet, upon these garments, prosecutors based their case that she didn't go home, but rather stayed up all night in her office, brooding and planning her suicide for the morrow.

Who were the three men in suits outside Digna's office the night before her murder? One was talking into a cell phone or radio; another appeared to be on lookout at the door. When Silvia Mariñelarnea asked one of them what he wanted, he said they were looking for "Javier." The Prosecutor's Office did not produce these men and their presence remained a mystery.

Modesta Aguilera Mejía, the cleaning lady who lived upstairs, described the fat man she saw at the door of the office at 31-A Zacatecas, just after 12:30 P.M. on the day of Digna's death. That was intriguing. Her report was considered important by the first detectives investigating the murder, who placed him at the crime scene around the time of the murder and considered him a suspect.

But in the final report, Aguilera's evidence had changed. She now apparently saw a skinny guy in a suit. I asked Sales, in March 2002, about rumors I'd been hearing about this eyewitness (I didn't know her name at the time) and he told me she was "mistaken," and that she'd merely seen a man delivering flyers. The police spent endless hours on these flyers and Sales emphasized it was important that they were still in the door frame at the end of the afternoon when lawyer Gerardo González climbed the winding staircase and discovered Digna's body. He was operating under the theory that Digna died between 1 and 3 P.M. and the flyers were proof she was alone at the time and that nobody had entered to kill her. However, I interviewed Sales just as the suicide theory was gathering steam. It would later evolve into the new forensic conclusion that Digna died in the morning, which made the flyers completely irrelevant to either suicide or murder.

The police report filed in January 2002 was specific: Modesta Aguilera saw a *fat* man, according to detectives who interviewed her in the first weeks. I found it interesting that a fat man—*"El Cuarterón"*—was cited in *El Sur*'s story about hit men from Guerrero being hired to kill Digna. One would think the police might have placed some importance on this coincidence instead of insisting that Digna's activities in Guerrero had nothing to do with her death.

Earlier police reports were discounted. Evidence of contusions on Digna's body, which according to police investigator Patricia Bulgarín indicated "a violent struggle," no longer existed. Reports of two guns evaporated. I asked Sales about the two-gun theory and he said that only one weapon was found at the scene, and that it was Digna's. She apparently procured it for her protection, pulling it out, wrapped in a towel, to show her brother Ismael, a few days before her death. We don't know where she got it and police abandoned efforts to identify its origins.[4]

And who moved Digna's body? Police grilled Gerardo González, Dr. Jorge Arturo de León and others who were at the crime scene. Sales later explained this rather large problem for a suicide theory—how *does* a corpse move itself?—by insisting that only Digna's head had been moved.

But Dr. de León, a friend of Digna's, thought her body looked "arranged" and that her killing was a professional hit. "This is not just any case," he said. "This is a political case and we are dealing with professional, well-informed assassins who know the system, who know the routine." He believed it was preposterous to imagine that Digna waited five minutes, with a bullet hole in her leg, before standing up to kill herself, which was what she supposedly did. Plus, there would have been blood everywhere. It was, he said with contempt, "not a believable version."

There were rumors that Digna's fingers were arranged in a "V," and that it was the mark of a Guerrero death squad. However, Dr. de León did not see her hands and it appeared to be, at least based on my interviews, a rumor without basis. What was important, however, was that Dr. de León did not see Digna's hands because they were not visible. They were stuffed under the couch, which was a remarkable and unexplained feat for Digna to have accomplished with a bullet in her brain.

He grieved over his friend long after her death. "Look, let me tell you something," he told me during our last interview in Mexico City. "I was not surprised at all when she went into the conflict zone of Guerrero. She was very brave, especially considering that the death threats against her were linked to Guerrero. It shows her courage and the commitment she felt toward people. I always believed that Digna was born with a special vocation different from other people because no one else had this courage to persevere, even though it might cost her life. I feel honored to have shared such a large part of it with her."

There was more unexplained evidence. To wit:

Digna's headband was found just inside the office door—proof, said the suicide theorists, that she placed it there to simulate a struggle. But why wouldn't she have taken the trouble to mess up her office even slightly more? And Digna was supposed to have been holding her coat (which she appeared to be doing) because she had stuffed it in her mouth to stifle her cries. Why would she worry about noise when she was firing a gun? Toronto police inspector Gary Ellis suggested she might have had her coat because her assailants intended to take her somewhere else to kill her—but their plan was foiled. It was only a theory but it made more sense than biting down on her navy topcoat.

DNA tests were done on traces of saliva found on three death threats left in Digna's mailbox in her last months of life. The results were male, and from different individuals. Police tested Jesús Ochoa and several of Digna's other brothers, colleagues, and friends Gerardo González and Lamberto González Ruíz, and her boyfriend, Juan José Vera, without finding a match. How did they explain away this male DNA? It made it difficult to build a case that Digna Ochoa was sending death threats to herself.

"Yes, it is a big puzzle," Sales told reporter Alberto Nájar. "It is only speculation but I could say to a friend, 'Hey, *amigo*, seal these envelopes for me, would you?'"5

* * *

The special prosecutor's report—"The Story of Digna Ochoa y Plácido"—was buttressed with assorted testimony, forensic reports, photos, police drawings, and a video of a supposed suicide. It brimmed with gossip, innuendo, inconsistencies, rumors, and false-hoods. "It tries to legitimize its conclusions by de-legitimizing a human being," observed a report by the Federal District Human Rights Commission. Digna was portrayed as an unstable, depressed, and joyless soul, who barely functioned as a human being, let alone as a lawyer. She was predisposed to taking her own life and should have been hospitalized. She was diagnosed as having schizophrenia and all manner of other mental imbalances by experts who conducted postmortem psychiatric examinations.

Prosecutor Guerra "said that ninety-five percent of her report, or something like that, was based on scientific proof," observed attorney Pilar Noriega. "But what scientific proof is there in doing a study of the personality of someone who is already dead and you don't have in front of you?"6

It was stressed repeatedly by Guerra that no single piece of evidence was paramount and that the verdict of suicide, or rather "probable suicide," was reached through the weight of all the facts. But Digna was described as if she lived in a vacuum. The fabric of her life was simply ignored. There was no mention of her plans to attend a little girl's birthday party on Saturday morning, meet with prisoners at Almoloya in the afternoon, or see her boyfriend, Juan José Vera, Saturday night. Gone was her promise to help the villagers of the Sierra Madre or find medical attention for a blind boy.

Instead, her early life was examined in great detail, notably a suicide letter she supposedly wrote to her sister Carmen and former boyfriend Adrián Lagunes when she was in her twenties. He was married and allegedly cheating on his wife but, some fifteen years after the fact, managed to morph into a paragon of veracity for the prosecution. I don't want to spend a long time on Digna's early years, especially her love life, because I don't think they are relevant to her murder in 2001. However, claims that she tried to kill herself and wrote suicide letters should be addressed.

I knew about this old boyfriend. Juan José told me she mentioned him one afternoon at her apartment when he was surprised by a photograph he found of her with former president Bill Clinton. "Digna, *who are you?*" he asked her. She began telling him about Kerry Kennedy's book on human rights defenders and about meeting Clinton at the Kennedy Center for the Performing Arts in Washington.

"And then, very seriously, she said, 'If you have any problem with my professional life we can end this now.' And I told her, 'That's not what I am asking you about, or what I want, but it isn't everybody who gets to stand beside Bill Clinton to have a photo taken,'" he recounted to me, several months after Digna's death. "We talked some more and I said to her, 'It doesn't frighten me who you are. I love you [and] it doesn't matter what you do.' She told me about how she was kidnapped and had such a difficult experience when she was young in Veracruz. She said she had a boyfriend who was frightened off when he found out about it and left. . . . He distanced himself from her and she lost him. So she was afraid that if I knew who she really was, I would break up with her. But I said, 'Neither of us is twenty years old. We are mature adults and I love you.' . . . That day, when I got home, I sent her an e-mail—'Digna Ochoa, you grow bigger in my eyes every day.'"

Digna's sister Carmen told Blanche Petrich that no suicide letter ever existed. "I kept every letter and postcard that she ever sent me, from that time period as well, because she was living in Xalapa and I was in Coatzalcolcos. They were all very loving and enthusiastic. . . . Never—never!—did she ever mention something as horrible as taking her own life."[7]

The original copy of this purported letter, apparently dug up by the Sales team, has never been released, and the Ochoa family has yet to see it.

In 1987, Digna was taken to a hospital with a wound in her neck. That was the early suicide attempt touted by the prosecution. "I know what happened because it was me who found her unconscious," Carmen explained to *La Jornada*. She said she arrived with her son to visit Digna one day, and Digna was waiting inside her apartment. "My little boy pushed the door open really hard. She was right behind it, and it caught her on the neck. She was bleeding."[8]

According to the prosecutor's theory (which weighed heavily in portraying Digna as a ticking suicidal time bomb), she was not kidnapped in 1988, as she claimed. Rather, she made up the story, either to mask a breakdown or to match the kidnapping and torture of her father whom she worshipped—or both. Their report ignored witnesses from the period who said Digna described having been kidnapped and raped, including making the charges at a press conference. It also conveniently omitted any reference to the most critical element of her life at the time, which was her political activism, instead turning her into a cliché of a hysterical woman.

The summer of 1988—a particularly turbulent year in Mexican politics—Digna was an adviser to the Cárdenas Democratic Front, a national coalition named for Cuauhtémoc Cárdenas from the center-left PRD, and working to elect an alternative to the ruling party and its (then) five decades in power. Cárdenas lost the famously stolen elections that year, Carlos Salinas from the PRI was president-elect, and the country was roiling with political unrest and repression by the military, police, and the death squads. Into the morass, Digna disappeared in August, resurfacing weeks later in Jalapa to give a press conference at which she denounced her kidnappers as members of the state judicial police. In her report on the press conference, Veracruz journalist Regina Martínez described Digna on first reference as "political adviser" to the Democratic Current, thus establishing her *bona fides*.

Digna filed charges but Veracruz authorities failed to investigate. Whoever wrote the section of the 2003 prosecutorial report dealing with Veracruz went into Sherlock Holmes mode, opining that "no investigation was ever begun, very possibly due to a lack of truth in her testimony, which was taken in its entirety by the State Attorney General's Office."[9]

Digna Ochoa was betrayed twice—by the Attorney General's Offices of the state of Veracruz, where her life began, and in the Federal District, where it ended. Nobody in authority gave any credence to her account. Consider what happened:

Digna Ochoa, twenty-four, held a press conference in Jalapa to report she had been abducted and raped by police and the Prosecutor's Office didn't bother to investigate. And yet Renato Sales, who boasted about his record defending human rights in Mexico, found this acceptable. Indeed, he used the lack of an investigation to prove that Digna had never been kidnapped in her home state of Veracruz. It would seem he was missing the forest for the trees. Neither did Margarita Guerra find anything amiss. The twenty-first-century PRD government in Mexico City appeared unable to look back at PRI authorities in Veracruz in 1988 and notice the lack of a proper investigation into very serious allegations.

* * *

Where in Margarita Guerra's report—anywhere in the report—was the Digna Ochoa known to her family, friends, and colleagues? Her goofiness, practical jokes, courage, generosity, and her meticulous attention to legal details—they were all missing from its pages. She was a romantic, she was trying to lose weight, she bought her first pair of running shoes during her last summer with Juan José, she was in the midst of incorporating her practice as a litigation lawyer. "Digna wasn't a schizophrenic or obsessive-compulsive or anything else they called her," Pilar Noriega told *Proceso* magazine as the suicide theory bubbled to the surface. "She was a woman dedicated to her work and to the defense of human rights campaigners. Her work was unquestionable."

Pilar was one of Digna's closest friends. "She was many things," she told me in her office during one interview in 2002. "On the one hand, she was very gentle in how she approached a case but on the other she could be tough. She had a strong character and when she was dealing with difficult issues, she was very tough. But the thing is, she didn't appear like that. She was intransigent— more than intransigent, she could be rigid—but then she had her sweet voice. She was very committed to her work, she was religious, and because of it she had this spirit of sacrifice. She liked to make jokes. . . . Some people had the idea that Digna was very delicate, something that she wasn't at all, but it all depended on which side of Digna you got to know."[10]

Pilar described the complexities of the human being. In the hands of Renato Sales and Margarita Guerra, such shades of

427

humanity turned into the boring black and white of the unimaginative.

Pilar also described Digna as "someone who knew what it was like to go without. She knew what it was like to go hungry."

That was how I knew she meant what she promised the villagers of the Guerrero mountains. She would be back, she told them two weeks before her murder.

* * *

Nothing in her life was off-limits to Mexico City prosecutors, not even her religion. Police psychologist Arturo Mendoza Vega[11] devoted considerable attention (his work was included in Guerra's report) to the premise that Digna sought death as a martyr for Christ. His proof of this dark and bloody purpose was found in notations in her own hand, such as "Love your enemies and pray for those who persecute you," or "Live according to Jesus Christ." Mendoza Vega reproduced a dozen or more of these scriptural stalwarts and sacred homilies, all highlighted in enthusiastic bold type. Suspicion of the Catholic Church, not uncommon among members of Mexico's professional and political elites, appeared evident in his report, as it did in other documents related to Digna's case. Reading his theories, I had the same sense as when Renato Sales sparked images of nuns committing mysterious acts in secret behind cloistered walls. (Suspicion mixed with fantasies. She wore red for blood and white for purity.) Perhaps the struggle between Church and State in a country colonized by Spain and the Catholic Church created neurosis and, to tweak Leo Tolstoy, every neurotic country was neurotic in its own way. But this theme of suspicion of the Church contrasts with the line of mutual respect between Mexican authorities and Jesuits close to Digna Ochoa, a line that ran unbroken through the story of her life and death and that, in my opinion, contributed to her undoing.

* * *

Digna spent eight years with the Dominican nuns of the Incarnate Word before leaving the order in March 1999. There were rumors about her sexual proclivities and innuendo about this former nun who took a lover. There was gossip that she'd been kicked out of the convent.

I visited with Sister Brigitte Loire Brétault in a pretty little convent house in the south of Mexico City in April 2002. We talked about Digna's time with the Dominicans. She had planned to take her final vows in early 1999; however, the sisters felt she wasn't ready, that she needed another year to mature, and they asked her to delay this final step. She got angry at the suggestion, telling them "if they didn't think she was ready to take [her vows] then, a year wasn't going to change anything."[12] Digna was like that, hotheaded at times, and it wasn't surprising to the small congregation that she reacted in this manner.[13]

Before Sister Brigitte finished her story, let me touch on this hotheaded aspect of Digna's character. Since her murder, she has come to be seen by many as a saint. She may have been a saintly personification of courage, but I don't think she would want to be remembered as one-dimensional. She could get mad easily, as the sisters who lived with her knew well. She could be boastful, as when she was triumphant with friends about having bested the soldiers and their lawyers at the *careo constitucional* (judicial hearing) in the Montiel/Cabrera case in Iguala, Guerrero. She could be uncompromising in her lack of tolerance for the religious shortcomings of others, as Pilar mentioned in an interview long after her death.[14] And she could be foolhardy and impetuous. I watched the video of her last trip into the mountains of Petatlán and saw her rushing to confront soldiers or taking notes on passing military vehicles. Even knowing her fate, I wanted to cry out each time, "Digna, stop!" as if the outcome could be different.

She was a real person, a human being with foibles, faults, and idiosyncrasies. That doesn't mean she wasn't also an extraordinary person.

"To talk about Digna is to talk about human rights because that was central to who she was," Sister Brigitte told me, on that soft spring afternoon in 2002, with birds twittering outside in the garden. She was an artist, French-born, and her beautiful canvases filled the rooms. In one of them there was a small "shrine" to Digna.

"Digna could not stand injustice," she continued. "Her motivation was to defend people who were unjustly condemned. Her work was her life. . . . She was a person full of joy, but from the moment she began to receive death threats, she was frightened. But there was no going back, because she felt she had to finish what she started."

In 1997, Digna spent six months in the Dominican mother-house in France and the nuns asked her to stay. There was no danger for her there. However, she told them that she could not, and that her life was in Mexico.

Sister Brigitte was not comfortable discussing the internal affairs of her order. But she felt it would be worse to say nothing and leave Digna undefended. The police interviewed her for five hours, pushing her to condemn Digna. "I know what they wanted me to say about Digna. But I told them that it was a personal decision for her to leave," she said. "We respected her decision because it was the most important decision in a religious life. Vows are forever and you cannot go back. It was her decision and it was a difficult thing, both for her and for us. It had been eight years since her novitiate and nine years in total with us."

I asked Sister Brigitte what she thought of the suicide theory.

"Suicide is desperation. There is no way out except by the leaving of your life. And we can understand people who abandon the struggle. But there was nothing of that in Digna's character—nothing at all. It is barbarous to invent such a line, and then to investigate it."

When Sister Brigitte said this, I thought about a comment by lawyer José Lavanderos about the so-called suicide. He'd worked with Digna for more than a decade and knew her well. "I can't believe she created this theatrical scene to make it look like murder. . . . If Digna wanted to commit suicide, she would have just killed herself and left no doubts about it. She would have just taken the pistol and—*poof!*—killed herself."

* * *

Prosecutors not only clung to the suicide theory, they did so with duplicity. While Mexico City authorities were saying publicly that they were open to all lines of investigation, Renato Sales was pushing suicide behind the scenes. I had no doubt after interviewing him for the first time, in March 2002, how the case would unfold.

Neither did Leo McGrady. He was part of the Canadian and British human rights team that met with Margarita Guerra in April 2003, three months before she issued her report. She argued at that time that Digna killed herself, describing the strange manner of her suicide—a shot to the thigh and then to the head—"as a peculiar way which was gender-related. We thought it was so ridiculous, it was almost embarrassing to have given credence to it in the first place," McGrady would later tell me. He didn't buy the theory that Digna committed suicide like a girl.

"The suicide theory in outline was absurd, and the closer you scrutinized it, the more absurd and preposterous it became. While they seemed hooked on it, it was as if it was contrived by half a dozen people—a theory comprised by a committee that never bothered to meet."[15]

Margarita Guerra stripped Digna's life of political meaning, just as she earlier played her part in obliterating the significance of murdered Mexico City judge Abraham Polo Uscanga. There was only a fleeting reference to Digna's work for the Cárdenas Front during her early years, and none to her activism in the National Congress of Campesinos.[16]

It was the same story in Guerrero. Police discounted any possibility that her legal investigation could have led to murder. She promised villagers in the Sierra Madre to "knock on doors" on their behalf. This was interpreted to mean that she had no power, threatened nobody, and therefore did not present anyone with a motive for murder. The Prosecutor's Office allowed Guerrero leads to slip away. In his report for the Inter-American Human Rights Commission, law professor Pedro Díaz urged Mexico City authorities to take a statement from a witness from Guerrero, a certain Estéban García Castro. Digna's brother, Jesús, wanted this man interviewed because he apparently had information about a Guerrero hit man hired to kill her—someone other than the two men named in the report by *El Sur*, which claimed a *cacique* hired them for the job.

The potential witness, García Castro, traveled from Guerrero to Mexico City to give his statement, but was turned away by prosecutors: They informed him he wasn't carrying the right identity papers. The Prosecutor's Office was not interested, even though he might have been able to shed light on the case, not to mention that he was right there on their doorstep.

The Prosecutor's Office also refused to act on a petition by Jesús Ochoa, made through the family's lawyer, Bárbara Zamora, to exhume the bodies of the two alleged hit men. The family wanted the DNA tested to see if it could be matched to saliva on three death threats that Digna received prior to her murder, and which tested positive for male DNA.

Several human rights organizations examined Digna's case, including the Federal District Human Rights Commission, the Inter-American Human Rights Commission and San Francisco–based Global Exchange. All exhorted investigators to seriously pursue leads in Guerrero—to no avail. There was a jurisdictional problem for Mexico City authorities in the state of Guerrero, as we saw when soldiers surrounded a team sent by Sales. But every jurisdiction failed Digna. The Díaz report, for example, criticized the Defense Secretariat and, by extension, the army high command, for obstructing the investigation.

Special Prosecutor Guerra tried to distance Digna from the case of Rodolfo Montiel and Teodoro Cabrera and efforts to bring soldiers to justice on torture charges. "Since she cannot entirely eliminate a role for Digna Ochoa in their defense," wrote British scholar John Gledhill, "she simply marginalizes her participation as part of a team effort, before citing testimonies from the released peasant activists that Digna Ochoa never talked to them about having problems with *caciques* or military personnel."[17]

Guerra's report was overkill. It diminished Digna to such a degree that it appeared all she did for the real lawyers was keep the coffee hot and make photocopies. I could attest, however, to Digna's role at Miguel Agustín Pro Juárez Human Rights Center as a skilled human rights lawyer and the lead attorney in the Montiel/Cabrera case. Her role was very real. In January 2000, when asked about the case, PRO director Edgar Cortez told the *Toronto Star:* "You have to talk to Digna Ochoa about that."

The report built a case that Digna tried to make her death look like murder. However, one was tempted to ask, if she was trying to do that, wouldn't she have made public the final death threats she received? Instead, against the advice of her friends and lover, she kept them a secret.

* * *

I thought the original teams of detectives were dismissed because they weren't doing a good job on the case. But I had come to believe that these detectives, despite a distinct lack of grace at times, ended up following the right leads—toward Guerrero. In the early days, they put great stock in the crime-of-passion theory (looking at Juan José Vera as their chief suspect, or imagining a jilted lesbian lover) and they didn't follow procedure with any precision. The Inter-American Human Rights Commission report identified, among other problems, that the crime scene wasn't properly protected (somebody stepped on a shell), Digna's body was moved before medical readings were taken (some never were), and the chain of custody of the evidence was compromised. Detectives even managed to drop the gun, damaging it, although it was not clear which team did this. However, as serious as these errors were, the commission concluded that they were due to systemic problems in the Mexican justice system. Within that system, the first teams were plodding along in a direction indicated by the events of Digna's life, especially the last three months of her life, which are the benchmarks of any credible investigation (as Margarita Guerra herself pointed out once, in an interview with Blanche Petrich). They were slouching toward Guerrero, and toward an intellectual mastermind behind the homicide.

Instead what happened? The focus shifted away from Guerrero. Edgar Cortez was not happy with the first two teams of detectives (under Nicolás Chávez) because, as he told me, the Prosecutor's Office would not share all the evidence with PRO, which had been given special assistant (*coadyuvante*) status in the case. Sales also mentioned that he took over because Edgar Cortez complained about a lack of regard for human rights by the investigators. As a result, on December 10, 2001, Renato Sales was put in charge of the case and the suicide theory began to percolate. Edgar argued that his complaints were based on a need for justice in the investigation. As it turned out, there was no justice for Digna.

I don't know why this happened. It may have been that Edgar's motives, and those of others who led PRO over the years, were benign, and the story simply ended badly. "I think people in PRO feel a certain guilt toward Digna," said Dr. de León. As her friend sees it: "They didn't give her the institutional blanket of protection that she needed. They left her on her own, and this was a very grave error. Without that protection, Digna was very vulnerable. She lived alone on her MacArthur scholarship. She had many plans, but she was completely alone, and the people who wanted to kill her knew that."

There was a puzzling aspect to PRO's involvement in the investigation. The notion of suicide emerged on the first night when, standing in the courtyard at 31-A Zacatecas, Alfredo Castillo was overheard telling his boss, Edgar Cortez, that Digna had committed suicide. Víctor Brenes, a human rights lawyer and Digna's friend, was shocked, blurting out: "You can't say that."[18]

Digna's relationship with PRO's leadership was problematic, certainly from March 2000 when, unbeknownst to her, the psychological profile was done by Mexico City police. Relations with PRO worsened into the crisis that clouded her growing fame later that year. She wrote anguished e-mails from Washington to Edgar, and to Chuche Maldonado, mentor, friend, and former PRO director. There were other issues with PRO. It was suggested that lawyers at PRO took a dim view of Digna's potential involvement, at the time of her death, in the defense of other members of the Organization of Peasant Ecologists of Petatlán, beyond Rodolfo Montiel and Teodoro Cabrera. I think it's true from what I found out in Guerrero that PRO didn't want Digna taking on more cases in the state, even though the center had no plans to take on the cases themselves. My colleague, Swedish journalist Petter Bolme, and I learned that people were warned not to talk about Digna's work there, at the risk of losing favor with PRO, a very powerful organization supported by international groups and governments.[19] The sentiment from people (who knew better than to talk on the record) was that PRO controlled the lion's share of the funding from human rights organizations abroad and if it decided to cut a group off, money would simply dry up, although there's no record they've done so.

Digna's family, especially her older brother, Jesús, continued to be angry with PRO, as were several of her friends. Dr. de León found it disturbing that Edgar did not acknowledge the death threats she received in the last months of her life. "On the nineteenth of October, I was one of the first people to testify to police about them," he said. "I told them she had received death threats in August because she came to see me about them. I explained all this to PRO and, instead of coming to me to ask me to tell them more about these threats, Edgar said publicly a few days later that Digna stopped receiving death threats before her murder."

I concluded that PRO's leaders turned against Digna after the Mexico City police did their secret psychological profile in March 2000. It determined that she was not a credible witness and was likely the architect of her own kidnappings and death threats in 1999.

I believed that this profile, written without benefit of a clinical examination of its subject, was integral in setting the course of Digna's life, from her exile in the United States, her return to Mexico, and the subsequent loss of police bodyguards shortly before her murder. It was not made public and elicited only a brief mention in the report by Guerra (which focused instead on similar conclusions in other psychological studies commissioned by the Prosecutor's Office).[20] But I think that this report was the key piece of evidence in showing how Digna was perceived by insiders—in the offices of the Mexico City attorney general and among those associated with the Miguel Agustín Pro Juárez Human Rights Center. On the afternoon he showed it to me, Renato Sales said that Edgar Cortez was aware of its existence from the beginning, telling me that this was routine since PRO lawyers had received death threats, and were under the protection order, as was Digna, of the Inter-American Human Rights Court. Edgar knew, and I think others did too, including former Jesuit priests Chuche Maldonado and David Fernández. In Felipe Cazals's film about Digna, all three men expressed hostility toward Digna.[21]

"She was a restless person, never satisfied with what she was told. 'Hey Digna, leave this alone, don't get into this.' She always had an answer," said Chuche Maldonado, speaking into the camera.[22] Is that what they said to her? "Hey Digna, leave Guerrero alone."

David Fernández expressed the frustration that Digna Ochoa didn't know her place. "It seems to me that Digna had a propensity for impudence," he told Cazals. "This was apparent in the confrontation with security forces, the judicial powers. She bordered on impudence."[23]

I think former Jesuit priest Enrique Flota knew too. Did he tell others? It would go a long way toward explaining why President Vicente Fox appeared to take such a muted stance on the assassination of one of the country's foremost human rights defenders. He acted as if there was something he wasn't saying publicly. It would also explain why the president's human rights expert, Marieclaire Acosta, moved from staking the credibility of her government's human rights record on solving Digna's murder to appearing blasé on the issue just a few weeks later.

Flota's role was intriguing. An adviser to both the Sales and Guerra investigations, he was the first to tell me about problems with Digna's account of her 1999 kidnappings. The psychological profile was done when his friend Samuél de Villar was attorney general for the PRD government in Mexico City. Enrique Flota was also the first to suggest to me that Digna committed suicide. He had an important role, along with Sales, in leading journalists to that conclusion.

Did these men, part of a brotherhood Digna could never aspire to enter, read the police report in 2000 and irrevocably turn their backs on her? It appeared so, although Digna always believed they did it over the telephone threat involving her nieces in the summer of 2000. They almost succeeded in destroying her, she wrote from Washington, where death threats and acts of aggression failed. Could human rights defenders accept a flimsy report—a ridiculous profile that took issue with a failure to wear makeup in the jungle—over the credibility of one of their own? The profile assumed that Digna had neurotic relations with her family and no close friends, based on her unwillingness to chat about her private life with security forces during questioning about a crime committed against her.

The language of the March 2000 profile—she was part of a team, instructed by others, it became the "Digna Ochoa case"— echoed through every report until the final psychological profiles commissioned by Guerra. (Remember, Guerra accepted two out of three reports, threatening to lay charges against psychiatrists who didn't agree with her.) The language echoed Edgar's own views. His opinion about the "team" was expressed repeatedly and with such vehemence during our interview that I concluded he was envious of Digna's rising star.

Did they all writhe inside with each new accolade—Amnesty's Enduring Spirit Award, the relationship with Kerry Kennedy— heaped upon the shoulders of (to them) this drab and inferior little woman who spoke with the accents of the Veracruz lower classes and who, at varying times, had worked for each of them? They, better than anyone, knew her every weakness. David Fernández was quoted as saying that he was "not going to permit them to make a martyr of Digna."[24]

"If I had doubts about Digna, I would not have asked her to leave the country," Edgar told me. "I took this delicate decision for her to leave the country because it seemed to be that she was under threat. . . . I repeat again: I never doubted her. If I had ever doubted her, we could not have made the denunciations we made."

He spoke carefully. He knew what was at stake. It would be a critical omission, worthy of investigation, if the director of a major rights organization did not pass on new findings to international authorities in a case involving a court ruling against Mexico by the Inter-American Human Rights Court in San José, Costa Rica.

But wasn't this exactly what Edgar did? His denial about doubting Digna was contradicted by people I interviewed in Washington, as well as by his own comments later to the *New York Times*. Furthermore, in his testimony to the Prosecutor's Office, he appeared disdainful of Digna's account of phone calls saying her nieces had been kidnapped on July 24, 2000. He declared that, on that day, shortly after 3 P.M., Digna arrived in his office, sat down, and, when asked what had happened, "she began to cry and then she fainted." Edgar immediately told his secretary to call Chuche Maldonado, who arrived promptly, and Digna apparently recounted what happened in the presence of both men.

Edgar told the police she said she'd been at her office at PRO that morning, but went home to pick up a computer disk she needed. While there, around 10 A.M., she answered her cell phone to hear the voice of one of her nieces speaking and then, "an unknown voice told her that nothing would happen to them if she followed his instructions."[25] A few moments later, she got a second call and was told her nieces were being held hostage on the roof of her apartment building. She went up and found nothing there. She returned to her apartment and got on the intercom to tell the doorman to ask her security squad to leave, which it did. Edgar continued: "She waited for the next call in which she was told to leave her apartment and walk along Colima Street, at least according to her account. Along her route, a man approached her, took her arm, and walked with her. *Licenciada* Digna Ochoa said she couldn't give a description of this person, and yet she walked from Colonia Condesa to Colonia Roma, a better part of the trip, accompanied by this man. She also said that, at one point, a second person walked with them but she couldn't identify him either. Along the way, according to her account, the first person said that she shouldn't worry because further along they would turn over her nieces to her. Finally, around Puebla and Orizaba streets in Colonia Roma, these people told her to go away. According to her same account, *Licenciada* Digna Ochoa walked along Puebla toward Insurgentes Avenue, where she got a taxi and came to the PRO offices." There she broke down.

"At that time, I believed her story," Edgar told police. However, he went on to recount that he subsequently doubted her because "one of the first things we did was to ask for a record of the calls to her cell phone and, in the information referred to us by the telephone company, there was no record of calls in the time specified in *Licenciada* Digna Ochoa's account."

The calls, of course, wouldn't have necessarily shown up on Digna's records and rights defenders have a history of poor relations with phone companies in Mexico. However, Edgar's account was curious for other reasons. He was critical of Digna's inability to describe her assailants, without considering any possible rationale. He made it sound like they were on a Sunday stroll. Couldn't each of these men have slipped in beside her, telling her to keep walking and looking straight ahead? He made no effort to explain why Digna might have dismissed her security squad. It was plausible she was told, "If you want to see your nieces alive, get rid of your bodyguards and do what we say."

He condemned Digna, noting that the "incident made it clear that her capacity to deal with a risky situation was minimal, in that she dismissed her security squad, she followed [the men's] orders, and she didn't make any attempt to contact any member of PRO." So she fabricated the entire episode and yet showed poor judgment in handling its danger? Was it possible that Digna was so scared that her only concern was the safety of her young nieces? She talked about this horrible day with Eva Alarcón in Guerrero shortly before her murder. She said she dealt as best she could with threats to her own safety but the thought that her nieces had been kidnapped was almost more than she could bear.

Margarita Guerra concluded that evidence from the events of July 24, 2000, "places Digna Ochoa's version of events in doubt."

Her report stressed that she "failed to officially denounce the incident to the police." Digna was kidnapped twice in 1999. Both times, she went to the police. Nothing good came of either experience. This time, worn out and, as she told J.J. and her closest friends, feeling completely hopeless that the police would help, she did not. Instead, she went to Edgar and Chuche. They sent her to Washington and cut off communication.

* * *

When Digna's police bodyguards had problems with her in 2000, they sought the advice of Edgar Cortez.[26] Digna apparently had a bad attitude. She didn't appreciate her bodyguards (one remembers her accounts of how they fell asleep and ran out of gas) and was seen to have rolled her eyes at their driving. Digna's every muscle spasm was observed and reported. She slammed a door, maybe twice, had a quick temper, and wanted to go places not authorized by Edgar in prior consultation with these guards.[27] When they complained about Digna, he told them "to be patient and that he would have a talk with Digna."

It turned out that these police bodyguards were telling investigators in the Prosecutor's Office about Digna's instability, lack of friends, and dysfunctional family. One report from January 2000 said that Digna went to the Tapo bus depot in Mexico City to meet "three indigenous-looking women"—her mother, her sister, and her aunt. In the opinion of these pseudopsychiatrists, she greeted her sister and aunt with an appropriate degree of warmth. However, "she was not very effusive with the woman she called *mamá*, kissing her only on the cheek." Guerra's report determined that she had a "dysfunctional relationship" with her mother.

One wonders if Digna knew her police bodyguards were reporting back to her boss at PRO.

* * *

In the years since Digna's murder, PRO has moved away from some of its sensitive cases of years past and slipped into a more "establishment" persona. Perhaps, if the case arose today, the center still would undertake the defense of *ecologistas* Rodolfo Montiel and Teodoro Cabrera, but it has expanded its portfolio. PRO holds seminars on PRD policy matters close to the heart of Mexico City Mayor Andrés Manuel López Obrador and routinely releases position papers on such issues as Daylight Saving Time and water conservation in the capital city.

"Well, we're more diversified," Edgar explained, when I asked him about this shift in the PRO agenda. "We maintain our work in the area of civil and political rights . . . but we have also branched out into the areas of economic, social, and cultural rights. We feel that there are many issues concerning these areas that deserve attention, and so what we have done is simply widened our focus of interest."

Not Digna's cup of tea. I doubt she would recognize PRO, spruced up and wearing a jacket and tie. She might have reacted impudently.

In November 2003, on the second anniversary of the release of peasant ecologists Montiel and Cabrera, PRO released a major report on the case, praising President Vicente Fox for his farsighted action—and neglecting to mention Digna's name. The omission caught my eye, given that Fox acted only as a result of national and international pressure in the aftermath of Digna's assassination. Ethel Kennedy, whose own husband Robert was assassinated, commented that it was sad Digna had to die in order for them to be free.[28]

Not long after the PRO report, Petter Bolme, who'd worked with me on Digna's case for a time in 2002 and was now living in Stockholm,[29] was about to visit Mexico City. I asked him to go and see Jesús González, PRO media relations director, and ask him about the report. As it turned out, he interviewed González by telephone. He had called and left a message, identifying himself as a reporter and asking to speak about Digna Ochoa. Just as he was about to return to Sweden, he got a return phone call.

He sent me a transcript of the interview and I include it here because it seemed to encapsulate how Digna Ochoa was remembered by the organization she loved so dearly:

"This is Jesús González from Center Pro. You had left a message last week. Sorry for not getting back to you until now. What can I help you with?"

"I have a couple of questions related to the last report you did on the *ecologistas* case."

"Yes, go ahead. What do you want to know?"

"Could you please tell me why you don't mention Digna Ochoa at all in your last report on the case of the *ecologistas?*"

"Well, I don't understand why we should mention her in the report. Do you have any reason for us mentioning her?"

"Wasn't she the lawyer for the *ecologistas?*"

"There were many lawyers involved in the case."

"Didn't she perform the *careo* (judicial hearing) when the military admitted that they had tortured the *ecologistas?*"

"She was just one of many lawyers. I don't see any reason for mentioning her in particular in this case. This [the report on the Web site] is not the space to talk about Digna. If she would have had any relevance to the case we would have mentioned her, but this is not the space to talk about her."

"But wasn't it her death that actually led to the presidential pardon of Rodolfo and Teodoro, as well as the pardon of General Gallardo?"

"Well, that might be true but we can't know for a fact that her death had any influence in Fox's decision to pardon the *ecologistas*. It is only a hypothesis and we can't put down hypotheses in our report. Excuse me, but are you interviewing me? You never said that this was an interview. I will not allow you to use anything that I said and if you do, I will deny it. You should have asked me for an interview."

"What? Yes, I told you I had some questions about Digna. Say for the sake of things we start over and you give me your official view on why you didn't mention Digna in the report. What would you say then?"

"I wouldn't say anything."

"So I can write that you don't have anything to say?"

"No, you can't write that. I have no comments and if you want a formal interview, you will have to put it in writing and send it to me. Then I will pass it over to one of our lawyers who can give you a formal answer."[30]

* * *

I am convinced that Digna Ochoa was murdered and that there has been a cover-up. In that case, there remain unanswered questions about why so much time, effort, and energy was spent on ensuring that her death be ruled a suicide. The reason may be the most obvious: fear. There is a body of expert opinion that argues that those who aren't corrupt don't want to take on powerful interests in Guerrero (with their links to a national network of friends in high places) or the power of the army, which, as shown by countless human rights investigations, conducts itself with impunity. And there is a very real, gritty, and legitimate fear of the death squads, which, the record shows, also largely operate with impunity.

While I don't know who killed Digna Ochoa, I believe her death was linked to her work in Guerrero, and that it threatened to expose the unholy alliance between the military and certain special interests—private, profitable, and illegal interests. But just as easily she could have been eliminated for her involvement with other clients, notably the Cerezo Contreras brothers, who were arrested in conjunction with August 2001 bombings at Banamex branches and charged with committing terrorist acts.

Digna herself talked about these "special interests." In September 2000, she told the Enduring Spirit awards dinner at the Beverly Wilshire Hotel in Los Angeles that she'd always wanted to be a lawyer fighting for truth and justice. "Later, I learned that due to the rampant corruption and impunity in Mexico, it was not sufficient to be innocent, to be right, and to have the law on your side, but it was necessary to fight against an entire government structure that defends very specific political and economic interests."

At all costs, the Mexico City Attorney General's Office avoided serious examination of these interests. Human rights lawyer Lamberto González Ruíz perfectly summed up that reticence: "There is a very old and persistent tendency among judicial agents to turn the victim into the killer when they investigate crimes related to repression, or if the case is just too difficult."

* * *

Many placed the blame for the lack of justice for Digna with Mexico City Mayor López Obrador and his PRD administration. In the opinion of Guerrero journalist Maribel Gutiérrez: "He is responsible for the people who were in charge of the investigation who were hiding information and, the most dangerous thing, erasing evidence in order to avoid any possibility that others would discover who killed Digna Ochoa."

Sergio Aguayo, acclaimed author and political scientist who received death threats after Digna's murder, wrote a compelling analysis of the case.[31] He began by stating that Attorney General Bernardo Bátiz was a "profoundly honest man" and a member of a center-left political party that was sensitive to human rights issues. However, he wents on to say that "the most worrying and serious aspect" of the suicide verdict was that it came five years after the Democratic Revolutionary Party won municipal elections in Mexico City, with a promise, among others, to investigate the death threats against the Miguel Agustín Pro Juárez Human Rights Center, which had begun in 1995.[32] The PRD was supposed to adhere to a higher standard than its predecessors had done.

These death threats were never investigated by the PRD government in Mexico City or by the federal government, either under the Institutional Revolutionary Party of Ernesto Zedillo or the National Action Party of Vicente Fox. They were ignored despite a strong report by the Federal District Human Rights Commission, which was sent to Mayor López Obrador in April 2002, six months after Digna's murder. This report criticized incompetence in the Mexico City Prosecutor's Offices, as well as a pattern of complete indifference to investigating the death threats received by PRO between 1995 and 2000. It cited administrative practices "that are not only illegal, but contribute—and have permanently contributed—to the existence of vice, corruption, and arbitrary actions that have made our judicial system the Achilles' heel of the Mexico City government. . . . Not only does it not contribute to the preservation of human rights, but actively disregards them."[33]

The commission called on the López Obrador government to take urgent action to clean up the Prosecutor's Office, especially in view of its failing efforts to investigate the assassination of Digna Ochoa.

López Obrador, like his federal counterpart, Fox, was swept to office on high expectations. He followed Cuauhtémoc Cárdenas, the first democratically elected mayor, who stepped down from municipal politics in 2000 to run against Fox. But he failed to heed the commission's pleas. López Obrador ignored five years of death threats against PRO lawyers, including Digna, just as he failed to insist on a legitimate investigation into her murder. He said publicly that he was satisfied with the suicide verdict. His prosecutors and their leaky boat of an investigation were the butt of jokes in Washington and they had dashed hopes of change, once again, in Mexico. On a grassroots level, few think Digna Ochoa committed suicide, just as few think a capital city transportation chief shot himself—twice—in the heart.

"The death of Digna Ochoa reproduces exactly what has been

seen in other famous crimes," wrote Aguayo. "As the conclusions that they deliver are not technically reliable, they are quickly refuted, leaving a cloud of intense distrust hanging over the protagonists. There is something worse than an abuse of power. We are confronted with the consequences of a discredited judicial system riddled with vice that nobody seeks to eradicate. Digna Ochoa was an attorney seriously committed to human rights who courageously fought against the same incompetence that, ironically and sadly, still hounds her even after her tragic death."

Bárbara Zamora resigned as lawyer for the Ochoa family in March 2003, after what she characterized as a direct threat from the López Obrador government. The family had special status in the case and she was being kept abreast of developments in Digna's investigation (which were also being leaked to the media). When she publicly expressed suspicion about new evidence being found by prosecutors (the little plastic bag of white powder, the letters clipped from newspapers), Attorney General Bátiz warned her she could be charged with obstruction of justice. "I couldn't interpret that as anything else but a threat," she said, adding that she would never have imagined such actions from a government of the PRD.[34]

Bátiz publicly pooh-poohed the notion that Digna's work touched interests important enough to want her dead. He said that he had thought so in the early days but that he changed his mind once the suicide theory took root in the Prosecutor's Office. He was a former professor at the Jesuit-founded Ibero-American University, reportedly a religious man, and maybe he had no reason to doubt a theory presented to him by Renato Sales, and which had the moral backing, in my opinion, of the highly regarded Jesuits who founded and directed the PRO center. That same logic for believing in the suicide theory also applied to Jesuit-educated president Vicente Fox.

In Digna's corner in the investigation—well, there was nobody. "We're not necessarily married to the [idea] that what we are saying is the absolute truth. It's the legal truth, arrived at with all the elements that it contains, in good faith, and with the intention of knowing what really happened," Bátiz told a joint press conference with Margarita Guerra, in July 2003.

The legal truth but not the absolute truth? Sounds like Prime Minister Jean Chrétien's line upon visiting Mexico on a free-trade tour in 1995 that *their* democracy is not *our* democracy. It is my belief that Digna Ochoa—who is after all the one who was dead here—deserved the absolute truth.

* * *

General José Francisco Gallardo was a hero in Mexico and abroad, a former international prisoner of conscience who spent eight years in jail for accusing the army of corruption and human rights crimes. He believed that Mayor López Obrador backed down for pragmatic political reasons and ambitions. "The Mexico City government doesn't want to investigate the military because they don't want to challenge them," he said.[35] He knew that Andrés Manuel López Obrador aimed to be president of Mexico and "he doesn't want to confront the army because he knows he can't become the next president if he does so. They all believe you can't win an election without the army. But I think that's wrong—and that one must confront the army."

Gallardo had no doubt that the order by President Fox to release him in February 2002 stemmed from the international outcry after Digna's murder, and that she paid for his freedom with her life.

This man, who knew better than anyone the dark capabilities of the state, never doubted Digna's accounts of her kidnappings in 1999. That same year, a kidnapping attempt by army intelligence agents against one of his sons was foiled by happenstance—the lucky intervention of local police in Mexico City. The ensuing police report, which slipped through before it was censored, cited the names and military identification of the perpetrators of the attempted kidnapping, who were turned over to army justice, where they and the cases against them vanished.

"Who could have carried out such a kidnapping—the army," he told me in Mexico City. "It is all documented and yet the army arrived and said that nothing happened because the soldiers were on a mission. And the police covered for them. The Prosecutor's Office covered for them. The army covered for them."

General Gallardo shared Digna's belief that agents of the state were behind her kidnappings, even as others naively clung to the view that such deeds were not possible in Mexico. "There is one line they didn't investigate at all, and that is the military," he said. "Digna investigated military abuse and torture and had been tortured herself. So there was a clear abdication of responsibility when they failed to investigate the army in her death."[36]

* * *

The ultimate responsibility, though, must rest at Los Pinos, upon the broad shoulders of Mexican President Vicente Fox. He promised to reform Mexico, to protect human rights defenders as never before, and, upon this oath, the people welcomed him with open hearts.

But Fox had his own interests to protect. As British academic John Gledhill concluded in a report on Digna's murder, "Fox was careful not to disturb the deeper arrangements of power that had emerged under the old regime, since Fox and his team were pragmatists who had benefited from the 'system' as previously established."[37]

This was the very system—*el sistema*—that Fox pledged to dismantle. It was obscure and shadowy, and little had been revealed about who controlled it, even by Mexico's finest journalists. "There seems to be a pact," Maribel Gutiérrez told me one day, in the offices of *El Sur* in Acapulco. "I don't know if there are superior forces, above the president, who are running things in

Mexico. What I do know is that they all act the same. It doesn't matter if the president is Ernesto Zedillo from the PRI or Vicente Fox from the PAN—there is no change."

Gallardo said that there could have been, and that Digna's life could have been saved. "If the president had done something concrete to end impunity, I think nothing would have happened to Digna," he had told me. Moreover, he warned that as long as the military and local *caciques* continued to run Mexico in an environment of impunity, it was merely a matter of time before there was another massacre on the scale of the murdered women and babies of Acteal.

* * *

The assassination of Digna Ochoa continued to cast a pall over the human rights movement in Mexico. It had been eloquently argued by other writers that Digna was killed twice, first in the flesh and then through the campaign that smeared her memory with the suicide verdict.[38] In reality, she had been murdered many more times with the litany of assaults against human rights activists in Mexico.

By declaring that she died by her own hand—or, to be precise, the cowardly "probable suicide" ruling—authorities abandoned the country's other rights defenders. Lawyer Pilar Noriega identified this outcome right after Digna's murder. "Whoever killed Digna acted with the conviction and the certainty that they could say, 'Look, I can do whatever I want, and nothing is going to happen,'" she told José Gil Olmos, of the news magazine *Proceso*. "They feel sufficiently protected that they are not threatened, even having committed a crime of such magnitude."

The mass of conflicting and false information about Digna's death lead to confusion, particularly outside Mexico, and made it easier to paint shades of gray. *Are we certain she didn't kill herself?* Senior people from international rights organizations had expressed that doubt to me. *I am absolutely certain.* Adding to the climate of doubt was, to me, the part played in this drama by Edgar Cortez and others at PRO who meekly surrendered Digna to the investigation.

In the opinion of Canadian lawyer and rights defender Leo McGrady: "The real damage in this erroneous conclusion is that, in addition to Digna's case and her reputation, it has acted to chill the work of other human rights lawyers and activists in Mexico who already were laboring under very trying circumstances. It suggests that people who dedicate their lives to causes and issues are, in many cases, suspect and unbalanced and even deranged. We need to see it as an effort to discredit a body of work which is so vital to the process of change which Mexico is experiencing."

The message—that it was open season on rights defenders—could not be clearer. Pilar called the chilled atmosphere for human rights workers the "Digna effect." She said she knew human rights activists who, faced with death threats, had left the country. "Her murder was a warning to the entire human rights movement," said Pilar. "The message is that death threats come true. And, if you think of it that way, you are filled with horror and panic because . . . sooner or later, a threatened person is going to get assassinated."[39]

Digna's murder led to a huge international outcry. Fox began facing questions during foreign trips. "The feeling was that here in Mexico human rights defenders are assassinated," Pilar explained. "That is a serious matter. But if she committed suicide, then human rights defenders are not in danger, nor are social activists or civil organizations. And there is no longer that stigma. The suicide version eliminates any vestige of a threat toward critics of the system."[40]

* * *

One could argue that, once the suicide line was established,

Digna was betrayed again. The two nations that joined with Mexico in leaping into the era of free trade with fine promises essentially did nothing. When the North American Free Trade Agreement among Canada, the United States, and Mexico became law in 1994, politicians talked about democracy and freedom and the protection of human rights. They talked grandly—but they did not include human rights issues in the deal. "We hear so much about not needing to incorporate human rights into treaties on trade because—or so the theory goes—if you fully engage a country like Mexico on the trade front, respect for human rights will follow," said Leo McGrady. "But it's very hard to see anything but evidence which contradicts that proposition flowing from Digna's case."

He chose his words carefully: "Canada has, on a number of occasions, joined with Mexico in celebrating a new respect for human rights, in some measure sincerely, but also as a way of easing trade relations that would otherwise be more difficult. But Canada runs the risk of being accused of hypocrisy if the government doesn't take a stronger public stand when human rights are so flagrantly violated. And there is no more straightforward attack on someone's human rights than the murder of a person who dedicated her life to the advancement of human rights."

Canada should have stood up and be counted. Yes, he said, "it's laudable" that Canada participated in the review of evidence in her case by the Inter-American Human Rights Commission by sending the RCMP's Al Voth to Mexico City. But he said that the Pedro Díaz report should have been made public instead of being kept secret, thereby shielding Mexico from any criticism whatsoever. Apart from the moral and international legal issues, Canadian tax dollars helped support the commission's parent organization, the Organization of American States.[41]

For the U.S. government, there was an additional reason to

push for answers in Digna's death, said McGrady. "One of the concerns is that the activists [the *ecologistas*] who were the focus of her activities in Guerrero were involved with an American corporation [Boise Cascade] and a government should be concerned about the values and ethics of its corporations abroad."

Gail Davidson, who founded Lawyers' Rights Watch Canada in January 2000, argued that Mexico had failed to comply with its international legal obligations in Digna's case and that, as a result, Canada had a duty to comment. This obligation superseded issues of Mexican sovereignty, she said, citing UN and OAS declarations on human rights that bound Mexico to protect defenders and to investigate violations properly. The UN Charter implied a dialogue on issues between states by obligating its members to "achieve international cooperation" in the protection of human rights.[42]

Davidson talked about Canada's obligations in an interview from the group's Vancouver offices in May 2005. She was passionate. She had been tracking Digna Ochoa's case for three years, writing letters of protest and organizing two joint Canadian-British fact-finding missions to Mexico. "The Inter-American Commission on Human Rights and the Inter-American Court on Human Rights have confirmed that Mexico had a responsibility to protect Digna Ochoa and now has a responsibility to conduct an 'effective' investigation of the threats and assaults that preceded her death, and of her death herself," she told me. "Once there has been a serious violation of international human rights obligations, and the state in which the violation has occurred has failed to pursue— or adequately pursue—the required remedies, other states such as Canada have a responsibility to intervene."

* * *

While Mexico City prosecutors compiled mountains of paper on Digna's alleged suicide, Lawyers' Rights Watch Canada was

453

documenting abuses against activists, including attorneys like Digna. Horribly, she wasn't even the only rights lawyer to die in the autumn of 2001. About a month before her death, hired killers had pumped five bullets into María del los Angeles Tamés, twenty-seven, who was also a National Action Party politician in the State of Mexico. Her friends called her Marigeli and she was planning to go public with evidence of corruption by members of her own political party. In her case, a suspect, the former PAN mayor of her town of Atizapan, had been arrested and charged with masterminding her murder.

For the majority of cases, however, nothing changed. Rights lawyers and activists continued to be threatened, assaulted, kidnapped, "disappeared," and murdered while the government looked the other way. In Guerrero, where members of the peasant ecologists group lived in hiding just as they did during Digna's visit, rights defenders were targets. One case in particular summed up the government's disdain for human rights: Abel Barrera, from a small rights center in Guerrero,[43] had received death threats on numerous occasions and the Inter-American Human Rights Commission recommended that he be protected by the Mexican government. But his police bodyguards weren't given expense money, so he had to travel to remote mountain communities alone. "What good are guards who do not have the appropriate resources to protect the person they are supposed to be guarding?" asked a report by Global Exchange.[44]

Officials from the federal Attorney General's Office told an American rights delegation in 2002 that they had access to only three available cars in the state. When Barrera filed a complaint with the Inter-American Commission, federal officials investigated his finances and filed a false report that he owned "a hotel, three pharmacies, three autos and a ranch . . . and his guards filed a report claiming that Mr. Barrera would not provide them with discount lodging at a hotel they falsely claimed he owns."[45] It would be funny if it weren't so serious, if a life weren't at stake.

The Global Exchange report said: "The [federal attorney general] is more interested in investigating the personal lives of human rights defenders, and in using this information to slander the work of these defenders, than in providing them with adequate protection from death threats."

It was little wonder that people said Mexico was going backward. Over a two-year period since Digna's assassination—between 2001 and 2003—Lawyers' Rights Watch Canada had written letters to President Vicente Fox, Attorney General Rafael Macedo de la Concha, Mexico City Mayor Manuel Andrés López Obrador, and other high-level politicians, on behalf of fourteen Mexican lawyers and human rights defenders whose cases were being tracked by international agencies because they involve allegations against the state.[46] They had reports of confessions extracted through torture, and evidence of rapes, beatings, and extrajudicial killings, including the disappearance of Marcelino Santiago Pacheco, an indigenous activist from Oaxaca, who was last seen on April 27, 2003. He had been kidnapped and tortured once before, in 1997, allegedly by security forces. At the time of his disappearance in 2003, he was waiting to testify against the former governor of the state.

On May 6, 2003, Veracruz human rights lawyer Griselda Tirado Evangelico, who was a Totonac like Digna, was shot and killed while leaving her house in the early morning in the city of Puebla. She founded the Totonaca Independent Organization, was active in an indigenous center of higher learning, and planned to run as a candidate in municipal elections. She was in her early thirties; her little girl was ten. Others in her activist family had been threatened and Amnesty International put out a bulletin urging the Mexican government to protect them. There was no response.

Another case involved the death of a lawyer in Ciudad Juárez, where three hundred women had been murdered since the early 1990s. On February 5, 2002, defense lawyer Mario César

Escobedo Anaya, twenty-nine, was gunned down by police in that city, across the U.S. border from El Paso, Texas. He was defending a man accused of involvement in the murders of eleven women, and maintained that his client was tortured into giving a false confession. A few days before his death, he announced that he would file criminal charges against state officials for allegedly kidnapping and torturing the man.

César Escobedo died in his car, riddled with bullet holes, after police chased him through the city. They claimed he was shooting at them and they fired in self-defense. Elements of the case were achingly familiar. There were allegations of altered evidence. Photos taken at the scene by a journalist showed an unmarked police Jeep Cherokee with no bullet holes in it. The same vehicle was shown in another photo, this time with a bullet hole in the hood. There were threatening phone calls to Escobedo's home in the days before he died, as well as warnings that his office would be bombed. A state senator said the case bore all the marks of an "execution" of a lawyer for attempting to expose torture by the police. A witness apparently saw police shooting directly into Escobedo's car on the night of his death, yet no charges had been made.

This was just the type of case Digna would have been anxious to investigate herself. She would have fought for justice.

* * *

There was another name on the list of rights abuses—Bárbara Zamora, Digna's friend and fellow lawyer and a founder of the rights organization *Tierra y Libertad* (Land and Liberty). She began to receive death threats not long after Digna's murder, as did her law partner Leonel Rivero. They didn't know if the threats were related to the case of the Cerezo Contreras brothers, which Digna was working on with Bárbara at the time of her death. She'd met with Digna for the last time at the Zacatecas Street office on Wednesday afternoon, October 17, 2001. "Digna was very animated, joking around and very enthusiastic about the work that we were going to do together, as well as the possibility of taking on the cases of other prisoners from the mountains of Petatlán," she told me in Mexico City, five months after Digna's death. She said Digna thought they would work together on the cases of other imprisoned *ecologistas* and said she was hoping for funding from Harald Ihmig, the German aid worker and theologian who journeyed into the mountains with her.[47] "She talked about the future. She was full of plans. . . ."

Bárbara left several anguished messages on Digna's answering machine the day she died.

They were supposed to go together to Almoloya prison the next day, Saturday, October 20, to visit the Cerezo Contreras brothers, Hector, Alejandro, and Antonio, university students in their twenties, in preparation for a hearing the following Monday. Of course, Digna never made it.

Bárbara Zamora continued to represent the brothers, who were jailed on charges of setting off bombs at a Banamex branch and writing the name of a guerrilla group—the Armed Revolutionary Forces of the People (FARP)—at the scene. The bombings were said to be the work of rebels, but she believed it was a "black ops"—the handiwork of special army units.

The prisoners' siblings, Francisco and Emiliana, were trying to prove the brothers were being tortured in prison and had filed complaints that plastic bags were placed over their heads and pulled off at the last moment before asphyxiation. Emiliana Cerezo Contreras, who was a doctor, had received death threats at her home and office. "*We are coming to kill you,*" said voices on the telephone. Authorities refused to trace the calls. They said there were no records.[48]

When a judge dropped initial charges against her clients, they were charged with more sweeping terrorism charges. "But if the judge concluded they weren't responsible for the acts, they weren't responsible for painting 'FARP' on a wall," said

Bárbara Zamora. "Therefore, how could they be responsible for acts of terrorism that other groups did? It is all irregular and contradictory."

A young filmmaker named Emiliano Altuna, a Spaniard, tried to make a film about the Cerezo Contreras brothers for a university class in Mexico. He began to receive death threats. *"You are a prick, Emiliano, and we know where you live, we know what you do . . . so don't play dumb if you don't want to be involved in an accident . . . you live in a neighborhood where robberies and murders happen often so watch out because this is the only warning you'll ever receive. . . ."*[49]

He left Mexico in 2003, without completing his film.

Digna thought the case of the Cerezo Contreras brothers could be easily won, but still took the precaution of writing a will and sending it to her sister in Misántla a few weeks before her murder. She was merely being careful, she assured Esthela. "Weeds never die."

On March 18, 2002, Bárbara Zamora received an e-mail death threat that the government—yet again—said it could not trace. "It seems to us by the style and the words they used that they have no connection with Digna," Mexico City attorney general Bernardo Bátiz assured Blanche Petrich, in an interview in 2002. But that, it would seem, was not the point. Rather, the inescapable fact was that nobody knew who sent the threats and authorities who should have been protecting Zamora apparently lacked the will to find out.

Shortly after Digna's murder, the Inter-American Human Rights Commission recommended to the Mexican government that Bárbara Zamora and Leonel Rivero (among others) be protected. Mexican officials agreed in November 2001 to post armed guards outside their offices and to provide electronic surveillance. They failed to do so for Zamora.

However, authorities did provide Rivero with bodyguards. On April 6, 2002, his two bodyguards were beaten up outside his home. Their guns were stolen and assailants left one in handcuffs and the other locked in the trunk of their car.[50] They left a message for Rivero: *"We're going to fuck him."*

There was more terror to come for Rivero and his family:

February 18, 2003—a voice, apparently that of a child, was left on his office answering machine. It said, *"I think we're going to get you."* Just a child's prank, declared officials in the Prosecutor's Office.

March 15, 2005—Rivero answered his residence phone to hear a young girl's voice saying, *"You will die."* The next day, there were four more voice messages on the family line, apparently from the same person. *"Just because I am a girl doesn't mean that I don't know how to kill you."*

So it went and so it goes. There is no respite from the relentless brutality.

The assassination of Digna Ochoa resulted in the freedom by presidential decree of Rodolfo Montiel, Teodoro Cabrera, and General José Francisco Gallardo. But on the level of grassroots activism by her former friends and colleagues throughout the country—in the law offices at 31-A Zacatecas or Ciudad Juárez and in other places where the grunt work of human rights defenders is being done and lives are being lost—the record has not improved. It's getting worse and the proud, brave people of Mexico deserve better.

Epilogue

In February 2005, Digna's family won an appeal in a Mexican superior court to have her case reopened. The court ruled that Mexico City prosecutors did not examine all the facts of the case, including evidence that there was extensive bruising on her body, that she was moved after death, and that the crime scene wasn't protected by authorities.

The ruling came amid a push by national and international groups to reverse the suicide ruling, which included letters from Zapatista Subcomandante Marcos, in the jungle close to the border with Guatemala, to Bernardo Bátiz, attorney general of the Federal District and a stalwart of the government of Mayor Andrés Manuel López Obrador. "People said that if López Obrador won the presidential elections in 2006—and by the late spring of 2005 it was certain that he would be the candidate of the left—there would be a bright future for this able lieutenant."

Bátiz responded to the court's decision by saying "it is everyone's commitment to shed light on the investigation" into Digna Ochoa's death. Renato Sales, his deputy attorney general and still one of his most trusted officials, made similar comments to the media. However, within days, there were rumblings from the Prosecutor's Office that the ruling didn't mean that the entire case had to be reopened. Rather, only a small amount of evidence needed to be examined by detectives. Meanwhile, there were reports that Digna was killed by special agents within the Mexican Army.

Jesús Ochoa, now director of the Digna Ochoa Human Rights

Center in Misántla, welcomed the news. "It could be nothing less," he said of the ruling by the court. He pledged to keep on fighting for justice for his sister. He added, however, that he had no real confidence in the attorney general or the government of López Obrador. He held a minority view of the mayor, a widower since his wife died of lupus in 2003 and more popular than ever.

At the time of this new twist in the case, President Vicente Fox was preparing to fly to the United States to discuss trade and border issues, including a new security perimeter, with Canadian Prime Minister Paul Martin and U.S. President George W. Bush, at the presidential ranch in Crawford, Texas. President Fox was in the fifth and penultimate year of his *sexenio,* which most agreed, with a certain wistfulness, had lost its luster some time ago. The president was merely biding his time until the end. It didn't appear any longer as if there was much support for a presidential run by the First Lady, Martha Sahagún.

His attorney general, Rafael Macedo de la Concha, soon resigned, apparently over his failure to bar López Obrador from being a presidential candidate over a disputed ruling he had made as mayor in a land dispute. Perhaps it was the only battle the crafty army general had ever lost.

In Mexico's capital city, there was trepidation about the reported reopening of Digna's case. There was speculation that Mayor López Obrador, who only recently had been quoted as saying he was satisfied with the suicide verdict of Special Prosecutor Margarita Guerra, wasn't eager to face claims in an election campaign that his government had betrayed the country's foremost human rights lawyer, Digna Ochoa.

Likely he wouldn't have to. The country's human rights defenders were weary and worn down. They had fought on too many fronts and they fought alone. There was no institutional support for them from Canada or the United States, whose politicians heralded the arrival of democracy and freedom from fear with the free trade agreement more than a decade earlier.

In September, Felipe Arreaga, the most thoughtful of the *ecologistas*, was released from jail in Guerrero. He'd been there for ten months, charged with the long-ago murder of a *cacique*'s son. While Amnesty International praised the decision by a Guerrero court to acquit him, the human rights group warned that his life was still in danger. There were arrest warrants out for another dozen of his *ecologista* colleagues, just as there had been when Digna visited his mountains. Temporary restrictions had been lifted and wide-scale logging was booming again in the Sierra Madre.

In early October, the Inter-American Human Rights Court in San José, Costa Rica, upheld an earlier protection order for Bárbara Zamora and Leonel Rivero. As it had with Digna Ochoa, the Mexican government had petitioned the Court to have the measures lifted, this time failing in its efforts.

Two potential witnesses in a new investigation into Digna's death appeared to have moved on with their lives.

Edgar Cortez had left the Miguel Agustín Pro Juárez Human Rights Centre and was now director of the largest national network of human rights organizations in the country, *Todos los Derechos para Todos* (Rights for All).

Juan José Vera had remarried and once again moved out of his mother's large house in Mexico City. However, according to the will about which Digna advised his mother on the last night of her life, he should one day inherit the property.

As the fourth anniversary of Digna's death approached in October, memorial services were planned across the country. Although the court had ordered the investigation into her death re-opened, Mexico City officials had nothing new to report. In June, Digna's body had been exhumed and, a week later, Bernardo Bátiz told reporters it had revealed nothing new.

And, in the shadows, the death squads grew stronger, taking their victims as they pleased. Are they not invincible?

Toronto, October 19, 2005

Acknowledgments

I am particularly grateful to a triumvirate who worked on this book. Petter Bolme gave unstintingly of his time, expertise, and humor. He was in Sweden when I began my research, but thought nothing of jumping on a plane and flying across the Atlantic when I needed him. Leticia Flores Moctezuma assisted me in Mexico City, putting in long hours with grace and good cheer. Lety is fearless, and I thank Alejandro and Gil for lending her to me. Reem Algharabali transcribed and translated interviews and offered insights that enriched the project.

I want to thank several other friends: Donna Barne (Washington) was with me on the train from New York City and could be counted on for flawless research; Michelle Shephard (Toronto) was generous with her police contacts, which happen to be the best in Canada; Graciela D'Adamo (Toronto) evolved from translator to friend in the first year; Cheryl Fisher (Toronto) designed a sanctuary for me in which to write; Dr. Héctor Sánchez Castillo (Mexico City) turned out to be a very fine detective; Sara Sahr (Toronto) kept me fit and sane; and Dr. Sheila Grossman (Montreal) inspired by example.

My colleagues at the *Toronto Star*—notably John Honderich, Mary Deanne Shears, Joe Hall, and Bill Ryan—made it easy for me to work on the book and slip effortlessly back into the newsroom in Toronto. I am buoyed by the enthusiasm and support of John Ferri, Giles Gherson, and the eclectic Alison Uncles, as well as the talents of Linda Turner and the legendary Star switchboard, and Joan

Sweeny Marsh and her sleuths in the library. Others helped me in immeasurable ways, among them Sharon Burnside, Jimmy Atkins, Peter Martyn, Ian Urquhart, Ruth Valancius, Peter Power, Olivia Ward, Carol Goar, Carl Neustaedter, Peter Howell, Louisa Taylor, Bart LeDrew, Duncan Boyce, and Ann Tugnut. Mark Trensch helped bring me home. And thank you, Jennifer Wells.

This book was not what I expected it to be, although I suspect that is often the case. It required enormous amounts of patience. Harald Ihmig in Hamburg was unflappable and I will not forget his kindness.

Some people who helped me asked to remain anonymous. I thank them anonymously.

I admire many brave journalists in Mexico, first among them Maribel Gutiérrez and Blanche Petrich. Their courage and dedication to their craft are an inspiration.

A book is a team effort, and I am lucky to have had three special teams working with me. My agent, Bruce Westwood, was the one who told me, "You must write this book," and I depended greatly on his colleague Natasha Daneman. At HarperCollins in Canada, my publisher, Iris Tupholme, is a warrior in stilettos. She shared my vision from the start and protected it fiercely. My editor, Nicole Langlois brought her organizational skills and superb sense of language to Betrayed and I am indebted to Noelle Zitzer. Alison Woodbury, from Blake, Cassels & Graydon, is the perfectionist's perfectionist. I am deeply grateful to Philip Turner, editor-in-chief at Carroll & Graf Publishers in New York, for believing that stories like Digna's must be told. It was serendipitous that he first became acquainted with Digna as an editor on Kerry Kennedy's remarkable Speak Truth to Power, which I took as a sign. At Carroll & Graf too, it was a pleasure to work with associate editor Keith Wallman.

I relied on experts who, despite busy schedules, were enormously generous with their time. They include Gary Ellis, Dr. James Young, Dr. Paul Gentili, Dr. Peter Adamson, Robert Warburton, and the one-and-only Finn Nielsen.

I am grateful for the support of my family, especially my mother, my sister Wendy Trottier, my uncle, Robert Diebel, and my aunt, Audrey Smith. I wish my dad were here. Linda McQuaig and Kelly Toughill lived and breathed this book, and I am honored to call them my friends.

Chronology

1964–1970: *Sexenio* (six-year term of governance) of President Gustavo Díaz Ordaz

May 15, 1964: Digna Ochoa was born in Misántla, Veracruz.

October 2, 1968: Massacre of Tlatelolco in which hundreds of students were surrounded and gunned down by the Olympic Battalion in Mexico City, at the Plaza de las Tres Culturas. The Mexico City Olympics began as planned shortly thereafter.

1969: Sugar mill closed in Misántla and mill-worker Eusebio Ochoa led protest marches to the federal palace in Mexico City.

1970–1976: *Sexenio* of President Luis Echeverría

1974: Mill reopened and Eusebio Ochoa returned to work.

1976–1982: *Sexenio* of President José López Portillo

July 1, 1980: Eusebio Ochoa was arrested, tortured, and imprisoned on trumped-up murder charges for his union activities at the mill.

July 1981: Eusebio Ochoa was freed from prison without being declared innocent.

February 1982: Devaluation of the Mexican peso plunged the country into the worst economic crisis in its history. The Mexican situation, combined with similar crises throughout Latin America, would eventually lead to a restructuring of the hemisphere's debt and set the scene for the trade pacts to come.

1982–1988: *Sexenio* of President Miguel de la Madrid

1984: Digna went to law school in Jalapa.

September 19, 1985: An earthquake measuring 8.1 on the Richter scale rocked Mexico City, killing at least ten thousand and injuring tens of thousands more. There was widespread disgust and frustration at the mishandling of relief money by federal and Mexico City officials.

1986: Digna began working part-time for the Veracruz Attorney General's Offices.

1988–1994: *Sexenio* of President Carlos Salinas de Gortari

Salinas was declared the winner of the July election in Mexico's most controversial vote. He was widely seen to have stolen the vote from opposition candidate Cuauhtémoc Cárdenas Lázaro from the leftist PRD, leading to protests and unrest over the continued rule of the PRI. The army clamped down on the opposition. Political murders increased.

August 16, 1988: Digna Ochoa, who was politically active with opposition groups, was kidnapped in Jalapa, Veracruz. She had notified her family in preceding days that she had found a "black list" of union and political activists at the offices of the state attorney general.

September 17, 1988: At a press conference in Jalapa, Digna denounced her captors as state police officers and said she was raped. There was no investigation.

Digna left Jalapa for Mexico City. She worked with earthquake relief and joined the new Miguel Agustín Pro Juárez Human Rights Center, founded by Jesuits in Mexico City.

January 1, 1994: The North American Free Trade Agreement (NAFTA) became law in Mexico, the United States, and Canada. On the same day, the Zapatista rebels, led by Subcomandante Marcos, took five towns in Chiapas. The Salinas government responded with war planes and troops. Within a few weeks, the shooting war evolved into an uneasy truce.

March 1994: Presidential candidate Luis Donaldo Colosio, from the ruling PRI party, was assassinated in Tijuana during a period of many political murders. He was replaced as candidate by Ernesto Zedillo.

December 1994: The peso crashed.

1994–2000: *Sexenio* of President Ernesto Zedillo Ponce de León

1995: Death threats began to arrive at the Miguel Agustín Pro Juárez Human Rights Center directed at Digna Ochoa and others who were defending "presumed Zapatistas"—activists who had been arrested and accused of being guerrillas. The threats continued for the rest of the decade.

June 1995: Massacre at Aguas Blancas, Guerrero, in which seventeen campesinos were gunned down. Governor Rubén Figueroa Alcocer was later forced to resign.

July 1997: Cuauhtémoc Cárdenas won the first-ever elections in Mexico City.

December 22, 1997: Acteal Massacre in which a death squad killed forty-five people, mostly women and children, with guns and machetes in Acteal, Chiapas.

July 1999: Digna Ochoa was lead lawyer in the PRO judicial team defending Rodolfo Montiel and Teodoro Cabrera, peasant ecologists from Guerrero who had been jailed after confessing under torture to drug and weapons charges. They were political activists who had been involved in a roadblock campaign to cut off wide-scale logging in the Guerrero mountains. More death threats arrived at PRO offices. It was thought that they were linked specifically to the Guerrero case.

August 1999: Digna was kidnapped and held in a car in Mexico City before being freed.

October 1999: Digna was kidnapped by unknown assailants at her home in Mexico City, blindfolded, interrogated overnight, and left tied up next to an open gas tank. Mexico City police investigated. The Inter-American Human Rights Court ordered the

Mexican government to protect Digna, Edgar Cortez, and PRO lawyer Jorge Fernández Mendiburo after an investigation by its sister organization, the Inter-American Human Rights Commission in Washington. The Inter-American Commission had first recommended protection for Digna and the others in 1995.

March 2000: Using videotaped police interviews with Digna Ochoa, the Mexico City Prosecutor's Office conducted a psychiatric report on her. The report stated that she was not credible and suggested she had never been kidnapped. The report was shared with her directors at PRO but never shown to Digna. The report ignored Digna's political work and referred to the people defended by PRO as "parasites."

July 2000: Digna received anonymous phone calls saying her nieces had been kidnapped.

Also in this month, PAN opposition candidate Vicente Fox Quesada won national elections. It was the first time the PRI had not held power in seven decades.

August 2000: Digna was sent into exile in Washington, D.C., by her boss at PRO, Edgar Cortez. She worked for a rights organization, CEJIL. Her friends in Washington were angry about PRO's lack of support for her.

September 2000: Actor Martin Sheen presented Digna with Amnesty International's "Enduring Spirit" Award in Los Angeles. She was also honored at the Kennedy Center for the Performing Arts in Washington, D.C., in a play about human rights leaders adapted from a book by Kerry Kennedy. Digna was becoming well known and respected in human rights circles in the United States. Meanwhile, there were problems with PRO.

October 2000: After a meeting in Washington with Edgar Cortez, Digna left PRO. She remained in Washington.

2000–2006: *Sexenio* of President Vicente Fox Quesada

January 2001: The Fox government began legal proceedings to have the Inter-American Court protection order for Digna Ochoa lifted.

February 2001: Digna began corresponding by e-mail with Juan José Vera, who lived in Mexico City.

March 2001: Digna returned to Mexico City. She worked on her MacArthur Foundation Fellowship and began to take private cases. A love affair blossomed with Juan José.

August 2001: Court-ordered protection for Digna was lifted. She lost her bodyguards. She began making plans to work again in Guerrero. Death threats arrived again at her apartment.

September 2001: Digna Ochoa visited Teodoro Cabrera and Rodolfo Montiel in prison in Iguala and traveled to Guerrero. She lined up support from a German aid group through Harald Ihmig.

October 1–3, 2001: Digna returned to Guerrero and traveled to mountain communities. She met with fugitive peasant ecologists facing arrest warrants and promised to help by raising awareness in the United States. She returned to Mexico City.

October 16, 2001: Digna began work in the law offices at 31-A Zacatecas Street.

October 19, 2001: Digna was killed by a bullet wound to the head. She was found at 31-A Zacatecas, wearing red rubber gloves and with powder strewn around the office. The next day the first police report ruled homicide.

The case was under the jurisdiction of the Mexico City attorney general. An international outcry erupted and President Fox promised justice, as did Mexico City Mayor Andrés Manuel López Obrador. His attorney general linked her death to her work in Guerrero.

November 2001: Fox released Cabrera and Montiel without declaring them innocent.

January 2002: Mexico City officials ruled homicide in the case of Digna Ochoa for the second time.

February 2002: Fox ordered the release of high-profile political prisoner General José Francisco Gallardo Rodríguez, who was declared a prisoner of conscience by Amnesty and PEN Canada for Freedom of Expression.

March 2002: Mexico City officials suggested that Digna committed suicide.

June 2002: Renato Sales, top Mexico City prosecutor, resigned over dissatisfaction with his unofficial suicide verdict.

July 2003: Prosecutor Margarita Guerra y Tejada released her report, which said that Digna had committed suicide.

April 2005: A Mexican superior court ordered Digna's case re-opened.

June 2005: Digna's body was exhumed.

Notes

Prologue: "Every Bone in Her Body, Every Ounce of Her Being"

1 Interview with Kerry Kennedy, New York, May 8, 2002.
2 Everybody refers to the members of the Organization of the Peasant Ecologists of the Sierra of Petatlán and Coyuca of Catatlán (its full name) as *ecologistas*, or ecologists.
3 Alberto Nájar, "Crónica de los últimos días, Digna Ochoa en Guerrero," *La Jornada, Masiosare* (Sunday magazine), November 4, 2001.
4 Interview with Eva Alarcón, Petatlán, Guerrero, February 28, 2002.

Chapter One: "They Just Killed Digna"

1 It is also known as the Federal District Human Rights Commission. Mexico City and Federal District (D.F.) are interchangeable. Like its national counterpart, CNDH, it is autonomous.
2 Pilar was a senior inspector.
3 Pilar Noriega was never a PRO employee, always taking cases as an outside lawyer.
4 Interview with Digna Ochoa for the *Toronto Star*, January 25, 2000. The threats were also compiled in a report, "Chronology of Reports of Harassment at PRODH," by the Center for Justice and International Law, Washington, D.C.
5 Raúl Monge, "Primer crimen político del sexenio," *Proceso* magazine, October 28, 2001. (Cover headline: "Digna Ochoa, El Aguas Blancas de Fox.")
6 Interview with Denise Gilman, Washington, D.C., March 20, 2002.
7 Interview with Digna Ochoa for the *Toronto Star*, January 25, 2000.
8 Ibid.
9 Ibid.
10 Ibid.
11 The time of 7:39 P.M. was contained in the Mexico City special

prosecutor's report released in July 2003, and there was apparently no record of any earlier calls to police. My interviews, however, suggested a timeline in which police had been notified earlier, with Carmen Herrera, for one, calling from PRO offices closer to 7 P.M. But there was no way of confirming the time.

12 The Public Prosecutor's Office or Public Ministry (*Ministerio Público*) fell under the Mexico City Attorney General's Office and had the power to investigate and prosecute crimes.

13 David Vicenteño, "Cita PGJDF a militares por el caso Digna Ochoa," *La Reforma*, November 9, 2001.

14 Interview with José Lavanderos, Mexico City, April 9, 2002.

15 The procedure, literally called the "Act Covering the Removal of the Corpse," was carried out by detectives working for a special section within the Public Prosecutor's Office.

16 Leticia Fernández, "Indagan origen de arma en homicidio de Digna," *La Reforma*, October 21, 2001.

17 The prison was located in Estado de Mexico, the state that surrounds the Federal District. It had been renamed La Palma, but many people still referred to it as Almoloya.

18 Interview with Kerry Kennedy, New York City, May 8, 2002.

Chapter Two: *La Llorona*

1 These canals once flowed through the entire city. But after conquering the Aztecs, the Spanish filled them in, thus creating water problems that led to five centuries of intermittent floods and water supply shortages yet to be solved.

2 The legend of *La Llorona* was well known in Mexico; however, I found insight in *The Legend of La Llorona* by Hans Hereijgers, published on February 1, 2001, on the Suite University site, www.suite101.com.

3 As detailed in Chapter 1, the Public Ministry was synonymous with the Public Prosecutor's Office, under the umbrella of the attorney general. People reported crimes to the Public Ministry and the Prosecutor's Office investigated and lay charges. An excellent analysis of the system's short-comings is contained in "Legalized Injustice: Mexican Criminal Procedure and Human Rights" (Lawyers Committee for Human Rights and Miguel Agustín Pro Juárez Human Rights Center, 2001).

4 The material in this chapter is taken from reports published on the Web site of the Mexico Attorney General's Office of the Federal District, in July 2003. The material, which ran about three thousand pages, and was released by the final special prosecutor, was removed after two weeks to

be replaced by a summary of the case, plus a statement from Attorney General Bernardo Bátiz. This information also came from three interviews with prosecutor Renato Sales Heredia, in Mexico City, in the spring of 2002, in which I was shown police photographs and extensive documents.

5 Interview with Juan Carlos Plácido, Mexico City, April 6, 2002.

6 I examined a photo of the watch, which was among photos in the criminal investigation file, in the office of Renato Sales. The time suggested that Digna's body was already lying in the Public Ministry at 8:50 P.M., which would indicate rather speedy work at the crime scene. However, that was not definite since the watch could have stopped.

7 While Dr. Fernández went by the title of director of Mexico City's Medical Forensic Services, he was in charge of autopsies performed by the forensic teams. He referred to Dr. Pedro Estrada González, coordinator of expert services, as the coroner. However, Dr. Estrada's teams, which fell under the umbrella of the Mexico City Attorney General's Office, performed only the external examination of the deceased, which in Digna's case occurred on Chimalpopoca Street.

8 Pat Watson, "From Dust to Dust: Forget Gangster Talk—This Is How a Bullet Really Kills," *Toronto Sun*, March 31, 2004, reprinted from *Share*.

9 Dr. Paul Gentili, Toronto Western Hospital, July 10, 2003. Dr. Gentili, a neurosurgeon, provided amplification of the bullet's destructive path within the brain.

10 Interview with Dr. José Ramón Fernández Cáceres, Mexico City, March 8, 2002.

11 Interview with Juan Carlos Plácido, Mexico City, April 6, 2002.

12 Dr. Fernández described the statues outside the forensic science building; I also verified information at the Windows to the Universe Web site, http://www.windows.ucar.edu, through the University Corporation for Atmospheric Research.

13 The Federal District is synonymous with Mexico City. It is referred to by its Spanish acronym, D.F., which is pronounced *D-F-ay*.

14 Their findings were included in the special prosecutor's report released by the Mexico City Attorney General's Office in July 2003.

15 Comisión de Derechos Humanos del Distrito Federal, "Caso Digna Ochoa," *Gaceta*, Publicación mensual de la CDHDF, November 2001, No. 11.

16 *El Universal*, Mexico City, October 20, 2001.

Chapter Three: Smile, Life Is Marvelous

1 J.J. gave me Digna's e-mails, and the few replies he had kept.

2 J.J.'s e-mail records registered the time they arrived in Mexico, one hour behind Washington, or Central Standard Time. The hours have been changed to match the sender. His account with Microsoft's Hotmail didn't automatically save sent messages, which explains why he didn't have a record of his own correspondence, other than the few he kept.

3 The dates for J.J.'s correspondence were not recorded.

4 J.J. used "charlar," which means "to talk or chat". In this context, the verb also means "to chat" online.

5 French for "little message."

6 Masculine and feminine forms of "friend."

7 J.J. used to teach school full-time, but now taught only selected classes.

8 He was referring to the public outcry over Daylight Saving Time. He believed that the campaign by Mexico City Mayor Andrés Manuel López Obrador against DST (imposed by the federal government) had succeeded at last. He was, however, mistaken.

9 The IAHRC is the investigative arm of the Organization of American States and the most prominent human rights agency in the hemisphere.

10 Digna's work at the IAHRC involved researching cases that had been forwarded to the agency for consideration by, among others, the Miguel Agustín Pro Juárez Center in Mexico City. They would have been cases of alleged torture, kidnapping, rape, and extrajudicial killings in which the commission was being asked to petition the government involved to protect its citizens. These would not have been cases Digna would discuss with someone outside her tight circle, and certainly not with a virtual stranger.

11 Chain of Mexican stores, most with restaurants.

12 Mexico City's ancient and famous main square.

13 Interview with Juan José Vera, Mexico City, February 18, 2002.

14 Ibid.

Chapter Four: Don't Fail Us

1 Linda Diebel, "Who's Man Enough to Run Mexico? PRI's Labastida Stakes Manhood, Party Power on Outfoxing Rival," *Toronto Star*, May 6, 2000.

2 Ibid.

3 Ibid.

4 Ibid.

5 Julia Preston and Samuel Dillon, *Opening Mexico: The Making of a Democracy* (New York: Farrar, Straus and Giroux, 2004), p. 171.

6 Miguel de la Madrid, *Change of Course* (Mexican Economic and Cultural Foundation), 2004. The book was excerpted in the Mexican press and this particular quote was translated by Ginger Thompson, *New York Times*, March 9, 2004.

7 Linda Diebel, "A Force for the Future, Bright and Burly Politician Vicente Fox May Be the Man to Break the Institutional Revolutionary Party's Hold on Power," *Toronto Star*, February 11, 1996.

8 Ibid.

9 Enrique Krauze, *Mexico: Biography of Power* (New York: HarperCollins, 1997), p. 423.

10 Diebel, "A Force for the Future."

11 Alfredo Corchado, "Texans Helped Pull Off Fox's Defeat of PRI; They Tell of Secret Adviser Role," *Dallas Morning News*, July 9, 2000.

12 He would eventually lose the campaign.

13 Nick Swift, "'We lick no one's boots,' says Andrés Manuel López Obrador, Mayor of Mexico City," CityMayors, www.citymayors.com, 2004. Mayor López Obrador was runner-up in the 2004 World Mayor Contest.

14 Linda Diebel, "A Paradise Lost to Pollution: Politics Fuel the Degradation of a Once-fertile State," *Toronto Star*, February 25, 1996.

15 While allegations continued to swirl about the Tabasco mess, and may well surface in the 2006 elections if Roberto Madrazo runs for president, there were no convictions in a Mexican court.

16 Julia Preston and Sam Dillon present an interesting analysis of the forces of change in Mexico in *Opening Mexico*.

17 Linda Diebel, "Cleaning Up Mexico's Reform Pact Aims to Halt Pattern of Corruption, One-party Rule," *Toronto Star*, August 7, 1996.

18 Much of this section is taken from my article "Kissinger's 'Truly New World Order'" in the *Toronto Star*, February 7, 1993.

19 Ibid.

20 Walter Isaacson, *Kissinger* (New York: Simon & Schuster, 1992), pp. 746–747. The book is an excellent source on the sweep of Kissinger's power in the hemisphere and throughout the world.

21 Diebel, "Kissinger's 'Truly New World Order.'"

22 Ibid.

23 Ibid.

24 Ibid.

25 Report by Talli Nauman, in *Borderlines* 82, for Global Exchange, October 2001.

26 Report by the Miguel Agustín Pro Juárez Human Rights Center, Mexico City. In 1992, 35 percent of the Mexican population was living in poverty; by 2000, that figure had risen to 52.4 percent.

27 Canadians fought the battle over free trade in the 1988 election campaign. In the United States, free trade didn't become a hot-button issue until the 1992 presidential race. Unions feared the loss of jobs to cheap Mexican labor and Democratic candidate Bill Clinton, running against incumbent President George Bush, waited until the last moment in October to announce his support for the deal. Labor supporters, who had thought he'd go the other way, were dismayed—but voted for him anyway. One lingering memory of the campaign was the squeaky voice of Ross Perot, Texas billionaire and independent candidate, warning about the "giant sucking sound" of jobs going down the tubes to Mexico post-NAFTA.

28 Ross Perot testified at Capitol Hill hearings that the Salinas government purposely delayed the decision to allow the peso to float on capital markets until after the Mexican elections in August and the American elections in November. Nobody wanted Mexico crashing and free trade examined during the U.S. vote in November 1994. Thus, the new Zedillo administration inherited the crisis.

29 Linda Diebel, "Shadow Hangs Over Mexico's Economy; There Are Signs Everywhere the Mexican Miracle May Be Faltering," *Toronto Star,* April 5, 1995

30 Interview with General José Francisco Gallardo, Mexico City, February 20, 2002.

31 Sting's haunting song, "They Dance Alone," is about *los desaparecidos.*

32 This account is based on my own reporting from Mexico City, as well as widespread Mexican press accounts and an excellent chronology, "What's Going On in Mexico Today Is Beyond Fiction," by Peter Lupsha, emeritus professor at the University of New Mexico, WGBH Educational Foundation, 2005.

33 Linda Diebel, "Perils of Paulina, She's in Eye of Mexican Storm, Family Dogged by Rumors of Crime and Corruption," *Toronto Star,* December 3, 1995.

34 "Under the Shadow of Impunity," Amnesty International, March 1999.

35 Amnesty International (Canada) news release, April 6, 1999.

36 Raúl Monge, "El primer crimen político del sexenio," *Proceso,* October 28, 2001. (Cover headline: "Digna Ochoa, El Aguas Blancas de Fox.")

477

37 Kerry Kennedy, *Speak Truth to Power: Human Rights Defenders Who Are Changing Our World*, with photographs by Eddie Adams (New York: Umbrage Edition, 2005), pp. 194–199.

38 Ibid.

39 Interview with Kerry Kennedy, New York, May 8, 2002.

40 By the time the book came out, Digna had left her Dominican order in Mexico City.

41 The award is given by the Chicago-based John D. and Catherine T. MacArthur Foundation.

42 The award presentation, including Digna's speech, is taken from Amnesty's U.S. Web site, www.amnestyusa.org.

Chapter Five: Candle in the Wind

1 Juan Manuel Venegas, "Por Separado, el papa Juan Pablo II recibió a Vicente Fox y Martha Sahagún," *La Jornada*, October 19, 2001.

2 Ibid.

3 Sergio Aguayo Quezada, *La Charola: Una historia de los servicios de inteligencia en México* (México City: Editorial Grijalbo, 2001), p. 271.

4 Comisión de Derechos Humanos del Distrito Federal, "Caso Digna Ochoa," *Gaceta*, Publicación mensual de la CDHDF November, 2001, No. 11.

5 By 2005, the foundation, in combination with another Sahagún charity, had $12.5 million in the bank, including a large amount in a U.S. fund. The amount raised questions about Sahagún's work and her political ambitions, which she continued to deny.

6 ANSA, *Listindiario*, October 23, 2001.

7 Ibid.

8 S. Lynne Walker, "A Grim Message: Murder of Human Rights Activist Shakes Mexico," *Copley News Service*, November 4, 2001.

9 Its full name in Spanish is Organización de Campesinos Ecologistas de la Sierra de Petatlán y de Coyuca de Catalán.

10 "Legalized Injustice," Mexican Criminal Procedure and Human Rights, Appendix V, p. 148.

11 "Digna," video by Carlos Mendoza, Canal 6 de Julio, Mexico City, 2002.

12 Bernardo Bátiz did not elaborate on the "huge investments" involved.

13 "Digna," video by Carlos Mendoza.

14 Julia Preston and Sam Dillon, *Opening Mexico: The Making of a Democracy* (New York: Farrar, Straus and Giroux, 2004), p. 287.

15 Alejandro Angeles Jiménez, "Aguas Blancas Massacre: Supreme Court Blames Figueroa," *The News*, April 24, 1996. In *Opening Mexico*, p. 288,

Preston and Dillon quoted from what they called an "extraordinary" Supreme Court report on the massacre. The court found the first shot was not aimed at the police, but was "an order or signal for the police to fire their automatic weapons in a barrage on defenseless civilians. . . . The police acted coldly and arrogantly, completely in command of the situation." The judges said that Figueroa sent in state officials to the scene "not to investigate and identify those responsible, but rather apparently to hide them and create information confusion."

16 Ginger Thompson, "Fighters for the Forests Are Released from Jail," *New York Times,* November 9, 2001.

17 Ginger Thompson, "Mexican Human Rights Lawyer Is Killed," *New York Times,* October 22, 2001.

18 Among the groups were Human Rights Watch, Robert F. Kennedy Center for Human Rights, Global Exchange, the Mexican League for the Defense of Human Rights, the Mexican Academy for Human Rights, PRO, and the Center Fray Franciso de Vitoria.

19 The court, based in San José, Costa Rica, is the judicial arm of the Organization of American States (OAS) and mandated to rule on human rights cases in the hemisphere. Before cases get to the court, they must first pass through another OAS body, the Washington-based Inter-American Human Rights Commission. The commission receives petitions about alleged abuses and, after reviewing the evidence, can recommend so-called "precautionary measures." In so doing, the commission warns a member government that the life of one of its citizens is in danger, that the state itself may be implicated, and that protection should be provided. But it is not mandatory and, in cases of "extreme gravity and urgency," such as Digna's, the commission has another option. It can turn up the heat by sending the file to the San José court and seeking stronger "provisional measures." The court ordered Mexico to implement these measures to protect the lives of Digna Ochoa, Edgar Cortez, Mario Patrón, and Jorge Fernández.

20 Miguel Agustín Pro Juárez Human Rights Center.

21 Interview with Digna Ochoa for the *Toronto Star,* Mexico City, January 18, 2000.

22 Center for Justice and International Law, Washington, D.C., Chronology of threats compiled in collaboration with the San Miguel Agustín Pro Juárez Human Rights Center and posted on the CEJIL Web site, www.cejil.org/PRESS/dignachrono.htm.

23 Ibid.

24 Interview with Tamryn Nelson, Washington, D.C., March 21, 2002.

25 Ibid.

26 Special prosecutor's report, Mexico City Attorney General's Office, July 2003, first section, p. 236.

27 Interview with Juan José Vera, Mexico City, February 18, 2002.

28 Interview with Juan José Vera, March 28, 2002. Blanche Petrich also reported Digna's concerns about the pregnant bodyguard in *La Jornada*.

29 Hector, Alejandro, and Antonio Cerezo Contreras.

30 Interview with Juan José Vera, Mexico City, February 18, 2002.

31 Known in Mexico as the Ejército del Pueblo Revolucionario.

32 Interview with Marieclaire Acosta, Mexico City, March 11, 2002.

33 Ginger Thompson, "Critics question closing of Mexico rights office," *New York Times*, April 23, 2003.

34 Fox had promised a "truth commission"—in the tradition of South Africa, Chile, Rwanda, and Kosovo—to uncover the crimes of the past. It did not materialize, although he appointed a special prosecutor, Ignacio Carrillo Prieto, who took over vowing that not even former presidents would be immune from prosecution. But it turned out they were. Carrillo tried to bring former president Luis Echevarría to trial on the charge of genocide for the 1971 shootings of students. The Supreme Court ruled in 2004 that it was too late to do so. There would be no accounting, either, for the Tlatelolco massacre of students in 1968.

35 Denise Dresser, "Mexico Stubbornly Denies Its Dark Past," *Los Angeles Times*, February 27, 2005. Denise Dresser is a professor at the Autonomous Technological Institute of Mexico and a former member of the Mexico Citizens' Advisory to the Special Prosecutor (Carrillo Prieto) for Crimes of the Past.

36 While Fox's office commented, it was four days before the president himself spoke.

Chapter Six: *Los Papás*, Mrs. Nobody, and the Fat Man

1 Blanche Petrich, "Que se haga justicia, exige la madre de Digna Ochoa," *La Jornada*, Mexico City, October 22, 2001.

2 Interview with Viviana Krsticevic, Washington, D.C., March 19, 2002.

3 Interview with Kerry Kennedy, New York City, May 8, 2002.

4 Petrich, "Que se haga justicia, exige la madre de Digna Ochoa."

5 Lawyers Committee for Human Rights bulletin, December 2001.

6 Sergio Aguayo Quesada, *La Charola: Una historia de los servicios de inteligencia en México* (Mexico City: Editorial Grijalbo, 2001).

7 "Texto Integro de la Amenaza," *El Universal*, November 1, 2001.

8   Marion Lloyd, "After Warnings Mexican Activist Slain," *Boston Globe,* October 28, 2001.

9   Bátiz said he was investigating the leaks, as he would when further leaks complicated the case in March 2002.

10 Interview with Rafael Álvarez, Mexico City, March 5, 2002.

11 Interview with Sister Brigitte, Mexico City, April 15, 2002.

12 *Police* is an easy catch-all term but they are, in fact, investigators from the Prosecutor's Office, which is part of the Public Ministry and under the jurisdiction of the Attorney General's Offices in the Federal District.

13 Interview with Raquel Mendoza, Mexico City, April 19, 2002.

14 Among strict conditions for loans placed on countries by the International Monetary Fund (IMF) and the World Bank are cuts to social programs, including education. During the strike, which was marked by violent demonstrations, many students carried signs denouncing the IMF and the World Bank, as much as the university administration and the government of President Ernesto Zedillo, for pushing to enforce tuition fees at the state-run university.

15 Special prosecutor's report on Digna Ochoa, section titled, "Papás de la UNAM," Attorney General's Office of Mexico City, July 2003. The Mexico City Attorney General's Office posted about three thousand pages of evidence on its Web site in July 2003. Some sections have titles and some are numbered, while others are not. The material was removed about two weeks later, to be replaced with a summarized version of a report by special prosecutor Margarita Guerra. Throughout, I refer in footnotes to this material as "special prosecutor's report," although only a part of the work actually was produced by Guerra's team.

16 Blanche Petrich, "Pendiente, indagar si como penalista Digna supo algo que la hizo *saber demasiado* de algún *intocable*," *La Jornada,* June 21, 2002.

17 Special prosecutor's report, July 2003, first section, p. 261.

Chapter Seven: The Train from New York City

1   Kerry Kennedy, *Speak Truth to Power: Human Rights Defenders Who Are Changing Our World,* with photographs by Eddie Adams (New York: Umbrage Edition, 2005), p. 198.

2   Linda Diebel, "Mexico's Littlest Victims of War: Death Squads Target Women, Children to Wipe Out Resistance," *Toronto Star,* March 7, 1998.

3   The officer in question was Julio César Santiago Díaz, retired army brigadier general, chief adviser to the Public Security Police in Chiapas, and director of the State Auxiliary Police. The translation of his comments is taken from "Always Near, Always Far: The Armed Forces in

Mexico" (Global Exchange, CIEPAC, Cencos, 1999), p. 124. Chapter 9, "The Armed Forces in Chiapas," is based on an earlier report in *Proceso* magazine, No. 1113, March 1, 1998, p. 7, as well as other sources. A photograph on the cover of the March 1 issue of *Proceso* shows paramilitary agents carrying arms and escorted by two Public Security Police officers. *Proceso* also said that Santiago Díaz told reporters that "officers from the Public Security Police had gone to a border community . . . to buy AK-47s, R-15s and M-16s, [and] that they were later brought to municipalities in the Highlands region, principally Chenalhó, where they were sold to paramilitary groups that operate in the area. . . ." He also said (and the translations are all from Global Exchange, p. 124) that "the same police force assigned to the area, as well as state police officers and ex-members of the Mexican Army, have been the principle suppliers of high-powered arms to paramilitary groups that operate in the region . . . [and that] soldiers from the 31 Military Region of Rancho Nuevo were hired to give training to indigenous anti-Zapatista militants." Another soldier told reporters that the paramilitaries were "openly tolerated" because "there had been orders from above."

4 "Mexico: Under the Shadow of Impunity," Amnesty International, March 1999.

5 "Always Near, Always Far," Global Exchange, p. 102. As this report indicates, there are estimates that go much higher; however, the consensus among experts is roughly seventy thousand troops since the Zapatista uprising in 1995. The Mexican Defense Secretariat does not release troop size figures.

6 Linda Diebel, "Axworthy Urges Human Rights Team for Chiapas: Death Squad Slayings Suggest Situation Worse," *Toronto Star*, April 18, 1998.

7 The massacre of El Charco (The Puddle) occurred June 6/7, 1998, in the village of that name in Guerrero. Human Rights Watch had denounced the case as a mass execution, in which soldiers surrounded a schoolhouse where villagers were asleep, and began shooting. The villagers had been holding a grassroots meeting, a so-called educational session, with members of ERPI (People's Insurgent Revolutionary Army). Eleven people died and five were injured. Eyewitnesses told HRW that civilians were shot dead as they lay wounded on the basketball court. The military version of events, in which it was described as a confrontation between soldiers and guerrillas, had been adopted unchanged and unchallenged by the office of the federal attorney general. The federal government "refused to undertake an independent investigation," said the report by Human Rights Watch.

8 Linda Diebel, "Mexican Land Wars: In Their Struggle for Justice, the Indians of Veracruz Are the Victims of Repression, Torture and Murder," *Toronto Star*, June 25, 1995.

9 The money went to the Mexican government for use on social programs in the poorest states, which were states with large indigenous populations. The sterilization brigade took its funding from the program.

10 Details on the Ejido Morelia case were taken from the Web site of Miguel Agustín Pro Juárez Human Rights Center, Mexico City, "PRODH Cases Brought Before the Inter-American Commission on Human Rights" at www.sjsocial.org/PRODH.

11 By August 1999, there were twenty-one thousand internal refugees in Chiapas, according to a report ("The Displaced Population in Chiapas" by Gustavo Castro and Onécimo Hidalgo) cited in "Always Near, Always Far."

12 Diebel, "Mexican Land Wars."

13 Details are provided at the Web site of the Miguel Agustín Pro Juárez Human Rights Center, Mexico City, "PRODH cases brought before the Inter-American Commission on Human Rights" at www.sjsocial.org/PRODH.

14 Much of this account is taken from my report in the *Toronto Star*, June 25, 1995.

15 Ibid.

16 Ibid.

17 In 2005, Joe Hall was deputy editor at the *Toronto Star*.

18 Web site of the Miguel Agustín Pro Juárez Human Rights Center, Mexico City, "PRODH Cases Brought Before the Inter-American Commission on Human Rights."

19 Ibid.

Chapter Eight: The Bricklayer's Daughter

1 Interview with Juan José Vera, Mexico City, March 26, 2002.

2 *Gringa* usually means American woman but it can refer to any foreigner.

3 Interview with Juan José Vera, Mexico City, March 26, 2002.

4 Hugh Thomas, *The Conquest of Mexico* (London: Pimlico, 1993), p. 444.

5 Ibid, p. 110.

6 Ibid, p. 109.

7 Ibid.

8 Ibid.

9 Interview with Jesús Ochoa, Misántla, Veracruz, February 23, 2002.

10 *Don* is a form of respect shown to older men.

11 The information is contained in the joint thesis by Jesús and Carmen Ochoa, "La Defensa de un Preso Político" ("The Defense of a Political Prisoner"), for a BA in Social Sciences, Escuela Normal Superior Justo Sierra Mendez, 1985.

12 Ibid.

13 Kerry Kennedy, *Speak Truth to Power: Human Rights Defenders Who Are Changing Our World*, with photographs by Eddie Adams (New York: Umbrage Edition, 2005), pp. 194–199.

14 Jalapa, the capital of Veracruz, is spelled both Jalapa and Xalapa.

15 Digna Ochoa, "Criminal Aspects of the Juvenile Offender," Veracruz University, Faculty of Law, Xalapa, Veracruz, 1989. She defended her thesis on May 12, 1989, at 6:30 P.M., before a jury consisting of *Lic.* Salvador Martínez Martínez, *Lica.* Virginia Luna Aguilar, and *Lic.* Jorge Machado Rivera. *Lic.* is the abbreviated form of *Licenciado*, which is the honorific for someone with a law degree. The feminine form is *Licenciada*. In Mexico, it has evolved to the point where anyone with a university degree can use it, and usually does.

16 Kennedy, *Speak Truth to Power*, pp. 194–199.

17 Regina Martínez, *El País*, September 17, 1988. This clipping is not online but is contained in *La Jornada*'s newspaper library in Mexico City.

18 Ibid.

19 Special prosecutor's report, "Historia de Digna Ochoa y Plácido" ("The Story of Digna Ochoa y Plácido"), Mexico City Attorney General's Office, July 2003.

20 Ibid. Although the file was meant to cast Digna in a negative light, it was very useful in revealing facts about her life during that period.

21 Ibid.

22 Regina's report ran in *El País* in Jalapa, September 17, 1988, as well as in *La Jornada*.

23 Interview with Regina Martínez, Jalapa, Veracruz, February 4, 2002.

24 Special prosecutor's report, "The Story of Digna Ochoa y Plácido."

25 Interview with Rafael Álvarez, Mexico City, March 5, 2002.

26 As Latin America correspondent for the *Toronto Star* from 1995 to 2002, I wrote extensively about the murdered women of Juárez, interviewing the families of the victims, as well as politicians and police. Police mixed up files, lost evidence, and, in some instances, spoke in a cavalier manner about the victims. Meanwhile, women continued to be found murdered, a situation that continues to this day, while the vast majority of the homicides remain unsolved. It is very much a political issue as Ciudad Juárez is unable to cope with the influx of people moving to the city

to work in the border *maquilas,* or free-trade factories, which have
exploded in northern Mexico since free trade began in 1994. The infrastructure of the city was built for a few hundred thousand and not the
three million who now live there. The safety of women in the city is
compromised by the lack of adequate transportation from the factories, a large enough police force, or even proper street lighting along
their routes home. These concrete problems are exacerbated by the
failure of political leaders, both in the state of Chihuahua and in the
federal government, to consider putting a halt to these murders a
national priority.

27 "Images of Repression: A Critical Time for Human Rights in Mexico,
1996–1998," Miguel Agustín Pro Juárez Human Rights Center, Mexico
City, 1998.

28 Ibid.

29 Interview with Rafael Álvarez, Mexico City, March 5, 2002.

30 "Images of Repression."

31 This was in early 2002. A more permanent memorial was later built at
Digna's grave.

Chapter Nine: Bad Breath, Bomb Threats, and War in Paradise

1 Linda Diebel, "Gag Order: Mexican Rights Workers Who Challenge the
Government Face Campaign of Terror," *Toronto Star,* January 30, 2000.

2 Ibid.

3 National Security and Intelligence Center.

4 Patricia Bulgarín, a senior investigator with the PGJDF, was involved in
Digna's case in both 2000 (the kidnappings) and in 2001 (her murder). I
tried to interview her on both occasions without success, despite many
messages left over several weeks.

5 Diebel, "Gag Order."

6 "Legalized Injustice: Mexican Criminal Procedure and Human Rights,"
Miguel Agustín Pro Juárez Human Rights Center, Mexico City, and the
Center for Justice and International Law (CEJIL), Washington, D.C.,
May 2001, p. 148. (The center was named for Miguel Agustín
[1891–1927], a Jesuit priest and martyr who was arrested, charged with
sedition, and executed in Mexico in 1927, at the height of the Cristeros
War.) The information in "Legalized Injustice" is based on a PRO
report, "Represión institucionalizada contra defensores de los bosques;
el caso de Rodolfo Montiel y Teodoro Cabrera, Campesinos Ecologistas
de la Sierra de Petatlán y Coyuca de Catatlán," October 7, 1999.

7 Ibid.

8 "Legalized Injustice, Mexican Criminal Procedure and Human Rights," p. 148.

9 Interview with Maribel Gutiérrez, *El Sur*, Acapulco, June 26, 2002.

10 "The Unchanged Face of Guerrero," Global Exchange, Delegation Report, July 9, 2001.

11 Diebel, "Gag Order."

12 "Military Injustice: Mexico's Failure to Punish Army Abusers," Human Rights Watch, December 2001.

13 "Always Near, Always Far: The Armed Forces in Mexico," Global Exchange, San Francisco, 1999.

14 The statement was posted at the time on the company's Web site, www.boisecascade.com, and quoted in the *Toronto Star*, January 30, 2000.

15 "Digna," video by Carlos Mendoza, Canal 6 de Julio, Mexico City, 2002.

16 The quoted sections are British scholar John Gledhill's interpretation of Digna's message in "The Two Deaths of Digna Ochoa: A Window onto the Violences of Power in Neoliberal Mexico," School of Social Sciences, University of Manchester, 2004. I could find no better way to summarize Digna's statements.

17 Telephone interview with Laurie Freeman in Washington, D.C., November 2004. Laurie Freeman is the author of "Troubling Patterns: The Mexican Military and the War on Drugs," a study by the Washington Office on Latin America (WOLA), September 2002.

18 "The Unchanged Face of Guerrero," Global Exchange. "In 1997, estimated personnel was between 25,000 and 45,000, and there is no indication of a reduction of troop presence since that time."

19 *La Jornada*, Mexico City, April 1, 1998. This translation of his comments is contained in "Always Near, Always Far," Global Exchange, pp. 100–101.

20 There were two laws: the General Law for the Establishment of the Bases of Coordination for National and Public Security Systems and the Federal Law Against Organized Delinquency, which is another word for organized crime, usually involved with guns and drugs.

21 Blanche Petrich, "Que se haga justicia, exige la madre de Digna Ochoa," *La Jornada*, Mexico City, October 21, 2001.

22 The relevant section is Article 13, Section X, of the Mexican Constitution.

23 "Report on Guerrero," Global Exchange, San Francisco, November 23, 1999.

24 Linda Diebel, "'Dirty War' Closes in on Mexico Resort Zone," *Toronto Star*, August 25, 1996.

25 Ibid. Canadian Holy Cross father Albert Mahoney, who had served in Mexico for more than twenty years, was among those deported.

26 "Images of Repression: A Critical Time for Human Rights in Mexico, 1996–1998," Miguel Agustín Pro Juárez Human Rights Center, p. 21.

27 Eduardo Albarran Orozco, "Interview with Digna Ochoa," *El Sur/La Jornada*, October 13, 1999, translated by Global Exchange.

28 Translation by Global Exchange, www.globalexchange.org.

29 According to "Always Near, Always Far: The Armed Forces in Mexico" by Global Exchange, the event occurred on April 20/21, 1999, after two hundred soldiers set up camp near the Mixtec barrio of Nuevo San José. The campesinos, Evaristo Albino Téllez, twenty-seven, and Antonio Mendoza Olivero, twelve, were picking corn when they were "riddled with gunfire." They made it to a field next to a river where they died, leaving a trail of blood to the site of the shooting. The next day, soldiers raped Mendoza's grandmother, fifty, and Albino's sister-in-law, thirty-three, according to testimony, when they went to the cornfield to look for the missing men. The military characterized the actions as "attacks on narco-cultivators." A report by the Defense Secretariat said: "Military units arrived at a poppy plantation, where five individuals . . . opened fire against the military personnel." The rapes were denied.

30 Other Mexicans who know the Sierra agree with her analysis. Carlos Montemayor, historian and author, told the *Toronto Star* in August 1996: "The government clamps down, but they don't improve health, education, agriculture or bring in electricity or running water. On the contrary, they have left Guerrero isolated in misery. If they don't do something, I believe the amount of guerrilla activity will increase. Armed insurgency is not an expression of ideological manipulation. It is the voice of hunger, fear, cold, injustice and exasperation."

31 Carlos Montemayor, *Guerra en el Paraíso* (Mexico City: Seix Barral, Biblioteca Breve, 1997).

32 General Jesús Gutiérrez Rebollo was arrested in February 1997. He was so cocky that he posed for photographs with druglord Amado Carrillo (full name Carillo Fuentes), a folly that helped convict him.

33 "Always Near, Always Far," p. 200. It's estimated that 70 percent of the cocaine sold in the U.S. and Canada is shipped through Mexico.

34 Linda Diebel, "Mexico's Dead Drug Lord Still Inspires Terror, 'Lord of the Skies' Leaves More Questions Than Answers—and a Bitter War of Succession," *Toronto Star*, July 20, 1997.

35 DFS and CISEN are the Mexican equivalents of CSIS (Canadian Security Intelligence Service) in Canada and the FBI (Federal Bureau of Investigation) in the United States.

36 The group is called Relatives of the Detained, Disappeared and Victims of Human Rights Abuses.

37 Interview with Enrique González Ruiz, *Vértigo*, Mexico City, April 30, 2005.

38 Careos constitucionales, Proceso Penal: 61/99 Iguala, Mexico.

39 All testimony is taken from court transcripts.

40 Human Rights Watch, "Military Injustice, Mexico's Failure to Punish Army Abuses," Volume 13, Issue 4 (B), December 2001.

41 The group posted an article about the award to Rodolfo Montiel on its Web site, www.goldmanprize.org.

42 Sam Quinones, "Imprisoned Mexican Wins Honor: Environmental Prize Goes to Farmer for His Fight Against Logging," *New York Times*, April 5, 2000.

43 The human rights foundation is based in Washington, D.C.

Chapter Ten: "Which One Is Digna?"

1 Inter-American Human Rights Commission, Washington, D.C., December 18, 2001.

2 "Mexican 'Prisoner of Conscience' Freed," *BBC News*, February 8, 2002.

3 The Center for Public Integrity, Washington, D.C., 1998.

4 José de Cordoba, "Military Coup: Mexican Army Takes Greater Public Role as Democracy Grows—From Drug Lords to Lice, It Tackles the Problems Other Institutions Can't—Evolution, Not Revolution," *Wall Street Journal*, New York, January 31, 2000.

5 Linda Diebel, "A Convenient Little War," *Toronto Star*, April 16, 1995.

6 It has been renamed the Western Hemisphere Institute for Security Cooperation. The name notwithstanding, the school is infamous for having groomed graduates who helped establish dictatorships throughout the hemisphere and were involved in massacres. It was dubbed "The School of the Assassins" by the Panamanian newspaper, *La Prensa*. The Global Exchange Study "Always Near, Always Far: The Armed Forces in Mexico" points out that by the end of the 1990s, Mexico had the largest number of personnel training at the school. The study says: "These personnel have been trained in extortion, physical and psychological torture, gathering military intelligence, command operations, sniper skills, interrogation techniques, terrorism, urban guerrilla strategies, counterinsurgency, low intensity warfare, irregular war, jungle operations, counterintelligence, training, internal defense, psychological operations, anti-drug operations, among others."

7 It translates as the Aeromobile Special Forces Group. "Always Near, Always Far" says that between 1996 and 1999, about thirty-two hundred GAFE soldiers graduated from a counterinsurgency course with the U.S. Seventh

Special Forces Group known as the Green Berets. Today, Mexico also has its own schools for training special forces and, according to the Center for Public Integrity (report, September 1, 2004), has created 109 GAFE groups.

8   The Center for Public Integrity, September 2004.
9   Diebel, "A Convenient Little War."
10 Delegation Report, Global Exchange and The Mexico Solidarity Network, May 2002.
11 Ibid.
12 Ibid.
13 Ibid.
14 Earthhope, January 6, 2005.
15 Interview with Eva Alarcón, Petatlán, February 28, 2002.
16 Ibid.
17 Maribel Gutiérrez, "La PGJDF desechó pistas en Guerrero," *El Sur,* June 26, 2002.
18 Interview with Eva Alarcón, February 28, 2002.
19 Alberto Nájar, "La línea del *narco*, las secuelas de un crimen," *La Jornada, Masiosare,* November 11, 2001.
20 *La Jornada,* Mexico City, November 11, 2001.
21 Alberto Nájar, "Crónica de los últimos días, Digna Ochoa en Guerrero," *La Jornada, Masiosare,* November 4, 2001.
22 *La Jornada,* Alberto Nájar, Mexico City, November 4, 2001.

Chapter Eleven: Suicide?

1   Interview with Gabriel Figueroa Sales II by Fred Sales, *In Motion Magazine,* 1998.
2   S. Lynne Walker, "Fight for Truth, Justice Put to Film, Death of Rights Attorney Raises Disturbing Questions," *The San Diego Union-Tribune,* July 27, 2004.
3   Interview with Víctor Brenes, Mexico City, February 19, 2002.
4   Ibid.
5   Blanche Petrich, "La operación inicial del EZLN, *La Jornada,* January 5, 1996.
6   "Legalized Injustice: Mexican Criminal Procedure and Human Rights," Miguel Agustín Pro Juárez Human Rights Center and Lawyers Committee for Human Rights, Washington, D.C., May 2001, p. 127.
7   "Chronology of Reports of Harassment at PRODH," Center for Justice and International Law, Washington, D.C., www.cejil.org/ PRESS/dignaochoa.
8   Interview with Víctor Brenes, Mexico City, February 19, 2002.

9 Marcela Turati, "Tiene El CISEN Ficha de Ochoa," *Reforma,* October 25, 2001.

10 Liberation Theology was advocated in a 1968 document from a meeting of Latin American bishops in Medellin, Colombia, during a time of military dictatorships in Latin America. Joe Gunn, director of the Office of Justice, Peace and Missions for the Canadian Conference of Catholic Bishops, said the theological treatise did not advocate violence. However, he said that its adherents said that they could see why, due to "structural injustice," people would be driven to violent actions. At its core, Liberation Theology criticized the violence of the social-political order against the poor. It argued that the way to achieve holiness was to be close to the struggles of the poor, helping to build water systems and generating plants, rather than preaching in august buildings. Liberation Theology evolved in Latin America in Brazil and other nations enduring military dictatorships. Cardinal Ratzinger and others in the Church hierarchy had full papal support in denouncing Liberation Theology; Pope John Paul II, for instance, criticized the rebel Sandinistas in Nicaragua and was a vocal supporter of General Augusto Pinochet in Chile. Some theologians believed that Pope John Paul failed to differentiate the struggles of Latin America from the violent boot of Communism in his native Poland and, indeed, in his final years, the pope softened his stance. The attack against Liberation Theology eased and Pope John Paul himself was a strong critic of what he called "savage capitalism." In April 2005, the College of Cardinals in Rome chose Cardinal Ratzinger to replace John Paul II, who had died ten days earlier. He emerged for the waiting crowd in St. Peter's Square as Pope Benedict XVI.

11 Enrique Flota used the terms "attorney general" and "prosecutor" interchangeably. The attorney general is the chief law enforcement officer of the Federal District.

12 Francisco Rodríguez, "Aportan en caso Digna indicios sobre suicidio," *La Reforma,* Mexico City, March 12, 2002.

13 Alejandro Lopéz Villanueva, from the Francisco Villa Popular Front.

14 John Gledhill, "The Two Deaths of Digna Ochoa: A Window onto the Violences of Power in Neoliberal Mexico," School of Social Sciences, University of Manchester, 2004.

Chapter Twelve: Saint Rosalie Talks to Jesus Christ in the Mirror

1 Juan de Arriola, a Jesuit priest and poet, was in fact born in the late seventeenth century. The rendition by Sales of his poem is not entirely accurate. The English version is my translation of his recitation.

2 The information about Saint Rosalie was taken from the Catholic Online Forum at http:forum.catholic.org.

3 Juan de Arriola, "Santa Rosalía ve a Jesucristo en el Espejo," from *Antología Poética de la Muerte* (México: Editorial Pax-México, 1967), with prologue and selection by Agustí Bartra. I translated Renato Sales's rendition of the poem as he quoted it; however, I noted that his recital differed from the 1967 version of *Antología Poética*. I don't know which edition was in the office.

4 Delegation report, "Global Exchange and The Mexican Solidarity Network," May 2003.

Chapter Thirteen: She Doesn't Wear Makeup, Does She?

1 Regina Martínez, *El País/La Jornada*, September 17, 1988, *La Jornada* library, México City.

2 Special prosecutor's report, "The Story of Digna Ochoa y Plácido," Mexico City Attorney General's Office, July 2003, referred in passing to the psychological profile done in the spring of 2000. Similar in their findings to the first psychological profile, further studies authorized by the Prosecutor's Office, led to the conclusion in July 2003 that the author of the death threats showed traits similar to Digna's. Two paragraphs were quoted as a setup to the other psychological profiles ordered by special prosecutor Margarita Guerra. Renato Sales had also ordered a profile. Digna was profiled to death. But the July 2003 report gave no indication that the initial psychological profile had had a great impact on Digna's life. Renato Sales obviously thought it important or he wouldn't have shown it to me—but he did, with no idea of its ultimate significance to the book I was writing.

3 Interview with Jesús Ochoa, Misántla, Veracruz, February 23, 2002.

4 Interview with Juan José Vera, Mexico City, February 8, 2002.

Chapter Fourteen: The Shunning

1 Interview with Tamryn Nelson, Washington, D.C., March 21, 2002.

2 Just as Fortune 500 companies have their pick of the legal crop, the world's leading rights agencies choose from a deep field of applicants who want to make a career in this field of the law. Competition is fierce and it is common to find lawyers from Ivy League schools, as well as other respected universities, in staff positions with Amnesty, Human Rights Watch, or the Inter-American Commission, both at headquarters and in postings. Denise Gilman, another example, graduated from the Columbia Law School and, in 2005, left CEJIL to

accept a post teaching human rights law at Georgetown University in Washington, D.C.

3 Denise, who used to be with the Inter-American Human Rights Commission, met Digna in Mexico in 1995, getting to know her well when she coordinated the project on torture in Mexico with PRO ("Legalized Injustice: Mexican Criminal Procedure and Human Rights") for the Lawyers Committee for Human Rights. Ariel, who used to work for CEJIL, met Digna in Mexico in the mid-1990s, and kept in touch with her.

4 Interview with Denise Gilman, Washington, D.C., March 20, 2002.

5 The details are confidential.

6 Interview with Denise Gilman, Washington, D.C., March 20, 2002.

7 Interview with Ariel Dulitzky, Washington, D.C., March 21, 2002.

8 Interview with Tamryn Nelson, Washington, D.C., March 21, 2002.

9 Interview with Viviana Krsticevic, Washington, D.C., March 19, 2002.

10 Interview with Denise Gilman, Washington, D.C., March 20, 2002.

11 Interview with Mario Patrón, Mexico City, March 6, 2003.

12 Interviews with Canadian police sources.

13 Sergio Aguayo Quesada, *La Charola: Una historia de los servicios de inteligencia en Mexico* (Mexico City: Editorial Grijalbo, 2001), p. 272.

14 Special prosecutor's report, "The Story of Digna Ochoa y Plácido," Mexico City Attorney General's Office, July 2003. All e-mails in this chapter are contained in the report.

15 Ibid.

16 Kerry Kennedy, *Speak Truth to Power: Human Rights Defenders Who Are Changing Our World*, with photographs by Eddie Adams (New York: Umbrage Edition, 2005), p. 197.

17 Special prosecutor's report, "The Story of Digna Ochoa y Plácido."

18 Interview with Denise Gilman, Washington, D.C., March 20, 2002.

19 Interview with Tamryn Nelson, Washington, D.C., March 21, 2002.

20 Ibid.

21 Interview with Ariel Dulitzky, March 21, 2002.

22 Interview with Denise Gilman, March 20, 2002.

23 Ibid.

24 Ibid.

25 Ibid.

26 Interview with Juan José Vera, Mexico City, March 26, 2002.

27 Ibid.

28 E-mail from Digna Ochoa to Ariel Dulitzky, September 16, 2001.

29 Interview with Denise Gilman, Washington, D.C., March 20, 2002.

Chapter 15: The Hit Man from Guerrero

1 Blanche Petrich, "Se prepara el escenario para sostener la tesis de *suicidio* de Digna Ochoa, *La Jornada,* April 28, 2003.

2 Ginger Thompson, "Rights Lawyer's Odd Death Tests Mexican Justice," *New York Times,* June 3, 2002.

3 The case was very sensitive and, through sources, I learned that the investigation was delayed after the initial trip to Mexico City by Pedro Díaz in early 2002 while the parameters for the investigative team were being clearly defined.

4 Special prosecutor's report, Mexico City Attorney General's Office, July 2003.

5 John Gledhill, "The Two Deaths of Digna Ochoa," School of Social Sciences, University of Manchester, 2004.

6 Alberto Nájar, "La línea del *narco,* las secuelas de un crimen," *La Jornada, Masiosare,* November 11, 2001.

7 Ibid.

8 Gledhill, "The Two Deaths of Digna Ochoa."

9 Special prosecutor's report, Mexico City Attorney General's Office, July 2003.

10 Ibid.

11 Special prosecutor's report, Mexico City Attorney General's Office, July 2003.

12 Maribel Gutiérrez, "Testigo: tirador de la sierra de Petatlán mató a Digna Ochoa, dice un testigo," *El Sur,* June 5, 2002.

13 Borges was working with a BOM unit, part of a network of Mixed Operational Bases (BOM according to its Spanish acronym) that were set up in 1995 as counterinsurgency units. Rights organizations that have studied the military in Mexico see this blending of security teams as evidence of further militarization in the country. I have cited the report "Always Near, Always Far: The Armed Forces in Mexico" by Global Exchange as a good source of information on the military. An authority who has written extensively on the Mexican military is Roderic Ai Camp, in particular in *Generals in the Palacio: The Military in Modern Mexico* (New York: Oxford University Press, 1992).

14 Nájar, "La línea del *narco.*"

15 Interview with José Reveles, Mexico City, March 4, 2002. He said that military commanders often start a business while they are still in the army, in order to have extra income when they retire.

16 The Bátiz team interviewed Maribel Gutiérrez, the author of the *El Sur* reports, but it is not clear who else they interviewed in Guerrero at this time.

17 Ibid.

Chapter 16: Margarita Guerra y Tejada

1 Blanche Petrich, "Entre inconsistencias, la PGJDF se acerca a una conclusión polémica sobre el caso Digna," *La Jornada,* June 20, 2002.

2 Blanche Petrich, "El caso Digna Ochoa se cerrará cuando tenga pruebas irrefutables," *La Jornada,* October 17, 2002.

3 Interview with Denise Gilman, Washington, D.C., March 20, 2002.

4 The group describes itself as a committee of Canadian lawyers dedicated to upholding advocacy rights and the rule of law. The Bar Human Rights Committee is the international human rights arm of the Bar of England and Wales, concerned with the protection of the rights of advocates and judges around the world. Leo McGrady made the April 2003 trip with Nadeem Ahmad and Jennifer Green from Britain.

5 Interview with Leo McGrady, March 13, 2005.

6 "Mexican Lawyer's Death Likely a Suicide," Associated Press, Mexico City, July 19, 2003.

7 Special prosecutor's report, "The Story of Digna Ochoa y Plácido," Mexico City Attorney General's Office, July 2003.

8 Ibid.

9 Lawyers' Rights Watch Canada, draft report, Vancouver, B.C., 2005.

10 "El de Digna fue un 'suicidio simulado,' asegura la fiscal Guerra," *La Crónica de Hoy,* July 19, 2003. While Guerra referred to Digna's death as a "simulated suicide," it would have been a "simulated homicide."

11 "Mexican Lawyer's Death Likely a Suicide," Associated Press. Guerra made the remark in an interview with AP.

12 Marion Lloyd, "Activist's Death Seen as Suicide: Investigation Findings on Crusading Lawyer Provoke Suspicion," *Boston Globe,* July 19, 2003.

13 LRWC letter, September 2, 2003.

14 Informe de la verificación de la prueba técnica en la investigación de la muerte de Digna Ochoa y Plácido, CIDH, May 27, 2003.

15 "Mexican lawyer's death likely a suicide," Associated Press.

16 Blanche Petrich, "Caso Digna; resultado vergonzoso, por ahora," *La Jornada,* July 21, 2003.

17 Ibid.

18 The remarks by David Fernández in the film by Felipe Cazals were translated by Harald Ihmig.

19 Interview with Víctor Brenes, by e-mail, August 2002, plus special prosecutor's report released in July 2003.

Chapter 17: The Experts: The Coroner, the Scientist, and the Cop

1 In January 2005, Dr. Young accepted a post as senior adviser to Anne McLellan, federal minister of public safety and emergency preparedness.

2 Twenty-four Canadians died that day, among 2,792 who perished in the Twin Tower attacks.

3 Another 184 people perished when a third plane slammed into the Pentagon, in Virginia near Washington, and 40 more when a fourth hijacked plane went down in a Pennsylvania field.

4 Dr. James Young, interview with Can West Interactive, August 2002.

5 Interview with Dr. James Young, Toronto, September 10, 2002.

6 Al Voth is a forensic specialist based in Edmonton, Alberta. He joined the RCMP in May 1974, and though he didn't specialize in forensics until 1991 (working as a highway patrol officer and on various emergency response teams), he won a 1978 competition giving him the title of "Best Shot in the RCMP." As well as an article on shooting and another on test firing a ruptured shotgun, he has written two novels, *B-ZONE* and *Mandatory Reload*, both published by Trigger Press International.

7 The translation of segments from Al Voth's report is my own.

8 He is now a superintendent with the Toronto Police Service.

9 Special prosecutor's report, Mexico City Attorney General's Office, July 2003.

Chapter 18: Cover-up?

1 Four teams of detectives released four reports, working under three prosecutors. The lead prosecutors were Nicolás Chávez (under Deputy Attorney General Alvaro Arceo Corcuera), Renato Sales, and Margarita Guerra.

2 Various reports totaling some three thousand pages were posted to the Internet home page of the Federal District Attorney General's Office in July 2003. The posting followed the press conference of Special Prosecutor Margarita Guerra and contained her report, "The Story of Digna Ochoa y Plácido," plus assorted documents, including forensic material, statements to police, and photographs. Despite its breadth, it is a selective posting and much material is missing. That summer, having wrapped up my research, I was dismayed at the prospect of having to wade through three thousand pages. However, the material proved to be a mine of valuable information. It stayed on the home page for two weeks, and then was removed, citing concerns by the Ochoa family. A statement by Bernardo Bátiz remained on the site, accompanied by a summary of

Margarita Guerra's "undisputed points of evidence," which essentially bolstered the Sales case.

3   Blanche Petrich, "Pendiente, indagar si como penalista Digna supo algo que la hizo *saber demasiado de algún intocable*," *La Jornada*, June 21, 2002. Petrich had four stories in *La Jornada* on June 21. In "Puede ser real que algunas de las amenazas a Digna Ochoa no fueran verídicas, señala Bátiz," she interviewed Bátiz. He said that "be it suicide or be it homicide, what she did for human rights, what she defended, what she left, that's what will live on." She asked him about press reports about a "supposedly psychological profile" of Digna. "Does it exist?" Bátiz said that work was "very advanced" on such a profile. However, when Petrich asked how long the PGJDF had had this profile, Bátiz replied, "Since very close to the beginning of the investigation." It may be that he was referring to the profile compiled in 2000. In the third article, "La pesquisa sobre Digna Ochoa, entre las más 'cuidadosas y abiertas' hechos en México," Bátiz was quoted as saying that Renato Sales was the first to alert him to the suicide theory. In the final piece, "Entre inconsistencias, la PGJDF se acerca a una conclusion polémica sobre el caso Digna," Petrich examined theories in the case and pointed out inconsistencies.

4   Ballistics testing did not negate the possibility that more than one gun was used in the crime. There were three bullets but only one could be positively identified as coming from the firearm found under Digna's legs. The other two projectiles were too badly damaged to make a positive match, and could have been fired by a weapon with a similar rifling design, which is the raised portion inside the barrel that marks the bullet as it travels down the barrel bore. RCMP expert Al Voth made this point in his contribution to the Díaz report for the Inter-American Human Rights Commission. According to expert Robert Warburton, who reviewed the Voth report for me, it was only a possibility the bullets came from another gun. But it's interesting in light of early reports of two guns. I haven't been able to get my first reaction to the photo Sales showed me—"it looks like a toy"—out of my mind. I've covered military coups, guerrilla groups, and armies all over Latin America and the Caribbean (notably Haiti) and I am reasonably familiar with weaponry. The gun in the first photo Sales showed me was small and looked like a toy. The gun in the photo released by the Special Prosecutor's Office in July 2003 looked deadly and dangerous—not at all like a toy.

5   Arturo Cano and Alberto Nájar, "Caso de Digna Ochoa, el martirio o la peor hipótesis," *La Jornada, Masiosare*, June 2, 2002.

6   Interview with Pilar Noriega, *Revista Rebeldía*, Mexico City, March 2005.

7 Petrich, "Pendiente, indagar. . . ."

8 Ibid.

9 Special prosecutor's report, "The Story of Digna Ochoa y Plácido."

10 Interview with Pilar Noriega, Mexico City, February 26, 2002.

11 His report, which is reproduced in "The Story of Digna Ochoa y Plácido," was dated June 28, 2002. Eight days earlier, Guerra gave an interview with Blanche Petrich in which she said she was going to have new and more complete psychiatric reports on Digna completed because the work done for Sales was done by only one psychiatrist. Either Mendoza Vega (who is a psychologist) completed his work in eight days, or his was the one put together under the Sales team—the one also referred to by Attorney General Bernardo Bátiz in an interview during that same period. Guerra not only didn't discard its contents, she relied heavily on them. No medical professional in Mexico conducted a clinical analysis of Digna, and yet she was—in absentia—analyzed to death.

12 Interview with Sister Brigitte, Mexico City, April 15, 2002.

13 The fact that the nuns asked Digna to wait a year shows how serious they were about their vocation, even though a prime concern was always increasing their numbers. In the spring of 2002, when I saw Sister Brigitte, there were only eleven Dominican nuns in Mexico City. A Mexican friend was with me and Sister Brigitte—who is mother superior of the small convent—gave her a not very subtle grilling to ascertain if she might be a candidate for the Dominicans. We smiled about it later.

14 Interview with Pilar Noriega, "Tiempo de Digna," *Revista Rebeldía*, February 2005.

15 Interview with Leo McGrady, March 13, 2005.

16 El Congreso Nacional de Campesinos is one of Mexico's foremost organizations fighting for land rights.

17 John Gledhill, "The Two Deaths of Digna Ochoa," School of Social Sciences, University of Manchester, May 2004.

18 Blanche Petrich, "Caso Digna: resultado vergonzoso, por ahora," *La Jornada,* July 20, 2003.

19 In 2002, for example, PRO's financial contributors included, among others, the British and Danish embassies in Mexico, the MacArthur Foundation, the Swedish organization Caritas Suecia, Secours Catholique, Pan Para el Mundo, the Tides Foundation, and the Angelica Foundation.

20 Guerra mentioned the study in the context that Digna's character met the psychological profile of the person sending threats to the PRO offices. A buzz about the existence of a psychological report began early under Sales, but it was always believed that his team was having the report put

together. In an interview with Attorney General Bernardo Bátiz in June 2002, Blanche Petrich asked about its existence and he said it was being written as they spoke. Later in the interview, he said that the Sales team had the psychological information since its inception, without explaining the apparent discrepancy.

21 Felipe Cazals, *Digna: Hasta el último respiro (Digna: Until the Last Breath)*, Grupo de Comunicación Publicorp and Academía Mexicana de Derechos Humanos, which premiered at the Berlin Film Festival, February 6, 2004.

22 Ibid.

23 Ibid.

24 Petrich, "Caso Digna."

25 Special prosecutor's report, "The Story of Digna Ochoa y Plácido." The rest of Edgar's account is from the same source.

26 Ibid.

27 Ibid.

28 Robert F. Kennedy, Ethel Kennedy's husband and Kerry Kennedy's father, was assassinated in Los Angeles, California, on June 6, 1968, while campaigning for the Democratic nomination for president of the United States. His brother, President John F. Kennedy, was assassinated in Dallas, Texas, on November 22, 1963.

29 By the spring of 2004, Petter Bolme was with the Stockholm-based Global Reporting.

30 Transcript of telephone interview, forwarded by Petter Bolme, May 2004.

31 My fondest memory of Sergio Aguayo, whom I interviewed often, was a luncheon for *Toronto Star* former managing editor James Travers in Mexico City. Aguayo, with his sweet smile and courtly manners, juggled descriptions of an upcoming book, a recent interview with the Dalai Lama, and an overview of Mexican culture, religion, politics, and recent history for my guest, between sips of soup and a mere dalliance with his entrée. The restaurant was one of his choosing and I felt badly that his generosity kept him from eating. But he was passionate about infusing Jim, a newcomer, with a Mexican sensibility in one sitting.

32 Sergio Aguayo Quesada, *Digna Ochoa, "Suicide or Homicide?"* translated by Lisa E. Castillor for Global Exchange, (Mexico City: Ideas y Palabras, June 25, 2002).

33 Ibid. The Federal District Human Rights Commission report as cited by Sergio Aguayo.

34 Blanche Petrich, "Se prepara el escenario para sostener la tesis de suicidio de Digna Ochoa," *La Jornada*, April 28, 2003.

35 Interview with General Gallardo by Petter Bolme, by telephone, November 2004.

36 Ibid.

37 Gledhill, "The Two Deaths of Digna Ochoa."

38 Along with John Gledhill's report for the University of Manchester, titled "The Two Deaths of Digna Ochoa," there was also an article in *Proceso* magazine (June 23, 2002) called "The Deaths of Digna Ochoa" by Fabrizio Mejía Madrid.

39 Interview with Pilar Noriega, *Revista Rebeldía*.

40 Ibid.

41 Not only was I turned down by the RCMP in my efforts to interview ballistics expert Al Voth, but officials in both the Canadian mission at the OAS in Washington and the foreign affairs department in Ottawa declined to comment on the Digna Ochoa investigation. I sought information from the Liberal government of Prime Minister Jean Chrétien, before Paul Martin took over in late 2003.

42 Article 1.3 of the UN Charter.

43 Tlachinollan Center was based in Tlapa, Guerrero.

44 Delegation report: Mexico, Global Exchange, and The Mexico Solidarity Network, May 3, 2002.

45 Ibid.

46 They were, according to Lawyers' Rights Watch Canada, human rights advocates Marisela Ortíz Rivera, Evangelina Arce, Marcelino Santiago Pacheco, Ernesto Ledesma Arronte, and Arturo Resquenses Galnares; and lawyers Mario César Escobedo Anaya, Sergio Dante Almaraz, Samuél Alfonso Casellanos Piñón, Beatriz Casas Arellanes, Bárbara Zamora López, Leonel Guadalupe Rivero Rodríguez, Griselda Tirado Evangelico, Luz María Lluvias Flores, Raúl Crespo Cassarubias, Osiris Marlene Avila Arellanes, and Bernardo Sánchez Cruz. Lawyers' Rights Watch reported receiving an answer from authorities that security measures were in place in only one case, that of Arturo Resquenses Galnares, an advocate with Christian Action for the Abolition of Torture, who received telephone death threats and reported being under surveillance by armed people.

47 At the time, Harald Ihmig was with FoodFirst Information and Action Network (FIAN), an organization based in Germany and focused on helping people get the tools and supplies needed to feed themselves.

48 Interview with Francisco Cerezo Contreras, Mexico City, February 19, 2002.

49 Peace Brigades International, "Threatened for Filming a Documentary

on the Cerezo Siblings," *PBI México Project Information Bulletin*, April 14, 2003. The organization provides unarmed protection for rights defenders who are at risk. Emiliano Altuna's experience was also reported by Lorraine Orlandi: "Young Filmmaker Faces Death Threat in Mexico," Reuters, April 24, 2003.

50 Lawyers' Rights Watch Canada.

Selected Bibliography

The following books are cited in the text or endnotes of *Betrayed*. For information on other sources, such as newspapers, journals, and reports, please refer to the Notes section.

Isaacson, Walter. *Kissinger: A Biography*. New York: Simon & Schuster, 1992.

Kennedy, Kerry, with photos by Eddie Adams. *Speak Truth to Power: Human Rights Defenders Who Are Changing Our World*. New York: Umbrage Editions, 2005. www.speaktruth.org

Krause, Enrique. *Mexico: Biography of Power*. New York: HarperCollins, 1997.

Loaeza, Guadalupe. *Las reinas de Polanco*. Mexico City: Cal y Arena, 1988.

Montemayor, Carlos. *Guerra en el paraíso*. Mexico City: Seix Barral, 1997.

Poniatowska, Elena. *La noche de Tlatelolco*. Mexico City: Biblioteca Era, 1971.

Preston, Julia, and Samuel Dillon. *Opening Mexico: The Making of a Democracy*. New York: Farrar, Straus and Giroux, 2004.

Selected Bibliography

Quezada, Sergio Aguayo. *La Charola: Una historia de los servicios de inteligencia en México*. México, D.F.: Editorial Grijalbo, 2001.

Thomas, Hugh. *The Conquest of Mexico*. London: Pimlico, 1993.

Recommended for further reading

Aguilar Camín, Héctor, and Lorenzo Mayer. *In the Shadow of the Mexican Revolution: Contemporary Mexican History, 1910–1989*. Austin: University of Texas, 1993.

Ai Camp, Roderic. *Generals in the Palacio: The Military in Modern Mexico*. New York: Oxford University Press, 1992.

Brown, Jonathan C. *Oil and Revolution in Mexico*. Berkeley and Los Angeles: University of California, 1993.

Castañeda, Jorge G. *The Mexican Shock: Its Meaning for the United States*. New York: The New Press, 1995.

DePalma, Anthony. *Here: A Biography of the New American Continent*. New York: Public Affairs, 2001.

Paz, Octavio. *The Labyrinth of Solitude*. New York: Grove Press, 1961.

Rivera, Guadalupe, and Marie-Pierre Colle. *Frida's Fiestas: Recipes and Reminiscences of Life with Frida Kahlo*. New York: Clarkson Potter, 1994.

Index

Endnotes are cited as follows: 485n6 indicates that the reference is to note 6 on page 485.

Index

and López Obrador, 460
and Mexico City Human
Rights Commission, 295
and Petatlán incident, 308,
309
and Sales, 384, 447
and Zamora, 458
Bauche, Vanessa, 264
Bautista, Bernardino "Nino,"
250, 253, 380, 382
Bautista Martínez, Perfecto,
248, 250
Bautista Valle, Juan, 247, 254
Benevides, Elisa, 270, 271
Bermúdez, Sari, 116
Bernal, María, 97
black lists, 187–88, 215
"black ops," 209–10, 457
Blades, Rubén, 105
Blancarte, Roberto, 126
Boise Cascade Corporation,
3–4, 204–5, 207, 230, 380, 453
Bolme, Petter, 179, 321
as journalist, 161, 172, 237,
254
PRO interview about Digna,
435, 442–44
Sales interview, 279, 289–90,
296–99
Borges, Franz, 381–82
Brady Plan, 84
Bravo Montes, Jovita
Guadalupe, 322
Brenes Berho, Víctor, 342, 353
death threats to, 272–73, 275
on Digna, 360, 405, 435
at murder scene, 16–17, 23,
24, 46
and "presumed Zapatistas"
case, 270, 271–73
Brétault, Sister Brigitte Loire,
25–26, 142, 146, 387, 429–30
Brokaw, Tom, 107
Bulgarín, Patricia, 45, 202,
329, 392
Buñuel, Luis, 261
Bush, George (senior), 86,
477n27
Bush, George W., 85, 102–3,
117–18, 461

Cabañas, Lucio, 220
Cabo San Lucas (Baja California Sur), 110
Cabrera García, Teodoro, 4,
203, 221, 230–32, 276. See
also Montiel/Cabrera case
arrest and torture, 205–8, 229
and Digna, 266, 400

release of, 231, 379, 442–43
Cabrera González, Jesús, 251
Cabrera González, Sergio,
246–47, 251, 382
Cabrera Torres, Roberto, 251,
252, 382
Cacalomacán (Mexico State),
271
caciques, 380–81
army and, 211, 219, 250, 255
Digna and, 216, 255, 400
and drug trade, 254, 380
in Guerrero, 205, 207–8, 251,
253, 379, 444
impunity of, 444–45, 450
in Veracruz, 164–65, 170
Callos Esposito, John, 105
campesinos, 276. See also specific
organizations; ecologistas;
Indians; Montiel/Cabrera
case
and drug trade, 219, 254
in Guerrero, 4, 124–25, 163,
203–5, 219, 220
human rights abuses against,
189, 218
murders, 158–60, 215, 221,
224, 251, 380
opponents of, 215, 219
and timber industry, 122,
163, 219, 252–53
Canada
and human rights, 452, 453,
461–62
and Mexico, 91, 452
and NAFTA, 85
Cárdenas, Cuauhtémoc, 79,
426, 446
in federal elections, 72–73,
267, 278
in mayoral election, 45, 82
Cárdenas, José, 292
Cárdenas, Lázaro, 84
Cárdenas Democratic Front,
185, 426
Carlotta, Empress of Mexico,
115
Carrasco, Diódoro, 342
Carrillo Fuentes, Amado, 223
Castañeda, Jorge, 112, 136
Castañón de Salinas, Paulina,
97
Castillo, Alfredo, 336, 405, 435
Castro, Fidel, 83, 97, 101
Catholic Church, 77, 276, 428.
See also specific religious orders
Cavillo, Jorge, 308–9
Cazals, Felipe, 264, 361, 404–5,
436

CDHDF (Federal District
Human Rights Commis-
sion), 423, 432, 446
Center for Globalization
(Yale University), 78
Center for Justice and Interna-
tional Law (CEJIL), 48, 130,
141, 338, 345–46
Center of Investigation and
National Security. See
CISEN
Cerezo Contreras, Emiliana,
457
Cerezo Contreras, Francisco,
457
Cerezo Contreras brothers
case, 25, 121–22, 132–33, 444,
456–58
Cervantes, Enrique, 240
Chapa Benzanilla, Pablo, 97
Chapultepec Castle (Mexico
City), 115, 116–17, 120
Chávez, Nicolás, 256, 391, 413,
434
Chiapas, 181, 209–11. See also
Zapatista Army
army in, 89, 157–58, 160,
164–65, 209–10
death squads in, 156–58, 161,
278
human rights abuses in,
156–58, 192–93, 243
tourism in, 86–87, 88
Chicago School, 83
Chico Mendes Environmental
Award, 231
Chirinos, Patricio, 168
Chrétien, Jean, 99–100, 158,
448
Christian Action for the Aboli-
tion of Torture, 291, 499n46
Church. See Catholic Church
Cihuacoatl (La Llorona), 29–30,
41
cinturónes de miséria (slums), 88,
165
Círculo Rojo (news program),
379
CISEN (Center of Investigation and National Secu-
rity), 103, 113, 223
and Digna, 114, 139, 200,
275–78, 341–42, 352–53
Citibank, 132
Ciudad Juárez (Chihuahua),
191–92, 455–56
Civic Association for National
Revolution, 188
Clark, Ramsay, 210

504

Index

Index

Index

Index

Index